God's Grace and Human Action

God's Grace and Human Action
'Merit' in the Theology of Thomas Aquinas

Joseph P. Wawrykow

UNIVERSITY OF NOTRE DAME PRESS
Notre Dame London
1995

Library of Congress Cataloging-in-Publication Data

Wawrykow, Joseph Peter.
    God's grace and human action : 'merit' in the theology of Thomas
Aquinas / by Joseph Peter Wawrykow.
        p. cm.
    Includes bibliographic references.
    ISBN 0-268-01031-5 (hard : alk. paper)
    1. Merit (Christianity) 2. Grace (Theology) 3. Thomas, Aquinas, Saint.
1225?-1274—Contributions in theology. I. Title.
BT773.W38 1995
234—dc20   95-18777
                                                                          CIP

∞The paper used in this publication meets the minimum requirements
of the American National Standard for Information Sciences—
permanence of Paper for Printed Materials, ANSI Z39.48-1984

Contents

Preface

IN THE FOLLOWING PAGES, I have examined 'merit' in the theological writings of Thomas Aquinas. Medieval discussions of merit are important for at least two reasons. Taken in itself, the treatment of merit can provide an important barometer of central theological and anthropological convictions—about medieval notions of the dignity and possibilities of human existence, about the seriousness with which different authors consider the fact of sin and its lingering effects even in the life of the justified, and about the ways in which God can come to figure in human existence through grace. But the medieval discussions have taken on added significance because of their use in the Reformation and since. Luther's insistence on "justification by faith alone" was at the same time an attack on Catholic claims about the religious value of morally good acts; the sixteenth-century Catholic rejection of Luther also entailed the re-affirmation of the notion of merit, with its official proclamation at the Council of Trent.

It is thus not surprising that modern scholars, both Protestant and Catholic, have shown a certain fascination with merit. Some of the medieval analyses of merit, so significant in the working out of the divisions between the churches during the Reformation, have as a result been studied in considerable detail and indeed adequately. One might cite here the researches of Werner Dettloff into the teachings on merit of Scotus and Ockham and their followers, work that has found its echo in other scholars such as Bernd Hamm.[1] But while the topic of merit not been wholly neglected, it is the underlying conviction of this book that the teachings of Thomas Aquinas about merit have only imperfectly been understood. Indeed, that Thomas had more than one teaching on merit, corresponding to different stages of his theological development, has itself not been sufficiently appreciated. The imperfect state of research on Thomas's approaches to merit has thus had a twofold effect. The main lines of Thomas's soteriology, including his sense of the precise roles played in human salvation by God and the human person, remain only partially

---

1 Werner Dettloff, *Die Lehre von der Acceptatio divina bei Johannes Duns Scotus mit besonderer Berücksichtigung der Rechtfertigungslehre* (Werl, 1954), and *Die Entwicklung der Akzeptations- und Verdienstlehre von Duns Scotus bis Luther* (Münster, 1963); Bernd Hamm, *Promissio, Pactum, Ordinatio* (Tübingen, 1977). I have subjected Hamm's discussion of Aquinas on merit to critical scrutiny in my first chapter.

sketched. And lacking a precise depiction of what Thomas himself taught or an explanation of the version of merit that had evolved by the time of the *Summa Theologiae*, evaluations of the reception of Thomas—in the later middle ages, during the Reformation, indeed, even in the present—remain stuck at a somewhat elementary stage.

The present close study of Aquinas on merit accordingly has a twofold audience in mind. The book is directly addressed to those who seek to understand more adequately an important part of Thomas's theology, viewed in its own terms. The primary goal of the book is to delineate the precise function performed by merit in Aquinas's account of salvation and, concomitantly, to chart the development in his understanding of merit evident in the course of his theological career. This study has been motivated by my concern to evaluate Thomas's success in combining his assertion (in this teaching on merit) of the religious value of human action done in obedience to God's will with his unequivocal affirmation (at least by the time of the *Summa Theologiae*) that human salvation at every stage (predestination, initial justification, perseverance on the path to God, beatitude) is dependent on the free and gracious involvement of God in the life of the individual.

It is hoped that a second set of readers will also find this book of interest, those concerned primarily with the Reformation and the later reception of high medieval teachings. By necessity, however, my book must stay for these readers at the level of an invitation to further study, merely suggestive of the value of a better-informed examination of the ways in which later theologians encountered the thought of Thomas Aquinas on merit. Comparative comments are kept to a minimum in this book; apart from some suggestions about the differences between Thomistic *ordinatio* and Scotist *acceptatio*, I have not brought Thomas into dialogue with other medieval authors. Nor do I attempt here to demonstrate that later medieval and Reformation responses to Thomas, even those of his self-described adherents, may fall short of the mature teaching in significant ways. Before establishing his teachings, that argument would undoubtedly have been premature. Rather, mindful of the need for a thorough study of Thomas himself, I have been forced to be content with the careful, at times painstaking, re-evaluation of what Thomas wrote on merit. The invitation to scholars of the later middle ages and of the Reformation to reconsider the fate of the mature teaching comes, then, precisely in the delineation of this rather distinctive account of merit. My suspicion, one that needs testing by others, is that Thomas's later readers, both Catholic and Protestant, were in fact blind to much that was crucial in the mature teaching. Armed with this analysis of Aquinas on merit, modern scholars of the Reformation will perhaps be inspired to investigate anew the quality of later readings of Thomas on merit and grace.[2]

---

2   For the attempt to show what light might be cast by this new interpretation of Thomas's mature teaching about merit on the teaching of John Calvin, an

In preparing this study it did not suffice to examine only the *ex professo* treatments or major passages on merit in Thomas's corpus. Rather, I have read through Thomas's theological writings virtually in their entirety, impelled by the conviction that one can fully understand Thomas on merit at different stages of his career only when familiar with the development in his positions on such related doctrines as providence and predestination, grace, and hope. As will become evident over the course of the book, the genesis apparent in Thomas's teaching about merit to a large degree mirrors that in these related doctrines. Tempting as it is, with the advent of the *Index Thomisticus*, to allow the computer to do one's research, what might be gained in "statistical accuracy" through exclusive reliance on the *Index* would, in the end, be more than offset by a loss of a feel for the texture and flow of Thomas's theological argument. Sensitivity to Thomas's concerns and to the spirit of his theology of merit can be achieved only by studying in their entirety the works in which Thomas discusses merit. Attention to the changing nuances in his analysis of the crucial related concepts which serve as the background to merit and to the inter-relationships between these concepts and merit makes it possible to know what Thomas means by merit and determine why he has proposed the teaching which he has. Hence, I turned to the *Index* only at the end of my study of the writings themselves to insure that no pertinent texts had been overlooked and, moreover, to see whether Thomas had also discussed merit in any unexpected places (he does not).

The book is divided into four chapters. The first, through its extensive and sometimes detailed orientation to the literature, indicates the assured results of earlier research into merit (and related concepts), the questions that remain open, and the main lines of argument that will be pursued in the subsequent chapters. The first chapter also provides the opportunity to acknowledge my debt to such scholars as Lynn and Pesch (on merit), Bouillard and Lonergan (on grace), and Pfürtner (on hope). The second and third chapters offer close readings of the discussions of merit in the various works of the Thomistic corpus, considered in rough chronological order; hence, in Chapter 2, I discuss Thomas's teaching about merit in the *Scriptum Super Libros Sententiarum*, and, in the *De Veritate*, and, in Chapter 3, his analysis in the *Summa Theologiae*.[3] The structure of these

---

avowed opponent of Thomas on merit, about *sanctification*, see my "John Calvin and Condign Merit," *Archiv für Reformationsgeschichte* 83 (1992): 73–90.

3   Of the three major systematic works (the *Scriptum* on the *Sentences* of Peter Lombard, the *Summa Contra Gentiles*, and the *Summa Theologiae*) only the *Summa Contra Gentiles*, written between 1259 and 1264, lacks an extensive analysis of merit. In this work, Thomas is content to make only brief comments about merit, to the effect that it pertains to God's providence to reward and punish and thus that human activity can merit the reward of heaven offered by God; see Book III, chapters 139 and 140. However, the *Summa Contra Gentiles* is in many ways a seminal work, for in it Thomas

chapters differs slightly. By the time of the discussion of merit in the *Summa Theologiae*, Thomas has developed an account of merit that is thoroughly integrated into his basic understanding of God-human relations and of human salvation. Hence, before turning in the third chapter to the extended comments in the *Summa* on merit, it is first necessary to set the stage, beginning the chapter with Thomas's ideas about creation and grace. The discussion of merit in the earlier *Scriptum* and the *De Veritate*, on the other hand, stands on its own, and hence I have proceeded in Chapter 2 directly to the early account of merit. The final chapter is much more tentative and speculative in tone; here, I briefly suggest how the contemplation of Thomas's use of his principal sources, Augustine and scripture, may shed additional light on the genesis and inspiration of the mature teaching.

To anticipate the main claims: Certain features of Thomas's thought on merit remained constant throughout his career. "Juridical" aspects are always present. In the *Scriptum* and in the *Summa*, 'merit' consistently refers to the establishment of a right in justice to a reward from God. This view of merit is scripturally based in that Thomas advances a teaching on merit to explicate the biblical texts affirming God's just reward of good behavior. Even more striking, however, are the new insights informing Thomas's mature teaching about merit. First, the *Summa* emphasizes predestination and grace. The person who merits before God has been freely chosen by God to enjoy eternal life. Moreover, as the result of God's free predestination, God grants the elect the grace required to move him to the actions meritorious of eternal life. The new stress on predestination and grace reflects both Thomas's speculative gains on grace and the will and his reading of certain decisive writings of the later Augustine, in particular the *De Praedestinatione Sanctorum* and the *De Dono Perseverantiae*. Second, the *Summa* delineates the sapiential dimensions of merit. In accordance with the plan of the divine wisdom, God employs meriting to manifest the divine goodness in a special way, by the salvation of the individual through his meritorious actions. Thomas's portrayal of merit in sapiential terms permits him to conclude that the attainment of salvation though merits testifies not only to the dignity of the human person but even more to the goodness of God.

---

has fashioned new descriptions of concepts which will figure prominently in the formulation of his mature teaching on merit. It is in the *Summa Contra Gentiles* that he ascribes to providence and predestination for the first time a causal certitude which extends not only to general effects but even to all individual events. Moreover, he replaces in the *Summa Contra Gentiles* the relatively static view of grace offered in the *Scriptum* with a much more dynamic understanding, which stresses God's direct application of the human person to activity. Thus, in the following chapters, attention is drawn in the appropriate places to the contribution of the *Summa Contra Gentiles* to the changes in Thomas's theology of grace and of the relations of God and the human person.

Acknowledgments

THIS BOOK ORIGINATED as my 1988 Yale University doctoral dissertation. My dissertation advisor, Professor George Lindbeck, has been a reliable source of enthusiasm and wisdom from the project's inception. Of the readers of the dissertation, R. Emmet McLaughlin, now of Villanova University, read the text and notes with special care and offered invaluable editorial suggestions. The Social Sciences and Humanities Research Council of Canada and Yale University furnished generous fellowships during the initial years of my graduate education. The research and writing of the dissertation was supported by fellowships from the Charlotte W. Newcombe Foundation and the Mrs. Giles Whiting Foundation. The revisions, most of which were done at the University of Notre Dame, were completed during my stay at the Center of Theological Inquiry in Princeton; I am grateful to the Director, Professor Daniel Hardy, and his staff for their hospitality.

I have benefited greatly from the comments and suggestions of those colleagues at the University of Notre Dame who are interested in the theology of Thomas Aquinas: Professors David Burrell, C.S.C., John Cavadini, Kent Emery, Jr., Mark D. Jordan, and Thomas F. O'Meara, O.P. The faults remaining in this book are undoubtedly due to my own obstinacy. I am also grateful to the Chairman of the Department of Theology, Professor Lawrence Cunningham, for helping to create and sustain an environment in which research and teaching in the history of Christian thought and practice are valued.

Parts of Chapters 3 and 4 have appeared in articles in *Augustinian Studies* 22 (1991) and *Medieval Philosophy and Theology* 2 (1992); I am grateful to the editors for granting me permission to use this material.

Finally, I wish to convey my appreciation to my mother and parents-in-law for their encouragement, and to my wife, Dianne T. Phillips, for her unfailing inspiration.

Chapter 1

The Literature on Merit and Related Concepts

THIS CHAPTER has two principal goals. First, I review the secondary literature on merit in Thomas Aquinas, in order to identify the major problems and disputed questions confronting the interpreter of this aspect of Thomas's thought. Second, I examine some of the literature on related aspects of Thomas's theology. One of the gravest flaws of the literature on merit in Aquinas is that it views his teaching on this concept in isolation from the general flow of his thought. As I shall argue, however, it is only in its relation to other doctrines in his theology that Thomas's teaching on merit can be fully appreciated. In particular, we cannot adequately grasp what Thomas means by 'merit' and establish what role it performs in his thought without reading his discussion of merit in terms of and in dialogue with his teachings on grace and hope. Indeed, many of the developments in Thomas's teaching about merit reflect and incorporate the parallel developments in his thought about grace and hope. Hence in the second part of this chapter, I examine the literature on related themes which I find especially valuable for the correct interpretation of Aquinas's theology of merit.

Section I. The Literature on Merit

Modern students of Aquinas have by and large neglected Thomas's teaching on merit.[1] Apart from occasional discussions of isolated aspects

---

1   A number of writers on merit have noted the paucity of studies of this notion in Thomas. See, for example, B. Catão, *Salut et Rédemption chez S. Thomas d'Aquin: L'acte sauveur du Christ* (Paris, 1965), p. 49, n. 2: "La notion de mérite, bien qu'elle ait une place importante dans la théologie catholique et dans la catéchèse courantes, ne semble pas avoir attire l'attention des chercheurs modernes. La bibliographie en est encore extrêmement pauvre"; and A. Miralles, "La Perspectiva Sapiencial de la Teologia del Merito en Santo Tomas de Aquino," *Studi Tomistici* 13 (Rome, 1980): 293: "El estudio teológico del merito no está de moda en la actualidad. Basta sequir la literatura teológica de las dos últimas décadas para comprobar que no atrae la atencíon este capitulo de la doctrina cristiana sobre la gracia." Miralles repeats the observation in "El Gobierno Divino en la Teologia del Merito de Santo Tomas de Aquino," *Teresianum* 35 (1984): 73. On the other hand, B. Hamm, *Promissio, Pactum, Ordinatio* (Tübingen, 1977), p. 313, notes that in

of Thomas's analysis of this difficult area of theological discourse, as well as studies which review in passing this part of his soteriology, there have been but three book-length studies of merit in Aquinas in this century, and each of these works is seriously flawed.[2] The earliest of these, *Die Verdienstlichkeit der menschlichen Handlung nach der Lehre des hl. Thomas von Aquin* (1931)[3] by J. Weijenberg, is more a neo-scholastic philosophical defense of twentieth-century teaching about merit along Thomist lines than a serious historical treatment of the thought of Thomas himself.[4] Indeed, to the extent that Weijenberg incorporates genuine Thomistic insights, it is exclusively to the Thomas of the *Summa Theologiae* that he has turned. Yet, even his use of the *Summa* is unsatisfactory, for Weijenberg's polemic has caused him to distort Thomas's analysis of merit. For example, Weijenberg directed his argument against contemporary philosophical trends which seek to deny personal freedom (p. 38f.) or to reject objective moral norms which guide human behavior (p. 41f.; pp. 48ff.) As a result, much of Weijenberg's book rehearses those questions in the *Summa* (especially in the Prima Secundae) in which Thomas establishes the possibility of the good moral act in conformity with the will of God. And in his own analysis of the 'meritability' of human action Weijenberg places the stress on human freedom to do the good, that is, the "subjective" aspects

---

comparison with the literature on many other medieval thinkers, Thomas's teachings on grace and merit have received a relatively large amount of attention. I discuss Hamm's analysis of Thomas's teaching on merit in some detail later in this chapter.

2   In the first section of the chapter, I first review the major contributions in the secondary literature to the understanding of merit in Aquinas and then conclude with a brief enumeration of the main problems which confront the student of this aspect of Thomas's thought. I have not discussed in this chapter every article which treats in some fashion Thomas on merit; when an article examines a somewhat narrow or technical topic, I have postponed evaluating it until the appropriate place in a later chapter. Thus, for example, I shall comment on B. de Margerie, "La sécurité temporelle du juste," *Studi Tomistici* 2 (Rome, 1974): 283–306 and on B. Marino, "La reviviscenza dei meriti secondo la dottrina del dottore Angelico," *Gregorianum* 13 (1932): 75–108, in Chapter 3.

3   J. Weijenberg, *Die Verdienstlichkeit der menschlichen Handlung nach der Lehre des hl. Thomas von Aquin* (Freiburg im Breisgau, 1931). The page numbers in the text refer to this book.

4   Near the end of *Die Verdienstlichkeit* (p. 210), Weijenberg reflected on his method and purpose: "Wir waren bestrebt, nicht nur methodisch in die Fusstapfen des grossen Meisters zu treten, sondern auch den wahren Sinn seiner Lehre—so oft die Gelegenheit sich darbietet—zu betonen," this last against the misunderstandings of modern philosophy. In his study of merit, P. De Letter, *De ratione meriti secundum Sanctum Thomam* (Rome, 1939), p. xviii, referred briefly to Weijenberg's book; De Letter notes that Weijenberg's book is more theological (= philosophical) in intention than historical and that Weijenberg makes reference to the Fathers and church documents, as well as to Thomas's own teaching, to make the case for merit.

of merit.[5] Concomitantly, Weijenberg downplays the role of grace in merit, limiting it to "elevating" the morally good act to the supernatural order, to mere "adorning" of the good act in such a way that it can lay claim to a supernatural reward.[6] Thomas, of course, acknowledges that in the present dispensation it is the morally good act done in freedom which is meritorious. But as his discussion of merit in the *Summa* at the end of the treatise on grace suggests, Thomas puts much greater emphasis than does Weijenberg on the role of grace in establishing the possibility of merit. Thomas's analysis of grace in the *Summa*, as the inner effective working of the Holy Spirit on the will, is similarly much more dynamic than Weijenberg allows. In addition to his inadequate treatment of grace in the *Summa* and his failure to grant grace the leading role in merit, Weijenberg's value as an interpreter of Thomas on merit is further diminished by his tendency to establish key points of his argument (ostensibly based on the thought of Aquinas) by reference to the explicit statements not of Thomas himself but of early twentieth-century Catholic theologians, who, needless to say, may differ in crucial respects from the teaching of Saint Thomas.[7]

---

5   Weijenberg, *Die Verdienstlichkeit der menschlichen Handlung*, p. 158f., refers to free, morally good acts as the "material" cause of meritability. In the discussion of grace in the second section of this chapter, the notion of "material" causality, and the related "formal" causality of grace, will be explained. As will become clear, material and formal causality in terms of graced acts indeed have a place in Thomas's analysis. But by the time of the *Summa*, Thomas prefers to view the relation between grace and free acts more in terms of efficient causality. Weijenberg has more or less ignored this aspect of the relation between divine and human causality.

6   For a characteristic statement on this issue, see Weijenberg, *Die Verdienstlichkeit der menschlichen Handlung*, p. 116: "Das neue Leben der Gnade erhebt den Menschen in diese von Gott gewollte übernatürliche Ordnung, sie macht ihn des göttlichen übernatürlichen Lebens teilhaftig, und auf diese Weise gibt sie seinen guten Handlungen ausser der natürlichen und moralischen, einen neuen, höheren Wert m. a. W. sie sind verdienstlich bei Gott und für das ewige Leben, sie haben Recht auf einen übernatürlichen Lob." A similar statement is found on p. 109. On p. 172, Weijenberg refers to the need for both grace and free will in obstensibly more satisfactory terms by stating that grace is the main, free will the secondary, principle of meritorious action. However, given Weijenberg's tendency to view meritorious acts exclusively in terms of material and formal causality, this statement should be taken to mean that grace principally makes morally good acts meritorious because it grants them supernatural value. Grace does not work in isolation but elevates the individual's morally good achievements, which provide the matter of merit. In other words, Weijenberg here is not referring to grace's efficient causality in producing these good acts which are meritorious. For Weijenberg's understanding of merit as establishing a right to reward, see, e.g., pp. 151 and 154.

7   In his review of Weijenberg's book in the *Bulletin Thomiste* 1933, p. 772 (#947), Y. Congar has evaluated Weijenberg's work in rather negative terms: "L'auteur est loin d'avoir traité ou même touché toutes les questions que pose la doctrine du mérite. . . . Au point de vue doctrinal, l'ouvrage est insuffisant;

A more competent study of merit in Aquinas is Prudentius De Letter's monograph, *De Ratione Meriti secundum Sanctum Thomam* (1939).[8] The book is divided into three chapters, each of which, in the scholastic style, is arranged in a series of articles. The first chapter discusses what De Letter calls the "ratio moralis" of merit in Aquinas, by which he means the ordination of human acts to retribution by divine justice; the second chapter examines the "ratio physica" of merit according to Thomas, that is, grace and charity, the "ontological principles" (p. 49) ordained to a supernatural end; and the final chapter describes the relations between these two *rationes* in the teaching of St. Thomas. Although De Letter's work marks an improvement over Weijenberg's, since De Letter is more careful to base his examination of Thomas's teaching on what Thomas himself wrote, his treatment of merit too suffers from a number of deficiencies. First, De Letter has introduced a number of terms into his description of Thomas's position not found in Thomas's own teaching. As De Letter acknowledges in his conclusion,[9] the terms *ratio moralis* and *ratio physica*, for example, are not Thomas's but rather are employed in contemporary Catholic teaching on merit. Used to describe Thomas's teaching, such terms are somewhat misleading. More grievously, De Letter's work fails as history because of its incompleteness, inattention to chronology and lack of awareness of the development in Thomas's treatment of merit. De Letter only examines Thomas's *ex professo* discussions of merit in the *Scriptum Super Sententiis* and the *Summa Theologiae*. But Thomas discussed merit at some length elsewhere, and there is no reason to assume, as De Letter does, that his teaching remained identical. Additionally, De Letter's belief that Thomas's teaching on merit did not undergo development (with one exception) permits him to mix indiscriminately statements from the *Scriptum* with arguments from the *Summa*, ignoring not only the decade separating the completion of the *Scriptum* and the beginning of the *Summa* but also the methodological inappropriateness of such a procedure.[10]

au point de vue historique, il est franchement faible. On aura peine à lui reconnaître une véritable valeur scientifique."

8 Prudentius De Letter, *De ratione meriti secundum Sanctum Thomam* (Rome, 1939). The page numbers in the text refer to this book.

9 See De Letter, *De ratione meriti secundum Sanctum Thomam*, p. 149, where he remarks that it is the contemporary practice among theologians to refer to the "moral" or "juridical," and to the "physical" or "ontological" aspects of merit. See also p. xviii, where De Letter admits that he has organized the discussion of merit in Aquinas in the modern way, that is, in the manner in which contemporary Catholic theologians tend to discuss merit.

10 As will become evident in the following discussion of the literature on merit, there is an almost unanimous consensus among interpreters of Thomas that his thought on merit remained the same throughout his career. This belief allows his students either to restrict their comments to his teaching in a single work (usually the *Summa Theologiae*) or to mix statements from various works indiscriminately. But it is clear that Thomas's understanding of merit evolved. By establishing his teaching about merit in each of his major works

De Letter, like Weijenberg, is guilty of distorting the thought of Aquinas on merit. As De Letter observes, in the *Scriptum* Thomas argues that the form of justice governing theological merit is distributive, while in the *Summa*, it seems rather to be a kind of commutative justice involved.[11] De Letter therefore devotes most of his first chapter to recording the arguments used by Thomas in the *Scriptum* to establish merit as an instance of distributive justice, and then embarks on his own attempt to identify the species of justice governing merit in the *Summa*. It is clear that justice is involved to some extent in merit at all stages of Thomas's career—after all, even in the *Summa*, merit means the establishment of some kind of claim or right to a reward in justice.[12] But unlike De Letter Thomas in the *Summa* is hardly concerned to identify the species of justice governing this aspect of human-divine relations—it plays no part in his deliberations on merit in I-II 114, and he seems only to have mentioned that it is in fact "commutative" justice in merit in passing, elsewhere in the *Summa* (II-II 61, 4 ad 1). Thus, by focusing his energies on the precise identification of the kind of justice involved in Thomas's analysis in the *Summa*, De Letter has concentrated on a facet of Aquinas's thought about merit which no longer plays the central role it did in the *Scriptum*, that is, the determination of the kind of justice involved in merit. What is perhaps even more striking about De Letter's analysis is that his discussion of the kind of justice involved in merit is not complemented with a study of the *cause* of Thomas's changed ideas on justice in relation to merit. De Letter appears unaware of the implications underlying Thomas's eventual rejection of distributive justice in merit (a justice which requires that God observe a kind of equality of proportion between the divine reward and the merits of various people) in favor, by the time of the *Summa*, of what can be termed

---

approached chronologically, the genesis of his thought reveals itself.

11   Although distributive justice predominates in the discussion of merit in the *Scriptum* and commutative justice in the *Summa*, De Letter has also observed (*De ratione meriti secundum Sanctum Thomam*, p. 35) that in both works Thomas at times can argue that each kind of justice is operative in merit. The "flux" in Thomas's analysis is due, says De Letter, to his sense that God cannot be adequately fitted into any human category; the complexity of God-human relations as they are found in merit prevents Thomas from ascribing merit too firmly to one or the other type of justice.

12   On the basis of *In Sent.* III d. 18, a. 2, sol., De Letter says that meriting is to make something owed to one which is rendered by justice. However, De Letter also notes (p. 104) a second "definition" of merit in Aquinas, which describes merit in terms of *disposing* oneself for a reward: "Mereri est igitur reddere se capacem recipiendi finem, seu reddere se dignum praemio," for by making oneself worthy of a reward, one "disposes" for the reward. See also p. 83. De Letter does not try to arbitrate between these two "definitions" of merit or to say which is the more basic for Thomas. It is the great virtue of Lynn's study of merit in Aquinas, discussed below, that he has determined that for Thomas it is the making owed to one in justice, not the disposing for a perfection, which is Thomas's preferred definition of merit.

"commutative" justice, which requires a "quantitative" equality between merit and reward. The basic reason that Thomas ascribes merit to commutative justice in the *Summa* is Thomas's new emphasis in this work on the role of *grace* in creating the meritorious act and especially Thomas's more dynamic conception of grace as the inner action of the Holy Spirit directly upon the will. Whatever "equality" there is between the meritorious act and its reward (and hence the possibility of commutative justice in merit), Thomas argues, is due to the equality of dignity between God's grace and the divine reward. De Letter acknowledges that for the Thomas of the *Summa*, it is the action of the Holy Spirit which establishes equality between merit and reward (pp. 12, 18, 30, 93). But he does not follow up this insight with a consideration of how the *Summa*'s treatment of grace differs from that in the *Scriptum*, an endeavor which would explain why the *Scriptum* does not assert a basic equality between merit and reward. Rather, De Letter is content to say (p. 19) that the teaching about the Holy Spirit does not appear in the *Scriptum* to explain the equality of merit and reward because in this work Thomas looks at merit only in terms of the free will and its actions (admittedly as aided by grace), while in the *Summa* Thomas looks at the entire reality of the meritorious act, including the ontological aspects of the human person raised by grace to God's level (see p. 30), and so is enabled to perceive the basic equality of merit and reward. It is not only a change of perspective, however, which accounts for the shift in Thomas's thought. As we shall see in the discussion of Bouillard and Lonergan in the second part of the chapter, Thomas's teaching on grace underwent considerable development from the time of the *Scriptum* to that of the *Summa*, and the developments in his thought on grace are of direct significance for his teaching on merit. It is unacceptable to assume, as De Letter does, that Thomas always understood grace (and hence merit) in precisely the same way.[13]

---

13   Indeed, precisely with regard to the action of the Holy Spirit in moving people to their act, Thomas's thought shows development. In Lonergan's analysis, Thomas's invocation of the "motion of the Holy Spirit" represents his discovery of actual grace, a grace which is lacking in the *Scriptum*. In other words, Thomas could base the equality of merit and reward on the contribution and action of the Holy Spirit, as he does in the *Summa*, only when he had discovered this kind of grace as a complement to habitual grace. In a sense, De Letter's inattention to the development in Thomas's teaching on grace as one of the sources of Thomas's later teaching on merit is a result of the narrow scope of his study. Although there is considerable disagreement about the inspiration for the increased dynamism of grace in the later Thomas (as the review of Auer, Hamm, Pesch, Bouillard, and Lonergan later in this chapter will demonstrate), I believe that a fundamental inspiration here is Thomas's work in the 1260s on the Pauline epistles, in which Thomas would have read of the Christian being lead by the Spirit. Since De Letter did not consider these writings, he was less likely to notice the Pauline contribution to Thomas's teaching on grace which distinguishes the analysis in the *Scriptum* from that in the *Summa*.

Finally, De Letter's study of merit in Aquinas is unsatisfactory because it either neglects important questions in Thomas's account of merit or subjects them to insufficient analysis. For example, De Letter disregards the development in Thomas's teaching about the possibility of meriting the first grace. Although Thomists have long been aware that the *Scriptum* lacks the *Summa*'s adamant denial of the possibility of such meriting, and the *Scriptum*'s somewhat ambiguous language makes it difficult, as we shall see, to determine Thomas's own position on this type of meriting in the early part of his career, De Letter has completely ignored this problem in his exposition of Thomas's teaching.[14] Similarly, the problem posed by Thomas's use of the notion of a *divine ordination* to establish the possibility of merit in the *Summa* is a vexing one and has provoked a number of interpretations in the recent literature. However, although the divine ordination is the basis of meritability in the later work, De Letter does not attempt to offer a separate, detailed exposition of this term. He never defines the divine ordination and only mentions it in passing. Even when he uses the term, it is not really clear what he understands by it. In the majority of cases, it is evident that for De Letter the divine ordination refers especially to the "ontological principles," grace and charity, given to the individual by God to insure the individual's attainment of salvation (e.g., pp. 16, 23, 34); here the stress is on the intrinsic value of good works done in grace which directs or ordains these good works to the end of eternal life. On the other hand, at times De Letter seems to suggest a more "Franciscan" gloss on this term, speaking of God's acceptance through the divine ordination of good works done in grace as meritorious (e.g., p. 47). In place, then, of a clarification of the meaning of this crucial term, De Letter simply avoids the issue, using the term when his argument demands it (especially when he cites a text from the *Summa* in which the term is used) but not bothering to explain precisely what Thomas means when he refers in the *Summa* to God's ordination of human activity to the attainment of God.

William D. Lynn's *Christ's Redemptive Merit* (1962)[15] addresses a prob-

---

14 In his later article, "Merit of Congruity," *Bijdragen Tijdschrift voor Filosofie en Theologie* 18 (1957): 262—67, De Letter looked at the nature and objects of congruent merit as a systematician using Aquinas as the "foundation" of his reflections. From this article, especially pp. 267–68, it seems clear that De Letter does not believe that Thomas's thought on the question of the merit of first grace changed. Unfortunately, his account of this merit in Aquinas describes more the teaching in the *Scriptum*, in which it is possible to conclude from Thomas's statements that Thomas allowed for morally good actions performed by the sinner without grace to serve as "meritorious" dispositions for the bestowal of grace, than the *Summa*, in which Thomas excludes any merit of first grace and insists on the prevenience of divine grace even for the human actions which precede the infusion of justifying grace.

15 William D. Lynn, *Christ's Redemptive Merit: The Nature of its Causality according to St. Thomas* (Rome, 1962). The page numbers in the text refer to

lem debated by twentieth-century Thomists, concerning the manner of Christ's meritorious causality and, more precisely, why according to Thomas only Christ could merit in a strict or condign sense for others. On the one hand, Thomists such as P. Glorieux[16] have argued that Christ's meritorious causality must be seen in terms of instrumental causality— Christ could merit for Christians because as the instrument of the Divinity, he alone was able to cause in others the dispositions needed to receive grace. Other Thomists, however, refuse to identify meritorious and instrumental causality. For them, Christ's meritorious activity is strictly speaking simply to be viewed in terms of merit; that is, Christ's work as human establishes a right to reward, in which right those who are joined to Christ may share. In order to resolve this dispute, Lynn first examines Thomas's general teaching on merit. His strategy is to identify the formal effect of merit—either to create a disposition needed to receive grace or to establish a right to a reward—and then to apply Thomas's general teaching on merit to the more obscure problem of the nature of Christ's redemptive merit for human beings. Though heavily dependent on De Letter's study in this first part,[17] Lynn's treatment is more satisfactory in a number of ways. First, with respect to the principal concern of the first part of his book, Lynn has enumerated a great number of Thomas's texts on merit in which merit is discussed in juridical and then in "material" or dispositional terms, and shows conclusively that it is the former that merit entails a title to reward in justice, which is the basic one for St. Thomas (p. 7).[18] Second, Lynn's methodology is more acceptable than De Letter's, for Lynn is more careful to distinguish statements made in the *Scriptum* from those in the *Summa* and he has observed a number of instances in which Thomas's teaching in the later work seems to differ from that in the earlier (see e.g., p. 23).[19]

---

16   this book.

16   P. Glorieux, "Le mérite du Christ selon S. Thomas," *RSR* 10 (1930): 622–49.

17   Lynn refers approvingly to De Letter's book (*De ratione meriti secundum Sanctum Thomam*) on p. 3 and cites it repeatedly in his own study.

18   Lynn, *Christ's Redemptive Merit*, p. 7: "[I]f we turn to [Aquinas] and ask what he understands by merit, he will answer that merit has an essentially juridical character; it is the action by which one acquires a right in justice to a reward." After considering the texts in which Thomas speaks of merit in terms of the disposition for a perfection, Lynn repeats (p. 72) "that the formal effect of merit is not an interior modification rendering the subject apt for receiving a reward, but a right in justice to a reward." It should be added that while Lynn acknowledges the place of justice in Thomas's definition of merit, he does not conclude that Thomas's teaching is therefore "legalistic." In the ensuing review of the literature, we shall see that scholars such as Auer have argued from the role of justice in merit to a legalism in Thomas, while others, such as Pesch, in order to preserve Thomas from the charge of legalism, have tended to downplay the place of justice in Thomas's definition of merit. I shall return to the question of Thomas's "juridicism" in the concluding paragraphs of this section of the chapter.

19   *Ibid.*, p. 23; Lynn introduces his discussion of the manner in which Thomas

Third, Lynn is also aware that Thomas's analysis of grace is more dynamic in the *Summa*, causing him to emphasize more adequately the role of grace in merit in this later work (p. 29). Fourth, unlike De Letter, Lynn acknowledges that by the time of the *Summa*, Thomas's interest in categorizing the justice involved in merit had faded (p. 24). Accordingly, Lynn does not replicate De Letter's exhaustive effort to identify the kind of justice operative in the *Summa's* treatment of merit.

Fifth, Lynn not only notes that in the *Summa* Thomas makes repeated use of the concept of a "divine ordination" to ground merit and that the invocation of the ordination marks a significant improvement on the *Scriptum;*[20] he also makes some attempt to describe what Thomas means by this term. There is some difficulty, however, in establishing Lynn's precise definition of the *ordinatio* in Aquinas. He himself does not offer a systematic or sustained statement about the content of the ordination that establishes the possibility of merit in the *Summa*. Rather, Lynn's comments about the ordination are scattered throughout the first part of his book, and it is left to the reader to construct a unified picture. From the scattered comments about the *ordinatio*, it appears that Lynn attributes different levels of meaning to this term. First, 'ordination' in general refers to the fact that as a class, humans are capable of life with God. As rational beings, the beatific vision is not inimical to them, and attaining the beatific vision would satisfy their deepest needs and desires (p. 31). But, secondly, 'ordination' means more than simply the ordering of people in general to God as to their beatifying end; it means that God moves people to God's own level to the supernatural level and gives to them the power of grace

treats the condignity of merit in the *Summa*, as compared with the *Scriptum*, by saying that he will now "point out those elements of doctrine which differ from the presentation in the *Sentences* [sic]"; he then lists three differences, under the headings of the "justice of merit," "divine ordination," and the "motion of grace." Nevertheless, Lynn does not wish to speak of a substantial development in Thomas's thought. For him, Thomas's teaching remains constant throughout his career. Rather, in the *Summa*, it is a question only of refinement, of stating better or more systematically the same teaching on merit found in the *Scriptum*.

20   *Ibid.*, p. 30: "One of the most striking differences which exist between, [sic] the analysis of merit in the *Sentences* [sic] and in the *Summa*, is the great prominence given in the later work to the divine ordination." After these words, Lynn adds that the principal ideas involved in the ordination can also be found scattered throughout the *Scriptum* and *De Veritate*, but concludes that "the terms itself and the systematization of thought that it represents are characteristic of the *Summa*." When he says that the "principal ideas" here involved are to be found scattered throughout the *Scriptum*, he perhaps is thinking especially of the "promise" to which Thomas occasionally refers in the *Scriptum* when speaking of merit; see p. 30, note 64, where among others, texts mentioning this promise are cited (although none are actually quoted). In Chapter 2, in the discussion of the *Scriptum*, I clarify the degree of resemblance between the *ordinatio* of the *Summa* and the "promise" of the *Scriptum*.

and the theological virtues which makes possible acts pleasing to God. Lynn shies away from the term 'predestination,' and his own discussion of grace is too brief to ascertain how convinced he is of the gratuity of God's action vis-à-vis the human person. But it seems that in this respect, 'ordination' means for Lynn what 'predestination' means for Thomas in the later works: God chooses freely a person for life with God and then brings this person to God. In this regard, then, the ordination differs from grace. Grace stands to the ordination as the effect stands to its cause (p. 33). Finally, there is a third element in the "ordination" which grounds merit for Lynn. Not only does God choose people for life with God and therefore endow them with the grace which elevates them to the supernatural level, God also "ordains" that the good works which they do under the guidance of grace will be meritorious, deserving the reward to which people are ordained by God. In other words, the "ordination" establishes an order between merit and reward so that God will grant people rewards for the good which they do. Hence, as Lynn writes at one point (p. 43), the term 'ordination' covers a rich complex of ideas in Thomas: "By one and the same divine ordination, He has decreed to raise man to a supernatural state, endow him with grace, which is the principle of merit, and reward him for good works proceeding from grace."

Although his own description of this *ordinatio* in Aquinas is fragmented, Lynn's diverse statements about the ordination (if I have interpreted them correctly) are of great value to the student of merit in Aquinas. As we shall shortly see, there have been rather different analyses offered in the literature of the ordination which makes merit possible: Hamm, for example, identifies the ordination with grace itself, while Pesch likens Thomas's ordination to the *acceptatio divina* of Duns Scotus. But I think that the various statements about the ordination made by Lynn touch upon most of the crucial elements in Thomas's teaching. In particular, in any account of this aspect of Thomas's teaching about merit, it is necessary to stress both that, in the ordination, God chooses a particular person to enjoy life with God, and God establishes a connection between the good works done by this person and the reward rendered for these works.

Yet, while Lynn's interpretation of the ordination is the most satisfactory one offered in the literature, there are still problems with his treatment. First, Lynn has left almost completely out of consideration the relation of the ordination in merit to the divine wisdom—Lynn's discussion of the divine wisdom is restricted to its relationship to God's justice. As Lynn correctly reports, in Aquinas justice means to "render what is owed or due (*debitum*)." In creation, God determines by the divine wisdom to establish a creature of a certain type. Once this determination has been made, God "owes" it to the creature to give it all that is required for a being of this type. Since God freely determines to establish creatures, this "debt" owed to the creature in fact is reducible to a "debt" owed to God Himself.[21]

---

21   The discussion in the text summarizes *ST* I 21, 1 ad 3; see Lynn, *Christ's*

Similarly, having decided to save a rational creature, God "owes" it to the creature to provide all that is needed, including grace, in order to bring it to eternal life. In this vein, the good works done by the rational creature in grace establish a "debt," the debt of merit, to be requited by God. Although significant, this discussion of the relation between justice and wisdom hardly exhausts the "sapiential" dimensions of Thomas's later thought about merit. Nor does it really tie the ordination to the divine wisdom in a completely satisfactory way—after all, these reflections about wisdom and merit are found throughout Thomas's writings, even in the *Scriptum*, and as Lynn himself argues, it is only in the *Summa* that the divine ordination comes to play an important role in Thomas's teaching about merit. There is a deeper connection between merit and wisdom that goes unrecognized by Lynn but which shapes Thomas's entire presentation of merit in the *Summa*. As I argue in Chapter 3, Thomas's later theology revolves around the insight that God created the world for the manifestation of the divine goodness outside of God. Since the world is not God, it is unable to manifest the divine goodness as it exists in a simple way in God. Rather, in place of the unified goodness which is God, the divine wisdom has "formulated" a plan for the manifestation of the goodness of God in the creation. According to this plan, there is a diversity of goods in the world and each creature by its being and by its activity proclaims God's goodness in the way appropriate to it. Thomas's discussion of human salvation and merit depicts the human person's attainment of God by merit as a particular instance of the manifestation of the divine goodness according to the divine wisdom. That some rational creatures are able to attain to God Himself, and are able to do so by their good actions (merits) is due to the ordination of the divine wisdom for the manifestation of the divine goodness in this special way. Hence, a full discussion of the ordination that makes merit possible in the *Summa* must examine the role of merit, according to the divine wisdom, in the manifestation of the divine goodness, as well as establish how his ordination-talk in this part of his theology reflects and presupposes his use of ordination-language in describing the role of the divine wisdom in the creating and directing of things.[22]

Redemptive Merit, p. 41. I return to this passage in the first section of Chapter 3.

22 Perhaps the best way to describe the development in Thomas's thought about merit is to say that it becomes increasingly "sapiential." By this, I mean that by the time of the *Summa Theologiae*, Thomas interprets merit in terms of the divine plan, formulated by the divine wisdom, for the manifestation of the divine goodness outside of God. For Aquinas, that God creates is due to God's desire to disclose God outside of God. Similarly, God employs the goods of the world in their activities, by which they reach their ends, for this same purpose: God has ordained their beings *and* their characteristic activities *and* the attainment of their ends for the manifestation of the divine goodness. So too with merit: Not only has God decided to share God's life with certain rational creatures to disclose the divine goodness in a special way; God has

Second, Lynn's discussion of this ordination is weakened by his failure to support his argument with careful reference to the appropriate texts: He simply asserts, for example, that ordination entails an ordering of good work to its reward, without citing or examining the specific texts in the *Summa* in which Thomas makes this clear.[23] Nor is Lynn's treatment of the divine ordination adequate for showing its true significance for Thomas's teaching about merit. Lynn simply refers to the ordination of the *Summa* in the course of his own argument about the true meaning of merit as the establishment of the right to a reward from God: He mentions it as but another feature of Thomas's teaching about merit. But as Thomas's discussion of the ordination at the very beginning of the question on merit in the *Summa* suggests, the *ordinatio* is not merely another feature of Thomas's discussion of merit; it is the key feature that makes merit possible in the first place and is the focus around which Thomas has organized his entire discussion of merit in the *Summa*. Any discussion of the later teaching on merit which marginalizes the divine ordination has failed to grasp the central feature of Thomas's later teaching. Thus, while Lynn has pointed his reader in the right direction, there is a need for a more thorough examination of the divine ordination in merit which will fully explicate this element of Thomas's thought and accord it the prominence which it deserves.

Other features of Lynn's presentation of merit are similarly disappointing. First, like De Letter, Lynn is content with Thomas's *ex professo* discussions of merit, in the *Scriptum* and the *Summa*. Second, Lynn simply leaves important problems in Thomas's teaching about merit out of consid-

---

ordained that they will attain God by their meritorious acts, in this way also proclaiming God. In the *Summa*, Thomas has tied merit closely to his thought about creation, providence, and predestination; in discussing each, he employs ordination-language. I do not think it would have been possible for Thomas to employ the *Summa*'s teaching about ordination in merit in the *Scriptum*. It is true, of course, that by the "promise" of the *Scriptum*, Thomas is referring to the ordering of acts to their reward, and this is certainly part of the "ordination" which grounds merit in the *Summa*. But ordination also entails God's election of certain individuals for life with God and then God's moving of them graciously to God through their acts. In the *Scriptum*, Thomas's thought about predestination is not so precise—he seems to think of it in more general terms, as the setting up of a "structure" by which those who do what is in them are able to avail themselves of God's universal offer of grace and so enter the path leading to God. Moreover, by the time of the *Summa*, Thomas thinks of the grace which arises from the ordination/predestination of God in more dynamic and efficient terms, and less in terms of the formal causality which predominates in the *Scriptum*. Hence, it becomes possible for him to speak of merits (good acts caused by grace) without sacrificing the insight that *God* determines whom God will save and accordingly "works" out the salvation of the elect.

23   In Chapter 3, I consider such texts as *ST* I-II 5, 7c, and I 23, 5c, and show how they contribute to our understanding of the content of the divine ordination.

eration. As did De Letter, Lynn fails to discuss the vexing problem of the merit of the first grace in Aquinas. There has been some dispute in the literature about Thomas's position on this question in his earliest theology. In particular, it is not clear whether Thomas allows a congruent merit of the first grace in the *Scriptum*. But although Lynn acknowledges that Thomas offers different analyses in the *Scriptum* and the *Summa* of the order of causality between the motion of the will and the first infusion of grace in justification,[24] he ignores the problem posed by Thomas's ambiguous statements in the *Scriptum* about meriting the first grace. Most significantly, despite his recognition of the more dynamic conception of grace in the *Summa*, this recognition has not adequately informed Lynn's account of merit. For example, he has not directly incorporated this insight into an explanation for Thomas's downplaying of distributive justice as governing merit in his later work, being content to ascribe this development in Thomas's thought rather to some supposed conviction on Thomas's part by the time of the *Summa* that the aristotelian categories of justice were too narrow and rigid to explain the unique relation which exists between the human person and God as a consequence of merit (p. 24).

In addition to the three monographs, there have been a number of other studies which have also treated Thomas's teaching about merit. In them, we find echoes of some of Lynn's (and De Letter's) more important conclusions. There seems to be a consensus that for Thomas, the basic meaning of 'merit' is that it establishes a right or title in justice to a reward rendered by God for good human actions. E. Neveut, for example, says of merit that "est un droit et suppose un rapport entre l'oeuvre faite et la récompense,"[25] while P. Lumbreras defines merit as a "titulum" to a reward from God.[26]

---

24   See Lynn, *Christ's Redemptive Merit*, pp. 52–53, n. 23. Lynn notes that in the *Scriptum* and *De Veritate* the relation between human acts and the infusion of grace in justification is discussed in terms of material and formal causality; in the *Summa* human acts are seen as caused efficiently by divine grace. In the second section of this chapter, in the examination of Bouillard, the question of the relation between the human preparation for grace and the infusion of grace is discussed in much greater detail.

25   E. Neveut, "Du mérite de convenance," *Divus Thomas* 35 (1932): 3.

26   P. Lumbreras, "Naturale meritum ad Deum," *Angelicum* 19 (1942): 157. For Lumbreras, there are two species of merit, supernatural and natural. On the supernatural level, merit provides a title to a supernatural reward, in justice. A. Miralles, "El Gobierno Divino," p. 80, also underscores the justice involved in meriting and rewarding. See also R. Garrigou-Lagrange, *Grace: Commentary on the "Summa Theologica" of St. Thomas, Ia IIae, q. 109–14*, trans. F. Eckhoff (St. Louis, 1952), 366: "Merit can be defined either in the concrete or in the abstract. . . . In the concrete, it is an action to which recompense is due in justice . . . or a good work which confers a right to a reward. In the abstract, it is a right to a reward." On the other hand, Catão, *Salut et rédemption* p. 49, n. 2, refers to Lynn's work somewhat disapprovingly and cautions us not to make the meritorious quality of the good work something "extrinsic" to it; he wishes to underscore the real,

On balance, I believe that Lynn has effectively made the case for "right to a reward" as the basic meaning of merit and that there should be little dispute about the principal meaning of merit in Aquinas. Throughout this work I have assumed that this in fact is Thomas's working definition of merit.[27] Similarly, other interpreters of Thomas agree with De Letter and Lynn that Thomas's teaching about merit remained the same throughout his career. Unwilling to allow for real development in Thomas's thought, they will speak at most of a "shift in emphasis" in his discussion of this doctrine.[28] On the whole, this reluctance to perceive development in Thomas's thought is probably ideological, reflecting the inability of many Thomists of an earlier generation to accept the possibility that Thomas could change his mind or that his understanding of an issue could mature. Yet we find the denial of development in Thomas's thought about merit even in such a progressive student of Aquinas as Otto Hermann Pesch, who thinks that Thomas's understanding of merit basically remained the same throughout his career;[29] Pesch's success in maintaining this position is greatly facilitated by his almost exclusive concentration on the teaching

intrinsic ordination of morally good works to their end/reward. I return to Catão's discussion of merit near the end of this section of the chapter.

27   However, while other interpreters have agreed that merit means a right to a reward, not all have followed Lynn in concluding (*Christ's Redemptive Merit*, p. 7) that Thomas's understanding of merit is therefore "juridical." As we shall see in the discussion of Catão, Hamm, and Pesch below in the text, some students of Aquinas argue that his teaching about merit is only poorly described as "juridical."

28   See, e.g., Catão, *Salut et rédemption*, p. 64, n. 1, where Catão speaks of "un changement d'accent" in Thomas's teaching about merit, for in the *Scriptum* Thomas looks only at the act in itself while in the *Summa* he considers the transcendent source of the supernatural perfection of the act, the divine intervention in grace. In his recent articles on merit in Aquinas, "La Perspectiva Sapiencial de la Teologia del Merito en Santo Tomas de Aquino" and "El Gobierno Divino en la Teologia del Merito de Santo Tomas de Aquino," Miralles clearly rejects any suggestion of development in Thomas's thought. For example, he even rejects De Letter's claim that in the *Scriptum*, distributive justice predominates in merit, while in the *Summa* it is commutative justice which is operative—for Miralles, it is always distributive justice which is involved in merit. See "La Perspectiva Sapiencial," p. 297, n. 19 and "El Gobierno Divino," pp. 82 and 83, n. 35. Miralles is simply incorrect in this matter. Miralles's assumption that Thomas's teaching remains the same permits him to quote indiscriminately texts from all periods of Thomas's career to support his arguments.

29   In *Die Theologie der Rechtfertigung bei Martin Luther und Thomas von Aquin* (Mainz, 1967), Pesch, *Die Theologie der Rechtfertigung bei Martin Luther und Thomas von Aquin*, for example, claims (p. 660) that Thomas always denied even a congruent merit of the first grace, thus implying that the teaching of the *Scriptum* and the *Summa* fully mesh on this question. As will shortly become clear, ascertaining what Thomas in fact teaches in the *Scriptum* about the merit of the first grace is much more difficult than Pesch would allow.

on merit found in the *Summa Theologiae*. The most notable exception in this regard is the non-Thomist Bernd Hamm. Hamm believes that we can delineate a development in Thomas's understanding of merit, one which is characterized by an increased "Aristotelianism" and "de-personalization" in Thomas's thought. For my part, I agree with Hamm that Thomas's teaching about merit has undergone development but disagree about the characterization of this development. As I shall argue, Thomas's development is due especially to an increased familiarity with the theology of grace of the later Augustine.

However, in the remaining literature, some attempt has been made to fill the lacunae left by De Letter and Lynn and to offer different perspectives on Aquinas's teaching about merit. For example, we find in the literature much discussion of Thomas's teaching of the possibility of a merit of the first grace. Here, Thomists ask whether Thomas ever allowed for a merit of the first grace by a merit *ex congruo*. Congruent merit is merit in a weak or improper sense, and it depends as much on God's merciful willingness to reward earnest effort by human beings as it does on God's justice. The question, then, is whether Thomas ever thought that the earnest effort of *sinners*, those who exist outside of grace, in preparing themselves for the gift of grace was congruently meritorious of this grace. In the *Summa Theologiae*, Thomas does not explicitly discuss such a merit *ex congruo* of the first grace, and indeed his denial of the *facere quod in se est* in the sense of action performed by an autonomous human being who wishes to receive grace and his corresponding argument that even the preparation for grace is due to God's efficient prevenient grace[30] have caused most, but not all[31] interpreters of Thomas to conclude that there is no room for such a merit of the first grace in the later Thomas. In the light of these statements in the *Summa*, most would argue that the later Thomas affirms only a *meritum ex congruo* which presupposes a prior gift of grace. However, the evidence of the earlier *Scriptum Super Sententias* is more ambiguous, for in certain passages Thomas seems to allow for a congruent merit of the first grace. Moreover, his somewhat different treatment of the free acts of the human person that are required in justification in terms of material causality, as well as his explicit affirmation of the *facere quod in se est* on the part of the sinner in preparation for the gift of grace, at least makes it possible that Thomas in the early work did teach a congruent merit of first grace, a teaching which he later abandoned. This, in fact, is J. Rivière's conclusion.[32] He claims that while Thomas asserted in the

---

30   See the discussion of Henri Bouillard, *Conversion et grâce chez S. Thomas d'Aquin* (Paris, 1944) and B. Lonergan, *Grace and Freedom: Operative Grace in the Thought of St. Thomas Aquinas*, ed. J. Patout Burns (London, 1971) in the second section of this chapter.

31   See the discussion of Garrigou-Lagrange, *Grace*, below in the text.

32   J. Rivière, "S. Thomas et le mérite 'de congruo,'" *RSR* 7 (1927): 641–49. The page numbers which follow in the text refer to this article.

earlier treatment the possibility of natural good works performed without the aid of grace that can merit *ex congruo* the gift of grace (p. 643f.), in the later *Summa*, Thomas's recognition that even the imperfect preparation for grace is caused by grace (pp. 644, 648) and that the gift of grace cannot fall under merit (p. 647) but rather makes merit possible, reveals that Thomas has abandoned his earlier position (p. 648) and restricted his talk about such a congruent merit to the activities of the person endowed with grace (p. 646). While Rivière correctly draws our attention to the main stages of Thomas's thinking on the question, the value of his article is diminished somewhat by his failure to consider those other texts in the *Scriptum* in which Thomas seems to *reject* this teaching by denying the possibility of a merit of the first grace. Indeed, on the basis of such texts, interpreters such as Neveut[33] have concluded that since such a merit is meritorious in only a weak and attenuated sense, Thomas in the *Scriptum* preferred to deny a congruent merit of the first grace.[34]

A rather different evaluation of the material in Thomas about a merit of the first grace is provided by R. Garrigou-Lagrange in his commentary on the treatise on grace in the *Summa Theologiae*.[35] Basically, Garrigou-Lagrange disagrees that any development in this matter is present in Thomas, for he thinks that even in the *Summa*, Thomas has affirmed the congruent merit which he affirms in the *Scriptum*. In the face of the apparently explicit rejection of such a merit in the *Summa*, Garrigou-Lagrange is forced to make a series of distinctions about merit to support his case. Although Thomas mentions in the *Summa* two kinds of merit, *meritum ex condigno* (merit in the strict sense, based on justice) and *meritum ex congruo* (merit in a less strict sense, based more on friendship), for Garrigou-Lagrange there are in fact *four* kinds of merit discussed by Thomas in the *Summa*. First, there are two types of condign merit, that of Christ, which by reason of the divinity is absolutely equal to the reward which it deserves, and that of Christians, whose works by virtue of the divine ordination are proportioned to the reward of eternal life, although

---

33   Neveut, "Du mérite de convenance," p. 9. What Neveut means is that when Thomas in the *Scriptum* rejects a merit of the first grace, he is thinking specifically of this merit in a weakened sense, congruent merit. It may be, however, that when he explicitly rejects a merit at the beginning of the spiritual life, Thomas is thinking exclusively of condign merit, merit in a strict sense, and leaving open the possibility of a congruent merit, an imperfect merit, of the first grace.

34   As we shall see in the second section of this chapter, on the basis of a more intimate knowledge of the pertinent texts in the *Scriptum*, Bouillard has argued that even in this early work, Thomas denied even the congruent merit of the first grace. In Chapter 2, I argue for the fundamental correctness of Rivière's argument, by explaining how the passages advanced by Bouillard do not necessarily exclude congruent merit (see previous note).

35   R. Garrigou-Lagrange, *Grace: Commentary on the "Summa Theologica" of St. Thomas, Ia IIae, q. 109–14*, trans. F. Eckhoff (St. Louis, 1952). The page numbers in the text refer to this translation.

not equal to it. Similarly, there are two kinds of congruent merit. Congruent merit for Garrigou-Lagrange does not involve justice but rests on the mercy of God alone. The two species of congruent merit are determined by the state of those who so merit. For those who exist in grace and are at peace with God, God looks mercifully on their (natural) acts and treats them as congruently meritorious. Sinners, on the other hand, are not friends of God. But if sinners nevertheless try to please God, God will consider such actions as congruently meritorious in a broad sense and, so, mercifully reward these acts (p. 369). It is this latter type of congruent merit which "merits" in an attenuated sense the gift of grace, both here in the *Summa* and in the *Scriptum*. Despite the surface disagreement between the two works, they contain the same teaching (p. 369). Garrigou-Lagrange's attempt to preclude development in Aquinas's teaching is subtle and imaginative and, I think, utterly incorrect. Thomas is capable of great clarity and precision. If he had meant to present four types of merit and not two, he would have said so clearly. And if he had wished to allow a merit *ex congruo* of the first grace in the *Summa* despite his radical reinterpretation of the *facere quod in se est* there and his accompanying insistence on the need for grace to prepare for grace, he would have told us so and would have explained the meaningfulness of such an assertion in the face of his denial of the "ideological" underpinnings of this teaching in the *Scriptum*. Moreover, it is doubtful, given his perception of the relations between merit and justice, that Thomas would allow a congruent merit which has no connection to the divine justice. While congruent merit is not governed by justice to the same extent as is condign merit, and God's mercy is undoubtedly prominent here, it would be incorrect to excise any reference to justice in this kind of merit, as Garrigou-Lagrange does.[36] To be blunt, Garrigou-Lagrange's analysis in this regard, at least, is of strictly "archaeological" interest, since it reveals the lengths to which certain students of Thomas have gone to bring Thomas in line with what they take to be the requirements of later Church doctrine. In the recovery of Thomas's own teaching about the congruent merit of the first grace and the stages of that teaching, Rivière's analysis despite its failings is closer to the truth.

Other students of merit in Aquinas have contemplated Thomas's teaching in its totality and have provided analyses of some of its salient features, as well as of its essential spirit, that differ markedly from the descriptions provided by De Letter and Lynn. In his influential study of high scholastic theologies of grace and merit, *Die Entwicklung der Gnadenlehre in der Hochscholastik* (1951),[37] J. Auer has offered a series of observations about

---

36   In this regard, attention should be drawn to the comments of De Letter, "Merit of Congruity," p. 262; De Letter suggests that the justice of God most fully applies in condign merit, the mercy of God in the impetration of prayer, and that in congruent merit, there is a "mixture" of justice and mercy which is operative. See also Miralles, "La Perspectiva Sapiencial," p. 299.

37   Johannes Auer, *Die Entwicklung der Gnadenlehre in der Hochscholastik,* 2

Thomas's teaching on merit. Auer discerns in thirteenth-century scholastic treatments of grace two basic orientations. On the one hand, there is what Auer calls the "more personalistic" early Franciscan school, centered around Bonaventure, which is faithful to the Augustinian insights into the grace-event as the genuine personal interaction of God and the human person. In the Franciscan school, merit is accordingly discussed in terms of God's free self-binding in relation to humanity. Given the infinite distance between people and God, and God's freedom from any necessitation by creatures, there can only be merit before God because God has freely decided to accept as meritorious works done in grace and charity. On the other hand, the Thomistic school is less concerned with the personal elements of grace and divine-human relations. According to Auer, Thomas's theology of grace is much more abstract than the contemporary Franciscan and, because of the influence of Aristotle upon him, comes to describe grace primarily in ontological and naturalistic terms. Auer's distinction between Franciscan and Thomistic approaches to grace informs the comments about Thomas's teaching on merit scattered throughout his book. First, Auer asserts that Thomas de-personalizes grace and merit. The reliance on Aristotelian concepts and terminology such as 'habit,' 'quality,' and the general depiction of divine-human relations in terms of primary and secondary causality, have caused Thomas to pay relatively little attention to the personalistic dimensions of merit and grace (p. 63). Second, Auer argues that the *divina ordinatio* mentioned in the *Summa* is not the Thomistic equivalent of the later Scotist *divina acceptatio*. The Franciscan concern in invoking the *acceptatio* is to safeguard God's sovereignty in relation to the creation. As Scotus put it, "nothing created can necessitate God," meaning that even grace, which is created by God, need not make its possessor pleasing to God. Only the additional decision by God to accept people who are in grace makes their acts meritorious. In Thomas, on the other hand, under the influence of Aristotle, there is a much greater preoccupation with the intrinsic qualities of grace. As an Aristotelian, Thomas tends to view things in terms of their natures and ends. For Thomas grace denotes the formal quality which makes the rational creature acceptable to God. Moreover, its nature has an inner orientation to God. Thus, according to Auer, once someone has grace—due to God's predestination of the individual—by an inner necessity, that is, due to the intrinsic value and orientation of grace, acts done in grace lead to the attainment of the end of grace (pp. 80, 153f). Third, Auer argues that this understanding of the intrinsic worth of grace, in combination with Thomas's stress on the justice regulating divine-human relations in merit, has caused Thomas to teach a basically "juridical" and even legalistic theology of merit. Indeed, because of the greatness of grace, which is equal in worth by its very nature to the reward of eternal life, the individual by meritorious actions not only obtains a real right to a reward but in fact

vols. (Freiburg, 1942–51). All references in the text are to the second volume.

even succeeds in putting God in his debt, establishing a claim upon God for this reward.[38]

Otto Hermann Pesch, the great student of Luther and Aquinas, in a number of works has disputed Auer's analysis of Thomas's teaching on merit.[39] Pesch argues that Auer is guilty of gross distortions[40] in his presentation of Thomas's theology of grace and merit. Pesch rejects Auer's general contention that Thomas has paid insufficient attention to the personal dimensions of grace. As we shall see shortly in the critique of Hamm's analysis, it is necessary to insist with Pesch on the connection between the gift of (habitual) grace, described by Thomas in admittedly Aristotelian terms, and God's creative love for the human person. More pertinent for our discussion, Pesch rejects Auer's analysis of the meaning of the divine ordination which constitutes the basis of merit in the *Summa Theologiae*. In fact, Pesch is convinced that the Scotist *acceptatio* and the Thomist *ordinatio* are intimately related.[41] Thus, he writes that for Thomas, the divine ordination refers to the divine decision to treat works done in grace (that is, the human works which are instigated and guided by divine grace) as meritorious.[42] Pesch adds, however, that this "acceptance/ordination" does not stand over against or in isolation from grace. Rather, it is tied to grace as one of its facets, due to the decision of God.

---

38   Auer, *Entwicklung*, 2: 154 "Der Mensch hat darum, nicht personal gesehen, aber sächlich betrachtet, ein wirklichen Anrecht, eine Forderung an Gott auf Grund der Gnade."

39   Three writings by Pesch are significant for our problem: *Die Theologie der Rechtfertigung bei Martin Luther und Thomas von Aquin* (Mainz, 1967), p. 771 [= *Rechtfertigung*]; *Einführung in die Lehre von Gnade und Rechtfertigung* (with Albrecht Peters) (Darmstadt, 1981), pp. 103ff [*Einführung*]; and "Die Lehre vom 'Verdienst' als Problem für Theologie und Verkündigung," in *Wahrheit und Verkündigung: Festgabe M. Schmaus*, ed. L. Scheffczyk et al (Paderborn, 1967), p. 2: 1865–1907 ["Lehre"].

40   Pesch, *Rechtfertigung*, p. 772, n. 70: "Die Darstellung der Thomas-Lehre bei Auer zeigt freilich bedauerliche Vergröberungen."

41   For a discussion of *acceptatio* and *ordinatio*, see *Ibid.*, 708f. There is a great deal which recommends itself in Pesch's analysis, although I think that he has overstated the resemblance between *ordinatio* and *acceptatio*. Moreover, I am not sure that I can agree with his further claim, in "Lehre," 1904, that there is a historical link between Thomist *ordinatio* and Scotist *acceptatio*, in the sense that Scotus knew Aquinas's position but then "radicalized" it. Despite the similarities, a great deal more work must be done to establish the peculiarities of the position of each, as well as the extent of Scotus's knowledge of Thomas, before deciding the issue. It is more likely that Thomas and Scotus are working with a common source which they have then treated in their own way.

42   Pesch, *Rechtfertigung*, p. 775, n. 78: "Die ordinatio divina ist eine sozusagen zusätzliche Verfügung über das, was dem Menschen im Gefüge des causa prima-causa secunda Verhältnisses ohnehin allerst von Gott zukommt und Inhalt dieser Verfügung ist gerade der Lohn-Charakter und damit die personale Bewandtnis des Zukommenden."

When God predestines an individual to salvation, God provides the means to attain salvation, i.e., grace, *and* determines that this grace and the works it supports are "worthy" of eternal life.[43] In this view, then, grace does not necessitate God's reward of meritorious action. Works performed through grace are deserving of a reward because God has freely decided and ordained to ascribe this value to such works.[44]

In the light of this understanding of the divine ordination, Pesch is able to rebut the other claims made by Auer. First, Pesch rejects the argument that the discussion of merit as governed by justice in Thomas's writings means that Thomas's teaching here is "juridical" or legalistic. Good human acts done in grace are meritorious of reward from God precisely because God has decided to accept these acts as worthy of eternal life. In other words, God's promise, not an abstract system of justice which considers only the intrinsic value of works, lies at the basis of merit.[45] Thus, says Pesch, the divine ordination frees Thomas from the charge of ascribing to the human person the power of placing God in his debt. As Thomas says at one point in the article in which he first introduces us to the divine ordination that is the ground of merit (I-II 114, 1 ad 3), the debt owed in merit is owed to *God*, and in requiting merits, God is simply honoring the divine commitment to treat good works done in grace as meritorious. Such a view, continues Pesch, is in reality the very opposite of self-righteousness, and Thomas's approach to the possibility of merit results in "die Entleerung des Verdienstbegriffes von aller juridischen Bedeutung."[46] Similarly, this interpretation of the divine ordination enables Pesch to reject out of hand Auer's claim that Thomas's analysis promotes the de-personalization of grace and merit. Since meritability rests on God's free ordination and acceptance of acts as meritorious and God rewards acts which conform to the divine will, it is more accurate, according to Pesch, to say that Thomas in fact champions a deeply personal view of merit. When people in loving obedience fulfill God's will for them, God remains true to the divine promise (announced in the gospel) and rewards their deeds by bringing God's people into complete and direct personal union with God.[47]

---

43   *Ibid.*, p. 781.
44   *Ibid.*
45   *Ibid.*, p. 776: "Thomas lässt den Lohn als Antwort der Treue Gottes stehen und streicht den Anspruch durch. Sinn der Verdienstlehre des heiligen Thomas ist also nach dieser ersten, alles Weitere beherrschenden Antwort: Gott schenkt aus Treue zu sich selbst dem Menschen auf dessen Handeln hin ohne jeden Anspruch einen Lohn."
46   *Ibid.*, p. 780, n. 99. See also p. 775: "Die völlige Entleerung aller juridischen Vorstellungen, die mit dem Verdienstbegriff verbunden sein mögen, ist schwer zu überbieten."
47   See, e.g., Pesch, *Einführung,* p. 105: in merit and reward, ". . . es sich um eine Antwort der Treue auf Treue, das heisst: um eine Begegnung von Personen und auf personale Weise handelt. Dies ist der erste und alles Weitere beherrschende Sinn der Verdienstlehre."

In his recent book, *Promissio, Pactum, Ordinatio* (1977),[48] Bernd Hamm has attempted to reformulate Auer's analysis while taking account of at least some of Pesch's comments. Inspired by Auer's example,[49] Hamm has studied scholastic theologies of grace with an eye to delineating the basic orientations adopted by different medieval writers in discussing grace and merit. As in Auer, for Hamm there are two basic ways in which scholastic theologians approached the problem of merit. On the one hand, there are those theologians who ground the meritability of human acts in what Hamm calls God's "historical self-binding"[50]. Here, it is God's decision, made in eternity and announced and promised in history through the Scriptures, to reward good works, and not the intrinsic value of human acts, which is the reason why human actions may deservedly lead to eternal life. Agreeing with Auer, Hamm notes that this analysis is preferred by the Franciscans. On the other hand, other theologians have downplayed the significance for merit of the divine decision and have focused their discussion of the basis of merit on the intrinsic value of good works that are done in grace. As might be expected given his reliance on Auer, Hamm presents Thomas Aquinas as the "einflussreichste Vertreter" (p. 312) of this way of analyzing merit. For Hamm, Aquinas is able to argue for merit on the basis of the intrinsic value of grace because of his adroit exploitation of the Aristotelian teaching on natures and their finality, especially in the later works (including the *Summa Theologiae*). Indeed, Hamm argues that Thomas's thinking on grace underwent a development directly as a result of his greater use of Aristotelian material. In Hamm's view, whereas the *Scriptum* on the *Sentences* of Peter Lombard and other early works treated grace more strictly in neo-Platonic terms as the "participation" in the divine nature by which the human person is raised to God's level and made pleasing to God, the later writings on grace thanks to Aristotle exhibit a much more dynamic account of grace, viewing it especially in terms of its capacity to ordain and direct the human person and his acts toward God.[51] Secondly, it is this "dynamizing" of grace under the influence of Aristotle which makes possible the grounding of merit in the divine ordination in the *Summa Theologiae* and which correspondingly makes it unlikely that Thomas understands the divine ordination in a "Franciscan" sense, as Pesch had argued. Since by its very nature grace is directed or ordained to

---

48   Bernd Hamm, *Promissio, Pactum, Ordinatio* (Tübingen, 1977). The page numbers in the text refer to this book.

49   *Ibid.*, p. 3, notes the influence of Auer on his study. However, Hamm's study of Aquinas is superior to Auer's, at least in the sense that it is a more systematic presentation of Thomas's thought.

50   Hamm, *Promissio, Pactum, Ordinatio*, pp. 1ff., explains this notion of God's self-binding that is revealed in history.

51   According to Hamm, *Promissio, Pactum, Ordinatio*, because of Aristotle Thomas emphasizes the "immanent-teleological" (p. 334) quality of grace and asserts an "ontological" link between grace and reward (p. 313); see also p. 336.

its end, the vision of God, and by its nature is of equal worth, at least in a "virtual" or "potential" sense, to the gift of the beatific vision,[52] Thomas has no need to introduce an extrinsic aspect to this account of meritability, that is, to refer to a divine determination and promise, apart from grace, to treat human actions done in grace as worthy of eternal life. Such a divine decision would be superfluous in Aquinas.[53] Yet, finally, although Hamm agrees with Auer to this point about Thomas's basically Aristotelian conception of grace and about the interpretation of the divine ordination in the *Summa*, Hamm joins Pesch in disagreeing with Auer's further characterization of Thomas's merit-language as essentially "juridical" in tone. As does Pesch, Hamm takes seriously Thomas's statement in *ST* I-II 114, 1 ad 3, that in meriting, God is placed under debt only to God. But Hamm cannot quite agree with Pesch in the claim that Thomas has advanced a portrayal of merit in "personal" terms—it is best, he says, to reserve the epithet "personal" to accounts of merit, such as the Franciscan, in which the categories of grace and merit are themselves personal and not naturalistic. Instead, since Thomas stresses the naturalistic features of grace and since natures are joined both ontologically and by orientation to their ends, it is most appropriate to call Thomas's teaching on merit "ontological-natural," for in his account grace by its inner connection to its end brings the individual to eternal life (p. 336).

The differences between these interpretations of merit and the divine ordination in Aquinas are striking: On the one hand, Hamm and Auer identify the ordination with grace and refer to the intrinsic qualities and orientation of grace/*ordinatio*. On the other hand, Pesch likens the *divina ordinatio* to the Scotist *acceptatio*, and says that merit is possible for Thomas because God has determined to accept good human acts as meritorious of salvation. Which interpretation more adequately expresses Thomas's thought? To date, Pesch has not formally evaluated Hamm's discussion of the divine ordination in Aquinas or attempted to answer Hamm's criticism of his own approach.[54] But although his interpretation suffers from certain drawbacks,[55] I think that on balance Pesch offers the more satisfactory interpretation of the divine ordination in the *Summa*'s teaching on merit. In the following pages, I will re-formulate the essence of Pesch's position, in slightly amended form,[56] by exposing the serious flaws in Hamm's analysis.

---

52   Hamm, *Promissio, Pactum, Ordinatio*, p. 335. Here, Hamm is referring to the example given in *ST* I-II 114, 3 ad 3. I return to this text in my critique of Hamm below.

53   For Hamm's characterization of such a divine determination in Aquinas as "überflussig," see *Promissio*, p. 325.

54   In *Einführung*, p. 105, n. 121, Pesch notes Hamm's work and says that he nevertheless stands by his analysis; he makes no effort to refute Hamm.

55   I shall enumerate in detail the problems with Pesch's interpretation in the text below.

56   The most important emendation to Pesch concerns the relation between the

First, it is impossible to concur with Hamm's claim that Thomas's teaching about grace and merit reveals the receding importance of "personal" elements in his theology in the face of a growing Aristotelianism. Although Hamm mentions in passing Thomas's reference to such "personalist" ideas as the community of humanity and God established by God's grace and the adoption of people as children of God,[57] Hamm in effect ignores these and other "personal" features in his presentation of Thomas's account of merit and fails to consider how they have tempered the more "naturalistic" Aristotelian concepts and terms in a more personalistic direction, thus strengthening by default his claims about the de-personalization involved in Thomas's portrayal of merit. Yet there are indeed personalist features in Thomas's teaching on merit, and these features should not be ignored.[58] Even with regard to those notions which apparently suggest a more naturalistic vision of merit, Hamm's case is not as solid as it might first appear. At a couple of points, Hamm refers to Thomas's use in his grace and merit talk of the image of a seed which contains "virtually" its end[59]—as Thomas uses this in I-II 114, 3 ad 3, this is meant to convey to us a sense of the basic equality between the grace (seed) informing meritorious action and the glory (the tree which grows from the seed) which is the end of this action, and Hamm infers that Thomas's choice of this image to "explain" merit is governed by his Aristotelian sense of the finality of natures. While in I-II 114, 3 ad 3, Thomas does not explicitly cite the text which has inspired this usage, the parallel discussion earlier in the *Summa* clearly shows that, in his use of seed language for grace, Thomas is referring not to Aristotle, but to the Bible, to I John 3:9.[60] Thus, to adopt for the moment jargon similar to Hamm's, the use of seed imagery in the discussion of merit testifies not to the Aristotelian-naturalistic-ontological origin of Aquinas's theology of grace, but rather to the *biblical*-dynamic background of Thomas's thought.

Second, the value of Hamm's analysis is limited by the narrow focus of his treatment of Thomas's theology of grace. To use the old scholastic distinction, Hamm focuses only on created grace and neglects uncreated grace, the God Who lies behind the gift of the habitual and other graces possessed by people. In this regard, one might reasonably suggest that Hamm is guilty of a rather selective reading of the secondary sources which

---

ordination and Thomas's thought about the divine goodness and wisdom. Pesch pays insufficient attention to this relation and accordingly distorts somewhat the precise content of the divine ordination. For a brief introduction to this relation in Aquinas, see the critique of Lynn above.

57 See, e.g., Hamm, *Promissio*, 313.
58 Later, in the discussion of the understanding of merit advanced by Catão, I shall return to this question of the "personalism" of Thomas's teaching on merit.
59 See, e.g., Hamm, *Promissio*, 335.
60 For the earlier use in the *Summa* of the image of "seed" for grace and the explicit citation of I John 3:9, see I 62, 3c.

have furnished many of the details of his discussion. As we have seen, Hamm argues that Thomas's discussion of (created) grace is characterized by the increasing importance of Aristotelian categories, which accounts for the accompanying "dynamizing" of grace in Thomas. Pesch too speaks of increasing dynamism of grace in Thomas. But Pesch also penetrates deeper into Thomas's thinking about grace and makes abundantly clear that this new dynamic feature of grace is due not so much to the new, Aristotelian concepts undoubtedly exploited by Thomas in the formulation of his theology as to Thomas's effort to bring to expression his ever-firmer conviction of the active involvement of *God* in the life of those whom God has chosen to save and to bring to God. Indeed, Pesch clearly directs our attention to the dependence of created grace on God. The grace which transforms the human person, granting new capacities and leading the person to God (and for the analysis of which Thomas employs Aristotelian categories, among others) is itself the result of God's creative love which stands at the basis of personal salvation.[61] Similarly, Hamm's comments about the dynamism of grace in the later Thomas are akin at first glance to those made by Henri Bouillard in his *Conversion et grâce chez S. Thomas d'Aquin.*[62] For example, Bouillard notes that while the early Thomas preferred to focus on the formal qualities of habitual grace, the mature Thomas described grace more in terms of "motion." Yet Hamm misses Bouillard's fundamental claim in this regard,[63] that Thomas now prefers to discuss grace precisely in terms of a *divine* motion because Thomas wishes to lay bare, in the discussion of the grace given to people, the origin of this grace in the love of God Who freely becomes involved in human salvation and directly and personally sustains the movement of the individual in the return to God. Moreover, Bouillard surely is not oblivious to Thomas's use of Aristotelian categories in formulating his insight into the divine presence through grace in human existence. But Hamm fails to acknowledge Bouillard's further claim, that it is Thomas's greater familiarity, through his exegetical work in the 1260s, with the *Pauline* teaching on grace that has contributed to this new stress on the dynamism of grace. As Bouillard mentions, passages in Paul which speak of the Christian "acting by the Spirit" or as "led by the Spirit"[64] necessitated in Thomas's mind the shift in his description of grace. Only when one contemplates Thomas's language about grace in abstraction from its biblical moorings and Thomas's conviction of God's involvement in human salvation, can one conclude (as does Hamm) that the use of Aristotle leads to the "naturalizing" and "de-personalizing" of grace. A

---

61   See, e.g., Pesch, *Rechtfertigung*, pp. 781 and 628ff.
62   Bouillard, *Conversion et grâce chez S. Thomas d'Aquin* (Paris, 1944). Hamm cites Bouillard and Pesch as sources for his presentation of Aquinas in *Promissio*, p. 313, n. 232, and refers to them throughout his chapter on Aquinas.
63   See, e.g., Bouillard, *Conversion et grâce*, pp. 91 and 140.
64   *Ibid.*, 138.

complete and integral reading of Thomas, which grasps the inner connections of created and uncreated grace, however, manifests the fully personal quality of Thomas's understanding of grace.

Most significantly, Hamm's interpretation of the *divina ordinatio* in the *Summa* in terms of the "inner, ontological" quality of works done in grace is simply not convincing. Despite Hamm's denials, Thomas's thought here is surprisingly close to the contemporary Franciscan understanding of meritability as due to the free self-binding of God by which God accepts good works done in grace as meritorious.[65] Hamm argues that Thomas's understanding of the divine ordination is shaped by his general "creation-ontology": God decides to bring certain people to salvation and accordingly grants them the means, grace, which by its very nature is directed to its end (God). In the face of this "givenness of creation," God is bound as it were to complete this grace by the bestowal of the final end of salvation.[66] There is no denying that Thomas takes account of creation in the description of the history of human salvation—as a systematician, he indeed sees the connections between God's will to create and God's will to save. But Hamm's interpretation of ordination in terms of "creation-ontology" would only be compelling if the act of creation were necessitated for Thomas by the inner requirements of God's being and, moreover, if the actual form which the result of the act of creation takes were itself necesary to fulfill the divine will in creating. In Thomas, however, the act of creation is absolutely free,[67] and while the result of this act is surely not purposeless,[68]

---

65   As I have already indicated in notes 41 and 56 above, I do not believe that the Scotist *acceptatio* and the Thomist *ordinatio* are identical. Indeed, as will become abundantly clear in Chapter 3, I think that there are crucial differences between the two. My point against Hamm is that he has drawn the distinction between ordination and acceptation in the wrong place, and hence has failed to note the resemblance between the two.

66   Hamm, *Promissio*, p. 333: "Während die Franziskaner durch sie den Freiheitsraum Gottes gegenüber seiner Schöpfung hervorheben wollen, indem sie zwischen Schöpfungsordnung und via salutis des Menschen eine Reihe von heilsgeschichtlichen Verordnungen zwischenschalten, weist Thomas durch seinen ordinatio-Begriff nicht auf die Kontingenz freien geschichtlichen Handelns, sondern auf eine Schöpfungsontologie. Die innergeschichtliche Dynamik der ordinatio, die sich in der Bewegung von Gnadengeschenk zum ewigen Leben entfaltet, geht direkt auf den göttlichen Schöpfungsplan zuruck. Kurz gesagt: Es handelt sich nicht um eine externe Verordnung, die den immanenten Schöpfungsgegebenheiten erst entgegentrate, sondern um einen Faktor der immanenten Schöpfungsgegebenheiten selbst, der ihre ontologisch-naturhafte Finalität erklärt."

67   Thomas makes the statement that God's creation is unnecessitated and free throughout his corpus; *ST* I 19, 3c, is representative.

68   For Aquinas, the end of creation is the manifestation of God's goodness outside of God. See, for example, *ST* I 44, 4c; I 47, 1c (God brought things into existence so that the divine goodness might be communicated to creatures and re-enacted through them); and I 65, 2c (in which Thomas says that the

it is not necessary in the sense that the divine goal in creating could be achieved by God only by creating the world. The manifestation of the divine goodness, which Thomas consistently asserts to be the end of creating, could have been accomplished in any number of ways, in accordance with the multiplicity of "plans" for doing this found in the divine wisdom. That this world in fact has come into existence to manifest the divine goodness is due to God's free decision or ordination ("self-binding") to achieve the divine purpose in this particular way.[69] Moreover, the simple decision to create does *not* require that the world (and its constituents and their mutual order) take the actual form which it has. The plan or *ordo* of divine wisdom to manifest the divine goodness which has actually been implemented in creation manifests as fully as possible outside of God the richness of the divine goodness. But it was possible for creation to take other forms and exhibit a different order among things and still to manifest the divine goodness as fully as the present order of things now does. The divine wisdom "devises" a number of possibilities to show the divine goodness and the present form of the world/creation is due to God's determination to adopt the present course of action to achieve the divine will.[70] In addition, in establishing the world and the creatures in it, God does not "manipulate" pre-existing natures with intrinsic qualities in order to achieve the divine goal. Rather, to achieve the divine end, God establishes natures of different sorts (God freely determines that natures will be of a certain type) and, most critically, determines in the formulation of the divine plan that the acts of natures of a certain type will lead to pre-established ends; their natures *and* teleologies depend on God's ordination.

---

entire universe and each of its parts has God as its goal [*ordinatur in Deum sicut in finem*], inasmuch as through their working out of their peculiar destinies the divine goodness is represented for the glory of God). I shall return shortly to the importance of this conception of the purpose of creation for Thomas's teaching about merit; and in Chapter 3, I shall develop the relations between merit and God's creative activity as they figure in Thomas's later teaching about merit.

69   See *ST* I 25, 5c: "Cum potentia Dei, quae est eius essentia, non sit aliud quam Dei sapientia, convenienter quidem dici potest qoud nihil sit in Dei potentia quod non sit in ordine divinae sapientiae, nam divina sapientia rebus inditus . . . non adaequat divinam sapientiam, ut sic divina sapientia limitetur ad hunc ordinem. Manifestum est autem quod tota ratio ordinis quem sapiens rebus a se factis imponit a fine sumitur. Quando igitur finis est proportionatus rebus propter finem factis, sapientia facientis limitatur ad aliquem   determinatum   ordinem.   Sed   divina   bonitas   est   finis improportionabiliter excedens res creatas. Unde divina sapientia non determinatur ad aliquem ordinem rerum, ut non possit alius cursus rerum effluere ab ipsa. Unde dicendum est simpliciter quod Deus potest alia facere quam quae facit." See also *ST* I 25, 5 ad 1. I shall return to I 25, 5, in my discussion in Chapter 3 of the content of the divine ordination which grounds merit in the *Summa*.

70   For this point, see *ST* I 25, 6 ad 3, and the corpus.

To apply this to the question of grace and merit, God indeed predestines certain people to salvation and, accordingly, grants them the means, grace, by which they will attain this end. But that grace in fact is the means leading to God is due to the determination of the divine wisdom, not to the intrinsic qualities of grace. And, further, that grace has value for salvation, that the acts of grace bring the human person to the reward of eternal glory, is similarly due to the divine decision, in the plan of divine wisdom, to grant this value to graced acts. In other words, when we view creation in general and the gift of grace and salvation in particular as the later Thomas does, in the light of the free determination of God to manifest the divine goodness in a particular manner, it is possible to assert with Pesch against Hamm (and Auer) that as much as in the Franciscans, in Thomas's later work, the meritability of human actions is ultimately ascribable to God's free decision to treat such acts as meritorious. For Aquinas, this decision by God is in accordance with the divine will in creating and redeeming. In *ST* I-II 114, 1, where the notion of the divine ordination is introduced to explain merit, then, Thomas has inserted his teaching about merit into the framework of his understanding of God's free creation and redemption of the world. Just as God has freely determined to create and to create in a particular way, and just as God has freely decided to save certain people by drawing them into the life of God, so God has freely ordained to accept as worthy of eternal life the good which people do in the free movement to God. It is this reading of merit in terms of divine sovereignty and freedom, and God's purpose in creating and redeeming, which has allowed Thomas to "solve" the problem of merit and which allows us to grasp fully what Thomas means by the divine *ordinatio*.

And yet, while I believe that Pesch's approach is more satisfactory than Hamm's, there are at least three problems with his presentation of merit and the divine ordination. First, Pesch is surely correct when he dismisses Auer's claim that Thomas's teaching about merit is "legalistic." But this is not the same as concluding that Thomas's teaching is also not "juridical." Throughout his career, Thomas speaks of merit and reward as governed by justice; and as we saw in the discussion of Lynn, in such texts as *ST* I 21, 1 ad 3, Thomas speaks of the "debt" which is requited by God in justice. In his treatment of merit in Aquinas, Pesch, however, ignores such texts and accordingly underplays the role of justice in governing merit and reward in Thomas Aquinas. In Pesch's reading, it is difficult to see why Thomas would think that merit does create a *right* to a reward from God. Secondly, Pesch has not discussed adequately the role of merit in the divine plan for manifesting the divine goodness outside of God. In my own re-formulation of Pesch, I provide a more careful description of the role which Thomas wishes merit to play in the divine scheme; God has decided to manifest the divine goodness in a special way by sharing God's own life with predestined individuals and by having the elect come to God by their meritorious acts. Thus, God orders merit to the reward of eternal life.

Although he is justly famed for his characterization of Thomas's theology as "sapiential," when it comes to discussing merit, Pesch pays insufficient attention to delineating the sapiential aspects of Thomas's later thought about merit. Greater attention to the sapiential dimensions of the divine ordination in Aquinas, in turn, would have disclosed more clearly the limits of Pesch's analogy between the Thomist *ordinatio* and the Scotist *acceptatio*. Surely Pesch is right in dismissing Auer's and Hamm's too-simple contrast of Scotus and Aquinas. The divine ordination in Aquinas does bespeak the divine freedom and sovereignty in salvation. But in Aquinas the *ordinatio* of merit to reward is not merely "extrinsic" to the created order of things, as is the Scotist acceptation. Rather, God's ordination of merit to reward and of people to merit eternal life is but a special instance of God's plan to display the divine goodness outside of God in creating the world—the *ordinatio* of merit in Aquinas is intimately and directly related to the divine will, informed by wisdom, for creation. Finally, Pesch is incorrect when he suggests that the ordination of merits to reward from God is simply a facet of *grace*. As I argue in Chapter 3, the two are not the same, for grace stands to the ordination as an effect stands to its cause. Thus, while Pesch's analysis is superior to those of Auer and Hamm, it is not possible to give unqualified assent to his description of merit and ordination. There is need for a study of merit that is more sensitive to the actual context and to the exact content of Thomas's teaching about the ordination which grounds merit in the *Summa Theologiae*.

A final work deserving comment is *Salut et rédemption chez S. Thomas d'Aquin* (1965) by B. Catão.[71] Catão makes a number of observations about the meaning and importance of merit in Aquinas. First, Catão stresses that for Thomas, the meritorious act is identical with the moral act; people receive the reward of eternal life for doing the good perfective of their being, as determined for them by God. Hence, since God has made the human being a creature whose activities are loving and knowing, by loving and knowing in the appropriate way, people come to the end of their natures (pp. 48, 51, 52, 57). But, second, this end of their nature is not immanent, but rather transcendent (p. 59). This end is God Himself. God has promised God to those who live as humans should. Hence, when one fulfills the moral law of one's being, one receives from God the end set for human beings, God. Third, following on this description of the coming to the end of human existence, Catão characterizes Thomas's teaching on merit as "personalist" (p. 54f.). The doing of the good appropriate to human being, and the receiving of the good which is God Himself, involve the relations of two persons, God and the human being. For the one, being truly human means to act as God has willed. For the Other, rewarding human activity by sharing Himself, means the completion of God's plan for sharing divine life with new members of a "divine community." In meriting and rewarding,

71   B. Catão, *Salut et rédemption chez S. Thomas d'Aquin: L'acte sauveur du Christ* (Paris, 1965). The page numbers in the text refer to this book.

two persons interact at the most intimate level. And, finally, this "person-alist" understanding of merit means for Catão that ultimately it is incorrect to say that Thomas's teaching about merit is "juridical." As Catão says, there is no denying that Thomas employs the language of justice to describe merit. Thomas's use of such language is understandable, given the simi-larities between the relations of God and human beings in merit and between the two partners in a "just" relationship. Justice entails two partners; justice means rendering what is owed *to another*. So too in merit and reward, God gives the reward to another, to the one who merits. But, says Catão, justice and juridicism imply the imposition of an external law code, according to which citizens must strive to live. This is not the case with merit; to merit, people do not "live up" to a code imposed from outside; they simply act as they were designed to act, as truly human beings. Similarly, justice suggests an "objectivization" of relationships, in which it is most proper to speak of "rights" and "the due." But, adds Catão, in meriting and rewarding, God and the human are not bound by external rules; rather, they are interacting at the deepest, interpersonal level. Thus, concludes Catão, while acknowledging the presence of justice-language in Thomas's teaching on merit, it is best to deny that his analysis of merit is "juridical." Rather, what we should say is that Thomas has "borrowed" the language of justice and juridicism in order to express the personal relation-ship of love involved in merit and reward.[72]

Catão's relatively brief comments about merit in Aquinas are perceptive and insightful. First, Catão is correct in stressing the material equivalence of moral and meritorious action; although Thomas insists that moral action must be informed by grace and charity to merit, he also repeatedly makes the point that it is by living out the law of one's being that one attains heaven. As shall become evident, people are "ordained" to a twofold end: They are not only capable of the end which lies within the range of their natural powers; by God's grace, they can attain the deepest fulfillment of their desire to know and to love, by coming into the immediate presence of God in the next life. Thus, it is by pursuing the path which leads to this

---

72 Catão makes this point in a number of places, e.g., *Ibid.*, p. 59: "La béatitude est un don d'une personne, Dieu, à une autre personne, l'homme. Il est donc normal que pour exprimer l'acheminement vers la béatitude on emprunte le vocabulaire de la justice, en parlant de mérite"; p. 49, n. 2: "L'acte moral est appelé mérite,—un terme emprunté au vocabulaire de la justice,—parce que nous recevons la béatitude d'un Autre. Cette dualité de personnes fonde l'analogie avec la situation de justice et explique par là l'emploi du mot 'mérite'"; and p. 58: "Lorsqu'on parle de l'acte moral comme 'mérite,' il y a sans doute une analogie. La réalité qu'on désigne ainsi n'est pas de l'ordre de la justice à proprement parler. Elle appartient, on le verra, à l'ordre de la grace, de l'amour et de l'intimité inter-personnelle. Mais rien n'empêche de garder le vocabulaire de la justice, puisque dans le plus profond de nos rapports avec Dieu, persiste toujours une dualité de personnes et partout où il y a différence de personnes, on peut parler, ne serait-ce qu'analogiquement, de justice!"

higher end, by doing the acts of knowledge and love which most accord with the highest human powers, that people live as fully moral *and* as deserving of eternal life. In the Thomistic analysis, then, there is no equation of meritorious action with works of "supererogation." People merit by becoming authentically human, as this has been determined by the creator of human nature, God. Similarly, Catão is correct in emphasizing the "interpersonal" features of merit and reward: While from one perspective, the Thomist teaching about merit speaks about the development of the individual through good action, from another, it emphasizes that merit entails a new relationship between God and people. This relationship, at bottom, is best described as one of love: By God's love, God summons certain people to share God's own life, and interacts with these people in such a way (i.e., in grace) that these people can attain to God and to live "as God lives," in the personal knowledge and love of God in heaven. In return, people offer themselves lovingly in their acts to God, offering to God the honor which emerges from the service to God involved in morally good and meritorious action. Thus, Catão accurately terms Thomas's teaching "personalist": 'Merit' does describe a web of relationships between God and people, in which human beings attain their destiny through their encounter with God, first in grace and then in glory.[73]

---

73   A number of other students of Aquinas have referred to the "personalism" of his teaching about merit. See, e.g., Colman E. O'Neill, the editor and translator of the Blackfriars edition of *ST* III 16–26 (volume 50, 1965); in appendix 4, p. 238f., O'Neill offers his reflections on the personalist dimensions of merit in Aquinas. Similarly, G. Philips, *L'union personnelle avec le Dieu vivant* (Louvain, 1974), 273–74, insists on the personalism of merit in Aquinas. More recently, O'Neill's student, Romanus Cessario, *Christian Satisfaction in Aquinas: Towards a Personalist Understanding* (Washington, D.C., 1982), has offered more extensive comments about the personalism of Aquinas. With regard to his main topic, Cessario argues that Aquinas tends to understand satisfaction more "juridically" in the *Scriptum*—it is principally a matter of justice. In this analysis, there is an order set up by God which people are to observe. Sin disrupts this order and thus people owe God a debt corresponding to their sin. Here, then, satisfaction satisfies for the debt of justice, appeasing God, and so makes things "right" between God and people. As Thomas matures as a theologian, however, the juridical recedes in importance, and Thomas comes to describe divine-human relations more in terms of mutual love. In the first place, God lovingly makes it possible for people to attain to God. Moreover, God graciously establishes the means of human salvation: On the cosmic level, God sends Christ who in his own love for people offers himself up as the means of satisfaction for the sins of all; on the personal level, God establishes that the repentance of people, in which they lovingly accept the punishment of their sins, will return sinners to God's favor and join them to the Son in the mystical body of Christ, which permits them to share in the benefits of Christ. By the time of the *Summa*, Thomas has added one further element to this description of satisfaction. In God's love, God has made rational creatures capable of God by endowing them with the reason and will which makes them the "image of

But, on the other hand, there are serious problems with Catão's discussion of merit in Thomas Aquinas. First, Catão gives scant attention to the divine ordination which grounds merit in the *Summa*, and his treatment is arguably inconsistent. He occasionally seems to equate the ordination with the basic constitution of human nature, whose "laws" are to know and to love (p. 64, n. 2; p. 48), while in other places, he seems to equate ordination with the motion of grace (which, in fact, issues from the ordination [p. 65]). In any event, his analysis of the *ordinatio* is flawed. He does not establish the sapiential framework of Thomas's teaching about the ordination, and, as will become clear, it is wrong to confuse the motion of grace with its cause, the ordination and predestination of people to eternal life. Finally, Catão's assertion that Thomas's teaching about merit is not "juridical" cannot be accepted. Obviously, merit for Aquinas does not involve an "objectivization" of the relationship between God and the human person, nor does meriting mean an adherence to laws which are purely extrinsic to human life. But Thomas's use of justice-language is more than a mere "borrowing," and the description of merit as the establishment of a "right" to a reward is more than a simple argument from analogy. We can accept Catão's claims about the personalism of Aquinas and the moral quality of merit and still take Thomas's language at face value. When he speaks of merit in juridical terms, that is, as governed by justice, Thomas means what he says. When people merit, they do attain a right to the

---

God." Sin, however, mars this image. Hence, the satisfaction by which people free themselves from the damage of sin now comes to be seen as "image-restoring." It is in this context that Cessario refers in passing (especially p. 214) to the complementary role of merit in the later Aquinas; while satisfaction restores the sullied image of God, merit "perfects" it, for by one's meritorious acts one becomes more as God intends, indeed more "like God." Hence, by merit, by becoming what one is supposed to be and as God has willed, one is able to do God's will and achieve the end set for the person, God Himself as the reward of authentic human existence.

I agree with these authors (and Catão) that Thomas's teaching about merit is "personalist," at least by the end of his career. God offers the opportunity to human beings for complete realization, and by acting as they should as human and as the "children of God," people do enter by their merits into an intimate communion with God. However, as I shall suggest shortly, I think a preferable designation for Thomas's mature teaching about merit is "sapiential." True, merit does bespeak the realization of authentic human existence in union with God. But as I have already suggested in treating Lynn and Hamm, in the *Summa* Thomas especially wants us to read merit in terms of God's plan in creating and redeeming the world, and this plan, as well as its execution, is formulated by the divine wisdom precisely and primarily for the manifestation of the divine goodness. The advantage of calling Thomas's teaching "sapiential" is that it emphasizes that merit ultimately is designed to serve the realization of *God's* purpose in creation. The realization of the deepest needs of the human person in coming to God is involved in merit, but this is secondary and subordinate to the principal purpose of merit, the achievement of God's will.

reward to which their acts are ordained. Yet Thomas's juridicism is highly nuanced. Thomas speaks of merit and reward, and the justice between them, only *within* the context of God's love for people which brings these people to God. In other words, Thomas does not wish his statements about justice and merit to be read in isolation from statements about the mutual love between God and people. In merit and reward, God recognizes the right to reward from God that has been created through God's gracious and loving moving-out to people and drawing them into the special community of God's chosen people.

This review of the literature on merit in Aquinas reveals that there are three main problems which confront the student of this aspect of Thomas's thought. The first is more or less simply factual: Does Thomas affirm a merit of the first grace in the *Scriptum*? The claim of Garrigou-Lagrange that Thomas teaches a congruent merit of the first grace even in the *Summa Theologiae* may safely be dismissed as wishful thinking. The possibility that Thomas affirmed such a merit is confined to the earliest state of Thomas's career. The difficulty in determining Thomas's position is due to his (at least) seemingly contradictory comments in the *Scriptum* on this issue. At times, Thomas seems to reject congruent merit of the first grace, while at others he seems to allow it. In Chapter 2, it will be necessary to review all of the evidence on this issue and to decide whether in fact these diverse statements are compatible.

The second problem is somewhat trickier: How best may Thomas's teaching on merit be characterized? What is its "essential spirit"? Or, put another way, how significant is *justice* in Thomas's teaching about merit? In the literature on merit, the question of its spirit is most often posed in terms of the "juridicism" of Aquinas's teaching about merit. With Auer, for example, the assertion that Thomas's teaching about merit is juridical allows him to dismiss Thomas's approach to merit as overly legalistic. There are in fact two issues involved in evaluating the juridicism of Thomas's teaching on merit. First, as I have already stressed in my review of Catão, throughout his career, Thomas discusses merit and reward in terms of justice; God renders for merit according to the requirements of justice. I do not think that Thomas's references to justice are mere "borrowings" or analogous arguments. As I shall stress in the concluding chapter, Thomas advances his teaching about merit to uphold the biblical affirmation of the just judgment of human beings by God. Hence, in keeping with this purpose in affirming merit, I think that it is clear that Thomas wishes his comments about the justice in merit to be taken seriously. Merit creates a right to a reward, a right that is justly recognized by God and requited at the end of time. But, secondly, the undoubted presence of "juridical" elements does not mean that Thomas's thought about merit is "legalistic." Pesch (and Hamm) are quite correct in rejecting Auer's characterization of Thomas's position. Unfortunately, in those such as Pesch and Catão, who have grasped that merit for Aquinas does not "objectify" or "de-personalize" the relations between God and people, the recognition that Thomas's teaching about merit is not legalistic has caused them to underplay the juridical features undoubtedly present in his thought. One must give Thomas's statements about the justice of merit their full value without however concluding that this juridicism establishes the basic tone of Thomas's teaching about merit.

Finally, it is necessary to examine more thoroughly Thomas's teaching about the divine ordination that grounds merit in the *Summa Theologiae*. In one sense, as with the first problem, this is a merely "factual" question: What does Thomas mean by this term? As we have already seen, a number of interpretations of the divine ordination have been offered in the literature. My own position is that by the *ordinatio* which constitutes the basis of merit, Thomas is referring to God's free determination to ordain selected human beings to life with God which they are to obtain through good works done by grace. "Ordination" thus covers both predestination and the ordering of good works to their reward. But, at a deeper level, the correct understanding of the divine ordination involved in merit allows us to penetrate to the basic spirit of at least Thomas's later teaching on merit. When he uses ordination-language, Thomas inserts his teaching about merit into his consideration of the essential function of creation. God creates the world for the manifestation of the divine goodness outside of God, and each good in the world has been designed by the wisdom of God to display some aspect of the divine goodness. When he cites the divine ordination to establish the possibility of merit, Thomas is telling us that merit too plays a role in the manifestation of the divine goodness in accordance with the divine wisdom By the careful study of the divine ordination involved in merit, I will show in Chapter 3 the true spirit of Thomas's teaching about merit. Rather than being "juridical," his later thought is "sapiential," for in Thomas's interpretation God in the divine wisdom has designed merit to manifest the goodness of God in a special way.[74]

---

74   Despite their promising titles ("La Perspectiva Sapiencial de la Teologia del Merito en Santo Tomas de Aquino" and "El Gobierno Divino en la Teologia del Merito de Santo Tomas de Aquino"), the recent articles by A. Miralles do not satisfy the need for a study which demonstrates the sapiential dimension of Thomas's teaching about merit. (Incidentally, although Miralles does not acknowledge it, the second article is but a slight revision of the first, with entire paragraphs being reproduced word for word. In terms of content, Miralles's argument remains basically the same in the two articles. Accordingly, in the following I shall restrict my comments to the first article, "La Perspectiva Sapiencial"; the following page numbers refer to this article.) In Thomas, 'wisdom' refers to the contemplation of the highest cause and the ordering of lower causes in the light of this contemplation. In terms of Thomas's analysis of creation and redemption, wisdom refers to the plan formulated by God to manifest the divine goodness outside of God. This plan includes the bestowal of specific natures on different creatures, each of which reflects the goodness of God in its own way and the vocation of the rational

Section II. The Literature on Related Concepts

A. *Grace and Merit*

Quite apart from the deficiencies of, and the unresolved problems in, the existing literature on merit in Aquinas, recent research on related aspects of Thomas's teaching about salvation also necessitates a new examination of Thomas on merit. First, as has already been indicated in the review of the literature on merit in St. Thomas, there is need for a study of merit that pays more careful attention to the developments in his analysis of grace in general. For example, the research of Bouillard and Lonergan has succeeded in delineating the different ways Thomas understood and described grace at different times in his career. In *Conversion et grâce chez*

---

creature to life with God in order to manifest the divine goodness in a special way. By its meritorious acts of knowing and loving in this world, which reflect the divine action, the rational creature is brought to share God's vision of God. In this perspective, merits are viewed as rooted in the plan of the divine wisdom, to manifest the divine goodness through the God-aided activity of a creature by nature "capable" of knowing and loving God. Given the titles of his articles, one would have expected from Miralles an examination of merit which would have made all this evident, by emphasizing the sapiential aspects of Thomas's treatment and delineating the greater or lesser prominence of the divine goodness and wisdom in Thomas's various treatments of merit. Instead, Miralles ignores the role of divine wisdom as the presupposition of merit and offers in the "La Perspectiva Sapiencial" a rambling discourse on various features of Thomas's teaching on merit, all seen, more or less, from what Miralles calls the perspective of God (p. 293) (hence the "sapiential" of the title). The disorganization and lack of focus of this article detract from some of the valuable points made by Miralles in passing—e.g., that God's desire to manifest the divine goodness lies behind creaturely activity, including human merit (pp. 296, 293–94, 302) and that what God seeks from merit is the revelation of the divine goodness (p. 298); that in the *Summa* (at least) Thomas discusses merit in the context of heirship and the grace of adoption (p. 302); and that the *auxilium* of God is needed for performing meritorious acts (p. 300). Moreover, Miralles does not distinguish between the various stages of Thomas's teaching on merit. He seems to ignore the development in Thomas's teaching and cites indiscriminately from different works and different periods to summarize Thomas's teaching. While he notes Thomas's stress in the *ST*, e.g., of the divine *auxilium*, Miralles does not advert to the development in Thomas's thinking on grace and so does not note that the *Scriptum* lacks such a stress. Similarly, he does not explicitly mention whether the *Scriptum* or other early works share the *Summa*'s interest in discussing merit in terms of sonship. Finally, as was observed in note 28 above, Miralles makes a serious mistake regarding the type of justice which is operative in merit in the *Summa*: On p. 297, n. 19, he rejects De Letter's conclusion that in the *ex professo* treatment of merit in the *Summa* Thomas holds a commutative justice, in opposition to the *Scriptum*'s affirmation of a distributive justice in merit. Miralles seems unaware that in the Secunda Secundae, Thomas himself explicitly states that it is a kind of commutative justice which governs merit.

S. Thomas d'Aquin (1944),[75] Bouillard's topic is Thomas's treatment of the question of the preparation for the reception of justifying grace. In particular, Bouillard seeks to comprehend why Thomas believes such preparation on the part of the human person to be necessary and, secondly, whether and in what manner God or divine grace may be said to be responsible for the human preparation necessary for the reception of grace.[76] For Thomas, justification itself is viewed throughout his career in terms of Aristotle's treatment of the generation of form. In justification, according to the order of nature, God infuses grace (viewed especially as *habitual* grace) into the recipient; the infusion of grace, in turn, "causes" two acts on the part of the recipient, the movement toward God in formed faith and the movement away from sin in repentance. Finally, the process of justification culminates in the forgiveness of sins and the establishment of the sinner in the state of justice.[77] In terms of his problematic, then, Bouillard is especially concerned to determine for Thomas Aquinas the extent to which the human recipient of justifying grace is, along with God, the cause of the acts toward God and away from sin, the middle steps of the process of justification. These acts, says Bouillard, together constitute the "ultimate disposition" of the recipient for the reception of justifying grace. But Bouillard is also interested in those acts of the human person which precede the infusion of justifying grace and which of themselves are not the ultimate disposition for the infusion of grace but, as it were, "remote" dispositions ("la disposition eloignée")[78] for this infusion, leading up cumulatively to the ultimate disposition for which grace is granted. It is Bouillard's thesis that Thomas's teaching on the preparation for grace, remote and ultimate, evolved over the course of his career. In his book, Bouillard sets out both to portray and to account for the development evident in Thomas's various discussions of the problem of the preparation for grace.

To delineate the development, Bouillard divides his book into three main parts, each of which is again divided into a series of chapters. The first part studies the teaching on the preparation for grace in the early part of Thomas's career, especially the *Scriptum Super Sententias* and *De Veritate*. As Bouillard observes, just as Thomas views the process of justification itself as the generation of form, in these early works he discusses the prelude to justification, human preparation, in terms of the preparation of

---

75   H. Bouillard, *Conversion et grâce chez S. Thomas d'Aquin* (Paris, 1944). The page numbers in the text refer to this book.

76   Bouillard, *Conversion et grâce chez S. Thomas d'Aquin*, p. 2: "Quel est, selon saint Thomas, le rôle de la préparation à la justification? et est-elle l'effect d'une grâce divine?"

77   See Bouillard, *Conversion et grâce chez S. Thomas d'Aquin*, p. 24f. for the description of justification in terms of the Aristotelian theory of generation in the *Scriptum Super Sententias*. On p. 146, Bouillard notes that in the *Summa Theologiae*, justification itself is still viewed in terms of the generation of form.

78   See, e.g., Bouillard, *Conversion et grâce chez S. Thomas d'Aquin*, p. 27.

matter for the reception of form:[79] the form of grace (habitual grace) is finally infused when the "matter" into which grace is to be infused is adequately prepared, or disposed, for this form. Here, then, the human acts constituting the ultimate disposition for grace are viewed as "material causes" which lead to and dispose for God's granting of grace. For Thomas, this analysis of the preparation for grace in terms of material causality does not jeopardize the gratuity of justification or undermine the notion of God's prevenience. First, as material cause, human acts disposing for justifying grace receive their "meaning" from the habitual grace infused in the soul; these acts are ordained to the reception of form and are complete only when the form of grace is received (p. 46ff). Secondly, that the morally good acts preceding grace in fact lead to the gift of grace is due to a prior divine decision to grant grace in response to such acts. By the design of God and out of God's pure goodness, God has ordained that to those who do what is in them (facientibus quod in se est), grace will be infallibly infused in the soul, to a degree conforming to the actual effort of the recipient in preparing for grace.[80] Third, at this stage of his career, Thomas argues that divine providence always precedes, as it were, the human acts that either remotely or ultimately dispose for justifying grace, for providence creates and arranges the conditions and situations in which these human acts are aroused. It is important to note here that when he talks of the role of providence "disposing" the human person for the infusion of grace, Thomas allows that providence stimulates or occasions the appropriate human act which is either an ultimate or remote disposition to grace in one of two basic ways. *Either* divine providence arranges for external

---

79   Bouillard offers (*Conversion et grâce chez S. Thomas d'Aquin*, p. 27) an illustration from the Aristotelian physics which may help to see what Thomas is talking about here. Before air can receive the form of fire, it must be "prepared" for the reception of this form by being heated; when the air is sufficiently disposed by heating, the air may receive the form of fire. By analogy, the form of grace can only be received in the "matter" of the human soul when the human person is properly disposed for grace by good human acts.
      As Bouillard points out (pp. 21, 145), Thomas in the *Scriptum* and indeed throughout his writings advances a second reason for the need of a preparation for grace—God's desire to work in a way which will respect human nature. Since human nature is characterized by intentional activity, free morally good acts by the person which are directed to fulfilling human being and pleasing God are seen by Thomas as adequate preparation for grace. In his book, Bouillard discusses this second reason for the need for a preparation for grace only in passing.

80   As Bouillard observes (*Conversion et grâce chez S. Thomas d'Aquin*, p. 38), lying behind this affirmation of the *facere quod in se est* is the distinction between absolute and hypothetical necessity. Absolutely considered, the works disposing for grace need not result in the gift of grace; but because God has bound God to such an order, by hypothetical necessity—that is, as due to the free divine self-commitment to a particular order of affairs—such acts do infallibly lead to the gift of grace.

situations that evoke such an act, e.g., preaching, illness, or the like. *Or,* by providence, grace *inwardly* stimulates the human will to this act. At this stage of his thought, then, Thomas does not insist on the *interior* moving by grace of the soul to act.[81]

In the second part of the book, Bouillard examines the teaching of the works of the middle period of Thomas's career, in particular, the *Summa Contra Gentiles*. In Bouillard's estimation, the years 1260–71 were a time of great discovery for Aquinas, for Thomas now encountered certain theological and philosophical works that profoundly altered his understanding of grace. Bouillard enumerates three fundamental changes in Thomas's theology of grace emanating from the discoveries of the middle period.[82] First, Thomas now insists on the prevenience of grace and on the divine initiative in conversion. In this regard, Bouillard argues that Thomas was led to reformulate his language about the relation of divine grace and the free acts involved in conversion by his reading of certain long-neglected works of Augustine, *De Praedestinatione Sanctorum* and *De Dono Perseverantiae*.[83] In these writings, Aquinas discovered that Augustine had attacked a view of conversion advanced by certain Pelagians which at least superficially sounded like the view propounded by Thomas in his early writings. The Pelagians had asserted that the beginning of faith and conversion comes from human effort, while God perfects the work. Thomas naturally saw a similarity with his description of conversion in terms of material and formal causality. Hence, his discovery of "semi-Pelagianism" (the term coined in the sixteenth century to describe this view) through the reading of Augustine caused Thomas to cease describing the free acts required of the human person in conversion as the material cause of

---

81   See Bouillard, *Conversion et grâce chez S. Thomas d'Aquin*, p. 72. Bouillard refers to *In IV Sent.* d. 17, q. 1, a. 2, qc. I ad 1, and *De Veritate* 24, 15, as instances in the early works where Thomas describes providence or the prevenience of "grace" in this regard as "interior." Yet, as Bouillard notes (p. 73), in these early writings Thomas does not insist that this prevenient "grace" needed for the preparatory acts of the human person be an inward acting of God on the soul.

82   Bouillard, *Conversion et grâce chez S. Thomas d'Aquin*, has provided his readers with excellent summaries of the three main discoveries of the middle period on pp. 91 and 140.

83   Peter Lombard had quoted passages from these works but, according to Bouillard (*Conversion et grâce chez S. Thomas d'Aquin*, p. 111), had not cited texts especially suited to reveal the nature of what has come to be called "semi-Pelagianism." Bouillard thinks that Thomas probably had the opportunity to read these works of Augustine in their entirety while in Italy in the 1260s, in close contact with the papal court (and library). Incidentally, Bouillard (p. 121) does not think that Thomas knew the canons of the Second Synod of Orange at which semi-Pelagianism had been denounced; in this, Thomas shared the general medieval ignorance of Orange. I return to the question of access in Chapter 4.

conversion and, concomitantly, to insist that these free acts are themselves caused by God's grace.[84]

Secondly, Bouillard notes that in the middle period, Thomas starts to insist that the action of God which prevenes the free acts in conversion is itself immediate and interior to the soul. Thomas's earlier position, that divine providence may "move" the soul to these required acts either through external events or through inner movement, is now abandoned. According to Bouillard, crucial here was Thomas's reading of the *Liber de Bona Fortuna* where Eudemus (writing in the guise of Aristotle) had contemplated how it is that the prudent man actually begins to take counsel. If taking counsel is due to a previous counsel about taking this counsel, *that* taking counsel in turn would depend on a prior one and so on to infinity, and the taking counsel originally in question would never occur. Rather, the actual taking counsel or process of doing so must be set off by a divine initiative or instinct which applies the prudent man to this act (p. 123). Thomas read Eudemus in the light of his concern to ensure the divine initiative in conversion. Hence, Thomas now stated that unless the soul were moved to the free acts required in justification, these acts would not occur; and since the will is not moved necessarily by external events, it is God, the creator of the soul, who must move it interiorly to its act (pp. 124 and 132).

The third change in Thomas's discussion of conversion and grace is found in the way he now describes justifying grace. In the *Scriptum*, Thomas emphasized the formal qualities of grace, which perfects the soul and makes it pleasing to God. In the works of the middle period, grace is still habitual and still adds a formal perfection to the soul. But now Thomas describes grace less as a "habit" and more as the "motion" of God in the soul, by which God moves the soul to the acts bringing the human person to God.[85] Here, Bouillard suggests that it was Thomas's reading not only of Augustine's anti-Pelagian works but also his deeper study of the Pauline epistles which is of great significance.[86] The reading and contemplation of

---

84   As the previous discussion of the "prevenient" features of providence and grace in the early works has suggested, Bouillard does not believe that Thomas was guilty of "semi-Pelagianism" in the early work. Rather, Thomas is at most guilty of a looseness of language, due to his ignorance of the heresy of semi-Pelagianism. This is a rather common conclusion of students of Thomas—Pesch, for example, argues similarly—but it is hard to see how the discussion of free works which serve as the material cause of the infusion of justifying grace and, in general, the affirmation of the *facere quod in se est* in the early works does not in substance equal the semi-Pelagian position attacked by Augustine and unequivocally rejected by Thomas from the middle period on.

85   Bouillard (*Conversion et grâce chez S. Thomas d'Aquin*, p. 135) says that from the *Summa Contra Gentiles* on, sanctifying grace is still seen as a habit but adds that "cet aspect passe fréquemment au second plan; il se subordonne à celui d'action divine. La grâce sanctifiante est d'abord ce par quoi Dieu conduit l'homme à sa fin dernière."

86   As I pointed out above in the critique of Hamm, Hamm has failed to perceive

such texts as Romans 8:14 ("qui spiritu Dei aguntur") would, in Bouillard's view, naturally have led Thomas to view conversion and indeed the entire spiritual life of the human person as being under the active and immediate guidance of God.[87]

According to Bouillard, Thomas retained these discoveries of the middle period in the great work of his maturity, the *Summa Theologiae*. Compared to the *Scriptum*, the *Summa* reveals a clear formulation of divine prevenience in the conversion of the sinner to God. In the *Summa*, Thomas focuses almost exclusively on the ultimate disposition for the infusion of grace in his discussion of justification, and describes these free acts unequivocally as the effect of God's efficient grace (pp. 148, 150). Since the ultimate disposition is itself the gift of God, in the *Summa* there is no longer room for the *Scriptum*'s preoccupation with these acts as the *material* cause of grace emanating from the human person alone. Thomas instead stresses that these acts are caused by the divine motion, and without God, there can be no conversion. Even with regard to the remote dispositions for grace, Thomas ceases to treat human activity as the material cause of grace. Though Thomas spends much less time in the *Summa* discussing these acts, when he does mention them he also insists that they are effects of God's grace. Similarly, Bouillard says, in the *Summa* Thomas brings his teaching on grace and conversion more firmly in line with his belief in the certainty of divine predestination. In the *Scriptum*, Thomas had tended to describe predestination in rather general terms, as the "setting up" of a structure within which human activity had great scope. God had decreed that to those who do what is in them, God is bound to grant the gift of grace. The amount of grace granted to the individual is in accordance with the effort expended by the recipient in preparing for grace. In the *Summa*, this general structure established by God has given way to God's decision to elect certain people to share in the divine life. This election, Thomas continues, expresses itself in the divine motion, in moving the individual to the acts associated with the gift of grace. As Bouillard points out, this description of the gift of grace as the result or effect of predestination means that Thomas now ascribes to God's decision and action, not to human preparation, the degree to which any individual shares in God's own life. God not only elects someone to share in the divine life, God also establishes

---

the Pauline source and inspiration for many of the changes in Thomas's theology of grace.

87   Bouillard writes (*Conversion et grâce chez S. Thomas d'Aquin*, p. 138): "Il est facile de remarquer comment le texte de saint Paul: 'qui spiritu Dei aguntur,' que saint Thomas avait présent à l'esprit, lui a imposé l'idée et la formule: 'ex impulsu Dei aguntur.' Il était ainsi amené a concevoir la grâce, principe du mérite, non comme une forme permanente, mais comme l'impulsion divine, l'action continue de Dieu dans l'âme. C'est là, en effet, la notion paulinienne de la grâce. Saint Thomas ne renonce pas à la notion d'habitus. Mais, quand il se laisse guider uniquement par l'Ecriture, il l'oublie provisoirement ou du moins la rejette à l'arrière-plan."

the extent to which that individual will share in God, by allotting, according to the divine decision, the amount of grace God wishes that person to have.[88] Finally, with regard to this subordination of grace to divine predestination, Bouillard adds that in the *Summa*, Thomas's perspective in describing grace has undergone modification. In the *Scriptum*, the emphasis in speaking about grace is on grace as *created*, as a quality or habit given to the soul by which the soul is rendered pleasing to God. In the *Summa*, grace is still habitual, but the emphasis in the discussion of grace has shifted away from grace as created (grace as the end-term of divine love in the soul) to grace as the expression of the freely loving God who stands as the origin of salvation and who sustains in immediate and direct fashion the return to God at every stage.

Bouillard has been severely criticized for certain aspects of his analysis of Aquinas's teaching on grace. Above all, both Deman[89] and Lonergan[90] have challenged Bouillard's assertion that Aquinas does not know of an "actual grace" and that the divine motion of his later writings by which people are converted to God and disposed for the reception of grace is simply sanctifying grace, the habitual grace which is infused in justification but seen here from the perspective of God's work in justification (p. 176). Concomitantly, Bouillard asserts (*Conversion et grâce chez S. Thomas d'Aquin*, pp. 196, 202, 213) that the divine motion in this respect does not differ from the "general concursus" by which God reduces every creature to its proper act. The distinction between God's supernatural motion which achieves human justification and which leads people to supernaturally oriented acts and God's general ("natural") operation in the universe, says Bouillard, is an achievement of theology after Thomas. Although Bouillard offers his readers some observations on Thomas's linguistic habits to support his contention regarding the absence of an "actual" grace in Thomas, his principal argument hinges on what he says is Thomas's

---

88   Bouillard (*Conversion et grâce chez S. Thomas d'Aquin*, p. 150) has expressed
      well the basic difference between the teachings of the *Scriptum* and of the
      Summa. In the *Scriptum*, Thomas invokes the hypothetical necessity arising
      from God's establishment of a structure within which people dispose
      themselves for grace as providing the connection between human preparation
      and the gift of grace; "dans la *Somme*, au contraire, elle est assurée par une
      intention divine relative à l'*individu* qui est sauvé, par un *dessein particulier*
      et une *action interieure* au sujet qui se prépare. C'est parce que Dieu meut le
      sujet avec l'intention de le faire aboutir à la justification que celui-ci aboutit.
      Autrement dit, l'idée d'*election*, qui n'apparaît pas dans l'article parallele du
      Commentaire des Sentences, régne ici." Bouillard's words about God's
      predestination of *individuals* also provide a valuable corrective to the views
      of those such as Auer and Hamm who perceive in Thomas's later works a
      diminution of the personal dimension of grace.
89   See T. Deman, review of *Conversion et grâce chez S. Thomas d' Aquin*, by H.
      Bouillard, In the *Bulletin Thomiste* 7 (1943–44): 46–58.
90   B. Lonergan, *Grace and Freedom* (London, 1971). I discuss Lonergan's book
      in detail below.

insistence that human action on the supernatural level is possible only when human potencies are perfected by supernatural habits: Since the acts which are required in justification are supernatural, the *auxilium* by which God causes these acts must itself be habitual grace, which not only moves the sinner to repentance but infuses the habits which elevate the individual to the level of God (see pp. 74, 196). But as Deman and Lonergan observe, Bouillard is incorrect in his basic assumption. As Lonergan says,[91] Thomas in fact does know of instances in which supernatural acts arise from faculties which lack supernatural habits. In these cases, God simply causes acts of *sentire, intelligere,* or *velle* to be received in their respective faculties. Thus, to the extent that Bouillard incorrectly identifies divine motion and habitual grace as the one and the same sanctifying grace and does not recognize that divine motion may also refer to actual grace, his analysis of Thomas on grace cannot be endorsed. Indeed, the work of Lonergan on operative grace, to be discussed shortly, provides us with a much more satisfactory account of Thomas on grace and human freedom and, thus, is a more valuable guide to Thomas's analysis of the way in which God and the human person "interact" in the achievement of the deeds which, on other grounds, are accounted "meritorious."

Nevertheless, despite this deficiency in Bouillard's work, *Conversion et grâce* remains important for the correct analysis of merit. First, Bouillard has made some interesting observations about Thomas's position on the merit of first grace in the *Scriptum.* Bouillard stands with those Thomists who deny that Thomas ever affirmed the congruent merit of the first grace in the early works despite accepting the *facere quod in se est* to describe the disposition for grace. Rather, says Bouillard, careful reading of the pertinent texts in the *Scriptum* reveals that when Thomas talks of such a meriting of the first grace, he is simply *reporting* the positions of others (*Conversion et grâce chez S. Thomas d'Aquin,* p. 34)—"some say that people can merit *ex congruo* the first grace"—and does not take the additional step of accepting this position as his own. Indeed, according to Bouillard (p. 35), Thomas's real position on the possibility of meriting the first grace even in this attenuated sense of merit is revealed in such passages as II d. 27, q. 1, a. 4, where Thomas simply denies (apparently) the possibility of any merit without grace. Bouillard's argument here is suggestive and, indeed, given the reluctance of interpreters of merit in Aquinas such as De Letter and Lynn to grapple in a meaningful way with this issue, his willingness to pursue it is much appreciated. In Chapter 2, when I return to the question, I shall again refer to Bouillard's analysis and suggest why I think it is mistaken.

Second, and more important, Bouillard draws our attention to the fact that in his teaching on grace Thomas progressively stressed the prevenience of divine grace and the pre-eminence of God in the entire process of salvation. Bouillard, as Lonergan and Deman have shown, is wrong about

---

91   See Lonergan, *Grace and Freedom,* p. 26, n. 17.

actual grace in Aquinas. But in terms of the general development in
Aquinas's thought on grace, Bouillard is successful in observing the differences between the early and later teachings of Aquinas about grace. It is
correct to observe, as Bouillard does, that the "model" of grace changes in
the writings of St. Thomas. In the early work, grace is seen exclusively as
"habitual," and grace and free will are analyzed in terms of the relation
between form and matter. In the later work, while Thomas still affirms a
habitual grace, the principal paradigm is now that of motion, and the
moving or reducing of potency to act. *Both* aspects of grace, the formal/ha-
bitual and the actual, figure in Thomas's teaching about merit in the
Summa Theologiae; as we shall see in Chapter 3, Thomas has incorporated
his keener appreciation of the "dynamism" of grace and God as mover of
people to their acts into his analysis of merit in such a way as to allow to
human action its own (meritorious) causality while nevertheless affirming
that the granting of initial conversion and perseverance in God's grace until
the end remain the unmerited gift of God moving people to salvation. In
related fashion, Bouillard's perception that in the later work Thomas is
more successful in tying his general teaching on grace (including merit as
the effect of cooperative grace) to his teaching on election and predestination warrants inclusion in my treatment of merit in Thomas's thought.
Again, in Chapter 3, I shall pick up on this cue and highlight those features
of Thomas's analysis of merit which reflect his concern to view human
activity and meriting in the light of divine predestination.

Finally, Bouillard's book is a valuable aid to the study of merit in
Aquinas, for it suggests the inspiration for certain of the changes in
Thomas's treatment of merit. Central here is Bouillard's observation of the
increased use by Thomas of the anti-Pelagian writings, *De Praedestinatione Sanctorum* and *De Dono Perseverantiae*. Bouillard argues that it was
Thomas's knowledge of these works in their integrity—that is, not simply
through extracts in florilegia—that is responsible for the increased dynamism of Thomas's teaching on grace. I tend to agree, and think moreover
that the knowledge of these same works of Augustine is responsible for
certain of the changes in Thomas's treatment of merit in *ST* I-II 114.
Especially relevant in this regard is Thomas's incorporation of those
features of the salvific process which do *not* fall under merit, that is, the
gift of first grace and the gift of perseverance and the divine motion which
continues to move the converted person on the path to God. Especially in
the final chapter, I shall consider in greater depth the manner in which
Augustine's anti-Pelagian writings have shaped Thomas's later teaching
on merit.

Bernard Lonergan's *Grace and Freedom,* published originally as a series
of articles in the early 1940s and published in book form with editorial
modifications in 1971,[92] is a brilliant and penetrating study of the different

92   B. Lonergan, *Grace and Freedom: Operative Grace in the Thought of St.
     Thomas Aquinas,* ed. J. Patout Burns (London, 1971). The page numbers in

stages of Thomas's theology of grace. Focusing on the passages in Aquinas in which Thomas refers to grace as "operative" and "cooperative," Lonergan observes that Thomas's understanding of grace underwent development in the course of his career. In the early *Scriptum*, Thomas conceives of grace exclusively as habitual grace and says that this habitual grace is divided notionally into *gratia operans* and *gratia cooperans*. In the disputed questions *De Veritate*, Thomas continues to affirm a habitual grace which is divided into *operans* and *cooperans*, but also mentions an *actual* grace which is *cooperans*. In the later *Summa Theologiae* (I-II 111, 2), finally, Thomas affirms both actual and habitual grace, each of which is further said to be *operans* and *cooperans*. The purpose of Lonergan's study is to explain this development in Aquinas's teaching about grace, and to delineate the accompanying development in his understanding of the relation of divine and human causality.

With respect to *habitual* grace, Lonergan characterizes the development in Thomas's teaching as due to Thomas's increasing success in integrating the reflections of the Augustinian tradition on the moral impotence of the sinner and the psychological dependence of human freedom on grace into the more metaphysically sophisticated reflections of thirteenth-century scholastics on grace as a supernatural habit. In the Augustinian tradition, human freedom is viewed almost exclusively in theological terms. Stressing human sinfulness, freedom is seen as the freedom from evil and for good which is caused in the individual by God's grace. To meet the demands of the Pelagian controversy, Augustine further refined this notion of grace-caused freedom by noting that this grace is itself divided into "operative" and "cooperative" types. In Augustine, it is operative grace which makes the will which already exists to be a good will, while cooperative grace cooperates with the good will to give it good performance (p. 3). Augustine's medieval successors continued to discuss freedom in predominantly theological terms. Thus, for Anselm, justice is the rectitude of the will. Freedom is the maintenance of the rectitude of the will for its own sake and is itself due to grace (p. 6). For Lonergan, the preoccupation with sin made it difficult to provide a completely adequate theory of human freedom—what Lonergan calls the "philosopher's definition of liberty" (p. 12). The freedom to will or not to will, that is, freedom absolutely considered without reference to the debilitating effects of sin, was generally left out of account. Similarly, the question of freedom in sinning proved intractable (p. 7).

Like Landgraf and others, Lonergan sees the "discovery of the supernatural" at the turn of the twelfth to the thirteenth century as decisive for the more adequate account of human freedom and of grace, and of their mutual relations. As worked out by the scholastics, the supernatural refers especially to the order established by God's special self-communication to rational creatures, endowing them with participation in divine life and

the text refer to the book form of Lonergan's study.

directing them to God as their beatific end. From Philip the Chancellor on, scholastic theologians came to define this participation in the divine life that orders the rational creature to God in terms of the Aristotelian notion of habit (p. 19). Augustine's action of God on the sinner now was seen as habitual grace, perfecting the human soul and elevating it before God (*gratia elevans*). Similarly, sin was more clearly delineated as defection from this spiritual ordering of the person to God, as the renunciation of the grace which perfects being and makes the rational creature pleasing to God. But, adds Lonergan, the "discovery of the supernatural" also liberated speculation on the *natural* sphere and in particular on human freedom, for now it was possible to contemplate the intrinsic capacities of nature without immediate reference to theological considerations. As a result, the philosophic datum about the freedom of the will, the freedom to will or not, was incorporated into the analysis of human freedom.

When Aquinas began his theological work, the theorem of the supernatural had been worked out and grace defined in terms of habit. His discussions of grace and freedom reflect the accomplishments of the early thirteenth-century theologians. In the *Scriptum*, Thomas followed his thirteenth-century predecessors in stressing habitual grace as a *formal* cause. As the discussion of Bouillard has already made clear, in this early work Thomas allowed to the human person the capacity to do morally good acts that could serve as the material cause for the infusion of sanctifying grace. In this respect, habitual grace serves as form to the matter of these free acts offered up by the soul and grants these acts a formal perfection. It "elevates" these human acts to the supernatural sphere and thus endows them with a meritorious quality as pleasing to God. More fundamentally, habitual grace makes the person himself acceptable to God and makes additional acts acceptable to God as merits. Yet, as form, habitual grace also endows the human person with new being (*esse*), a kind of participation in the divine. And since *agere sequitur esse*, in the *Scriptum* Thomas also can describe habitual grace as an *efficient* cause. Habitual grace and the virtues infused with this grace incline the human person to acts of a distinctively supernatural cast. In terms of the underdeveloped theory of human action which Thomas maintained at this point (see the discussion below on actual grace), Thomas asserts in the *Scriptum* that as efficient cause habitual grace operates (inclines to) the inner acts of the soul, while also "operating" the exterior acts of the person (p. 30f.).

Using the terminology created by Augustine, Thomas adds in the *Scriptum* that habitual grace may also be viewed in terms of *gratia operans* and *gratia cooperans*. Considered as a formal cause, when habitual grace elevates the person to the supernatural order and makes the individual acceptable to God, it is "operative"; when it makes the person's acts acceptable and meritorious, it is "cooperative" (p. 31). Considered as an efficient cause, when habitual grace creates the act of will in the human person, it is "operative"; when it operates the exterior acts, it is "cooperative." Here, says Lonergan, we have the anomaly of a cooperative grace which "operates" (p. 32).

In *De Veritate*, Thomas altered his teaching about habitual grace. For example, he made a slight change in the description of this grace as a formal cause. He still asserts that the morally good acts which precede conversion are elevated to the supernatural order and made acceptable to God by habitual grace, and he thinks that this habitual grace continues to make human acts meritorious throughout the spiritual life. But instead of two functions of grace making the person acceptable to God (operative grace) and the person's acts acceptable to God (cooperative grace) as in the *Scriptum*, Thomas combines these two aspects in *De Veritate* and says that habitual grace formally elevates the human person (and thereby his acts), and he calls this grace *operans*. Thomas's discussion of habitual grace as *efficient* cause, however, underwent more profound alteration. This is due, in the first place, to Thomas's concern in *De Veritate* to articulate human freedom more clearly vis-à-vis the habits infused with grace. He still continues to assert that habits "incline" the soul and its powers to act. But he now acknowledges that this inclination does not translate into an inner necessity or operation. The human person remains free to act or not to act in accordance with the inclination of the habit. Thus, in *De Veritate*, Thomas no longer describes the causality of the habit, including habitual grace, as operating the act of the human person; rather, habitual grace as efficient cause is merely *cooperans*, cooperating, but not necessitating entirely, acts of a kind in the person (p. 36f.). Secondly, this re-definition of the interaction of habits and human freedom is due to Thomas's efforts to be more faithful to the data from the Augustinian tradition regarding human sinfulness. As Lonergan says, in the first enthusiasm over the "discovery of the supernatural" and the description of grace as habitual, the thirteenth-century scholastics tended to lose sight of the debilitating effects of sin (p. 46). In *De Veritate*, Thomas attempted to remedy this inattention to the power of sin. He argues that while the infusion of grace has indeed "transformed" the human person by introducing the individual into the life of God and granting the individual the capacity to act like God on the human level (referring here to the grace and the theological virtues whose acts imitate God's own acts of knowing and loving God), this transformation is never complete in this life, never matching the perfection known by the blessed who have attained to God. Rather, the propensity to sin, which marks the life of people before the gift of grace, retains its power even after grace. In this light, then, grace must counter the remaining sinful inclinations of the person, must heal the person of the remnants of sin (grace as *sanans*), by cooperating with the person in the struggle to become true to the new life begun in the individual by God (again, habitual grace as *cooperans*) (p. 55).[93] For Lonergan, the advances in Thomas's

93 As we shall see below, according to Lonergan, Thomas's reading of Augustine has also led him to assert in *De Veritate* a second kind of sanctifying grace,

thinking about habitual grace in *De Veritate* due to his increased perception of the continuing power of sin are offset somewhat by the loss in this work of the notion of grace operating the inner acts of the soul. Whereas in the *Scriptum* Thomas had incorporated the traditional Augustinian description of grace as operating good will and cooperating with good will to give good performance by stating that habitual grace as operative acts on the inner man but as cooperative acts on the outer, in *De Veritate* Thomas asserts simply that habitual grace is cooperative with respect to both inner and exterior acts of the soul and the person (p. 37). Lonergan suggests that this lapse is especially ascribable to the flux and uncertainty at this time in Thomas's thought about the nature and activities of the will (see below on actual grace).

By the time of the *Summa Theologiae*, however, Thomas had successfully incorporated all aspects of the Augustinian description of *operans* and *cooperans* grace into his treatment of habitual grace. First, Thomas's sense of sin had caused him by the time of this work to recast the relation between the free acts done in justification and justifying grace. Sin creates a predilection to sin, which leads to further sin. Of ourselves, we are insufficient to break the cycle begun by our sinful acts. In any given situation, our previous sin will incline us to sin again. To overcome the propensity to sin, then, God must directly intervene in the soul, destroying the habit of sinning and replacing it with a new orientation, the orientation to justice and the life of God which is created by grace and the virtues given with grace. In the works of the later part of his career (in the discussion of justification from the *Summa Contra Gentiles* on), then, Thomas re-asserts the Augustinian definition of operative grace as operating the good will of the justified by stating that in conversion, habitual grace effects the good acts which are required on the part of the recipient to re-direct his will to God as end. Thomas also retains the insight of *De Veritate* about habitual grace as *cooperans*. Once habitual grace as *operans* has changed the will from its wrongful attachment to the things of the world and turned it to God, habitual grace as *cooperans* cooperates with the good will, inclining it to the actions befitting the new life of the person in God and bringing the person to God. On the other hand, corresponding to the increased prominence of efficient causality in the discussion of habitual grace is a relative devaluation of formal causality. Thomas, of course, continues to affirm that habitual grace makes human acts meritorious by directing them to God as their end. But given the acknowledgment that grace causes the acts which occur in justification, Thomas in the *Summa* no longer ascribes this role to grace with regard to any acts which might precede the gift of grace. Rather, habitual grace formally "completes" in this way only the acts which themselves are done in the state of grace (p. 59f).

According to Lonergan, it is Aquinas's formulation of the concept of

an actual grace which is *cooperans*, for which we must pray to confirm us in this struggle against the power of sin.

actual grace (i.e., Thomas's *auxilium*) which provides even surer testimony to Thomas's speculative acumen. Whereas Thomas found the notion of habitual grace ready made, and thus had only to refine his understanding of this grace in the light of the dogmatic data, the formulation of actual grace is Aquinas's own accomplishment, and Thomas had to work out for himself the correct analogy of nature for this kind of grace (p. 63). Lonergan suggests that a number of developments in Thomas's understanding of related notions conspired to make possible his discovery of actual grace. First, Thomas perceived ever more acutely the value of the Aristotelian *premotion* for depicting the dependence of the world and its occurrences on God. In Aristotle, premotion is meant to account for the actual occurrence of causation. Given two entities, premotion helps to explain why it is that one exercises causation on the other only at a particular time and not earlier or later. In Aristotle, premotion refers to the creation or "manipulation" of the conditions in which actual causation may occur. Negatively, it entails the removal of some obstacle or impediment to causation which allows the occurrence of causation; more positively stated, it refers to the bringing of the two entities into the relation or proximity or disposition which facilitates causation (p. 71). As illustration, Lonergan offers the example of an iceberg at the Pole. The sun cannot melt it while the iceberg is at the Pole (that is, the sun does not cause its effect in the iceberg). For melting to occur, the relative position of the sun and the iceberg have to be changed. Either the sun will have to be moved over the Arctic circle or the iceberg will have to be moved toward the equator. It is the moving of either entity into the correct position which is the premotion necessary for the occurence of melting.

Throughout his writings, Thomas always maintained that God is "involved" in all operation in the world, including human acts. However, says Lonergan, the incorporation of the Aristotelian premotion into his teaching to suggest how God is the cause of all that occurs is a relatively late development. In the early *Scriptum* and *De Veritate*, for example, God's involvement in causation is restricted to God's creation and conservation of beings. There, the argument is that what causes the substance also causes the active potency; what causes the active potency also causes what the latter causes (p. 86). That is, the effect of some being which has been created and is sustained by God can also be attributed to the cause of that being, to God. By the time of the *Summa Contra Gentiles*, however, Thomas has made the Aristotelian premotion his own and uses it to suggest a more intimate involvement of God in all activity. In the later works, to explain why things come to exercise their causality, God is seen as the "cause of the causation" of every cause in the world in the sense of the Aristotelian premotion. God not only creates and conserves being, God also applies ('application' is the Thomist equivalent of the Aristotelian 'premotion') each thing so that it may exercise the type of causality appropriate to its nature. In this regard, Thomas tends to describe the relationship of the created nature to God as that of instrument to principal, efficient cause. While each type of creature retains its nature and exercises the kind of causality appropriate to it (whether voluntary or natural), that it in fact exercises its causality is due to God's applying it to its act.

Parallel to the incorporation of the Aristotelian premotion into the Thomist analysis of the relation between creaturely and divine causality, Lonergan observes, is the development in Thomas's understanding of the *causal* certitude of divine providence. As Lonergan points out, Thomist application and Aristotelian premotion are not simply identical, for in Thomas's later works, where he employs Aristotle's notion of premotion, application is viewed in terms of the Christian affirmation of divine providence, that is, God's plan and will for the world (p. 76). Again, as in the general understanding of God's operation in creaturely causation, Lonergan perceives a development in Thomas's understanding of divine providence (p. 78ff.). In the early *Scriptum*, the causality of divine providence is basically ignored. Although Thomas on occasion can speak of divine providence marshaling the circumstances which lead to the conversion of the sinner (see the discussion of Bouillard above, where it was observed that divine providence "prevenes" the acts of the sinner which serve as the material cause of conversion, by offering the external events—illness, preaching—which occasion these human acts), Lonergan observes that in the *Scriptum*, divine providence is viewed almost exclusively in terms of simple foreknowledge. In *De Veritate*, however, the causal aspect of divine providence receives more attention. Here, divine providence is seen more in terms of the actual working out through divine agency of God's plan in the world. Yet, in *De Veritate*, this "working out" is confined to general results, at least as regard contingent causes (including human acts in freedom). It does not pertain to each and every act or occurrence in the world. Thus, in this work, Thomas can argue for the certainty of the salvation of the elect, according to the causality of divine providence, but does not add that each act of the elect is causally certain. To ensure personal salvation, God will grant sufficient graces so that ultimately the individual will reach the goal set by God. But by the time of the *Summa Contra Gentiles*, Thomas has attained his mature position. Divine providence is certain, and this certainty extends both to general effects and to the particular acts of different kinds of agents (including the human agent, who acts in a voluntary manner). In the earlier works, a stumbling block to the assertion of the causal certitude of divine providence had been the objection that divine causality in such an extensive and direct way would be tantamount to destroying the causality of the creature. For example, it is proper to the human person that it is a free cause of its acts and that its effects are contingent, that is, they may or may not occur. But if divine providence is causally certain even with respect to particular, contingent events, it would seem that the acts of the human person would therefore no longer be contingent, for the efficacy of the divine causality would make them necessary. According to Lonergan, Thomas's ability to affirm the causal certitude of providence in the *Summa Contra Gentiles* is due to his firmer grasp of the implications of divine *transcendence* for divine causality (p. 79). The argument against the efficacy of the divine will trades on confusing God with the agents found in the world, who are subject to the conditions of time. Yet God is not involved in time. For God, there is no past, present, or future; rather, all that is, is "present" to God in an eternal "now." Thus, while it is certainly true to say (as Thomas does from the *Contra Gentiles* on) that God's causality "precedes" that of the creature, this involves not a temporal priority but one of the metaphysical order. Unless God applies the creature to its act, there is no act. This application, however, does not temporally precede the causation, for God lies outside of time. Similarly, Thomas came to perceive that the argument succeeds only when the efficacy of divine willing is not viewed against the background of the distinction between absolute and hypothetical necessity. Absolute necessity is that which stands in its own right, and this is incompatible with contingency. Hypothetical necessity, on the other hand, refers to actual conditions: If something (*A*) is so, then it is so (if *A*, then *A*). Given the "presence" of the world to God, it is only a hypothetical, not an absolute, necessity that God's willing "adds" to events in the world. And this type of necessity is not incompatible with the contingency of human events (p. 103ff.).

The third area in which development in Aquinas's thought facilitated the discovery of an actual grace is his understanding of the will, its freedom and acts. Thomas came to see the need to affirm two "first" causes, as it were, of the will in its act (p. 101). In the earlier works, Thomas had been content to refer to the work of the intellect as the mover of the will. The intellect considers the various courses of action possible in a given field of endeavor, opts for a particular course, and presents it to the will. However, Thomas became dissatisfied with a view of the will as a purely passive potency and perceived that there is no inner necessity that the will be moved by any object, including the object provided by the intellect, to choose a particular course of action. He saw, by the time of *De Malo*, that there was need to affirm a second cause of the will's act, one that determines the will actually to choose the course of action presented it by the intellect. Here, Thomas was greatly influenced by his reading of Eudemus's *Liber de Bona Fortuna* (p. 99). Contemplating the origin of the prudent man's decision to take counsel, Eudemus had concluded that it was a divine instinct that must set the process in motion. For Aquinas, once he had grasped more firmly the need for the divine premotion for the occurence of any action in the world, it was clear that the *initium consiliandi* discussed by Eudemus was but a special instance—that is, the case of willing—of the application by God of secondary causes to their act. Since the will's act is not necessitated by any (external) object, it must be determined *interiorly*; and this can be done by God alone, the creator of the will. Thus, in addition to the causality of the intellect specifying the act of the will, Thomas affirmed, from *De Malo* on, the causality of God determining (moving) the will to its act.

Moreover, Thomas attained a clearer grasp of the acts proper to will (p. 93ff.). In the earlier works, he is content to refer to the simple act of willing, without acknowledging different types of acts of will. In the later works, however, he refers to two types of acts issuing from the will: the willing of the end and the willing of the means to the end; this latter he ascribes to the *liberum arbitrium*. Corresponding to this clearer differentiation of the acts of will, Thomas also refines his notion of the will itself. Under Aristotelian influence, in the earlier works such as the *Scriptum*, Thomas seems to conceive of the will as a purely passive potency, which is moved to its act. By *De Malo*, however, he grounds the *human* freedom which he had always posited more firmly in an "active" power of the will to move itself. The will now is not only moved (*moveri*; *movetur*) by another, it also *se movet,* and sets the other powers of soul to act. In terms of the distinction, then, between the willing of the end and the willing of the means, Thomas in the late works argues that as to the first, the will is purely passive, moved to its act by the object presented to it by the intellect *and*, in a different way, by God applying it to its act. In the willing of the means, however, the will is also active, implementing the strategy which permits the attainment of the end.

Thomas's deepening reflections on divine premotion, God as transcendent cause and the causal certitude of providence and the nature and freedom of the will, all contributed to Thomas's formulation of actual grace. Thomas's articulation of this concept complements the development in his understanding of habitual grace outlined above. First, in the early *Scriptum*, Thomas thinks of grace exclusively as *habitual* grace. But in *De Veritate*, Thomas acknowledges in passing a second type of sanctifying grace, different from the habitual grace which is *operans et cooperans*. Under the influence of Augustine's exposition of the *Our Father,* in which Augustine stresses the need for even the justified, that is, one already in the state of grace (for Aquinas, Augustine's words would naturally be taken to refer to *habitual* grace), to pray for God's additional help to do good, Thomas affirms the need of an actual grace which is *cooperans*, confirming the justified in good, inspiring good thoughts and granting perseverance. At this stage of his thinking, however, Thomas does not yet conceive of an *actual* grace which is *operans*. For one thing, says Lonergan, Thomas was prevented from taking this next step because he had not yet worked out his understanding of will as both a passive and an active potency and, thus, did not yet distinguish clearly between the two acts of willing, the will of the end and the will of the means (p. 118). Accordingly, he simply propounds an actual grace which affects the will in an undifferentiated manner and calls this *cooperans*. But, secondly, Thomas had not yet worked out his notion of divine application or premotion nor had he grasped the pertinence of this for the discussion of willing. It was only in the *Summa Contra Gentiles*, when he had assimilated the Aristotelian premotion and referred it to human acts, that a grace preceding the conversion of the sinner, changing the will of the sinner (which appears to be actual grace but which may be the infusion of habitual grace), is proposed. However, in this and subsequent works in which this *praeveniens* grace in conversion is discussed, Thomas does not specify that this grace is *operans*. Only in the *Summa Theologiae* (I-II 111, 2) is the development completed. Along with the habitual grace which is both *operans* and *cooperans*, Thomas explicitly affirms a different kind of sanctifying grace, which later theologians designate "actual" grace, that too is explicitly said to be both *operans* and *cooperans*.

As Lonergan makes clear in his discussion of *ST* I-II 111, 2c, the teaching of this article constitutes a significant advance over the earlier analyses of grace and offers a fitting conclusion to the various streams of speculation which had contributed to the development of Thomas's teaching on grace. First, Thomas now offers his definitive statement on the meaning of both *gratia operans* and *cooperans*. In the *Scriptum*, the distinction between *operans* and *cooperans* was seen as being more or less equivalent to that between "prevenient" and "subsequent" grace, that is, it was viewed in terms of a temporal sequence. There, Aquinas had the precedent of Augustine's own usage. However, once he had worked out more clearly the nature of the will as not only a passive but also an active power, distinguished the acts of willing of the end and of the means to the end, and perceived the need for the Aristotelian premotion even in the case of the will, Thomas was prepared in the *Summa* to re-define operative and cooperative grace. In *ST* I-II 111, 2c, Thomas now says that operative grace is the grace that effects the will of the end, and here the will is said to be *mota et non movens* (the will as passive potency). Cooperative grace, on the other hand, has to do with the will of the means and the external performance of the acts attaining the will's end, and here the will is both *mota* (by grace) and itself moving (the other powers of the soul, and the organs of the body, to their acts) (p. 127). These new definitions, as Lonergan observes, apply equally to habitual and to actual grace. As *operans*, habitual grace changes the orientation of the sinner, granting the justified the new being and virtues which raise the sinner to the spiritual sphere and re-direct the soul to God; as *cooperans*, habitual grace works with the will, inclining the will and strengthening its performance as it wills the acts appropriate to the new being in God. As *operans*, actual grace changes the will, replacing its former will of its sinful ends by moving it to the new will of its proper end, of God; as *cooperans*, actual grace works with the justified, strengthening the human person in the deeds which in fact bring the person to God. In a sense, then, what Thomas has done in this article is fully to assimilate into his own teaching the distinction between grace as the cause of good will and grace as the cause of good performance which

Augustine had asserted in his original analysis of operative and cooperative grace.

Second, in *ST* I-II 111, 2c, says Lonergan, Thomas also makes clear that the work of actual operative grace is not limited to the special case of the conversion of the sinner. This grace is also involved in all the good willed and performed by the justified. In the tradition before Aquinas, the focus in the discussion of operative grace had been almost exclusively on the question of conversion and the respective roles of grace and free will. In this article of the *Summa*, of course, Thomas is still concerned to show how his new understanding of operative actual grace as the cause of the will of the ultimate end and of operative habitual grace as the infusion of new being ennobling and empowering the soul affects the understanding of human conversion. But when Thomas refers to the function of actual grace operating good will in conversion, he treats conversion as but one case in which actual grace is operative. He says that operative grace is seen "especially" (*praesertim*) in the conversion of the sinner, implying, as Lonergan notes (p. 123), that conversion is not the only instance in which actual operative grace is required for good will. Indeed, in the light of Thomas's conviction of the need for divine application to cause the causation of the will, it is clear that operative actual grace is required whenever the will wills a good end. Thus, actual operative grace applies the will also to the willing of the proximate good ends that refer the justified to God and directly promote the return of the justified to God.

Lonergan's *Grace and Freedom* is of enormous significance for the study of merit in Thomas Aquinas. In the first place, Lonergan confirms Bouillard's principal conclusion, that in Thomas's teaching on grace in general there is an increasing tendency to analyze grace in more dynamic terms. Obviously, Lonergan and Bouillard reached this conclusion in rather different ways. For Bouillard, Thomas alters the expression of his theology of grace in the light of his work as a historian and especially as a consequence of his discovery through deeper reading of semi-Pelagianism. Although Lonergan too refers at times to this aspect of Thomas's project as a theologian, noting Thomas's use of Eudemus and of Augustine in re-defining his solution to the problem of grace and freedom,[94] it remains true that Lonergan's Aquinas is much more the speculative theologian, working out his new position on grace as he works out his mature thought on related questions. Despite this differing evaluation of the significance of Thomas's historical work, Bouillard and Lonergan agree that in his

94   In *Grace and Freedom*, however, Lonergan has not addressed Bouillard's claims about Thomas's new use of *De Dono Perseverantiae* and *De Praedestinatione Sanctorum*. In discussing Aquinas's use of Augustine, Lonergan refers rather to his reading of *De gratia et libero arbitrio*. As far as I can see, there is no good reason for thinking that Bouillard's reference to Thomas's "integral" reading of these works as contributing to the re-statement of his position on grace is incompatible with Lonergan's own position.

discussion of grace and freedom, Thomas tends to place a greater emphasis on God's efficient causality and to relegate the formal qualities of grace to secondary importance.[95] Hence, in terms of conversion and the preparation for and infusion of first grace, Lonergan agrees with Bouillard that the early Thomas had viewed conversion in terms of the completion of matter by form, the gift of grace elevating the preceding free acts of the human person to the supernatural order, while in the later works Thomas depicts the relation of grace and the free acts in justification solely in terms of efficient causality. The affirmation of the *facere quod in se est* which accompanies the description of conversion in terms of formal causality explains why there is at least the possibility of some kind of merit of the first grace in the early works.[96] Similarly, as does Bouillard, Lonergan draws our attention to the increasing prominence of the causal certitude of divine providence in Thomas's writings and to Thomas's tendency to relate the life of grace more and more to divine providence and predestination. This, as I shall argue especially in Chapter 3, helps us to understand why in the discussion of merit in the *Summa Theologiae*, but not in the discussion of merit in the *Scriptum*, divine predestination has come to figure so prominently in the description of the conditions of human merit.

Yet Lonergan not only confirms important features of Bouillard's discussion of Thomas's theology of grace, he also corrects Bouillard and offers a more complete treatment of the relation between freedom and grace, by going beyond the confines of the single question of conversion. As we have seen, Bouillard denies to Thomas a knowledge of actual grace. Yet, as Lonergan makes clear, although Thomas does not use the term 'actual grace,' when Thomas speaks of the divine *motio* or *auxilium*, he is in fact thinking of a second type of sanctifying grace which differs from habitual grace.[97] Lonergan's more careful portrayal of the developments which both

---

95 See, for example, Lonergan's comment (*Grace and Freedom*, p. 41) that habitual grace tended to recede in importance as Aquinas worked out his notion of actual grace.

96 Unlike Bouillard, Lonergan does not offer his own position on the problem of the merit of the first grace in the *Scriptum*.

97 M. C. Wheeler provides an independent examination of actual grace in Aquinas in "Actual Grace according to St. Thomas," *The Thomist* 16 (1953): 334–60. Although written in the 1950s, this article indicates that Wheeler was unaware of the arguments of both Bouillard (and his denial to Thomas of an actual grace) and Lonergan (and his portrayal of the discovery by Aquinas of this grace). Wheeler's study suffers from the same inattention to chronology and development characteristic of certain Thomists of an earlier generation. Hence, she treats Thomas's statements about actual grace from different periods as of a piece. This naturally causes her to read later refinements into Thomas's earliest attempts at grasping actual grace. For example, on p. 343, she mistakenly reads *De Veritate* 27, 5 ad 1, in which (as Lonergan says) Thomas makes the anomalous assertion of a cooperative grace which operates on the will, in the light of the later distinction between the two acts of the will. But as Lonergan noted, Thomas only perceived this

habitual and actual grace experienced in Aquinas's writings is of direct relevance to the understanding of merit in St. Thomas. Consequently, Lonergan's work makes more understandable the teaching in *Summa Theologiae* I-II 114 about what the justified may or may not merit. In the eighth article of this question, for example, Thomas says that the justified can merit the increase of grace, while in the ninth article, he says that the justified cannot merit the grace of perseverance. At first glance, these two assertions may appear incompatible. After all, if one can merit more grace, which is the "condition" of salvation and which brings its possessor to God, why does Thomas deny the merit of perseverance? But in light of Lonergan's analysis, it seems clear that in the eighth article, Thomas is referring especially to *habitual* grace: Once habitual grace is freely infused, it is subject, as it were, to the same "laws," *mutatis mutandis*, which govern any habit. Repeated action of any kind serves to increase the possession of that habit. So, too, acts of charity, for example, merit the increase of this habit

---

distinction after the writing of *De Veritate*. Similarly, in treating of operative and cooperative grace, Wheeler refers to the two ways in which Thomas could distinguish between these two graces—in the early works, in terms of a temporal sequence of prevenient and subsequent; in the later *ST*, in terms of the willing of the end and of the choice of the means—without noting that the latter way is not present in the earlier works. However, her article is of value in that it offers an acceptable summary of Thomas's teaching about "actual" grace as this emerges in the later work.

In "Grâce et motion divine chez saint Thomas d'Aquin," *Salesianum* 12 (1950): 37–84, G. Ladrille examines the texts in Aquinas on grace in chronological order in the light of Bouillard's thesis. While acknowledging the value of Bouillard's work in tracing new themes and expressions in Thomas's teaching on grace, Ladrille, as had Deman and Lonergan (see notes 89 and 90 above), rejects Bouillard's conclusion that Thomas knows no actual grace. True, Ladrille concedes, Thomas does not affirm the modern Catholic "transitory" elevating actual grace. But Thomas does not strictly identify habitual and actual grace under the rubric of divine motion or *auxilium*. Moreover, Ladrille rightly criticizes Bouillard for restricting divine motion to the mere reduction of habits and potencies to acts. For Ladrille, actual grace does this, but also does more—it guides and protects the predestined, assures the moral goodness of his action and allows him to persevere in the good (p. 77). Finally, for our purposes, it is interesting to note that Ladrille acknowledges in passing the development which has occurred in Thomas's thought on merit *ex condigno*. In the *Summa* as opposed to the *Scriptum*, it is the motion of the Holy Spirit that establishes the equivalence between meritorious action and the reward involved in condign merit (p. 76f.). Although Ladrille does not go further with the question of merit, we shall see that Thomas's discovery of actual grace lies behind the later affirmation that a sort of *commutative* justice, not distributive (as in the *Scriptum*) is involved in condign merit. Interestingly, Ladrille makes no reference to Lonergan's work; in many respects, his treatment of Thomas on grace and freedom parallels Lonergan's earlier discussion, but in a more straightforward fashion.

in its possessor.[98] But in the ninth article, Thomas is referring especially to *auxilium* (which Lonergan designates "actual" grace). The denial of the merit of perseverance reflects Thomas's mature grasp of the need for the divine premotion in the accomplishment of any morally good act. Now, the divine motion which is necessary for the actuation of the will is not necessitated by any previous human action or good work. Rather, God moves the will to act solely in accordance with the divine plan for that individual. Thus, the good acts that merit the increase of habitual grace (a. 8) are themselves due to God's free, unmerited intervention moving the will to act and sustaining the person in the return to God (a. 9). In like fashion, Lonergan's analysis allows us to perceive that Thomas's development of the teaching on actual grace enabled Thomas to give new meaning to his assertion that human salvation, which in a sense is "merited," nevertheless remains throughout the gift of God. In the later works, not only must God move the sinner to the acts which accompany the initial infusion of sanctifying grace, God must also apply the justified to the meritorious action which leads to the fulfillment of the quest for salvation, reducing the habits infused in justification to acts befitting the return to God.

Finally, Lonergan's thorough study of grace in Aquinas serves to clarify Thomas's teaching on hope as this affects the teaching on merit. As we shall shortly see in the discussion of Pfürtner, a more adequate understanding of merit in Aquinas depends on relating his teaching on merit to his teaching on hope. In Chapters 2 and 3, I argue that Thomas analyzes hope differently in his early and later works. In particular, Thomas grounds the possibility of hope differently in the *Scriptum* than in the *Summa Theologiae* and the other later works, the disputed question *De Spe* and the *Compendium Theologiae*. In the *Scriptum*, the realization of the end of hope, eternal life, is possible in general terms because God has established the means, grace, by which the attainment of God may be realized. In the later works, Thomas discusses the possibility of hope in much more immediate and indeed "personal" terms. Hope is possible because the one who hopes confides in the God Who precedes, confirms, and sustains the human person in action. In the light of Lonergan's analysis of Thomas on *auxilium* and motion, it is not too difficult to conclude that this shift in Thomas's analysis of the possibility of hope reflects his keener appreciation of the function of "actual" grace in the effecting of human salvation. As these examples suggest, then, in Lonergan's *Grace and Freedom*, we have a reliable guide to the development of Thomas's teaching on grace, a teaching which provides the immediate background for the development of his teaching on merit.

---

98   In the appropriate place, I shall indicate how the increase of a theological virtue *differs* from the increase of an acquired virtue; see, e.g., the discussion of the increase of charity in the *Summa Theologiae* in Chapter 3.

B. Hope and Merit

Recent research on Thomas's teaching about hope similarly reveals the need for a new study of merit in Thomas Aquinas. First, the work of S. Pfürtner about Thomas's teaching about the certainty of hope, while illuminating certain facets of Aquinas on merit, creates new difficulties for the interpreter of this aspect of Thomas's theology. Pfürtner's *Luther and Aquinas on Salvation* (1961/64),[99] counters, among other things, the usual objection raised against the Catholic teaching that the human person must contribute in some fashion to his own salvation through the performance of meritorious actions (i.e., by doing works which somehow "earn" eternal life). This objection contends that the stress on merit constitutes a denial of the primacy of God in human salvation and places too much confidence in human powers of doing what is necessary to gain eternal life. And, it continues, because of the actual frailty of the human person and the attendant inability to do anything worthy of God, the initial over-confidence in human capacities implicit in the teaching on merit ultimately leads to despair over the very possibility of attaining salvation at all.[100] The primary purpose of Pfürtner's book is to demonstrate the fundamental agreement between Aquinas and Luther about the possibility of attaining certainty of personal salvation. Traditionally, both Catholics and Lutherans have concluded that there were no grounds for such certainty in St. Thomas on the basis of his argument, in *ST* I-II 112, 5, that a person could not know if he were in the state of grace; at best, one could have conjectural certainty of the possession of grace.[101] But Pfürtner perceives in Thomas's teaching about hope insights and concerns similar to the Lutheran teaching about personal salvation. As Pfürtner says, in his discussion of hope,

---

99   S. Pfürtner, *Luther and Aquinas on Salvation*, trans. E. Quinn (New York, 1964). The German original was published in 1961.

100 Any number of Protestant authors could be cited as posing this objection to the Catholic teaching on merit, going back to Luther himself. A relatively recent scholar who argues in this vein is J. Heinz, *Justification and Merit: Luther versus Catholicism* (Berrien Springs, Mich., 1981). As the subtitle suggests, in this book Heinz wishes to maintain the incompatibility of Lutheran and Catholic views on justification and merit. However, Heinz's scholarship, at least with regard to the Middle Ages, is shallow—it is difficult to take seriously someone writing in the 1980s who cites Karl Barth (p. 150) and A. von Harnack (p. 147) as authorities on Thomas's soteriology. Moreover, although he lists Pfürtner's book in his bibliography, Heinz seems unacquainted with Pfürtner's basic thesis. Heinz's argument on p. 18 and p. 18, n. 2, regarding the impossibility, in Thomas, of knowing whether one has grace (and hence the uncertainty of personal salvation) suggests that Heinz has not fully grasped that for Thomas, *hope* is the locus of such personal certainty. Similarly, on p. 100, Heinz advances the "insight" that common to Jews and Catholics is not only a teaching on merit but the uncertainty of salvation.

101 Pfürtner, *Luther and Aquinas*, 41f., observes that the Council of Trent followed Thomas in this belief.

Thomas asserts that hope, the gift of God by which we trust in God's mercy, offers the Christian confidence about his personal destiny.[102] This recognition of the function of hope in Aquinas, in turn, casts doubt on the validity of the traditional objection at least as applied to Thomas's teaching on merit, for this understanding of hope discloses that for Thomas, whatever one's "works," it is in God, not in oneself, that one will base his confidence about his eventual fate.[103] Yet Pfürtner's new account of Thomas on hope itself has precipitated significant unanswered questions about Thomas on merit (and hope). For example, what function does Thomas in fact want merit to perform in his soteriology, and is he successful in finding a place for merit and human achievement in a theology which places so consistent an emphasis on God's role in the attainment, and guaranteeing, of salvation?

Other features of Thomas's teaching on hope (especially in the *Summa*), only mentioned in passing by Pfürtner or not at all,[104] suggest, however, the general lines along which Thomas attempted to resolve the tension between hope and merit. On the one hand, in his teaching about the vice of presumption which is opposed to the theological virtue of hope, Thomas makes clear that the confidence in God engendered by hope must be (and will be) accompanied by good acts which manifest God's grace in the present life. For Thomas, presumption is based on an erroneous assessment of God's nature and of the quality of God's aid to people in this life. Proceeding from the contemplation of the divine omnipotence, presumption is a "twisted hope" (*ST* II-II 21, 2c) which judges that God's power is such that God can (and does) save people without their repentance (in the case of first grace) or their effort to pursue and do the good (in terms of life in the state of grace) (II-II, 21, 1c). For Thomas, the error here is twofold. First, it suggests that God in saving people disregards their nature as free agents. For Aquinas, however, it is an "axiom" that God acts upon every creature in accordance with its nature, and thus in saving people will act upon them in such a way that human freedom is preserved. Secondly, presumption in a sense diminishes God's grace rather than exalts it, for it fails to recognize that grace is not only God's gift of forgiveness to people but indeed divine power by which God transforms human life in the realization of the divine purpose for people. In other words, then, for Thomas correct hope and trust in God's mercy, as opposed to presumption, includes the recognition that a person must respond positively to the

---

102 *Ibid.*: "There can be no doubt that [Aquinas] brings under the heading of hope what Luther describes as trust."

103 *Ibid.*, 104–5: "Certainty of hope comes to the believer from God and his unswerving fidelity, his merciful turning to us, not from our own moral exertions or perfections."

104 On *ibid.*, pp. 157–58, Pfürtner acknowledges that he has left many questions about hope unanswered, including, he says, the problem of merit that he has only mentioned in passing. In a sense, then, this study is designed to complete the analysis of hope and merit only begun by Pfürtner.

promptings of divine grace in order to be saved; hope does not exclude meritorious behavior but entails it.

On the other hand, one's merit must not in turn provide an excuse for redirecting one's hope from God to oneself. In the return to God, whether in the act of hope by which one tends to God or in the meritorious act, one must always recognize and affirm that it is God Who takes and retains the leading role. This becomes clear in Thomas's discussion of the other vice opposed to theological hope, that of despair (II-II 20). For Thomas, despair, like presumption, is based on an erroneous judgment about God. While one may adhere to the general proposition that God can save people and does so by grace, the one who despairs lacks confidence that God is able to apply grace to him, because of certain peculiar limitations on his own part which supposedly make him unable to receive the divine mercy (II-II 20, 2 ad 2). Here, contemplation of the instability of the free will (II-II 18, 4 ad 3), of the capacity for sin of even the justified *viator* throughout the pilgrimage to God and thus for defection from, and opposition to, God, has replaced trust in the God who saves and constantly renews the existence of the justified. Consequently, for Thomas, whatever the good one freely does (under the influence of grace), whatever one's merit, it would appear that true hope will save its possessor from self-exaltation and reliance on self (and its woeful consequences), for it informs one's good works with the recognition that personal salvation exists as a possibility only because of God's power, not the person's, to overcome the evil in human existence and to transform and lead the person to God by divine grace.

These general reflections on the relation of merit and hope in Aquinas must be developed further, in order to grasp correctly the role of merit (and its limits) in Thomas's account of salvation. For example, the question remains open to what extent Thomas's analyses of hope, presumption, despair, and merit evolved over the course of his theological career. Indeed, it is one of the flaws of Pfürtner's presentation that he has failed to take account of the problem of development in Thomas's teaching. He assumes that Thomas's analysis of hope always remained the same and thus pays no attention to questions of chronology. Yet a good case may be made that Thomas re-formulated his position on the ground of the possibility of hope, a matter of direct significance for Pfürtner's thesis. The discussion in Chapter 2 of Thomas's teaching on hope in the *Scriptum* and in Chapter 3 of his analysis of hope in the mature writings will disclose that his description of the ground of hope differs at various stages of his career and that this difference has a direct bearing on the teaching about merit.[105]

---

105 In addition to the discussions of hope in the *Scriptum* and the *Summa*, Thomas also treats hope at some length in the *Compendium Theologiae* and the disputed question *De spe*. Chapter 3 demonstrates that their teaching is closer to that of the *Summa* than to that of the *Scriptum*. On *ibid.*, p. 95, Pfürtner cites a text from the *Scriptum* (II d. 26, q. 2, a. 4), in which it is stated that the certitude of hope is caused by the divine liberality, as if this text were

Similarly, it will be instructive to examine Thomas's use of tradition in his teaching—for example, in the *Scriptum* and the *Summa* Thomas has been forced to "re-interpret" in a benign fashion Peter Lombard's affirmation that the theological virtue of hope "arises from grace *and* merit," a statement whose obvious meaning not only conflicts with Thomas's view of hope as the unmerited gift of God but also seems to transform merit into the constituent of hope. Finally, in this regard, it will be valuable to ponder the import of Thomas's teaching about (filial) fear (II-II 19), the gift of the Holy Spirit (II-II 19, 9c) perfective of hope by which one shuns evil and pursues good out of fear of separation from God (II-II 19, 9 ad 1), and to consider its application in Thomas's writings to the account of the relation between hope and merit.

---

affirming the point made in the *Summa*, that human hope rests on the direct involvement and aid of God in sustaining the return to God. As I argue in Chapter 2, the text from the *Scriptum* is actually referring only to the fact that God has established the means, grace, by which the achievement of God is possible. In the *Scriptum*, Thomas does not mention the direct relationship which exists in hope between the human person chosen by God for salvation and God in the divine *auxilium*.

Chapter Two
The Early Teaching on Merit

THE ANALYSIS of Thomas's own teaching about merit begins with the consideration of the works from his earliest period (covering the years 1252–59). For the purposes of this study, the *Scriptum Super Libros Sententiarum* and *De Veritate* are the most significant of these. Other contemporaneous works, such as Thomas's *Commentary on the De Trinitate* of Boethius, while of value for our knowledge of Thomas's thought in general, make scant mention of merit and hence will not be discussed.

Section I. The *Scriptum Super Libros Sententiarum*

The *Sentences,* composed by Peter Lombard in the 1150s, offered to its readers a more or less systematic account of the truths of the Christian faith.[1] The Lombard divided the *Sentences* into four books, each of which was in turn divided into chapters. The further grouping of the chapters into "distinctions" was not accomplished until sometime before the mid-thirteenth century. The Lombard derived the basic organizational principles for the *Sentences* from Augustine, especially from *De doctrina christiana.* There (in Bk. I, chapters II and IV), Augustine had suggested that realities could be divided into *res et signa.* The *res,* in turn, could further be distinguished in terms of the *res, quibus fruendum est* (the things that should be enjoyed, that is, God), and the *res, quibus utendum est* (the things which should be used on the way to God, that is, the world and creatures). Taking Augustine's cue, Peter announces at the beginning of his work[2] that he has adopted the distinction between *res et signa,* as well as utilized the different dimensions of *res,* for his presentation of the faith. Hence, the first three books of the *Sentences* obstensibly discuss the Augustinian *res*; the final book, in which the Lombard looks at the sacraments and the last things, discusses Augustine's *signa.* Despite his pretensions, however, as has frequently been remarked,[3] the Lombard's division

---

1   See the recent critical edition by I. Brady, *Magistri Petri Lombardi Parisiensis Episcopi Sententiae in IV libris distinctae,* 3d ed. (Grottaferrata, 1971). The editors of Thomas's commentary on the *Sentences* (see note 8 below) also print a version of Peter's work, which differs from Brady's version in some details. Brady gives the chapters of the Lombard's original version, as well as the later distribution of these chapters into distinctions.

2   *Sententiae* Bk. I, d. 1 chaps 1 and 2.

3   See, e.g., M. Grabmann, *Die Geschichte der scholastischen Methode* (Graz,

is rather artificial and cumbersome, and in fact in the writing of the *Sentences,* Peter often lost sight of his organizing principles. In the rest of the work, he seldom refers to the *res-signa* division or explains a point in terms of it. Although the *Sentences* lack brilliance in style as well as in organization, Peter's work was enormously successful in the Middle Ages. By the time of St. Thomas, the *Sentences* had been adopted in theological "faculties" as, after the Bible itself, the crucial text for theological education. Once the student of theology had completed a series of "cursory" readings of certain biblical texts under the supervision of a regent master, he would pass to the "reading" of the *Sentences* itself, offering his own analysis of the truths of the Christian religion through his lecture on the Lombard's work. Only then would he himself be qualified for appointment as a regent master.[4] A number of reasons can be offered for the success of the *Sentences.* For example, although he ignores important authors, Peter offers in his work copious references and citations of the works of certain Patristic writers, especially Augustine, whose views, if not his actual words, are cited over one thousand times;[5] in the *Sentences,* then, the student of theology was introduced to many texts authoritative for the theological enterprise.[6] The *Sentences* also proved attractive since it offers abundant material for

---

1957), 2: 364.

4   For a good discussion of the role of the Lombard in theological education, see James A. Weisheipl, *Friar Thomas d'Aquino: His Life, Thought and Work* (Garden City, N.Y., 1974; repr. with addenda and corrigenda, Washington, D.C., 1983), pp. 67–77. There is some dispute among scholars of Aquinas about the years in which Thomas did his cursory lectures on the Bible; he may have served as "biblical bachelor" under Albert the Great in Cologne (1248–52), or spent the first two years in Paris (1252–54) lecturing on the Bible. If the latter is correct, then his commentary on the *Sentences* should be dated 1254–56, rather than 1252–56. For an indication of the success enjoyed by the *Sentences,* see F. Stegmüller ed., *Repertorium commentariorum in Sententias Petri Lombardi,* 2 vols. (Würzburg, 1947), which lists the commentaries produced on the *Sentences* in the Middle Ages.

5   For a description of Peter Lombard's sources, see J. De Ghellinck, "Pierre Lombard," in *DTC* 12, no. 2 (Paris, 1935), especially cols. 1989–90. There are some surprising omissions in Peter's sources. Despite the importance of the works of Pseudo-Dionysius for Hugh of St. Victor, for example, Peter Lombard cites Dionysius only twice (this should be contrasted with Thomas's own repeated reference to Pseudo-Dionysius in his commentary on the *Sentences*). Similarly Peter refers to the writings of Boethius only once, which again is surprising given the prominence of Boethius in such mid-twelfth-century theologians as Gilbert of Poitiers. Needless to say, Peter is almost wholly ignorant of the Greek Fathers.

6   The virtue of the *Sentences,* however, from a different angle is also its weakness. Like other medieval *florilegia,* in offering easily accessible extracts from important theologians, the *Sentences* made it tempting to forgo reading the entire writings of these theologians. One recalls Bouillard's observations about the importance of Thomas's direct encounter with the later writings of St. Augustine for the development of his own theology of grace; unlike many of his contemporaries, Thomas was not content with anthologies.

discussion and debate, not only because it covers the entire range of the faith, but also because Peter often reports discordant opinions without suggesting his own "solution," thus offering his readers considerable opportunity to exercise their own theological skills.[7]

In Thomas's *Scriptum* on the *Sentences*, which, as we have it, is Thomas's edition of the lectures he delivered in 1252–56 in fulfillment of the final requirement of his theological training, we have the most systematic expression of Thomas's theology at the earliest stage of his career.[8] Although Thomas notes Peter's claim to organize the truths of the Christian religion according to the Augustinian *res et signa* division, Thomas

---

7   Occasionally, Peter does venture his own resolution of difficult theological problems, and in the century following the writing of this work, lists of Peter's propositions which were at odds with the prevailing theological wisdom were compiled and published. For more on this matter, see Edward A. Synan, "Brother Thomas, the Master, and the Masters," in *St. Thomas Aquinas, 1274–1974. Commemorative Studies.*, ed. A. Maurer (Toronto, 1974), 2: 219–42.

8   I have used the edition of the *Scriptum Super Libros Sententiarum* prepared by P. Mandonnet (vols. I-II) and M. F. Moos (vols. III-IV) (Paris, 1929–1947). The Moos edition of the fourth book of the *Scriptum* terminates at distinction XXII. For distinctions XXIII to L of Book IV, I have used the Parma edition reprinted in the Supplement to the *Index Thomisticus*, vol. I (Stuttgart, 1980). Apparently, the Leonine critical edition of the *Scriptum* will not be available for some years to come.

     For each distinction, there are three parts to Thomas's commentary. First, in the *Divisio*, Thomas attempts to show how Peter Lombard has organized his discussion. Second, Thomas offers his own discussion of the issues raised by Peter. And, third, in an *Expositio*, Thomas offers brief comments on certain statements made by Peter. For our purposes, it is the second part, unfailingly the lengthiest in each distinction, which is the most important. The principal division of the second part is the question. There may be only one question in a distinction, or a number of questions. Each question is divided into articles, each of which in turn is composed of "objections" (*ob*), one or more arguments to the contrary (*sed contra*), a resolution of the issue raised in the article (*solutio*), and finally the responses to the objections first raised (*ad*). There is occasionally a further division of the second part of a distinction, the *questiuncula* (*qc*), the "little" question. In this, Thomas divides an article into separate, smaller questions. In citing a text from the *Scriptum*, the word '*In*' followed by a number in Roman numerals indicates the book of the commentary. The following number in Roman numerals, prefixed by a 'd,' refers to the distinction. The next number, in Roman numerals, prefixed by a 'q,' refers to the question. This is followed by an arabic numeral, prefixed by an 'a,' which denotes the article. The remaining information refers to the part of the article cited. Hence, *In II* d. XXVII, q. I, a. 3, sol., refers to Book II, the twenty-seventh distinction, the first question, the third article of this question, and the part of the article cited, the response. When a number follows the "sol.," this refers to a solution of one of the *questiunculae*. When there is only one question in a distinction (as there is in the example chosen), the article number can follow immediately after the distinction: *In II* d. XXVII, a. 5, sol.

suggests that a more accurate assessment of the Lombard's work is that he has looked at these truths in terms of God as the beginning and end of creatures,[9] an organization which suggests Thomas's own in the later *Summa Theologiae*. However, despite the intimations of the *Summa*, Thomas's *Scriptum* remains faithful to the order of discussion in the *Sentences*, and thus this early work of St. Thomas manifests significant differences in organization from that found in the *Summa*. In terms of the doctrines that most interest us here, for example, following the Lombard's lead Thomas discusses merit *ex professo* where the Lombard treats it, in the discussion of grace in Book II, while he postpones the analysis of justification until Book IV, d. XVII. In the *Summa*, the analysis of justification comes immediately before that of merit (*ST* I-II 113–14) and the discussion of merit there builds directly on that of justification. Similarly, Thomas discusses God's providence and predestination as does the Lombard in the first book of the *Scriptum* (d. XXXIX–XLI), but only discusses God's justice and mercy near the end of Book IV (d. XLVI). In the *Summa*, Thomas discusses these qualities of God in close connection with God's providence and predestination (*ST* I 21–23), thus making possible a more integrated approach to the attributes of God which figure so significantly in the later discussion of merit. Finally, as I point out in detail later in this chapter, the organization of the discussion of hope in the *Scriptum* differs markedly from that in the later work.

A. In II *d. XXVII, q. I, aa. 3–6*

Thomas's *ex professo* treatment of merit falls in the midst of his discussion of grace in the *Scriptum*.[10] As was observed in the first chapter, while

---

9   See, e.g., *In I* d. II, *divisio textus*, in which Thomas says that theological doctrine is about things according as they proceed (*exeunt*) from God as their principle and are related (*referuntur*) to God as to their end.

10   Thomas's treatment of grace in the *Scriptum* covers *In Sent.* II d. XXVI to *In Sent.* II d. XXIX and includes many of the topics treated in the treatise on grace in the *Summa Theologiae* I-II 109–114, albeit in different order. In d. XXVI, he considers the nature, subject, and divisions of grace, while in distinctions XXVIII and XXIX he treats the need for grace at different stages of "salvation" history (e.g., before and after the Fall). Throughout the discussion, 'grace' as the effect of God's love in people is understood by Thomas exclusively as *habitual* grace. The notion of an actual grace or at least a different modality of grace, grace as *auxilium*, is completely absent. The few instances in the *Scriptum* in which Thomas refers to the *auxilium* of grace or of God must not be read in a technical sense as the equivalent of the later *auxilium* of the *Summa*. When he uses the term here (see, e.g., *In II* d. XXVIII, q. I, a. 3 ad 5; *In III* d. XL, a. 3 sol.), he is *not* speaking of God reducing the person to his act or moving the person to the correct use of his powers, but rather is speaking broadly, of the help which God offers people to achieve God. In the use of *auxilium* in the *Scriptum*, Thomas is probably inspired simply by Peter Lombard's remarks about the grace which is *adiutorium* or *auxilium*. See, for example, Bk. II, d. XXIV, chapters 140 and 141. Later in

Thomas can later speak of grace as the efficient cause of human action,[11] when he speaks of grace in this early work he is thinking especially of the *formal* qualities of grace. The human person has the opportunity to attain the direct vision of God. God has created this being as a *rational* creature, which means that the person is *capax Dei*, capable of reaching the direct vision of God which God always enjoys.[12]

---

this chapter, I shall indicate why the lack of an *auxilium* in the technical sense is significant for Thomas's teaching on merit in the *Scriptum*.

11   When referring to grace as efficient cause, Thomas prefers to say that grace "disposes" or "inclines" the person to his act. See, e.g., *In II* d. XXVI, q. I, a. 5 ad 2, where Thomas asserts that grace is the "efficient" cause of good acts; *In II* d. XXVI, q. I, a. 5 ad 3, in which Thomas states that grace "inclines" the *liberum arbitrium* to good acts; *In II* d. XXVIII, q. I, a. 1 ad 3, where he notes that God through habitual grace aids (*iuvat*) us to act well; and *In III* d. XIII, q. I, a. 1 sol., in which Thomas says that grace perfects the soul for work. Recall Lonergan's comments about the inadequate notion of the will which is found in the *Scriptum*.

By the time of *De Malo*, a work of the middle period, Thomas will have worked out a view of the will as both an active and a passive power. As passive, it is moved by the object provided by the intellect and, in a different way by God, to the willing of the end; as active, it moves itself to the choice of the means. As we shall see in Chapter 3, this nuanced view of the will will have important repercussions for Thomas's analysis of the meritorious act. In the earlier *Scriptum*, on the other hand, Thomas views the will solely as passive, moved by the object presented to it by the intellect (and "disposed" by habitual grace to certain acts). Given the rudimentary notion of the will in this work, Thomas is unable here to offer a detailed consideration of the relation of the will and grace, such as he will in the later *Summa Theologiae* I-II 111, 2c. Rather, he is forced to speak in general ways of grace disposing or inclining the person to act. As Lonergan observed, at this stage of his career Thomas is convinced that action will normally follow on this inclination because of the passivity of the will.

12   Thomas refers to people as *capaces Dei* or *capaces gloriae* in any number of places in the *Scriptum*. See, for example, *In III* d. XXVIII, a. 2 ad 3, and *In III* d. XXVIII, a. 4 sol. The basis of this "capacity" is God's creation of rational creatures in the divine image. The "image of God" denotes the rational creature's imitation of God through his intellectual activity. Since the human being has a mind, it is possible for him to share, by God's grace, in God's self-knowledge by viewing the divine essence directly. This vision will fulfill the rational creature's deepest yearning for knowledge. In the background of this discussion of the capacity of rational creatures for God's own life lies the distinction between the two ends of human life, the natural and the supernatural. The "natural" end lies within the unaided capacities of the human being. It is natural for the person to know the truths accessible through the evidence of the senses. The "supernatural" end is what transcends human nature—it is God's own life and activity. To come to this supernatural end, Thomas adds, the person must rise to the supernatural level, and this occurs through grace. Grace "proportions" the soul to God as to its special end. The distinction between the natural and the supernatural ends of human activity remains a constant feature of Thomas's discussion of grace and merit throughout his career.

However, to realize this opportunity for life with God, it is necessary for

However, Thomas's analysis of the way in which the person obtains grace and "rises" to the supernatural level differs in the earlier and later works. As we shall see, in the *Summa Theologiae* Thomas will also speak of the human person's "capacity for God," and on this basis state that all people are "ordained" to eternal life. However, in the *Summa* Thomas makes it abundantly clear that the actual attainment of eternal life is due to God's ordination in a different sense. God ordains or predestines selected individuals to attain life with God and then grants them the grace which converts them to God and moves them along the road to God. Here, the salvation of individuals is clearly shown to be dependent on God's free predestination of them, God's ordination of them in a special way. The matter is not so clear in the *Scriptum*. In the *Scriptum*, there are occasional texts which will speak of God's predestination in terms which evoke the *Summa*. For example, Thomas teaches in a few passages that God will so manipulate circumstances that one chosen by God to come to eternal life will in fact convert; see *In II* d. XXVIII, q. I, a. 4 sol., and ad 1. On the other hand, in the *Scriptum* we also find statements which are quite at odds with the later teaching of the *Summa*. Thomas says that our freely performed acts (that is, not efficiently moved by grace) in *aliquo modo* are also a cause of the infusion of grace, in the sense that when a person on his own initiative disposes himself for grace, and so becomes "worthy" of grace, God then gives grace. See, e.g., *In IV* d. IV, q. I, a. 3, qc. IV ad 1. I shall return to Thomas's affirmation of the *facere quod in se est* in the *Scriptum* in the detailed discussion of *In II* d. XXVII, a. 4. As Thomas says in a few places (e.g., *In IV* d. XLVI, q. II, a. 2, qc. II ad 4), God has *promised* to give grace to those who so prepare themselves. In other words, by God's free self-binding, God has established a structure by which human freedom and activity are granted the greatest value. The person must decide to prepare for grace. If he does, then he enters on the path which leads to heaven. Coupled with this "promise" is Thomas's teaching about predestination in terms of God's antecedent and consequent will. By God's antecedent will, God wills all people to be saved, in the words of I Timothy 2:4, and makes the universal offer of grace. But when people do not prepare themselves for this grace, that is, when they do not stop sinning (sin creates an obstacle to grace), by God's consequent will God does not will their salvation; God only wills/predestines those to salvation who respond correctly to the general offer of grace. See, e.g., *In III* d. XXXII, a. 2 sol. and ad 4. This analysis of predestination in terms of God's consequent will is fairly prominent in the *Scriptum*. In the *Summa*, however, Thomas does not connect the two notions and, as we shall see, his analysis of predestination is quite different, making it clear that God's willing of salvation is in no way as "reactive" as the earlier teaching makes it sound. In the third chapter, I return to this question when I consider the suggestion of Arfeuil that Thomas's teaching about predestination remained constant throughout his career, and that it is the *Scriptum*'s teaching which most adequately expresses Thomas's mind. For a much more accurate description of providence and predestination in Aquinas, see the fine article by W. Ysaac, "The Certitude of Providence in St. Thomas," *Modern Schoolman* 38 (1961): 305–21. At any rate, the different approach to predestination in the *Scriptum* grants to Thomas's affirmation that all people are *capaces Dei* a much greater importance than it has in the *Summa*.

the person to be raised by grace to God's own level[13]—God as end transcends the natural capacities of the human being, lying beyond the scope of normal human activity.

Thus, in discussing grace as operative and cooperative,[14] Thomas observes that as operative, grace elevates the person to the supernatural order, making its possessor pleasing to God and orienting his being to God. Likewise, as cooperative, grace adds a formal perfection to the person's *works*. Just as the person is now pleasing to God and is endowed with supernatural dignity by operative grace, so too by cooperative grace his works are pleasing to God. Through the added dignity of cooperative grace, which "proportions" these works to God, human action is now treated as *meritorious* before God.[15] Hence, in the *Scriptum* when he turns to the *ex professo* treatment of merit, which is the effect of cooperative grace,

---

13 For assertions of grace as *elevans*, "bridging" the gap between the natural and supernatural and raising the person to a transcendent order of existence, see *In II* d. XXVI, q. I, a. 3 sol., in which Thomas says that grace elevates human nature to a higher kind of life, raising the essence of the soul to a "quoddam divinum esse, ut idonea sit ad divinas operationes"; *In II* d. XXVIII, q. I, a. 1 sol., in which Thomas asserts that for merit, the *liberum arbitrium* must be raised by a habit, grace, "qui etiam naturae facultatem excedit"; *In III* d. XXIII, q. 1, a. 4, qc. III ad 1, where Thomas states that although people are naturally ordained to God (see the previous note), the theological virtues are necessary to orient people to God as to their supernatural end; and *In IV* d. V, q. I, a. 3 sol., where Thomas states that "gratia elevat hominem ad vitam quamdam quae est supra conditione omnis naturae creatae." Similarly, there are numerous texts in which Thomas refers to the *formal* perfection wrought by habitual grace. See, for example, *In III* d. XIII, q. I, a. 1 sol., in which he states that grace "perficit [the soul] formaliter in esse spirituali," according to which the soul is now similar to God; and *In II* d. XXIII, q. I, a. 1 sol., in which Thomas states that through the gift of grace, people are made "children of God," and in a way "divinae naturae consortes." The last phrase is meant to be a conscious allusion to II Peter 1:4, which remains a favorite biblical text for Thomas throughout his career to describe the work of grace. In Chapter 3, on the *Summa Theologiae*, I note passages in which Thomas also refers to this text. For other discussions of the formal perfection of grace in the *Scriptum*, see *In III* d. XXVII, q. II, a. 4 sol. IV, and *In III* d. XXVIII, a. 3 sol.

14 Thomas's detailed discussion of habitual grace as operative and cooperative is found in *In II* d. XXVI, a. 5. In addition to the formal perfection worked by grace both as operative and as cooperative, Thomas discusses in this article these graces merely in terms of 'prevenient' and 'subsequent' grace, that is, in terms of a temporal order.

15 Thomas makes these points in *In II* d. XXVI, a. 5 sol. and ad 2. In the response of this article, as well as in ad 4, Thomas also describes the *efficient* causality of operative and cooperative grace, stating that operative grace causes the inner act of the will, while cooperative causes the "exterior" act of the will. In view of the undeveloped notion of the human will, this is as far as Thomas will (and can) go in the *Scriptum* in discussing the relations of will and grace in action. Incidentally, in the discussion of these graces in the *Summa* (I-II

Thomas wishes to explain precisely how the good acts performed by the person in grace are meritorious before God.[16]

111, 2c), Thomas will retain the language of "inner" and "exterior" acts, despite having realized a more sophisticated view of the will. See note 11 above. In the first part of Chapter 3, I discuss the difficulty posed by the retention of this language. For an additional statement that operative grace makes its possessor formally just and pleasing to God, and cooperative grace his acts meritorious, see *In II* d. XXIX, q. I, a. 1 ad 2.

The *Scriptum* is replete with affirmations of the need for grace in meriting. See, for example, *In II* d. XXVI, q. I, a. 4 sed contra 2, where Thomas says that grace is the *principium merendi*, and *In II* XLII, q. II, a. 4 ad 2, where he states that it is the principal cause of merit; *In II* d. XXVI, q. I, a. 5 sol., *In II* d. XXVIII, q. I, a. 1 ad 1, and *In II* d. XXVIII, q. I, a. 2 ad 6, in which he asserts that without grace there can be no merit; and *In III* d. I, q. I, a. 2 ad 5, *In IV* d. XIV, q. I, a. 4, qc. I ad 1, and *In IV*, d. XV, q. I, a. 2 ad 1 and ad 4, in which he affirms the "infinite" power of grace because grace makes it possible to merit the infinite reward, God Himself. In some texts in which Thomas describes the need for grace in meriting, he mentions that by grace people are "adopted" as children of God to whom the inheritance of eternal life, which belongs naturally to God, is now "owed." See, for example, *In III* d. X, q. II, a. 1 sol., and *In III* d. X, q. II, a. 2 sol. In the *Summa Theologiae*, Thomas will restate this relation between merit and sonship but will work the idea into the *ex professo* treatment of merit itself. In the *Scriptum*, Thomas adds that not only grace, but the theological virtue of charity, is necessary for merit. In Thomas's analysis, the theological virtues "flow" out from habitual grace. While grace perfects the essence of the soul, the theological virtues perfect the powers of the soul, through which human acts are executed. Of the theological virtues, charity is the most important, because it directs the acts of the person directly to God; see, e.g., *In II* d. XXXVIII, q. I, a. 1 ad 1, and *In IV* d. XLIX, q. V, a. 1 sol. For Thomas's affirmation that charity is the *root* or *principle* of meriting, see *In III* d. XXXV, q. I, a. 4 sol., and *In IV* d. XLIX, q. I, a. 3, qc. II sed contra 2. Thomas discusses the need for charity in the meritorious act in such texts as *In II* d. XLI, q. I, a. 5 ads 3 and 6, and *In IV* d. XV, q. I, a. 3 sol. III, where he says that charity makes good works pleasing to God. Thomas retains his conviction about the need for charity in meriting throughout his career. For statements in the *Scriptum* about the need for both grace and charity for merit, see *In II* d. XLI, q. I, a. 2 sol., and especially *In III* d. XXX, a. 5 ad 1, in which Thomas says that grace is the *remote* principle, charity the *proximate* principle of meritorious action.

16 A constant feature of Thomas's discussion of merit is the emphasis on another element, in addition to grace and charity, that must be present for merit: human freedom, the ability to choose freely the course of action desired for people by God to attain God. It is the *liberum arbitrium* which distinguishes the human being from other creatures. Non-rational creatures are set on their proper course of action by instinct, and they do not conform to (or withdraw from) this course of action by a free act of will. They simply follow this course of action. People, however, as agents with will are able to devise any number of strategies for action, not all of which are conducive to fulfilling the human being in the manner God intends. For Thomas, this ability to opt to act as God wills, this mastery over one's actions, creates along with grace and

Thomas's *ex professo* treatment of merit in the *Scriptum* occurs in *In II* d. XXVII, q. I, aa. 3–6. In the first two articles of this distinction, Thomas had been concerned with (theological) virtue, looking at the definition of virtue offered by Augustine which had been so influential in the Middle Ages. While the juxtaposition of virtue and merit in a single distinction may strike us as odd—and, indeed, in the *Summa*, Thomas has discussed these topics in separate questions[17]—Thomas's concern here is to be faithful to the Lombard's text. In distinction XXVII of the second book of the *Sentences*, Peter contemplates the transformation wrought by God through grace. He notes that God's gracious action establishes the principles of virtuous action in us, citing Augustine's definition of virtue, that "virtue is a good quality of the mind by which someone rightly lives, and which no one uses badly, which God alone operates in a man." The Lombard then notes that because of God's creation of the virtues in the justified, the redeemed person is subsequently able to act in the proper way, that is, he is now able to act meritoriously. Thus, in prefacing the discussion of merit in this distinction with a consideration of virtue, Thomas is simply following the Lombard, although Thomas is more careful than Peter to stress that Augustine's definition of virtue is applicable to *theological* virtue alone.

Thomas has structured his discussion of merit around the questions of the *objects* of merit. By showing what "parts" of the spiritual life, the journey of the soul to God,[18] can be merited, Thomas hopes to establish why good moral actions are in fact meritorious.[19] Each of the four articles devoted to merit considers a different object of merit. In the third article, Thomas considers the end of spiritual existence, the beatific vision, and asks whether a person can merit eternal life condignly. In the fourth article, he turns to the beginning of the spiritual journey, the first entry into the state of grace which is the presupposition of life with God, and asks whether the infusion of grace is merited by one who lacks grace. In the fifth article, Thomas's topic is the merit of the one already in the state of grace. Can

---

charity the possibility of speaking about merit. For affirmations of the place of free choice or the will in meriting, see *In III* d. XXX, a. 3 sol., *In II* d. XXXV, q. I, a. 4 sol., and *In II* d. XXXIX, q. I, a. 2 ad 2. In such texts as *In III* d. XXVII, q. II, a. 4 sol. III, Thomas reflects on the need for an action to be voluntary for merit to arise. In *In II* d. XXVIII, q. I, a. 1 sol., and *In II* d. XXIX, q. I, a. 4 sol., Thomas mentions the need for grace *and* free choice in meriting.

17 In the *Summa* Thomas discusses theological virtue in I-II 62.
18 See *In II* d. XXXV, q. I, a. 3 ad 4, for the description of merit itself as "quasi quoddam iter in finem beatitudinis."
19 As mentioned earlier, for Aquinas the meritorious action is one in which the person acts in conformity with the law of human being as determined by God and thereby comes to the end of human existence, life with God. Thomas, it is clear, is unwilling to restrict meritorious action to the so-called supererogatory deed. For statements in the *Scriptum* in which Thomas tells us that a person merits when doing the moral good, see, e.g., *In I* d. XLVII, q. I, a. 3 ad 3, and especially *In I* d. XLVIII, q. I, a. 1 sol.

this person merit the increase of the grace which perfects the soul and readies it for the beatific vision? Finally, in the sixth article, Thomas asks a question raised in the schools from the mid-twelfth century on, the applicability of the merit of one person to another. He asks if it is possible to merit the first grace for another. Thomas's treatment, in terms of detail and the sophistication of the discussion of merit, is superior to Peter's rather broad and imprecise statements about merit. In his discussion of merit, as elsewhere in the *Scriptum*, Thomas exploits the discoveries and insights of a century of theological speculation since the Lombard.

In the third article of distinction XXVII, Thomas marshalls an impressive array of arguments *against* the condign merit of eternal life. In the first objection, Thomas suggests a "biblical" basis for the rejection of condign merit. In Romans 8:18, Paul speaks of the sufferings of the saints and asserts that these sufferings are not at all equal (*condignae*) to the reward which their sufferings shall gain for them. Hence, says Thomas, since the deeds of the saints are considered most meritorious, if they fall short of condignity, then all merit must be inferior in value to the reward of eternal life.[20]

In the second objection, Thomas also focuses on the word 'condign' in order to make the case against condign merit. The word 'condign' denotes an equality between a work and its reward. But the end of human action

---

20 *In II* d. XXVII, q. I, a. 3 ob 1: "Aliquis non possit ex condigno vitam aeternam mereri per actus virtutis. Primo per id quod habetur ad Rom., VIII, 18: 'Non sunt condignae passiones huius temporis ad futuram gloriam quae revelabitur in nobis.' Sed per passiones quas sancti sustinent maxime merentur. Ergo videtur quod nullus ex condigno vitam mereatur." Elsewhere in the *Scriptum*, Thomas also touched on the sufferings of the saints and explained why they are meritorious. It is because the saints, those who exist in grace, have *willingly* or *voluntarily* accepted the suffering which they must endure and suffer for the sake of God. See, e.g., *In II* d. XXXVI, q. I, a. 2 ad 5, and *In II* d. XVII, a. 5 ad 4; *In II* d. XL, a. 4 ad 1, is also of relevance here. For the "voluntary" aspect of meriting, see also note 16 above. In speaking of suffering freely *propter Deum*, Thomas introduces an important idea that will be found throughout his career when he considers merit. The deed which is meritorious of reward from God is done primarily not for the reward but for the sake of God. If the work were done because one desired the reward, the work would then proceed from a selfish motive. But in speaking of doing the deed for God's sake, Thomas is able to incorporate the idea that it is in "losing oneself" that one finds oneself. By acting as God wills for the reason God wills, one does achieve the end ordained for one's being. In Aquinas, the preferred locus of this discussion is his analysis of the theological virtue of *charity*. By charity one tends to seek the good of another—one wills good for the other. Hence, the more perfectly charity becomes rooted in the person, the more one wills the good of another, that is, the more one wills God and seeks to do what God wills for human being. See *In III* d. XXIX, a. 4, sol. See also note 15 above, in which passages in the *Scriptum* in which Thomas calls charity the root or principle of merit are cited. Charity is emphasized because through it, one can will the end which God wills and which God wills one to will.

is God Himself. Since God infinitely transcends the person and anything the person might do, condign merit of eternal life from God is impossible.[21] In the remaining objections (objections 3–5), the arguments proposed by Thomas are even more radical. If valid, they would not only eliminate condign merit of eternal life. They would eliminate all merit whatsoever between the human person and God. In these three objections, Thomas seems to be assuming a familiarity among his readers with the various features which are involved in merit in everyday life, that is, in merit between people. In brief, these normal features of merit are that in meritorious action, one is giving something to another which is not owed or due to the other; that by meriting, one makes the other into his debtor; and that merit entails being of benefit to the recipient of one's action. Having assumed a familiarity with the conditions of merit between people, the remaining objections seek to show why merit before God is impossible. Hence, the third objection observes that when a person works correctly, what he is doing is observing God's will for him and so offering to God what he owes to God. Since one who renders what he owes does not merit, there is no condign merit of eternal life from God.[22] Similarly, merit between people and God is impossible because merit means making another into one's debtor, and God is debtor to no one.[23] Finally, because of the divine perfection, God stands in no need of help from anyone and cannot be aided by another; thus again a crucial condition for merit, being of benefit to another, is absent from the relations between God and people.[24]

Despite the strong case which can be made against condign merit of eternal life, Thomas nevertheless affirms in this article the condign merit of the goal of spiritual activity, life with God. The response of article 3 is divided into three parts. First, Thomas reviews two answers given to this question by other theologians.[25] Second, he contemplates the truth in each

---

21 *In II* d, XXVII, q. I, a. 3 ob 2: "Condignum importat aequalitatem dignitatis. Sed impossibile est quod actus humanus aequatur in dignitate praemio vitae aeternae, quod est ipse Deus. Ergo videtur quod nullus ex condigno vitam aeternam mereri possit."

22 *In II* d. XXVII, q. I, a. 3 ob 3: "Ille qui reddit quod debet, non meretur ulterius praemium. Sed homo bene operans reddit quod debet, ut dicitur Luc., XVII, 10: 'Cum feceritis omnia quae praecepta sunt vobis, dicite: servi inutiles sumus: quod debuimus facere, fecimus.' Ergo videtur quod nullus ex condigno, recte vivendo, vitam aeternam mereatur."

23 *In II* d. XXVII, q. I, a. 3 ob 4: "A quocumque quis meretur, ille debitor sibi efficitur: quia praemium merito debetur. Sed Deus non potest effici debitor. Ergo apud ipsum nihil ex condigno mereri possumus."

24 *In II* d. XXVII, q. I, a. 3 ob 5: "Nullus meretur praemium apud eum qui eius opere nec iuvatur, nec iuvari potest. Sed Deus nostris bonis operibus non iuvatur, quia bonorum nostrorum non eget, ut in psal. XV dicitur. Ergo videtur quod apud ipsum mereri non possumus."

25 The "merit" which is the focus of this study is a *theological* concept. As used by theologians, the term refers to the right created by good human action to a supernatural reward from God. See also, e.g., *In III* d. XVIII, a. 2 sol., and

position. Finally Thomas suggests that he finds the affirmation of condign merit of eternal life from God more correct (*verius*), introducing in support of this conclusion his consideration of the kind of justice which is operative in merit and reward.[26] First, Thomas simply reports the divergent opin-

---

In III d. XVIII, a. 4 sol. In addition to this "positive" connotation of merit in a theological sense, Thomas can also use 'merit' to designate the *culpa* of sin. By one's sin, one "merits" punishment. See in this regard, e.g., *In I* d. XLIII, q. II, a. 2 ad 5, and *In II* d. XXXVI, q. I, a. 3 sol. In this usage of 'merit,' Thomas has biblical warrant. In the Vulgate, texts such as Hebrews 10:29 use merit in the sense of sin calling forth punishment from God. Similarly, the Lombard had also known the negative as well as the positive connotation of merit—see, e.g., Bk. II, d. XXX. Finally, Thomas occasionally uses "merit" words in a non-technical and non-theological fashion. Hence, he can speak of something "meritoriously" happening or being the case, where the adverb *merito* simply means "deservedly" or "rightly" so. See, e.g., *In II* d. XXII, q. I, a. 1 sol. The range of meanings which 'merit' can have—deserving a supernatural reward from God; the aspect of sin which deserves punishment; the non-technical sense of the everyday adverb—is reproduced in all of Thomas's writings throughout his career.

26   *In II* d. XXVII, q. I, a. 3 sol., reads as follows: "Circa hoc sunt duae opiniones. Quidam enim dicunt quod aliquis vitam aeternam non potest mereri ex condigno, sed ex congruo. Alii vero dicunt quod etiam ex condigno potest quis vitam aeternam mereri per actus virtutum. Dicitur autem aliquis mereri ex condigno, quando invenitur aequalitas inter praemium et meritum, secundum rectam aestimationem; ex congruo autem tantum, quando talis aequalitas non invenitur, sed solum secundum liberalitatem dantis munus tribuitur quod dantem decet. Videntur autem utrique quantum ad aliquid verum dicere. Est enim duplex aequalitas, scilicet aequalitas quantitatis et aequalitas proportionis. Secundum quantitatis aequalitatem ex actibus virtutum vitam aeternam ex condigno non meremur; non enim tantum bonum est in quantitate actus virtutis, quantum praemium gloriae, quod est finis eius. Secundum autem aequalitatem proportionis ex condigno meremur vitam aeternam. Attenditur enim aequalitas proportionis, quando aequaliter se habet hoc ad illud, sicut aliud, ad alterum. Non autem majus est Deo vitam aeternam tribuere, quam nobis actum virtutis exhibere: sed sicut hoc congruit huic, ita illud illi; et ideo quaedam proportionis aequalitas invenitur inter Deum praemiantem et hominem merentem; dum tamen praemium referatur ad idem genus in quo est meritum, ut si praemium est quod omnem facultatem humanae naturae excedit, sicut vita aeterna, meritum etiam sit per talem actum in quo refulgeat bonum illius habitus qui divinitus infunditur, Deo nos consignans. Illi tamen qui dicunt nos ex condigno vitam aeternam posse mereri, verius dicere videntur. Cum enim sit duplex species iustitiae, ut in V *Ethicorum*, cap. II, Philosophus dicit, scilicet iustitia distributiva et commutativa, quae in contractibus, ut in emptione et venditione: iustitia commutativa respicit aequalitatem arithmeticam, quae tendit in aequalitatem quantitatis; iustitia vero distributiva aequalitatem respicit geometricam, quae est aequalitas proportionis. In redditione autem praemii ad merita magis servatur forma distributionis, cum ipse unicuique secundum opera sua reddat, quam commutationis, cum Deus a nobis nihil accipiat; quamvis a sanctis quandoque inveniatur metaphorice dictum, quod bonis operibus regnum caelorum emitur, inquantum Deus accipit opera

ions on this issue. Some (*quidam*), he notes, say that there is no condign merit of eternal life; one can only merit God congruently ("Quidam enim dicunt quod aliquis vitam aeternam non potest mereri ex condigno, sed ex congruo"). Others (*alii*), however, think it is possible to merit eternal life condignly through virtuous action ("Alii vero dicunt quod etiam ex condigno potest quis vitam aeternam mereri per actus virtutum").

Completing this review of the two positions, Thomas adds brief definitions of "condign" and "congruent" merit. In condign merit, there is an equality between the reward and the merit, an equality which is graspable by and apparent to the reason ("Dicitur autem aliquis mereri ex condigno, quando invenitur aequalitas inter praemium et meritum, secundum rectam aestimationem"). In congruent merit, such an equality is absent. In its place is the liberality of the one who grants the reward to those whom it is fitting (*decet*) that such a gift be granted ("ex congruo autem tantum, quando talis aequalitas non invenitur, sed solum secundum liberalitatem dantis munus tribuitur quod dantem decet").[27]

Having reported the disagreement over this question, Thomas acknow-

---

nostra, ut acceptans ea: et ideo verius dicitur quod ex condigno meremur quam quod non ex condigno."

27   In *In IV* d. XV, q. I, a. 3 sol. IV, Thomas offers a somewhat more comprehensive discussion of the difference between 'condign' and 'congruent' merit. After noting that merit means "to make it just that something be given to a person," Thomas states that 'justice' here can be taken in two ways. First, 'justice' can have a proper meaning, inasmuch as the reward respects a *debitum* which exists on the part of the recipient (*ex parte recipientis*). The second sense of 'justice' bears only a similitude to the first (*quasi similitudinarie*) because it respects not a *debitum* in the recipient, but a debt *ex parte dantis*—it befits (*decet*) the one giving something to give it although there is no *debitum* in the first sense, that is, no *debitum* in the recipient, whcih must be requited. In this latter sense, 'justice' is used as Anselm had defined it, as "decentia divinae bonitatis." It pertains to the divine goodness to give someone something, even though that someone does not possess a "right" to the reward. Having spelled out these two meanings of 'justice,' Thomas adds here that 'merit' can similarly be spoken of in two ways: "Uno modo actus per quem efficitur ut ipse agens habeat debitum recipiendi. Et hoc vocatur meritum condigni. Alio modo per quem efficitur ut sit debitum dandi in dante secundum decentiam ipsius. Et ideo hoc meritum dicitur meritum congrui." Thomas goes on to say that the first kind of justice and merit presuppose the divine love. God must first have loved the person and granted grace to him before condign merit will come into play. As we shall shortly see, this is because the person and his acts must be "proportioned" to God before they can deserve a reward from God. Thomas also notes in the present text that people speak of the acts which *precede* grace as congruently meritorious, that is, meritorious in the second sense. However, Thomas states that because this is not really or properly "merit" inasmuch as justice here is not fully or truly justice, he does not call such acts "meritorious." Later in this chapter, in the discussion of article 4, I return to this and similar texts, in trying to ascertain whether Thomas nevertheless asserted the congruent merit of the first grace in the *Scriptum*.

ledges that there is truth in each position ("Videntur autem utrique quantum ad aliquid verum dicere") and shows the strength of each analysis. There are, he tells us, two kinds of equality. In the first, the equality is one of *quantity*—one thing is equal in size to another. If we are thinking of this kind of equality when we speak of condign merit, then there can be no condign merit between people and God. While there is good present in virtuous actions, this good quantitatively falls short of the good involved in the beatific vision of God. This, then, is the truth in the position of those who say that there can only be congruent merit between people and God. The other kind of equality to which Thomas refers in this article is one of *proportion*. Here, the equality is established by equal treatment for the same kind of work. The ruler of a community, for example, observes this equality of proportion when he gives the same amount to those who have equal needs and rights, while granting lesser amounts to those whose rights are less. If we think of the equality of proportion, says Aquinas, it is possible to affirm condign merit before God. God grants the same reward to those who have done the same virtuous action and who therefore have merited in the same way. God's observance of the same measure insures the equality of proportion.[28]

Given that equality may be proportionate as well as quantitative, Thomas is able to assert in the third part of the article that those who affirm the condign merit of eternal life are more correct ("Illi tamen qui dicunt nos ex condigno vitam aeternam posse mereri, verius dicere videntur"). Merit, as we have seen in Chapter 1, is a matter of justice. The reward is rendered for what is owed to a person.[29] Drawing on the authority of

28   In the *solutio* of the present article, Thomas informs us that the "proportion" between merit and reward is created by grace and the theological virtues: He speaks here of the habit *divinitus* infused by God which directs one to God. I shall return shortly in the text to the rather limited role of grace in Thomas's *ex professo* consideration of meriting. For Thomas, God offers the same reward to like actions. The action of one will be equal to and like that of another when the degree of difficulty in the act is the same, the same effort to do the act is expended (see *In III* d. XXIV, a. 3 sol. III) *and* the act is performed by people who have the same amount of grace. As will become clear in the next two articles, the amount of grace which a person has is dependent on the degree of effort which the person has expended to obtain grace and then to increase it. Hence, when two people have the same amount of grace, this is because each has prepared himself equally for his grace. In his mature teaching, Thomas will change his analysis, and insist that the degree of grace which a person has is due to *God's* decision to give that person a specified "amount" of grace.

29   In the *Scriptum*, Thomas occasionally offers brief "definitions" of merit in passing, in which he makes clear that merit involves justice. See, for example, *In III* d. XVIII, a. 2 sol., where Thomas offers the following definition in the context of discussing the merit of Christ. In justice, he says, two people are required, the one doing (*faciens*) justice and the one suffering (*patiens*) justice. The action proper to the one doing justice is to render to each what is his own. "Patientis autem iustitiam actio propria est facere sibi debitum quod est ei

Aristotle (*Ethics* V), Thomas describes two species of justice, commutative and distributive. Commutative justice is found in commercial transactions, such as buying and selling; here, the equality which is the basis of justice is an "arithmetical" equality, in which the purchase price equals the value of the thing purchased. Despite some metaphorical statements in the tradition about the saints "purchasing" heaven by their deeds,[30] it is not commutative justice which governs Christian merit. As Thomas had already agreed, those who affirm a mere congruent merit between people and God are correct in the sense that they deny the "quantitative equality" of the Christian's good deeds and God's reward. The other kind of justice, distributive justice, is based on what Thomas calls a "geometrical equality," one in which a proportion is observed; and this, he states, is the kind of justice which is operative in merit. God renders to each person according to his works and distributes the same reward to people of equal right. Thus, Thomas concludes, in terms of distributive justice, it becomes possible to speak of merit and reward between people and God and, moreover, to say that the works of people are "equal" to God's reward, at least by the equality of proportion.[31]

per iustitiam reddendum: et hoc proprie mereri est." In *In IV* d. XV, q. I, a. 3 sol. IV, which was discussed in note 27 above, Thomas begins the discussion of condign and congruent merit by saying that merit is "actio qua efficitur ut ei qui agat sit iustum aliquid dari." In his *ex professo* treatments of merit, both in the *Scriptum* and in the *Summa*, Thomas shies away from such brief "definitions" of merit, preferring the more extended treatment of the various aspects of merit which is possible in the *ex professo* analysis. Nevertheless, Thomas always insists that meriting involves justice.

30   In *In II* d. XXVII, q. I, a. 3 sol., Thomas notes statements in the tradition which would seem to suggest that by their good works the saints do "buy" heaven. He advises us that such statements must be taken metaphorically. Only if they are read as straightforward, literal descriptions of the relation of people and God is it necessary to limn a place for commutative justice in human merit. Similarly, in *In IV* d. XXV, q. III, a. 2, qc. I ad 1, Thomas also rejects the equation of merit and *emptio*, and thus precludes commutative justice in merit.

31   Thomas discusses commutative and distributive justice in a number of places in the *Scriptum*. See, e.g., *In III* d. XXXIII, q. I, a. 3 sol. II, and *In III* d. XXXIII, q. III, a. 4, qc. V ad 2. He also treats distributive justice in *In I* d. XLI, q. I, a. 3 ad 2, and the relation between creation and this justice in *In I* d. XLIV, q. I, 1. ad 2. In the discussion of creation and justice, Thomas says that God's decision to make a creature of a certain type means that God has established a *debitum* which is to be requited by God in justice. Given that the creature is to be of such a type because of God's will, God "owes" to that creature all which belongs to a creature of that type. Hence, in creating God observes distributive justice with regard to all creatures of given types. Thomas will retain this insight throughout his career. From the *Scriptum* to the *Summa*, whenever he mentions the justice involved in creating, he says that it is *distributive* justice which God observes. Until the Prima Secundae of the *Summa Theologiae*, Thomas will also make the same claim about the justice in merit. He will consistently argue that it is distributive justice which God

In the light of the argument that condign merit is governed by distributive justice, Thomas is able to answer the objections originally raised against condign merit. Thomas's basic approach is simple and straightforward. The objections would apply only if condign merit were governed by commutative justice; but since it is distributive justice which is operative in merit, these objections pose no threat to the acceptance of condign merit.

observes in rewarding the merits of Christians, and indeed in this regard he draws a parallel with the justice involved in creation. One of the principal differences between the treatment of merit in the *Scriptum* and in the *Summa* is that in the *Summa* Thomas is more willing to speak of merit before God as under a kind of commutative justice.

In the *Scriptum*, however, Thomas mentioned only in passing that it is possible to ascribe merit before God to *commutative* rather than to distributive justice. In *In IV* d. XLVI, q. I, a. 1, sol., Thomas repeats the analysis of distributive and commutative justice which is familiar to us from the parallel discussions elsewhere in the *Scriptum*. Commutative justice normally involves an equality of quantity between act and reward, and since there is the greatest inequality between God and people, commutative justice cannot govern human merit before God. On the other hand, human merit before God is possible because of *distributive* justice. God is just and recognizes our merits because God gives to equal merits the same reward. To this point, the present text simply repeats the teaching found elsewhere in the *Scriptum*. However, Thomas now adds that though commutative justice "properly" has no role in merit and supernatural reward, because of the lack of the equality of quantity, sometimes we speak of the "equality" of commutative justice in a different sense and hence do affirm commutative justice in meriting. We speak of an "equality of proportion" being involved in the commutations or dealings between people of unequal dignity. Hence, the son who strictly speaking is inferior to the father cannot give to the father something equal in quantity to the father's reward. But the son can nevertheless obtain something as a reward from his father when he tries his best. Just as he tries his best to help his father, his father responds by "doing his best" and giving something in return to his son as a reward. This "equality of proportion" in the acts of son and father, who each act to the fullness of his own capacity, comes under commutative justice, says Thomas, and adds that we can speak of merit and reward between people and God in the same way. When people do their best, God "matches" this and does God's best, offering in return for the work a heavenly reward according to the dictates of commutative justice. However, although Thomas can speak here of commutative justice in merit, he has hardly anticipated the argument of the *Summa*. In the *Summa*, Thomas will assume not an "equality of proportion" between merit and reward but an equality of *quantity*, an equality which has been established by the dignity and value of grace. In this text of the *Scriptum*, Thomas makes no mention of grace as needed for commutative justice and, as we have seen, he denies the equality in quantity of merit and reward. Hence, the present text simply denotes Thomas's recognition that it may be possible to speak of commutative justice in meriting without the accompanying perception of what he will come to see as the true ground of this possibility, the intrinsic worth of God's grace. Thomas also allows for commutative justice in ad 4 of the present text (*In IV*, d. XLVI, q. I, a. 1, qc. I ad. 4).

Hence, the Apostle's words about the lack of equality between the sufferings of the saints and their future reward are directed to the *quantity* of the good involved in these acts. Their present pains shall be compensated by the much greater good of heaven. Paul leaves out of consideration the proportion of the reward of heaven to these good works and so the equality in meriting and reward which facilitates condign merit.[32] Likewise, the fourth and fifth objections, which had seemed to undermine the very possibility of merit, lose their force once we grasp the species of justice involved in condign merit.[33] If commutative justice ruled merit, we would have to speak of merit "making God into one's debtor" (ob 4 and ad 4) and "giving God some benefit or help" of which God stands in need (ob 5). In commutative justice, the one partner in the transaction accepts something from the other (*solutio*), something which the partner wants or needs and for which the partner now has to repay with something of equal worth. But in distributive justice, there is no need to speak of the partner becoming the "debtor" of the one who merits or the partner deriving some benefit from the deed. Indeed, as applied to human merit before God, by distributive justice God remains unaffected, as it were, by merit. Merit places God under no obligation or debt—and in requiting merit God Himself manifests the greatest liberality. God freely doles out rewards to meritorious recipients.[34] One can speak of justice here, and so merit, because God gives these rewards justly. In accordance with distributive justice, God gives equal rewards for equal merit, and so observes a proportionate equality in the distribution of rewards.

When compared to the parallel treatment in the *Summa*, it is apparent that Thomas has offered in the *Scriptum* a rather different analysis of the merit of eternal life. First, the *Scriptum*'s discussion is truncated and telescoped. Indeed, in the *Summa* Thomas has spread the material treated in *In II* d. XXVII, q. I, a. 3, over three distinct articles: In *ST* I-II 114, 1, he

---

32   *In II* d. XXVII, q. I, a. 3 ad 1: "Apostolus per dictum suum intendit excludere aequalitatem quantitatis: quia non est tanta acerbitas praesentium passionum quam gaudium futurae gloriae." In ad 2 of this article Thomas argues similarly against the objection that the meaning of the word 'condign' as "equal in dignity" necessarily precludes condign merit before God. He states that the "equality of dignity" implied in the word 'condign' need not involve an equality of quantity (and hence commutative justice); it may refer only to an "equality of proportion," which is covered by distributive justice and so Thomas is able to speak of condign merit before God.
33   I discuss the third objection and response of this article below.
34   *In II* d. XXVII, q. I, a. 3 ad 4: "Dicendum quod in iustitia commutativa ille apud quem quis meretur, efficitur debitor ei qui meretur, ut patet in illis qui operationes suas locant in servitium aliorum; sed in iustitia distributiva non requiritur ratio debiti ex parte eius qui distribuit: potest enim ex liberalitate aliqua distribuere, in quorum tamen distributione iustitia exigitur, secundum quod diversis, prout eorum gradus exigit, proportionabiliter tribuit." Below, I observe that Thomas in fact offers an alternate answer to the fourth objection.

grapples with the fundamental problem of the very *possibility* of merit. In the second article, he considers the need for *grace* for the merit of eternal life. And in the third article, he establishes the manner in which human acts done in grace are *condignly* deserving of heaven. Because he has adopted a more relaxed and systematic approach in the *Summa*, Thomas is able to re-distribute the different parts of *In II* d. XXVII, q. I, a. 3, over the three articles in the *Summa*. Thus, the third, fourth, and fifth objections of the *Scriptum*'s article are found almost verbatim in *ST* I-II 114, 1, while the first and second objections are re-positioned in *ST* I-II 114, 3.[35] Likewise, the first *sed contra* of *In II* d. XXVII, q. I, a. 3, which refers to a biblical text (II Timothy 4:8) affirming God's just judgment of human beings as the basis of accepting the condignity of the merit of eternal life, as well as the thrust of the *solutio*, which maintains the condignity of merit, are placed by Thomas in *ST* I-II 114, 3, in the *Summa*'s discussion of condignity.[36]

Not only has Thomas organized his material differently in the two works. In crucial details he also offers substantially different arguments about merit. Mention has already been made about the most obvious difference between the *Scriptum* and the *Summa*. On the one hand, in the *Scriptum* Thomas establishes the condignity of merit by identifying the kind of justice involved in merit. There can be condign merit because God requites the merits of human beings according to the dictates of distributive justice, which renders to people who are equally deserving the same reward for their works. On the other hand, in the *Summa* Thomas is no longer concerned to determine the kind of justice which is involved in merit in order to demonstrate the condignity of the Christian's merit. Rather, Thomas grounds his teaching about merit in the divine *ordinatio* which predestines certain people to eternal life and orders their works done in grace to the reward set for people by God as their goal (a. 1). He then shows that merit is condign by considering the *grace* which issues from God's ordination for people and which endows their deeds with "equality" (condignity) to the reward of their acts, eternal life with God. Thus, in the one work, there is a great interest in the *justice* which governs merit and reward. In the other, while justice is still involved, the overriding concern is to display how merit and its condignity depend on God, on God's *ordination* and on God's action upon the individual through *grace*.

---

35 The third objection is repeated in *ST* I-II 114, 1 ob 1. The thrust of the fourth objection is restated in *ST* I-II 114, 1 ob 3. The fifth objection, which denies that God can be aided or helped by our merits, is substantially taken over in *ST* I-II 114, 1 ob 2. *In II* d. XXVII, q. I, a. 3 ob 1, which cites Romans 8:18, is repeated in *ST* I-II 114, 3, ob 1, while the *Scriptum*'s ob 2 is found in *ST* I-II 114, 3 ob 3.

36 Thomas cites II Timothy 4:8 in I-II 114, 3 sed contra, and argues for the condignity of merit to its reward of eternal life in the corpus of the third article of I-II 114. In my final chapter, I return to Thomas's claim that he is moved to affirm merit by the scriptural evidence about the just judgment of God.

It may be objected, however, that the difference between the *Scriptum* and the *Summa* has been overstated; after all, scholars such as Lynn have suggested that the *ordinatio* which is so important in the *Summa* is in fact found, albeit in less systematized form, in the *Scriptum*. Attention can be directed to the response to the fourth objection in the present article, in which Thomas refers to a "promise" by God which is involved in merit. In the fourth objection, the possibility of merit had been denied because meriting means placing another in one's debt, and God is debtor to no one. In the fourth response, Thomas is somewhat uncertain about the correct answer to this objection—he offers two possible solutions, each equally plausible, without deciding between them. The first has already been mentioned above—the objection would hold only if merit were governed by commutative justice, which entails putting another in one's debt.[37] The second answer, however, invokes a concept which has hitherto gone unmentioned in the article. There is merit because of the "promise" which God has made to reward good acts.[38] Thus, because God has promised to reward these acts—and while Thomas does not make this explicit, it is likely that he wants us to realize that God has *freely* promised to reward merit—it is quite legitimate to speak of God being a debtor to the one who merits. This is what God wills.[39] Yet, while the *ordinatio* of the *Summa* surely includes the idea that God has ordered good works to their reward, the *ordinatio*

---

37 See note 34 above.
38 In addition to the present text, Thomas speaks of a "promise" which is involved in meriting in *In IV* d. XLVI, q. I, a. 1, qc. III sed contra 2, where he ascribes the idea to Anselm. Peter Lombard also had spoken of God being a *debitor* to people by a promise in Bk. I, d. XLIII of the *Sentences*. Note the striking similarity between Peter's and Thomas's language in this regard. Both say that God is not made a debtor to us because of good works *nisi forte ex promisso*, that is, because God has promised to reward good works. The words *"nisi forte"* need not indicate hesitation on Thomas's part to accept this affirmation of a promise which grounds merit. Rather, they indicate that speaking of God as debtor is unacceptable *except* when we stretch the term 'debtor' to include the debt which follows on God's freely offered promise. Thomas's uncertainty between the two answers given in ad 4 has to do, rather, with his own uncertainty about which position best meets the objection raised against merit. He does not doubt the truth of either claim made in ad 4. While Thomas does not often use the language of "promise" to speak of the relation between merit and reward, the idea is certainly found in his works throughout his career. For Aquinas, it is a given that by divine providence every act is ordained to its appropriate reward, whether supernatural good or punishment. The ruler of the universe, God, has established that all acts obtain their just deserts. It seems that the success of Auer and Hamm in drawing a sharp distinction between the Franciscan and Thomist schools on merit is achieved in large degree by ignoring Thomas's statements about the ordination of divine providence in this regard.
39 *In II* d. XXVII, q. I, a. 3 ad 4: "Deus non efficitur debitor nobis, nisi forte ex promisso, quia ipse bona operantibus praemium repromisit; et ideo non est inconveniens, si ab ipso quis mereri possit, ex quo aliquo modo debitor est."

involves much more, and the *Scriptum* lacks many of these additional elements. As was stated in the first chapter and will be argued in detail in the third, there are many facets to the *ordinatio* which makes merit possible in the *Summa*. It not only orders works to their reward. It also denotes God's predestination of certain people to achieve eternal life in order to manifest the divine goodness outside of God in a special way. And it determines the extent of the grace which the beneficiary of God's love will receive and which is active in the person's life, thereby also determining the degree of beatitude to which the person will attain. The *ordinatio* of merit became the crucial feature of Thomas's doctrine only when he was convinced of the absolute priority of God in salvation and acquired the means to express this conviction in a thoroughly plausible way. Thomas was able to base his teaching on the divine ordination only when he made the salvation of the individual subject in every regard and at every stage to the divine predestination. Thomas's position on predestination in the *Scriptum* (and indeed throughout the works of the early period) is somewhat fluid. On the one hand, in the early stage of his career, Thomas wished to distinguish God's providence from God's predestination to salvation. Providence is more or less restricted to God's knowledge, and does not entail the exercise of will and causality over occurrences in the world. Thomas will even say that some contingent events fall *outside* of the control of divine providence.[40] Predestination, on the other hand, does entail the exercise of God's causality. Thomas will allow that due to predestination, the eventual salvation of an individual is assured. But when he speaks of predestination in the *Scriptum* he does *not* insist that God's predestination is also causally certain with regard to every act of the predestined. Rather, God's will ensures the achievement of eternal life by an individual; and Thomas will even suggest in a few places that by the divine will God "guides" an individual to convert to God.[41] But that a person does the good

40 See, e.g., *In I* d. XL, q. I, a. 2, sol.
41 For the most part, in his various discussions of providence and predestination in the *Scriptum*, Thomas's principal concern is to distinguish the two. He does this by equating God's providence with the divine knowledge (which does not of itself imply causality), while arguing that predestination also involves causality, for it means the ordering of a rational creature to a specific end, heaven. Yet, in a few places, Thomas will speak of providence guiding a rational creature in such a way that it will convert to God, as God wills. In such passages, he seems to be allowing for the causality of providence and making providence the equivalent of predestination. Note, however, that in these relatively infrequent texts, Thomas says that providence guides or shapes the action of the individual *either* through external *or* through internal influence. In the *Scriptum* he does not insist, as he will from the *Summa Contra Gentiles* on, that God's predestination must issue in an *inwardly* effective call of the individual converting the person to God. For texts in the *Scriptum* that testify to the role of providence/predestination in the conversion of the individual, see *In II* d. XXVIII, q. I, a. 4 sol., and ads 1 and 2; and *In IV* d. XVII, q. I, a. 2, qc. II ad 2, in which Thomas says that God

in conformity with God's desire at any particular time falls outside the scope of divine predestination. It is up to the person to employ the grace given to him to do what God wills. God does not will/cause the doing of this particular good. Thomas makes *this* additional claim about God's involvement in every good act only in the writings of the early 1260s on.[42]

In the *Summa*, there is the most intimate connection between the *ordinatio* involved in merit and grace: As the equivalent of predestination, the ordination is the cause of grace, and because God ordains someone to achieve eternal life (through this person's merits), God's grace consequently moves the individual to the acts which bring him to God. In other words, the teaching about the divine ordination involved in merit in the *Summa* assumes the causal certainty of each act of the individual in accordance with predestination; and as we have just seen, the *Scriptum* lacks this teaching about divine predestination: In the *Scriptum* God's predestination does not *move* the individual to each one of the acts which brings him closer to God.

Similarly, when he uses *ordination*-language in the *Summa* Thomas consciously is tying his teaching about merit to his more general considerations about the creation of the world. For Aquinas, God has created the world for the manifestation of the goodness of God outside of God: The creation is designed to show God's goodness, and each being in the world, as well as its activity, discloses as best as it can some facet of the divine goodness. In the *Summa*, Thomas tells us that the same holds for merit as

---

prevenes the good will which precedes justifying grace either by punishments or by some "aids" (*auxilia*), which can be interior or exterior. By external influence Thomas understands God's manipulation of the circumstances of a person's life so that the person decides to convert to God. Later, we shall see that in *De Veritate* Thomas continues to assert that God's aid in conversion can be either external or internal.

42   From the 1260s on, Thomas is willing to speak of providence and predestination in the same terms: Both involve knowledge *and* God's effective causality. Predestination now comes to be consistently characterized as the part of providence which has to do with the ordination and effective moving of certain rational creatures to the end of eternal life. Providence, on the other hand, denotes God's plan for all creatures and God's effective direction of all creatures to their ordained end. In the works of his maturity, Thomas insists not only on the causal certitude of the results of providence and predestination, but also on the causal certitude of each and every effect of providence and predestination. No action, whether necessary or contingent, eludes the divine causality which guides the world to its end. As we shall see especially in the third chapter in the discussion of the *Summa Theologiae*, Thomas's conviction of the extent and certainty of providence and predestination will permit him to re-define his teaching on merit in a striking fashion. My depiction of the "trajectory" of Thomas's developing understanding of providence and predestination is greatly indebted to W. Ysaac, "The Certitude of Providence in St. Thomas." Lonergan's comments about operative grace and predestination in *Grace and Freedom* have also proved very helpful.

well: Meritorious activities by their similarity to God's activity reflect the divine activity. And most significantly, God has ordained that the meriting by people of eternal life shall also disclose the divine goodness in a special way. In broad terms, there are present in the *Scriptum* some foreshadowings of the *Summa*'s insistence on the divine goodness as the motive of all which God does vis-à-vis the world—the divine goodness is cited as the motive of creation, for example.[43] But what we do not find is Thomas discussing important theological issues, including merit, in the light of the divine motive in dealing with the world: Thomas does not "read" merit in terms of the divine goodness and God's purpose in creation. Indeed, Thomas passes over every opportunity in the present article where he might have tied merit to the divine goodness. For example, in the *Summa* when he answers the claim that merit means helping someone and so cannot apply to human-divine relations, Thomas agrees that God does not need our help but he also observes that this is not why God has ordained merit: In our merit, God seeks only God's own honor, for merit is designed in its own way to display the goodness of God.[44] Similarly, the observation of the connection between merit and the divine goodness allows Thomas to solve the problem of God's "indebtedness" in a more satisfactory way than he has in the *Scriptum*. In the *Summa*, Thomas will not concede, as he does in the first part of ad 4 of *In II* d. XXVII, q. I, a. 3, that through merit God in any way becomes a debtor to people. Rather, in the *Summa* Thomas refers to God's ordination of merit to reward and suggests that in requiting merit, God indeed is a *debitor*, but a debtor not to us but to *God*, for God in order to manifest the divine goodness through merits has promised to God to requite merits with their appropriate reward.[45] Given

---

43   For discussions of God's goodness as the end of creation and the purpose of God's dealings with the world, see in general *In I* d. XLV, in which Thomas treats of the divine will. See also *In II* d. I, q. II, aa. 1 and 2, where Thomas considers how creatures reflect in their own way the divine goodness which exists in unified fashion as God. Thus, even at this stage of his thinking, Thomas evinces a recognition of the significance of the divine goodness and wisdom for theology. But Thomas's recognition of the general importance of the divine goodness and wisdom has not yet been applied to particular questions in theology, including the question of merit. Hence, one way to characterize the difference between his earlier and later teachings about merit is to say that his later teaching has become much more "sapiential"—Thomas is especially concerned to show how merit reflects and proclaims the goodness of God in accordance with the dictates of the divine wisdom.

44   *ST* I-II 114, 1 ad 2: "Deus ex bonis nostris non quaerit utilitatem, sed gloriam, idest manifestationem suae bonitatis; quod etiam ex suis operibus quaerit. Ex hoc autem quod eum colimus, nihil ei accrescit, sed nobis; et ideo meremur aliquid a Deo, non quasi ex nostris operibus aliquid ei accrescat, sed inquantum propter eius gloriam operamur."

45   *ST* I-II 114, 1 ad 3: "Quia actio nostra non habet rationem meriti nisi ex praesuppositione divinae ordinationis, non sequitur quod Deus efficiatur

these important differences in teaching, it is simply not possible to accept
the suggestion that Thomas could have advanced the divine ordination as
the basis of merit in the *Scriptum*; the structuring of the discussion of merit
around the divine ordination as in the *Summa* becomes possible only
because of the discoveries of the middle years about providence, predestination, and grace, and Thomas's own maturing as a theologian in the years
separating the composition of the two works.

The absence of a fully thought-out teaching on the divine ordination in
fact has forced Thomas in at least one place in this article in the *Scriptum*
to offer an inadequate analysis of one aspect of merit. The third objection
had rejected merit because by the acts which would be "meritorious," all
one is doing is to offer to God what one owes to God, service, and one does
not merit by doing what one should. Now, in the *Summa* Thomas will refer
to the divine ordination to explain the possibility of meriting by doing one's
duty to God: God has ordained that following the law of one's being as
human and as Christian will bring the person meritoriously to the desired
end, life with God, and so doing what one should for God is in fact
meritorious before God. In the *Scriptum*, on the other hand, Thomas must
adopt a rather different approach. Thomas's answer in the third response
of the present article is difficult and should be quoted in full:

> etiam reddendo quod debet, meretur aliquis; in hoc enim aliquis
> apud Deum meretur in quo etiam vitae laudabilis apud homines
> constituitur. Actus autem iustitiae est laudabilis, sicut et aliarum
> virtutum; unde etiam actus iustitiae meritorius est, quamvis qui-
> dam hoc quondam negaverunt, et tamen actus iustitiae in reddi-
> tione debiti, etiam quod homini debetur, consistit; quamvis enim
> illud quod reddit quod debitum est alteri suum non sit, nihilominus
> tamen modus operationis in quo fundatur, et ius merendi, et laus,
> ipsius reddentis est, qui voluntarie et propter bonum iustitiae
> reddit.

What Thomas here seems to be assuming is that there is an intrinsic
connection between what is praiseworthy before other people and what
"merits" before God. The act of justice, the rendering of what is owed (to
God), is praiseworthy, just as are the acts of the other virtues, and so when
the act of justice is correctly performed—willingly and for the sake of
justice—it then deserves reward from God. Thomas's response here is
somewhat bewildering and arguably beside the point. The objection had
noted that when a person does something for another which is not owed to
that other, that other, not someone else, owes the action a reward. The
response however speaks, as it were, of *two* different "beneficiaries" of the
act, other people, who find the doing of the action aimed at God praiseworthy, and God, for whom the good act is done. It simply *assumes*, moreover,

simpliciter debitor nobis, sed sibi ipsi, inquantum debitum est ut sua
ordinatio impleatur."

that what other people find praiseworthy, God will deem meritorious and precisely because other people find the doing of one's debt to God deserving of praise. But Thomas offers here no evidence, whether biblical warrant or philosophical considerations, that this is in fact the case. Thomas's analysis here is rather feeble, to say the least, and the answer of the *Summa* in terms of the divine goodness will mark a great improvement.

In addition to the different organization and the lack of a teaching about the divine ordination, one final aspect of Thomas's teaching in *In II* d. XXVII, q. I, a. 3, likewise distinguishing the *Scriptum* from the *Summa,* also demands comment: Thomas's relative neglect of the role of *grace* in condign merit. We shall see that in the *Summa,* Thomas makes the case for condign merit of eternal life on the basis of the intrinsic worth of grace: By habitual grace, the person and his acts are raised to the supernatural level and given a dignity equal to the reward of these works; moreover, as *auxilium,* grace means that involvement in human actions of the *Holy Spirit,* to whom eternal life belongs naturally. Thus, when the Spirit causes a person to do the good, by the involvement of the Spirit these acts deserve what belongs naturally to the Spirit, eternal life. In the *Scriptum,* on the other hand, Thomas makes only a fleeting mention of the need for grace in condign merit. In the *solutio,* when he speaks of the equality of proportion which is involved in condign merit he adds an important proviso: Human acts are proportionate to eternal reward provided the merit and the reward are in the same *genus,* which is established when the acts which are meritorius issue from the virtues (grace and the theological virtues) which are divinely infused by God. Only if these virtues are present will human action be directed to, or proportioned to, God.[46] Other than this comment,. however, the role and need for grace in condign merit pass unnoticed in the *ex professo* treatment of merit in the *Scriptum.* At one level, Thomas's neglect of grace in this article in the *Scriptum* may simply be due to a lapse in the young Thomas as a systematician. As we have already seen, in the *Scriptum* Thomas emphasizes the formal qualities of habitual grace, telling us how grace "endows" its possessor with supernatural being and gives his being and works new dignity before God. Given this under-standing of grace, Thomas could very well have incorporated his view of grace into his teaching on merit, reflecting how grace elevates human acts to God's own level and so makes them "condignly" deserving of heaven. But even though the discussion of merit comes in the midst of the treatise on grace, Thomas almost wholly ignores grace when he speaks of condignity and so fails to evaluate satisfactorily the contribution of grace to the condign "meritability" of human action. Yet, at a deeper level, Thomas's

---

46 *In II* d. XXVII, q. I, a. 3 sol.: ". . . dum tamen praemium referatur ad idem genus in quo est meritum, ut si praemium est quod omnem facultatem humanae naturae excedit, sicut vita aeterna, meritum etiam sit per talem actum in quo refulgeat bonum illius habitus qui divinitus infunditur, Deo nos consignans."

neglect of grace here perhaps is explicable rather by the rudimentary state of Thomas's understanding of grace itself. As we have already seen in Chapter 1, the major difference between Thomas's earlier and later teachings on grace is the absence of the grace of *auxilium* in the early works and the stress in the later works on God's dynamic involvement through *auxilium* in the life of the Christian. I think it is fair to characterize this progression in Thomas's thought as due to his firmer sense of the place of the source of (habitual) grace in the life of the Christian: Thomas has been able to complete his analysis of created grace because his focus has shifted in the treatise on grace to *God*, uncreated grace, whose love is the source of the grace in the individual and whose active involvement in the Christian's life makes the attainment of God a reality. By showing that *God's* love is the proper starting-point of the consideration of human salvation and merit, Thomas is able in the *Summa* to argue for the condignity of merit to reward on the basis of the equal worth of merit and reward. In the *Scriptum*, on the other hand, since Thomas has not grasped the basic subordination of the religiously significant acts of human beings to the God who moves them to their acts, and moves them for the purpose of bringing them to God, Thomas evaluates these acts not by the power of God, their principal mover, but by the power and dignity of the people who do these acts. Hence, since there *is* an infinite distance between people and God, there is no possibility of arguing that these good acts are "condignly" meritorious, if we take the equality here as one of a "quantitative" worth; only God-moved and -controlled acts could possess such an equality. Instead, Thomas is able to speak only of a "proportion" between human acts and God's reward, and so must assert that the merit between people and God must be governed by distributive justice, which does not require this quantitative equality between act and reward for condign merit.

In the next article, *In II* d. XXVII, q. I, a. 4, Thomas turns his attention to the beginning of the spiritual life, asking if the human person can merit the first grace. As was observed in the first chapter, there is considerable dispute in the literature about Thomas's teaching in the *Scriptum* about the merit of the first grace: Some Thomists such as Bouillard and Neveut argue that Thomas never allowed a congruent merit of justifying grace, while others such as Rivière believe that in his early writings Thomas did assert the beginning of the spiritual life to fall under merit. The *possibility* that Thomas taught the congruent merit of the first grace is created by his affirmation in the *Scriptum* of the *facere quod in se est*.[47] For Thomas, God has promised that to sinners who do their best, by trying to do good and to

---

47   Thomas affirms the *facere quod in se est* throughout the four books of this "commentary" on the *Sentences*. For this affirmation, see, e.g., *In I* d. XLVIII, q. I, a. 3 sol., in which Thomas states that while the doing of one's best does not make or create grace, it is within our power to dispose for God's grace; *In I* d. XLVIII, q. I, a. 3 ad 1, where he asserts that when one does one's best, God's aid does not fail a person; *In II* d. IV, q. I, a. 3 sed contra 3, and *In II* d.

avoid further sin, God will grant the grace which will free them of their sin and elevate them to God's own level.[48] In this analysis, the good works of

---

XXVIII, q. I, a. 4 sol., where he explains that for doing one's best, all that is required in the person is the *liberum arbitrium* which constitutes the basic ability to turn to God; and *In II* d. XXIX, q. I, a. 3 ad 3, where Thomas says that God gives more grace to the one who is more disposed for this grace by his preparatory action. For other affirmations of the *facere quod in se est*, see *In II* d. XXVIII, q. I, a. 3 ad 5; *In II* d. XXXIII, q. II, a. 2 sol.; *In III* d. XXV, q. II, a. 1, qc. I ad 2; and *In IV* d. XX, a. 1, sol. I. When he speaks of people doing their best to prepare for grace in the *Scriptum*, Thomas is assuming that it lies within the power of the human person to move himself to such preparatory acts: God may in fact manipulate the circumstances of the person's life in such a way that a person will be inclined to convert to God (see note 41 above), but this manipulation of circumstances does not "necessitate" one doing one's best—this remains the responsibility and task of the human person. In the *Summa*, on the other hand, Thomas speaks of God's operative *auxilium* working the conversion of the sinner—given God's free predestination of the sinner to salvation, grace inwardly accomplishes the conversion to God at the predetermined time, inwardly moving the sinner away from sin and to God. In *ST* I-II 111, 2c, Thomas will say that this operative *auxilium* moves the sinner, and the sinner is simply moved—in conversion, the sinner does not also move himself to God. Consequently, in the *Summa* Thomas has presented an analysis of conversion in which it makes less sense to use the *facere quod in se est* to describe the human contribution to the movement to God; people are simply moved to God by an inwardly operative grace. In the *Scriptum*, of course, Thomas also speaks of a role for grace in conversion: Grace can mean the manipulation of the external circumstances of a person's life in accordance with divine providence so that a person will decide to convert. 'Grace' can also refer to God's offer of salvation to all human beings: God wills all people to be saved and so makes available to all the grace required for salvation (see note 12 above). However, it is crucial that the person respond correctly to this undifferentiated offer of salvation: Only by preparing oneself for grace is the grace offered by God to all appropriated by the individual. Moreover, the amount of grace appropriated by the individual is itself determined, according to the *Scriptum*, by the degree of preparation worked by the individual on his own behalf. Hence, in certain texts in the *Scriptum*, Thomas argues that both God and people are the *cause* of grace: God offers the grace needed for salvation, and people obtain this grace by readying themselves for its infusion. In this vein, see, e.g, *In I* d. XLI, q. I, a. 3 sol., and ads 1 and 2; *In I* d. XLI, q. I, a. 4 ad 3; *In III* d. XXXI, q. I, a. 4, sol. I (where he states that the amount of charity infused in a person directly corresponds to the effort expended by the individual to prepare for grace and the theological virtues); *In IV* d. IV, q. I, a. 3, qc. IV ad 1; *In IV* d. IX, q. I, a. 3, qc. IV ad 1; and *In IV* d. XIV, q. I, a. 2 sol. I.

48　Thomas grounds God's aid in response to good moral behavior by the sinner on the divine promise to so respond in *In IV* d. XLVI, q. II, a. 2, qc. II ad 2: "Deus enim hoc promisit ut peccatoribus veniam petentibus venia largiretur." Without this promise, there would be no "need" for God to acknowledge the moral effort of the sinner with the gift of grace—after all, the sinner by definition lacks the "proportion" to supernatural reward which is required for

the sinner are viewed as the necessary preparation for the formal perfection of habitual grace. In the generation of any form, the matter in which the form is introduced must be readied or disposed for the form; until the matter is suitably disposed, the form cannot be generated. Hence, in the infusion of habitual grace, the good works stand as the material cause of this infusion: Once the sinner disposes himself for grace by doing what is in him, by God's promise God is bound to grant justifying grace and so perfects the soul.[49] The question then is whether the good works of the sinner which are professedly *dispositional* for the infusion of grace and which make the doer "worthy" of grace [50] are also *meritorious* of grace in at least some fashion.

The ambiguity about Thomas's teaching is created by his somewhat discordant statements on the issue in the *Scriptum*. Thomas addresses the problem of the merit of the first grace in a relatively large number of texts. In some of these texts, Thomas mentions that there are theologians who do call the acts which ready the sinner for grace "meritorious"; these naturally good acts merit *congruently* the infusion of the first grace. In certain of these cases, Thomas simply reports this opinion and does not

---

meriting a reward from God. But given the promise of God by which God "obligates" God to respond to such actions by giving grace, there is a conditional necessity on God's part to give grace.

49   For the analysis of justification in terms of the generation of form, see the review of Bouillard's study of Aquinas in Chapter 1. Thomas will depict the "contribution" of the individual in justification in terms of "material" causality throughout his career. The basic difference between his teaching in this regard in the early works and that in the later, is that by the time of the *Summa Theologiae* Thomas will insist that this preparation of the "matter" of the soul for the infusion of habitual grace is itself worked by God's grace of *auxilium*. When he writes of the *facere quod in se est* in the *Scriptum*, Thomas is usually thinking of the disposition of matter for its form. However, he can also describe this doing of one's best in terms of the *removens prohibens*. In such texts as *In IV* d. XIV, q. II, a. 2 ad 1, and *In IV* d. XVII, q. I, a. 2, sol. II, Thomas states that there is a barrier to the reception of grace, which must be removed if grace is to enter the soul. The way in which the barrier is "knocked down" and the soul "opened" to grace is, of course, by ceasing from sin and doing one's best, all of which is pleasing to God and is appropriate for the reception of grace.

50   For the statement that by doing one's best, one becomes worthy (*dignus*) of the gift of grace, see *In IV* d. XVII, q. I, a. 1, qc. IV ad 3. There are, of course, different degrees of worthiness: The worthiness of one who is in the state of grace and whose acts are condignly worthy of God differs from the "worthiness" of a sinner who nevertheless is trying to amend his life; similarly, the "worthiness" of such a sinner differs from the "dignity" of one who remains obstinate in his sin. In the case of one doing his best, while he falls short of the dignity of the justified person, he still is superior to one who shows no inclination to stop sinning. To such a one, God grants grace, and this person has become "worthy" of grace, by being less "unworthy" of God's merciful action. For this consideration of the degrees of worthiness, see *In II* d. XXVII, a. 4 ad 4.

take a stand on the issue: He does not explicitly reject the position of these other theologians, nor does he explicitly adopt this view as his own; he simply tells us that some wish to describe these acts as "meritorious."[51] His silence here, however, may indicate his approval of this position; such is the view of Rivière. In other passages, on the other hand, Thomas not only reports this theological position, he also *seems* (at least) to deny it, saying that one cannot merit the first grace from God.[52] Finally, there are other texts in the *Scriptum* in which Thomas does not report that some theologians affirm a congruent merit of the first grace, but simply tells us that he himself is unwilling to speak of a merit of the first grace. In II d. XXVII, q. I, a. 4 sol., in fact, is such a text. Thomas's answer here builds nicely on the analysis offered in the preceding article. In a. 3, *solutio*, Thomas had stated that for merit to occur, the deed and the reward must be found in the same genus; in other words, both must be "supernatural." On this ground, Thomas had stated that condign merit of eternal life presupposes the grace which "proportions" human action to the supernatural reward of heaven and places human action in the same "genus" as this reward. In a. 4, *solutio*, Thomas again repeats that for merit, the act must be "proportioned" to the reward. Now, by definition the "natural" act of the sinner lacks grace and so is not proportioned to any supernatural reward, including the reward of grace itself. Thus, Thomas states here categorically, because of the "ontological" gap between God and creatures and the difference between the natural and supernatural orders of existence, "donum gratiae nullo sub merito cadere potest eius qui in puris naturalibus est." To nail down the case against a merit of the first grace, Thomas adds in passing a second reason, new to the discussion of merit in the *Scriptum*, why the naturally good act does not suffice for the merit of grace—he states that not only the gulf between the natural and the supernatural prevents merit, so too does human *sin*; although Thomas does not explicate why sin precludes merit, this is presumably because sin increases the *disproportion* between the sinner's acts and God's reward.[53] Thus, Thomas concludes

---

51 One such text is in fact found in the present article. In *In II* d. XXVII, q. I, a. 4 ad 4, Thomas writes that to those who have created a *dispositio* to grace through their efforts, God gives grace, and he adds that "ex quo dicuntur quoddammodo ex congruo gratiam mereri." In this text, Thomas does not indicate any disagreement with the description of the *facere* in terms of congruent merit. See also *In II* d. XXVII, q. I, a. 6 sol. ". . . et hoc modo dicitur quod actibus talibus non meretur quis gratiam sibi ex condigno, sed solum ex congruo."

52 See, for example, *In IV* d. XV, q. I, a. 3, sol. IV, where he notes the view that the disposition for grace is sometimes said to be congruently meritorious but adds that this is not really or properly merit and so there is no merit of the first grace.

53 *In II* d. XXVII, q. I, a. 4 sol.: "In omni qui meretur exigitur ut actus eius sit aliquo modo proportionatus ad id quod meretur; nullus enim meretur nisi id quod secundum suam conditionem potest eum contingere: sicut servus non meretur a domino ut in hereditatem filiorum admittatur, sed ut mercedem

this *solutio*, there is no merit of the first grace; rather, all we should speak
of here is a *habilitas* or disposition which the good moral action of the sinner
creates for grace.[54]

54   suam recipiat. Gratia vero omnino conditionem humanae naturae excedit:
quod patet ex eius effectu, quia ducit in finem quem nulla creata natura per
se attingere potest, propter quod dicitur I Cor., II, 9: 'Quod oculus non vidit,
nec auris audivit, nec in cor hominis ascendit quae praeparavit Deus iis qui
diligunt illum.' Unde donum gratiae nullo sub merito cadere potest eius qui
in puris naturalibus est, et multo minus eius qui in peccato deprimitur."
In II d. XXVII, q. I, a. 4 sol.: "Sed tamen opera bona ante donum gratiae facta
praemio suo sibi proportionato non carent; causant enim quamdam
habiliatem ad gratiam . . ." Note that Thomas here says that good works done
before grace is received do have a "proportion" to grace. The language is a bit
loose and perhaps unfortunate—after all, a reader may conclude that Thomas
is referring to the same "proportion" between works done in grace and the
reward of eternal life which allows for condignity (a. 3), even though in the
first part of the present article he has made clear that non-graced works lack
such a "proportion." Rather, Thomas is referring here to the controlling
"insight" of the *facere quod in se est*—it is appropriate that God give grace to
those who demonstrate an interest in and willingness to receive such grace.
By doing their best, people orient themselves, "proportion" themselves, to
grace; it is a different kind of "proportion," therefore, to which he here refers.
For other texts in which Thomas allows that people can dispose for grace but
simply denies a merit of the first grace, see *In II* d. V, q. II, a. 1 sol.; *In II* d.
XXVII, q. I, a. 4 ad 5; *In III* d. XXXIV, q. I, a. 6 ad 6; *In IV* d. XLVI, q. I, a. 2,
qc. III ad 2; and *In IV* d. XLVI, q. II, a. 2, qc. II ob 4.
    In the present article, Thomas notes other "results" of doing one's best in
preparation for grace: ". . . et secum etiam quamdam honestatem, et
iucunditatem, et pulchritudinem habent, in quibus praecipue eorum
praemium consistit; et aliqua etiam per accidens causant, ut bonorum
temporalium affluentiam, aut aliquid huiusmodi: quia frequenter, ut
Gregorius dicit, *Moral.*, lib. V, cap. 1, Deus in hoc mundo remunerat eum qui
praemium futurae gloriae non meretur, ut sic nullum bonum irremuneratum
inveniatur." With regard to the *honestas* and *iucunditas*, Thomas seems to be
referring to what he will call in the fifth article the *praemium concomitans*
of a good act; I shall examine this idea more fully when treating article 5. The
other "reward" of good action done outside of grace mentioned in article 4 is
even more interesting: Thomas says that *per accidens* such people obtain
some temporal good as a reward from God. Thomas will also mention
temporal goods in return for such good works in *In IV* d. XV, q. I, a. 3 sol. IV,
where he in fact calls these good works "congruently" meritorious. In the
Summa, Thomas will devote an entire article to the merit of temporal
prosperity; see *ST* I-II 114, 10. The comparision between *In II* d. XXVII, q. I,
a. 4 sol. and I-II 114, 10, is illuminating of the distance which separates the
Scriptum and the *Summa*: As we shall see in Chapter 3, in 114, 10, Thomas
structures his discussion of temporal rewards around the conviction of God's
control of all events and judgment over them by the divine providence. Thus,
people obtain what they deserve as the direct result of their actions, all in
accordance with divine providence. In the *Scriptum*, on the other hand, there
is no allusion to the role of providence here, and Thomas is content to make
the point in passing that even the unjustified merit some temporal goods from

Thus, on the one hand, there are passages in the *Scriptum* in which Thomas arguably permits a congruent merit of the first grace, while on the other, there are texts such as the present article which seem to rule out any merit of this grace. How are we to correlate these different statements on the issue? For an adequate resolution of the problem, it is absolutely necessary to be attentive to the different degrees of entitlement covered by the term 'merit.' 'Merit' in its fullest sense is *condign* merit, in which the person who receives a reward from God possesses a right to that reward according to the dictates of distributive justice. In the *Scriptum*, Thomas says that this is merit in the "proper" sense—it is most fully meritorious of reward. At a lower level is merit in an "improper" sense, or incomplete merit; this is congruent merit.[55] In this merit, while justice is to some extent still involved, God's liberality is even more to the fore.[56] In *condign* merit, God's liberality, of course, is also present: God freely rewards good acts which are proportioned to God. Justice enters because in rewarding different acts, God offers greater or lesser rewards in accordance with the greater or lesser goodness of the acts. In congruent merit, on the other hand, the *proportion* between merit and reward which makes condign merit possible is missing: Since the works of the sinner are natural and do not emerge from the virtues divinely infused by God, good works and reward are not of the same genus and so do not call forth/deserve reward from God. And yet justice is not completely lacking: Since the good works of the sinner are directed to the reception of grace and create a *habilitas* for grace, and since God has promised (freely) to give grace for such

---

God. In Chapter 3, I shall briefly discuss the teaching of Thomas's *Commentary on Job* on this issue, and show how Thomas's teaching there anticipates, but still falls short of, his mature teaching in the *Summa*.

55   For the assertion that condign merit is most fully or *proprie* merit, see *In III* d. IV, q. III, a. 1 ad 2. For the comment that congruent merit *per se loquendi* is not merit, see *In III* d. XVIII, a. 6, qc. I ob 3; in *In IV* d. XV, q. I, a. 3 sol. IV, Thomas mentions that by congruent merit one disposes for grace but adds that "properly," this congruent merit is not merit. In *In III* d. IV, q. III, a. 1 sol., Thomas makes the point that only *large* do we say that the preparation for something is meritorious of it.

56   The basic idea in congruent merit is that it befits God's generous nature, it is congruous with God's mercy, for God to give a reward to a person in recognition of that person's good efforts. In the *solutio* of the sixth article of the present distinction, Thomas suggests that there are in addition "degrees" of congruent merit. In the sixth article, Thomas is discussing the merit of the first grace for another. He says here that one can congruently merit the first grace for another and adds that this is more meritorious than when someone is said to congruently merit the first grace for himself. The reason for this greater "merit" in the congruent merit for another is that the one who merits for another is in the state of grace and so his acts have a greater worth than those of a sinner who is trying to please God. In both kinds of congruent merit, however, the key element is God's liberality and willingness to acknowledge such acts as merits.

preparation, we can speak, in a diminished sense at least, of these good works "deserving" the reward of grace from God.

With these comments on condign and congruent merit, and on the degree of justice involved in each, it is possible to offer the following reconciliation of Thomas's disparate statements in the *Scriptum*. When Thomas denies the merit of the first grace, he is thinking first and foremost of *condign* merit, merit in the truest and strictest sense of the term. He denies condign merit here because preparing oneself for grace does not create a right for this grace according to justice; the proportion required for distributive justice is strictly speaking lacking. Similarly, in those passages in which Thomas denies the merit of the first grace after mentioning those who have asserted a congruent merit of the first grace, he is again thinking principally of condign merit. In mentioning congruent merit, he is not absolutely denying also the congruent merit of the first grace. Rather, in such passages he is denying that congruent merit is really merit, if we mean by 'merit' that which is governed by justice between the one who rewards and the one who merits—that is, merit in the "proper" sense of the term, condign merit. Now, these passages *would* nevertheless be decisive for our question if in the *Scriptum* Thomas simply did away with congruent merit altogether; in this vein, if he argued that since congruent merit is not "really" merit (because it is not merit in the truest sense), it would be better not to speak of it at all, then these comments about congruent merit and the first grace would be compelling. But Thomas himself makes use of a "congruent" merit in other, less-controversial contexts[57] and while he does not disguise his predilection for *condign* merit as the only authentic merit, he is nevertheless willing to speak of the "right" involved in congruent merit. Hence, I believe that in those passages in the *Scriptum* in which Thomas seems to allow for a congruent merit of the first grace, he is doing more than simply reporting the opinion of other theologians (e.g., Bouillard) or mentioning a possible position without committing himself to it. I think that he himself has implicitly accepted this merit, albeit an imperfect merit, of the first grace. Indeed, whether he wishes to admit it or not, Thomas has provided ample space for such a merit of the first grace in his early theology. Given his affirmation of the *facere quod in se est* and his stress on the need to create a disposition for the infusion of grace, which will follow infallibly because of the divine promise, even though he nowhere explicitly avers the congruent merit of first grace, he has *de facto* incorporated a teaching of the congruent merit of the first grace into the theology

---

57		See, for example, *In III* d. IV, q. III, a. 1 ad 6, where he speaks of the congruent merit of the Blessed Virgin Mary, and *In II* d. XXVIII, q. I, a. 6, where Thomas speaks of ordinary Christians meriting congruently the first grace for others. Thus, when we describe congruent merit according to the Thomas of the *Scriptum*, we must underline that this merit falls short of the justice and dignity of condign merit (see the texts listed in note 55 above) but that it still makes sense to speak of it as 'merit,' as the texts listed in the present note prove.

of merit in the *Scriptum*. Those who do their best thereby congruently merit the grace which follows such action.

Given the need to prepare for grace and the *de facto* acceptance of a congruent merit for oneself, the question remains why Thomas is so reluctant to speak of a merit of the first grace. The answer is to be found in the first *sed contra* of the present article. Here, Thomas states that what is given for merit is not given *gratis* and what is not given *gratis* is not grace. On this basis, Thomas denies the merit of the first grace. In this *sed contra* Thomas has not made reference to any biblical material. But in the parallel places in his other writings in which he makes a like argument about the incompatibility of 'grace' and 'merit,' Thomas often cites certain texts from Romans (especially 11:6), in which Paul asserts that justification is not owed to works but is given freely by grace. Thomas is probably thinking here of such texts. Thomas consistently interprets Paul to be speaking of the first grace by which people are justified. Paul, in Thomas's reading, does not mean to exclude the merits which issue from God's grace by which people attain God. Thomas desires to be a good disciple of Paul: He wants justification to be solely "by grace." Thus, while the logic of his own position in the *Scriptum* should have caused him to affirm explicitly a congruent merit of the first grace, his desire to be faithful to the Pauline teaching has led him simply to deny the condign merit, the "real" merit, of the first grace and to leave unmentioned that we can in fact speak of a lesser or imperfect merit, congruent merit, by which the acts of the sinner obtain a "right," albeit a faint one, to the reward of grace from God. Nevertheless, implicit in his analysis of justification as requiring the self-willed deeds of the sinner in preparation for grace is the teaching that these good works of the sinner do merit congruently the first grace.

In *In II* d. XXVII, q. I, a. 5, Thomas directs his attention to the "middle" of the journey to God: He asks whether a person who has grace can merit the increase of this grace. Thomas's discussion of this question in the *Scriptum* is difficult, and differs strikingly from his analysis of the same question in the *Summa*. The point of departure for the later analysis is the depiction of how habits in general increase, and then to display the difference between the increase of acquired virtue and of infused virtue (habitual grace and the theological virtues). Habits in general are said "to increase" when they become more deeply rooted in their possessor. For the acquired virtues, a person disposes himself for the virtues by doing acts of a certain kind; once enough of these acts have been done so that the person has a steady disposition to act in that way, he is said to "have" that virtue. Similarly, once a person has an acquired virtue, continued and more fervent action of a type increases the possession of that virtue so that in future one is more inclined to act in the way conformable to the virtue. In the case of *infused* virtues, this basic analysis of the increase of the virtue is repeated, with one crucial difference. Again, acts of a kind dispose one for the appropriate habit: The good acts of the sinner ready the sinner, make him "worthy" (*dignus*) of the grace which frees him from sin and raises him to God. And yet grace and the theological virtues are not "natural," falling directly under the unaided acts of people. Rather, these are supernatural entities, created by God; and thus, while the acts of people dispose them for grace and charity, God must "create" grace and charity and give these to the person who is disposed for them.[58] The same holds for the person who already has grace and charity: By acts in keeping with grace and charity, this person disposes himself so that he can receive more grace. Moreover, in the later works, Thomas explicitly says that this increase is "merited." For one who is in grace, disposing for more grace deserves its increase. But since grace and charity are supernatural, the increase of grace must be received from God, the source of grace. People merit the increase of these virtues, and God gives the increase.

In the discussion of this problem in the *Scriptum*, many of the elements of the later analysis are already present. In the fifth article of d. XXVII, Thomas agains speaks of the need to "dispose" oneself for the increase of grace, through acts which issue from the infused habits of grace and charity.[59] Similarly, while he does not develop the distinction between acquired and infused virtues, he does state here that grace is increased through *God*'s response to meritorious action: People dispose themselves, and God deepens their possession of grace.[60] Finally, Thomas is quite willing to call the disposition for more grace by one who possesses grace "meritorious"—this disposition does deserve this reward.[61]

But, on the whole, in this article Thomas offers a different analysis of the merit of the increase of grace. Determinative of this different analysis is the problem which Thomas finds most troublesome when we speak of the increase of grace: How is it that the one act which merits eternal life *also* merits a second reward, the increase of grace? Can one act be remunerated twice? In the *Summa*, Thomas solves this problem through the deft use of the image of the "journey." The end of the human journey is God,

---

58   Recall, however, that in the later works, this preparation for the infused virtues is itself worked by God's operative *auxilium*; see note 47 above.

59   *In II* d. XXVII, q. I, a. 5 ad 4: "Homo habens gratiam non dicitur posse proficere in melius, quasi ipse gratiam sibi augmentet, cum augmentum gratiae a Deo sit; sed quia homo potest per gratiam acceptam augmentum gratiae mereri, disponendo se, ut majoris gratiae capacior fiat."

60   *In II* d. XXVII, q. I, a. 5 ad 3: "Tam augmentum gratiae quam etiam ipsius infusio est a Deo: sed tamen aliter se habent actus nostri ad infusionem gratiae et augmentum ipsius: quia ante infusionem gratiae homo nondum est particeps divini esse; unde actus sui sunt omnino improportionati ad merendum aliquod divinum, quod facultatem naturae excedat: sed per gratiam infusam constituitur in esse divino; unde iam actus sui proportionati efficiuntur ad promerendum augmentum vel perfectionem gratiae." In ad 4 of this article, quoted in the previous note, Thomas also says that God gives the increase of grace.

61   See *In II* d. XXVII, q. I, a. 5 ad 3, quoted in the previous note, and ad 4, quoted in note 59 above.

and God is merited through good moral action. Now, in a physical journey, when one travels to a destination, one also passes through all the points in between. In terms of the spiritual journey to God, the 'points in between' is the grace by which one is readied for the beatific vision. The more grace one has, the more perfected one is for the vision, and so the more of the vision one will enjoy. One obtains, as has been said, more grace through merit. Hence in the later works Thomas's analogy of movement on a journey allows him to show how the same act can have "two" rewards—there is the principal reward which is eternal life. And there is the reward which is ordained to eternal life, the increase of grace which readies one for eternal life. By the same act, one merits eternal life and the increase of grace.

In the *Scriptum*, on the other hand, while surely acknowledging that grace readies one for heaven, Thomas has failed to adopt the simple strategy of a "subordination" of ends/rewards to explain how one act can have two rewards. In the absence of this rather obvious device, Thomas is forced in *In II* d. XXVII, q. I, a. 5 *solutio*, to advance a more elaborate analysis to eliminate the problem.[62] His first move in this article is to draw an analogy between merit and reward, and *culpa* and *poena*. There is a twofold *poena* for each *culpa*: an external penalty which is inflicted by a judge for the misdeed; and a second penalty which is interior to the wrongful act, "accompanying" (*comitatur*; *concomitans*) it or arising from it more intimately than the external reward. In this latter regard, Thomas refers to the "remorse of conscience and other things of this sort" (. . . *conscientiae remorsus, et huiusmodi*) which plague the sinner because of his act; the idea is that such things are intimately bound to the *culpa* and are produced or effected by it. So too Thomas says, is there a twofold reward for the merit of the Christian. The one reward is clearly distinct from the work and is rendered for it by God. This is eternal life and "whatever is

---

62 *In II* d. XXVII, q. I, a. 5 *solutio*, reads as follows: "Sicut culpae redditur duplex poena: una quae comitatur ipsam culpam, ut conscientiae remorsus, et huiusmodi, secundum quod Augustinus dicit in lib. I *Confess.*, cap. XIII quod inordinatus animus sibiipsi est poena; alia quae infligitur exterius a judice Deo vel homine; ita etiam duplex est praemium respondens merito: unum quod comitatur ipsum actum meritorium, ut ipsa delectatio boni operis, et similia; aliud quod pro bono opere redditur a Deo vel homine, ut vita aeterna et quidquid hoc modo redditur. Ad hoc autem duplex praemium diversimode actus meritorius ordinatur: quia ad primum praemium est proportionatus secundum formam suam; verbi gratia, ex hoc ipso quod est actus ab habitu perfecto procedens, delectabilis est; unde in principium actus reducitur sicut in causam: sed ad praemium quod exterius redditur, ordinatur secundum proportionem dignitatis tantum; ut qui tantum meruit, tantum remuneretur in quocumque bono, et qui tantum peccavit tantum puniatur. Secundum hoc ergo dico quod per actum meritorium contingit mereri augmentum gratiae sicut praemium concomitans naturam actus meritorii, cum naturale sit ut omnis actus possit in acquisitionem vel augmentum similis habitus vel effective vel dispositive."

rendered in this way."[63] The second reward is more closely bound to the
act and accompanies it, arising from the doing of the act. Here, Thomas
gives the example of the "delight" which is caused by the good deed and
which one takes in it, and other such "attendant features" of good action.
The relations between merit and reward in the two cases, then, are rather
different. As we have seen in the third article, in the merit of the "exterior"
reward, the good work is rewarded because of its worth (*dignitas*), with
God rendering equal rewards for acts of equal dignity. In the other relation
of merit and reward, the reward is determined not by the dignity of the
work, but according to the "principle of merit," the habits of grace and
charity from which the act proceeds,[64] and the human freedom which
performs the act.[65] As Thomas says in the *solutio*, in this relation the
reward is proportioned to the "form" of the act, which is provided by the

---

63   For a reader who approaches the *Scriptum* informed by the teaching of the
      Summa, the "whatever is rendered in this way" (*et quidquid hoc modo
      redditur*) mentioned in the *solutio* may make one think of the grace which is
      ordained to the obtaining of eternal life. This, however, would be to render
      the rest of the *solutio* superfluous: The rest of the *solutio* only makes sense
      and is necessary given Thomas's conviction here that the merit of the increase
      of grace must occur in a way different from the merit of heaven. It may very
      well be that when Thomas refers to what is rendered in the way that eternal
      life is rendered, he is referring obliquely to the rendering of first grace for
      congruent merit. In the next article, Thomas mentions how one can merit
      congruently for another from God, and this occurs in a way which is similar
      to the merit of eternal life; and, as I have just argued, I think that in the
      Scriptum Thomas probably accepts a congruent merit of the first grace for
      himself, where again God renders a reward, grace, in the same way as God
      renders eternal life for condign merit. The principal problem with this
      suggestion on how to interpret the present phrase, however, is that God's
      rendering for condign merit and for congruent merit are not in fact exactly
      alike—in condign merit, the distributive justice of God predominates. The
      similarity between the two arises because the reward for each comes "from
      outside," from God.
64   *In II* d. XXVII, q. I, a. 5 sol.: "Ad primum praemium est proportionatus
      secundum formam suam; verbi gratia, ex hoc ipso quod est actus ab habitu
      perfecto procedens, delectabilis est; unde in principium actus reducitur sicut
      in causam." See also note 15 above for texts in which Thomas asserts that
      grace and charity are the *principia merendi*.
65   *In II* d. XXVII, q. I, a. 5 ad 2: "Quando actus meritorius se habet ad praemium
      solum in ratione meriti, tunc verum est quod sicut quis per unum actum
      eiusdem rationis meretur praemium, ita et per alium. Secus autem est
      quando actus meritorius se habet ad praemium non solum ut meritum, sed
      quodammodo ut causa, et sic se habet actus meritorius ad augmentum
      gratiae; unde non oportet quod quilibet actus meritorius augmentum gratiae
      mereatur: quia non in quolibet actu meritorio invenitur illa conditio per quam
      ex actu consequitur augmentum habitus; sed solum in illo actu quo quis utitur
      accepta gratia secundum proportiones suarum virium, ut in nullo gratiae Dei
      desit per negligentiam." See also note 16 above for Thomas's assertion of the
      need for human freedom for merit.

"causes" of the act, that is, grace and freedom. Hence, when an act proceeds from a greater habit of grace, it "produces" or effects a greater "interior" or concomitant reward: To use the example which Thomas prefers in the solution, from a more perfect habit of grace arises the accompanying reward of more delight in the work. Thomas concludes the solution by relating all of this to the present problem, the increase of grace. The increase of grace occurs in the same way as the "delight in the good work" which accompanies the doing of the work. Because the act proceeds from a perfect habit, grace, it effects (dispositively) the increase of that habit and gives the doer more grace.

In the responses to the objections, Thomas is more careful to distinguish the way in which good works produce "delight in the work" and grace; here, Thomas ties this analysis in with the features of his understanding of the increase of habits which will remain constant throughout his career. Thus, for example, he insists that the good work in grace produces the increase of grace by disposing for it. It does not cause it as an efficient cause (ad 4). Similarly, because grace is supernatural, while the act disposes for grace, God must give the increase (ads 3 and 4). But while these more familiar elements of his teaching make it more understandable, it seems quite clear that the present analysis is basically a misstep. For one thing, with the admission that it is *God* who must grant more grace, Thomas has more or less eviscerated the difference between the two meritorious relationships: In both, something exterior—God—must reward the merit and the reward comes to the act from outside. Similarly, surely the analogy between the "delight in the work" and the "increase of grace" cannot be taken too far. Indeed, Thomas arguably has paid such great attention to the delight in the work in the *solutio* precisely because this example works much better as illustration of this kind of relation between merit and reward than does the increase of grace. It makes sense to speak of a satisfaction or happiness over a good deed which emerges from the doing of the work. When one stresses that God creates grace and must infuse it and that people simply *dispose* for grace, not effect it, it is less clear how grace and its increase accompany the good deed in the same way. All Thomas has done here is to devise an over-elaborate scheme to solve a problem which only succeeds in confusing his reader—the later answer, much simpler and straightforward, will be in this regard infinitely superior.

Thomas completes the *ex professo* treatment of merit by examining the possibility of one person meriting the first grace for another; this discussion in the sixth article thus completes Thomas's treatment of the merit of first grace begun in article 4. In broad terms, Thomas's position on this question in the *Scriptum* is the same as that in the *Summa*, with one significant difference to be noted below. In the *solutio* Thomas states that only one person, Christ, can merit the first grace for another condignly. He adds that those in grace cannot merit the first grace condignly for another but are able to merit it congruently. In the *Scriptum*, Thomas's answer revolves

around a consideration of the possible causes of "insufficiency." He starts
from general considerations to show why good works normally are "insufficient" to merit grace for another.[66] In general terms, insufficiency may
arise, in the first place, from the imperfection of the cause: The cause may
simply be incapable of producing the desired effect, as for example when a
fire which is too small fails to warm. Secondly, insufficiency may be created
by some impediment in the effect which blocks the cause's action. Hence,
a piece of wood which has been dampened by water will fail to catch fire.
Either the imperfection of the act or an impediment in the intended object
of one's merit can account for the failure of the merit of one person to apply
to another. With regard to the imperfection of the act, it may be that the
act belongs to a genus different from the intended effect. Thomas is
thinking here especially of the natural acts by which the sinner prepares
for the infusion of habitual grace: Since these acts are not supernatural
and so not fully proportioned to grace, they fall outside the genus of grace.
It is for this reason that a sinner cannot merit first grace for himself
condignly, although, as Thomas puts it here, "it is said" (dicitur) that such
acts congruently merit grace for oneself. Naturally, since these acts are not
condignly meritorious for oneself, they obviously will not avail for the
condign merit of the first grace for another. What, then, about the merits
of someone who already has grace? Do they extend condignly to the first
grace for another? Again, Thomas answers negatively. His basic argument
focuses on the "limited" nature of the grace possessed by the Christian.

---

66   The pertinent part of In II d. XXVII, q. I, a. 6 sol., reads as follows:
      "Insufficientia causae ex duobus contingere potest: vel ex imperfectione
      causae, ut quando ignis est parvus qui calefacere non potest; aut ex
      impedimento quod accidit circa effectum, ut si ligna aqua humectantur; et ita
      cum meritum quodammodo sit causa praemii, dupliciter contingit ut actus
      meritorius non sufficiat ad praemii consecutionem: vel ex imperfectione
      actus, vel ex impedimento eius qui praemium consequi debet. Sed imperfectio
      actus potest esse duplex: aut ita quod actus sit extra genus talis perfectionis
      quae meritum causat, sicut sunt actus gratiam praecedentes; et hoc modo
      dicitur quod actibus talibus non meretur quis gratiam sibi ex condigno, sed
      solum ex congruo; aut est in genere talis perfectionis, quae tamen propter sui
      parvitatem non sufficit ad merendum, et hoc modo dico quod actus habentis
      gratiam se habent ad acquirendam gratiam alteri; sufficit enim gratia ad hoc
      ut homo per eam sibiipsi mereatur, sed quod alteri mereatur, ad hoc non
      sufficit, nisi sit perfectissima gratia, aquae quoddamodo in alios redundet: et
      propter hoc dicitur quod Christus, de cuius plenitudine omnes accipimus,
      Joan., I, omnibus ex condigno meruit; sed nullus alius alteri ex condigno
      meretur, sed solum ex congruo; ita tamen quod est hic plus de ratione meriti
      quam quando aliquis dicitur sibi mereri gratiam ex congruo.
      Quantumcumque autem gratia perfecta sit quae opus meritorium causat,
      potest impediri effectus meriti vel praemii, dummodo dicatur unus alteri
      mereri. Sed dicitur aliquis alter vel alius dupliciter: vel secundum subjectum,
      sicut sunt diversae personae, et hoc modo constat quod etiam meritum
      Christi, nedum merita aliorum, in multis effectum non consequitur, propter
      eorum indispositionem . . ."

Clearly, the one who exists in grace possesses the requisite "proportion" to the end of grace, supernatural reward. But his grace is "small," sufficient only for the condign meriting of eternal life for himself. It is insufficient for the condign merit of grace for another. Only Christ, Thomas adds, can condignly merit the first grace for another. Since Christ's grace is "most perfect" (*perfectissima*), Christ alone can so merit the first grace for others because his grace *does* extend to such an effect. Although the average Christian cannot condignly merit the first grace for another, Thomas nevertheless does wish to encourage action on the behalf of others. Thus, he concludes this part of his answer by mentioning, without explanation, that the Christian can merit the first grace for another congruently. Presumably this is because the grace which is the cause of merit *can* extend to this effect.[67]

In the remaining part of the *solutio*, Thomas directs his comments to the "recipient" of the meritorious act. While Christ can condignly merit the first grace for another, and average Christians can congruently merit for others, this merit does not inevitably achieve its effect, for it can be blocked by some impediment in the intended recipient of this merit, by an *indispositio* of this other to the reward of grace. Thomas does not define the nature of this *indispositio* to grace in the present article, but from what we have seen in article four, by the impediment in the recipient he must mean both the absence of grace in that person, so that his being and acts are purely natural, not proportioned to grace, *and* the presence of sin in a person which makes him unworthy of grace. This *indispositio* or impediment to grace can be overcome by the person's doing of his best to prepare for grace, by resisting sin and doing good. Thus, when in the present article Thomas says that an impediment in the person can block Christ's condign merit of grace for him, or the Christian's congruent merit of grace, what he means is that such merit fails to achieve its effect because the person in question has himself failed to do what is necessary to receive grace. The acts of others can establish a right to the first grace. But the requital of this right

---

67   Thomas simply mentions Christ's possession of "the most perfect grace" and the *parvitas* of the grace of ordinary Christians without explaining the difference between these two graces. If Thomas had had at his disposal in the *Scriptum* a fully worked-out teaching on ordination/predestination, there would have been no difficulty in accounting for the difference. All Thomas would have had to do is note that Christ has been ordained to be the head of all Christians and the principal means of their salvation and that accordingly Christ's grace, which issues from this ordination, extends to the condign meriting of salvation for other people. On the other hand, the ordination of the individual Christian to a specified degree of salvation would have "explained" why his merit, in a condign sense, suffices for the individual alone. In the *Scriptum*, Thomas asserts that Christ's grace is greater than others and hence of greater effectiveness on the basis of the union of the two natures in Christ and thus the greater dignity of Christ's work. Correspondingly, for those who are not God there is less dignity and power to their work. In the next section, I shall return to the problems involved in the merit of Christ.

depends upon the person also preparing himself for the reception of this reward.[68]

This reference to an impediment blocking the reception of grace in *In II* d. XXVII, q. I, a. 6 *solutio*, helps us to perceive a principal difference in the orientation of Thomas's teaching about merit in the *Scriptum* and in the *Summa*. Thomas in fact has made a statement which is materially identical in the parallel discussion in the *Summa* of the merit of the first grace. In *ST* I-II 114, 6c, he states that the merit of one will be congruently meritorious of the first grace for another *provided* that there is no impediment in the other. Yet, as found in the *Summa* this statement is perplexing and difficult, for if taken seriously, it would seem to *eliminate* all such merit despite Thomas's affirmations to the contrary—after all, every person who lacks grace has an impediment to grace because he is a sinner who is at odds with God. More crucially, in the *Summa* the impediment to grace is removed not by the independent initiative and action of the sinner, but by God's *auxilium* effecting the conversion of the sinner: God decides to save someone and then does it. Yet the value of Thomas's comment in I-II 114, 6, about the impediment is that it forces us to recall Thomas's mature teaching about providence and predestination and the ordination which

---

68   In other words, while the evidence about the congruent merit of the first grace for oneself is arguably inconclusive, there is no question that there is nevertheless a merit which is involved in the reception of first grace, the condign merit of Christ and the congruent merit of Christians for others.

   In *In II* d. XXVII, q. I, a. 6 sol., Thomas completes his discussion of the impediment in the intended beneficiary of merit as follows: "Sed dicitur aliquis alter vel alius dupliciter: vel secundum subjectum, sicut sunt diversae personae, et hoc modo constat quod etiam meritum Christi, nedum merita aliorum, in multis effectum non consequitur, propter eorum indispositionem; aut secundum accidens et secundum rationem, sicut dicitur quod Socrates in foro est alter a seipso in domo, sicut ipse hodie est alter a seipso cras; et inde est quod quando aliquis hodie meretur vitam aeternam ut habeat eam in fine vitae suae, licet meritum sit sufficiens quantum in se est, tamen potest impediri ne effectum consequatur, per peccatum quod intervenit cras et post cras, ratione cuius dicitur praecedens meritum mortificatum esse. Sed praemium illud quod quis sibi meretur, quod est concomitans meritum, impediri non potest. Secundum hoc ergo patet ex dictis quod aliquis alteri gratiam mereri potest ex congruo et non ex condigno: nec tamen necessarium est quod ille gratiam accipiat, cum aliquis ei gratiam meretur." In terms of the problem discussed in the sixth article, the analysis of the second "alius" is irrelevant. Here Thomas is telling us why a person may not himself receive the reward of his merit—because he later sins and so creates an impediment in himself to the reception of his reward. In the *Summa*, Thomas will incorporate the substance of this material, as well as the information found in *In II* d. XXVII, q. I, a. 4 ad 3, into *ST* I-II 114, 7, where he asks whether the justified can merit a restoration to the state of grace after a fall from grace. In the *Summa*, he will deny such a possibility and insist that the return to grace will be a gift of God, just as the first entry into grace was due to the operative grace of conversion.

grounds merit. In the later works, God ordains the salvation of individuals and ordains the means of their salvation. God may ordain to use the prayers and actions of the saints to be the causes or occasions of the conversion of others: God may have determined to save others through the merits of others. Hence, in the *Summa* people are encouraged to help each other because God may have determined to use their acts in the furtherance of God's plan. If God has so ordained, then God removes the impediment to grace through the works of the saints. The statement about the impediment, then, directs us to God's causally efficient providence and predestination. The statement about the impediment makes it clear that the acts of the saints are not only meritorious of grace for others but attain their goal of the conversion of others provided that God wills to use them to this end.

In the *Scriptum*, on the other hand, the statement about the impediment in the beneficiary of this merit is not so difficult. Nor is Thomas making a point about the divine providence and predestination when he refers to this impediment.[69] Rather, given his affirmation of the *facere quod in se est* in the *Scriptum*, it is relatively easy to overcome the apparent difficulty posed by this reference to the impediment which might obstruct merit. When the person prepares himself for grace by avoiding further sin and doing the natural good, the merits of others for him do avail for his conversion. In the *Scriptum*, reference to the impediment is not designed to direct our thoughts to God and to the manner in which God employs human merits for the working out of God's plan. On the contrary, the thrust of Thomas's teaching runs in a different direction: The reference to the impediment is

---

69 Thomas *does* refer to divine providence in this article. In *In II* d. XXVII, q. I, a. 6 ad 5, he writes: "Frequenter contingit quod per orationem sanctorum hominibus offeruntur occasiones ut se ad Deum convertant et ad gratiam recipiendam praeparent; qua praeparatione facta, et gratia eis infunditur. Quamvis autem sanctis non orantibus homines salvarentur, si se praepararent ad gratiam, non tamen sequitur quod etiam praeparatis suffragia sanctorum non conferant: quia Deus hoc modo praevidit et ordinavit ut per horum merita illi gratiam accipiant." Note, however, that there is still a crucial difference between the *Summa*'s use of providence and the *Scriptum*'s. In the *Summa*, the divine providence must be invoked to solve the problem of the impediment. We are encouraged to act for others because God may have ordained to use our merit to eliminate the impediment to grace in another and work that person's conversion. In the *Scriptum*, Thomas does not try to relate the divine providence to the impediment in the intended beneficiary of merit. He is simply encouraging effort for another because God "frequently" uses this merit to convert people. But the impediment which prevents this merit taking effect must be removed, not by God, but by the person in question, through the good acts which express the sinner's decision to turn to God. It remains true, however, that the mention of providence in this response, *is* significant, for it marks the first inklings of Thomas's later teaching about merit which discusses and relates merit completely to the providence and predestination of God.

meant to encourage a person to work out his own salvation. To put it bluntly (and yet fairly, I believe), in the *Scriptum* grace and the supernatural reward of heaven are "there for the taking" through the gracious will of God. People must simply do their best, and they shall receive the appropriate response from God. In terms of first grace, by doing their best they dispose themselves for God's grace and arguably merit it congruently; in terms of more grace once possessed and the reward of heaven, doing one's best by the appropriate use of grace through the correct use of human freedom similiarly merits the highest rewards from God. The same holds in the discussion of merit for another—Thomas has placed the onus on people to do what is necessary to come to God. In this vein, he paints a picture of a "cooperative" effort to attain grace. By their acts, other people establish at least a congruent right to the first grace for a person. By his own acts, this other completes the task, removing from himself the barrier separating him from the end of others' merits for him, the first grace. Thus, in the sixth article we learn much about the difference between the *Scriptum* and the *Summa*: In place of the "global" perspective of the *Summa*, in which merits are viewed in their contribution to the divine plan and their service to God, in the *Scriptum* Thomas has adopted a perspective which focusses on the human person and his responsibility to come to God through his acts.

When we contemplate Thomas's teaching about merit as a whole in *In II* d. XXVII, q. I, aa. 3–6, two aspects of this teaching are particularly striking. First, Thomas's analysis of merit here is marred by a number of false steps and questionable assertions. The most significant of these is Thomas's attempt to define two "relations" between merit and reward, an "interior" and an "exterior" one, and then to relate merit to the reward of additional grace and to the reward of eternal life in terms of this twofold relation. The reward "accompanying" the performance of the act as both merited *and* caused by the act, however, is a concept of doubtful usefulness, and fortunately Thomas abandoned in his later works this youthful attempt to explain how a single act can have two rewards.[70] Secondly, Thomas's *ex professo* discussion of merit in the *Scriptum* is "monochromatic," lacking the depth and color found in the *Summa*. In the *Scriptum*, Thomas adopts a straightforward approach to merit, looking only at what the human person can merit from God—eternal life, first grace, the increase of grace, and grace for another. What he does not consider here is what the person *cannot* merit from God. In this, there is an enormous difference between the *Scriptum* and the *Summa*. In the *ex professo* discussion of merit in the *Summa*, Thomas is as concerned to show what

---

70   I would suggest that Thomas's relative neglect of the value and contribution of grace in evaluating condign merit of eternal life (a. 4) and inclusion of the second "alter" in the sixth article when discussing congruent merit for another are similarly unfortunate.

lies beyond the meritorious action of the Christian as to underscore the rewards of his merits; and this attention to the first grace and to the operative grace of perseverance discloses more clearly the true nature of his teaching on merit. By emphasizing that God maintains the Christian on the path to God freely and without concern for human merit, Thomas tellingly makes the case that human salvation is the gift of God. We do merit the end of salvation by our acts; but these acts are guided and sustained by God's free involvement in human activity in accordance with the divine plan. Without this added dimension in his teaching, the doctrine of the *Scriptum* remains rather flat and perhaps even misleading. It suggests the need for merit, but does not show the limits of this merit and so fails to emphasize adequately the full extent of the dependence of people on God for their salvation.[71] In the years separating the *Scriptum* and the *Summa*, Thomas will "discover" the grace of *auxilium* and divide it into operative and cooperative grace. Moreover, he will succeed in subjecting every human act effectively to the divine predestination as to its efficient cause, without eradicating human freedom in the process. With these tools at his disposal, in the *Summa* Thomas will be able to complete his teaching on merit by also emphasizing what cannot be merited through human acts.

B. In III *d. XVIII*

Thomas also offers detailed reflections on merit later in the *Scriptum*, in the course of his treatment of the merit of Christ (*In III* d. XVIII). Thomas's discussion of the merit of Christ is well-organized, and indeed at least in terms of organization, Thomas's discussion of the merit of Christ in the *Scriptum* is superior to that found in the *Summa Theologiae*.[72] In

---

71   As I have already suggested, the discovery of the grace of *auxilium* and its division into operative and cooperative will be of great moment in Thomas's formulation of his mature teaching on merit. With the operative *auxilium* of conversion and of perseverance, he will be able to show the limits of merit by insisting that the entry into grace *and* the perseverance in grace always remain the unmerited gift of God. Nevertheless, in at least one text in the *Scriptum*, Thomas has mentioned the limits of merit. In *In IV* d. XV, q. IV, a. 7, qc. II ad 3, Thomas says that our merits fall short of God's glory, and so he encourages Christians to pray to God to supply in God's mercy for the deficiencies of human merit. This, of course, is rather less than the *Summa*'s recognition of the need to hope and pray to God for the aid necessary to stay in grace. Yet it still reflects Thomas's awareness that the pilgrim to God must be aided by God if he is to complete the journey and be worthy of God. Later in this chapter, I shall contemplate Thomas's teaching about *hope* in the *Scriptum* and suggest how his teaching in this work differs from the mature teaching on hope (and merit) in the *Summa*.

72   In place of the closely knit discussion of the merit of Christ as found in the *Scriptum*, in the *Summa* Thomas has scattered the discussion of Christ's merit throughout the fifty-nine questions of the treatise on Christology in the Tertia Pars. For the location of the discussions of Christ's merit in the *Summa*, see note 185 of Chapter 3. Thomas also has a fairly lengthy

large measure, the superior organization of the discussion of Christ's merit in the *Scriptum* is due to Peter Lombard's own success in organizing the discussion of the merit of Christ in the *Sentences*. Among the scholastics, the merit of Christ had been the focus of intense debate for decades before the Lombard. It is likely that the scholastics had raised questions about the merit of Christ even before they had subjected the very concept of merit to sustained analysis. Hence, by the time that Peter turned to this question, there were well-established areas of dispute with regard to the merit of Christ, and Peter could describe the main points of the debate with relative ease. In turn, the discussion about the merit of Christ had reached its high point with the twelfth-century scholastics, and accordingly the ensuing century had added very little in substantive terms to the understanding of the question. When Thomas himself turned to the merit of Christ, he was able on the whole simply to follow the Lombard's approach and basic conclusions in examining this theological problem.

For the Lombard, there are three main questions to be resolved when speaking of the merit of Christ. The first was probably the first to have been raised in scholastic circles, precisely because it is the more obvious. Is 'merit' a useful term for soteriology, to describe Christ's work on behalf of people? Thus, Peter asks whether Christ could merit "for us" (*nobis*). The second question is more subtle and seeks to define the limits of Christ's merit. The scholastics also asked whether Christ merited *for himself* (*sibi*). Obviously, this second question reveals a certain sophistication. The scholastics had turned from the more obvious problem about the nature of Christ's work for people to the further question of the nature and "need" of Christ's work for himself. In this vein, there were manifest problems which had to be resolved: Given the affirmation of the divinity of Christ and the assertion of Christ's sinlessness and perfection, in what need would Christ stand of such merit? And since Christ's actions were the action of God and merits establish a right to a reward from *another*, how can we speak of Christ/God meriting from God? Finally, the scholastics of the twelfth century also sought to determine which of Christ's actions were meritorious. Did Christ merit by the Passion alone, or, were all of his actions performed as a man meritorious? Peter himself had no doubt that Christ did merit, not only for us, but for himself as well, and that all of his actions, not simply the Passion, were meritorious. In his own discussion of the merit of Christ, Thomas has benefited enormously from the Lombard's description of the extent and rewards of Christ's merit. His own discussion reflects and incorporates the concerns and insights of the Lombard and other twelfth-century authors on merit, with but minor modifications.

Thomas's treatment of Christ's merit in *In III* d. XVIII covers five

---

examination of the merit of Christ in *De Veritate*; I shall review the teaching of *De Veritate* later in this chapter. With the few exceptions to be noted in the course of the present section, Thomas's analysis of the merit of Christ remains constant throughout his career.

articles. In the second article of this distinction, Thomas builds on the argument of the first article, in which he has asserted that there is an action of Christ which is distinctively *human*,[73] to state that it was possible in general terms for Christ to merit. As human, Christ was capable of the freely performed acts which are necessary for merit. In the third and fifth articles of *In III* d. XVIII, Thomas then discusses the *locus* of Christ's merit. As had the Lombard before him, Thomas asks whether Christ as human merited in the first moment of his conception (a. 3). Having claimed that Christ so merited, he then asks in the fifth article about the merit of the Passion and its special significance. In this latter regard, among Thomas's concerns, again following the twelfth-century scholastics, was to demonstrate that the passion was not superfluous but in fact adds to the merit which Christ had accrued through his earlier works. The task at hand is to examine why the passion was necessary if Christ's earlier acts had already merited the rewards achieved by Christ. Finally, in the fourth, fifth, and sixth articles, Thomas examines the *beneficiaries* of Christ's merit. He first asks (aa. 4 and 5) whether Christ could merit *for himself*, and, naturally, Thomas's special problem here is to show why such merit is "necessary." Then, Thomas asks about Christ's merit for others: In the sixth article, he asks whether Christ by his acts merited for others the "opening of the door" of heaven, that is, did Christ's merit establish the right for all people to obtain God through union with Christ? In all, Thomas offers in *In III* d. XVIII an analysis of Christ's merit which exploits the insights of the *ex professo* treatment of merit in the second book of the *Scriptum*, as well as builds on the real insights of the twelfth-century teaching on the merit of Christ.

In *In III* d. XVIII, a. 2, Thomas asks whether in fact Christ could merit. To Peter Lombard's questionings about the beneficiaries and rewards of Christ's merit, Thomas has prefixed the more basic question about the very possibility of Christ meriting. In the second article, Thomas notes seven objections which would seem to preclude merit from Christ. While there are different nuances in these objections, at bottom we find in these objections but two fundamental strategies to discount the merit of Christ.

---

73   The significance of *In III* d. XVIII, a. 1, is that it in fact makes it possible for Thomas to speak of Christ meriting. 'Merit' is a category used only of agents of free choice who lack certain goods but by whose actions these goods can be obtained justly. If Christ were simply God, Christ would already as God possess whatever other people must merit from God. Similarly, if Christ lacked human freedom and were but the tool of God, we could not speak of Christ doing the free acts which are merits. But the full humanity of Christ allows theologians to speak of Christ meriting, for they then can focus on Christ as *human* using his will to merit something from God. Hence, while the first article says nothing directly about merit, it indicates why merit can be ascribed to Christ: By virtue of his human nature and the attributes appropriate to human nature, including the freedom of the will, Jesus Christ is a free agent able to act in accordance with God's will and so merit.

The first, which is followed in the sixth and seventh objections, trades on the divinity of Christ. Meriting means establishing a right to a reward, so that what was not owed to a person now becomes owed to that person through his acts. Moreover, when a person merits, he merits from another person. His works establish a right to a reward from God who eventually rewards the merit. Hence, to speak of Christ meriting, we would have to posit a reward which Christ by nature did not possess, and, most crucially, say that Christ establishes this right to a reward before a person who is completely other than Christ. The affirmation of the divinity of Christ, however, makes it impossible to speak of Christ meriting before God. As God, Christ possesses what belongs to God (the vision of God) naturally. Hence, Christ does not have to merit the vision of God because he already enjoys it as God.[74] Similarly, it is impossible for Christ to merit because Christ is himself God, and so there is lacking here the "alterity" necessary for merit; one cannot merit a reward from oneself.[75] While these objections possess some interest, they really pose no difficulty to the affirmation of Christ's merit before God. In the first article of this distinction, Thomas had restated the orthodox affirmation of the two natures of Christ. As both divine and human, it is necessary to speak of two "actions" in Christ, a divine and a human act. Merit involves the action of *humans* before God. Thus, while it is clear that as divine, Christ's divine actions do not merit before God, as human we can in fact say that Christ's works do have religious significance before God. Similarly, the humanity of Christ is not the divinity, and so Christ as man can merit from God. Hence, the sixth and seventh objections can only be raised by confusing the two natures, and therefore two actions, of Christ; and Thomas in the preceding article has warned against this confusion.[76]

---

74   The definition of merit as "making something owed" to oneself to which I refer in the text is taken from the beginning of *In III* d. XVIII, a. 2 sol.; I shall return to this "definition" shortly. For the objection to Christ's merit on the basis of his divinity, see *In III* d. XVIII, a. 2 ob 6: "Nullus meretur id quod suum est. Et propter hoc apud homines filii non merentur a patribus, sed servi; quia ea quae patrum sunt, hereditario iure competunt filio. Sed omnia quae Patris sunt, Christi sunt."

75   *In III* d. XVIII, a. 2 ob 7: "Nullus meretur a seipso. Sed quicumque meretur, meretur aliquid a Filio Dei. Cum ergo Christus sit Filius Dei, ipse nullo modo mereri poterat." The idea that meriting involves *two* partners is a fundamental one for Thomas's teaching about merit and will be found throughout his writings. It is the "alterity" here involved which permits him to subject merit to justice. As we saw in the first section of this chapter, in the *Scriptum* Thomas has occasionally lost sight of this, as when he speaks of the reward accompanying/issuing from the good work (see *In II* d. XXVII, q. I, a. 5 sol.). However, this is a youthful error which is not repeated in the works of the maturity.

76   In addition to *In III* d. XVIII, a. 1 sol., see *In III* d. XVIII, a. 2 ad 6: "Christus non meretur secundum Divinitatem, secundum quam habet quod omnia sunt sua; sed meretur secundum humanitatem, ex qua non habet quod omnia sua

It is the second strategy adopted in the objections which at first glance constitutes a more compelling case against the merit of Christ, for it focuses on an important feature of the *humanity* of Christ. In various ways, these objections deny the merit of Christ because they note that throughout his human life, Christ was a *comprehensor*. In medieval theology, there are two sharply defined states possible to people. The first is in this life, when people can work out their salvation. A popular way to characterize this state was to describe it as a *pilgrimage*, and to say that the one engaged in this pilgrimage is himself a traveler on the way to God, a *viator*. The second state of human existence is after this life. To those who have acted as God wills while a *viator*, God grants Himself, ushering the Christian *viator* into God's presence and joining the pilgrim to God. For the scholastics, including Aquinas, the pilgrimage of the first state has here given way to what is termed 'comprehension.' In viewing the essence of God and being joined immediately to God, people find their desires satisfied and their needs fulfilled. In attaining God, they are no longer on the way (*viatores*), they are now *comprehensores*, those who are joined in a most satisfying way to God and are living God's own life. Now, merit is restricted to the first stage of human existence, to the pilgrimage to God. When people merit, they are as it were taking the right "steps" which will lead them to God. There is no merit in the second stage, when people have come to God. Rather, this is the time of *reward*, when those who have merited God receive the just reward for their acts, God Himself.

The case of Christ, however, slightly differs from the norm: While other people must await the next life to see God (and so reap the rewards which they have merited), the scholastics were convinced that Christ as man enjoyed the vision of God while he was alive, indeed throughout his life. Hence, Jesus Christ did not have to wait for the beatific vision. Christ throughout his life on earth was a *comprehensor*. This affirmation about Christ had obvious implications for the discussion of Christ's merit. In particular, since only the *viator* can merit and Christ was always a *comprehensor*, there seems to have been no time in which Christ could merit, whether for himself or for others. Christ did not need to merit, nor could he merit, because he enjoyed the goal of merit, the direct vision of God. The remaining objections to the second article of d. XVIII draw this conclusion in one way or another. Some of these objections in fact simply make this case in a straightforward way. Hence in the first objection, we read that because Christ was a *comprehensor* throughout his life, he could not merit,[77] while in the third objection, the objection states that because Christ was created *beata* (and so was a *comprehensor*), there is no reason

---

sunt;" and ad 7: "Et per hoc patet solutio ad septimum; quia a Filio Dei meremur ratione Divinitatis suae, ex qua parte ipse non merebatur."

77 *In III* d. XVIII, a. 2 ob 1: "Christus enim semper fuit comprehensor. Sed comprehensoris qui est in termino, non est mereri, quia meritum est via ad terminum. Ergo Christus non meruit."

to speak of merit arising from Christ's action.[78] The other objections trade on features of 'comprehension' to dismiss the merit of Christ. Thus, for example, in the beatific vision the *love* which a person has for God which impels the movement to God in this life is heightened to its most complete degree. The beatific vision means the fullness of love. Hence, when we merit, we merit this fullness of love, which we shall receive in heaven. But since Christ was a *comprehensor*, Christ's love was always complete and so there is no place for his meriting the increase of this love. His love could not increase.[79] Similarly, as we have seen in the *ex professo* treatment of merit, meriting involves the correct use of the *liberum arbitrium*. People have many courses of action available to them, not all of which truly fulfill the law of human being. When people use their free choice correctly, they merit, and so draw closer to God. After this life, however, the free choice will find its rest, for in the beatific vision the person will have come into contact with the good itself. Since the will seeks the good and opts for it, in the presence of goodness itself, the person will be drawn irresistibly to the willing of God. In God's presence, there will be no possibility of the will opting for what is not God, for choosing as it were the wrong option with regard to God. Since, then, the will will be determined to the good infallibly, there is no room to speak of merit in the beatific vision. The will "has" to choose God. Thus, since Christ even in this life enjoyed the beatific vision, Christ's *liberum arbitrium* always was determined to the good, and so with Christ there is no place for merit arising from the correct use of the will. Christ "had" to will what Christ willed, God,[80] and thus could not merit.

In the *solutio* of *In III* d. XVIII, a. 2, Thomas counters these arguments against the merit of Christ in basically the same way as he will later in his other treatments of the merit of Christ, in *De Veritate* and the *Summa Theologiae*. He asserts Christ's merit because, he says, Christ was not only a *comprehensor*, Christ was also a *viator*. However, in the *solutio* Thomas

78 *In III* d. XVIII, a. 2 ob 3: "Anima Christi a principio suae conceptionis fuit beata, sicut modo est. Sed modo non meretur. Ergo nec unquam mereri potuit."
79 See *In III* d. XVIII, a. 2 ob 2: "Non potest esse idem meritum et praemium, sicut nec causa et causatum. Sed actus caritatis perfectae est praemium, quia est ipsa fruitio. Ergo cum in Christo fuerit caritas consummata, per ipsam mereri non potuit; et ita nullo modo merebatur, cum omnis meriti principium sit caritas"; and ob 4: "Quicumque meretur, merendo proficit quantum ad illud quod est principium merendi; quia caritas per meritum augetur. Sed caritas Christi augeri non potuit, nec ipse in spiritualibus bonis proficere. Ergo ipse non merebatur." In response, Thomas will agree that Christ's love could not increase and was identical with the love involved in the beatific vision, but nevertheless insist that this love as the principle of meriting permits Christ to merit some rewards from God.
80 *In III* d. XVIII, a. 2 ob 5: "Naturalibus non meremur, propter hoc quod sunt determinata ad unum. Sed liberum arbitrium in Christo erat determinatum ad bonum. Ergo ipse per liberum arbitrium mereri non potuit; et ita nullo modo, cum omne meritum sit ex libero arbitrio."

is not content simply to insist that Christ in some way was a pilgrim in this world and so could merit. He takes the opportunity to remind his readers of the salient features of merit, to show why it is appropriate to speak of Christ meriting.[81] First, Thomas recalls to us that merit and reward fall under *justice*. The one who rewards merit is said to "do justice." 'Justice' means to render what is owed, and so the one who rewards is rendering what is owed (*debitum*) to merit. On the other hand, the one who merits is said to "undergo justice." This person makes something owed to himself, the reward, which must be requited by justice.[82] Hence, on this

---

81   The pertinent parts of *In III* d. XVIII, a. 2, sol., read as follows: "In iustitia duae personae requiruntur, scilicet faciens iustitiam et patiens iustitiam. Facientis autem iustitiam, reddere unicuique quod suum est actio propria est. Patientis autem iustitiam actio propria est facere sibi debitum quod est ei per iustitiam reddendum: et hoc proprie mereri est. Unde et id quod secundum iustitiam redditur, merces dicitur. Sed quia iustitia reddit unicuique quod ei debetur et in bonis et in malis; bona autem simpliciter sunt ea quae ad vitam aeternam pertinent, et mala simpliciter ea quae ad miseriam aeternam; inde est quod secundum Theologos meritum proprie dicitur respectu horum; quamvis magis proprie respectu bonorum dicatur meritum, demeritum vero respectu malorum. Ad hoc igitur quod aliquis mereatur, tria necessaria sunt scilicet agens qui meretur, actio per quam meretur et merces quam meretur. Et ideo ad meritum tria requiruntur. Primum est secundum comparationem merentis ad mercedem, et scilicet ille qui meretur sit in statu acquirendi mercedem. Et propter hoc illi qui sunt omnino in termino, nihil merentur, quia nihil acquirere possunt. Secundum est ex comparatione agentis ad actionem, ut scilicet sit dominus suae actionis; alias per actionem suam non dignificatur ad aliquid habendum, nec laudatur. Et ideo ea quae agunt per necessitatem naturae vel etiam per violentiam, non merentur. Tertium est secundum comparationem actionis ad mercedem, ut scilicet aequiparetur mercedi, non quidem secundum aequalitatem quantitatis—quia hoc requiritur in iustitia commutativa quae consistit in emptionibus et venditionibus—sed secundum aequalitatem proportionis quae requiritur in iustitia distributiva, secundum quam Deus praemia aeterna partitur. Actio autem proportionata ad vitam aeternam est actio ex caritate facta; et ideo per ipsam ex condigno meretur quis ea quae ad vitam aeternam pertinent. . . . Et haec tria in Christo reperiuntur. Ipse enim quamvis quantum ad aliquid in termino perfectionis fuerit, scilicet quantum ad operationes animae quibus beatus erat et comprehensor; tamen quantum ad aliquid defectum patiebatur eorum quae ad gloriam pertinent, inquantum scilicet erat passibilis anima et corpore et inquanturm erat corpore mortalis; et ideo secundum hoc erat viator in statu acquirendi. Similiter et omnis actus eius informatus erat caritate. Et iterum actus sui dominus erat per libertatem voluntatis. Et ideo omni actu suo meruit." In the *solutio*, Thomas is thinking of *condign* merit; this is the kind of merit appropriate to Christ. However, he also refers here in passing to other kinds of 'merit,' congruent and 'interpretative.' I have omitted for the moment his description of these merits. In a later note, I shall discuss Thomas's comments on these additional kinds of merit.

82   For another text in which Thomas observes the relation between merit and justice, see note 74 above. Thomas also relates merit and justice elsewhere

basis, Thomas states that in meriting, there must be present three "elements" for the acquisition of merit. There must be an *agent* who is capable of meriting, of making something owed to him; an *actio* which the agent performs in order to make something owed to him; and a *reward* (*merces*) which stands in an essential relation to the good deed and is rendered for it. When he speaks of an agent who is capable of meriting, Thomas is, in the first place, simply adopting as his own the claim of the objections of this article, that only the *viator* can merit. He states here that only the person on-the-way can merit the end of the journey. The person who is completely (*omnino*) at the term of the journey no longer merits this end. But, secondly, when he speaks of the capacity to merit he is also referring to the necessity of *freedom* for merit. There are various kinds of causes in the world. Some are simply moved to their act. We do not speak of such causes "meriting," for they contribute nothing of their own to the act; they are simply applied by another to it. For meriting, an agent must possess dominion over his acts and be able to apply himself to his act; where this dominion is lacking, so too is merit.[83] And yet, while it is essential that the agent be free, and a *viator*, this is not enough to guarantee merit. In *In II* d. XXVII, q. I, a. 3 *solutio*, Thomas had insisted that for condign merit, the works performed by the *viator* had to be *proportioned* to the intended reward of eternal life: merit and reward must belong to the same (supernatural) genus, and so merits presuppose grace and charity which endow human action with the requisite dignity. Thus in *In III* d. XVIII, a. 2 *solutio*, Thomas completes this review of the prerequisites of merit by adding that for merit the good act must be proportioned to its reward. He states here that the acts of the free agent who wishes to merit the end of the spiritual life must issue from the theological virtue of charity, which proportions his acts to God, for his merit to deserve this end.[84]

---

in this distinction; see, e.g., *In III* d. XVIII, a. 4, sol. I; and *In III* d. XVIII, a. 5 ob 1 and sol.

83   For texts in which Thomas insists on human freedom as a condition of merit, see note 16 above.

84   As I observed in note 81 above, in the present article Thomas refers to two other kinds of merit, congruent and interpretative, and describes how they resemble but fall short of true merit, condign merit: "Opera autem bona quae non sunt ex caritate facta, deficiunt ab ista proportione; et ideo per ea ex condigno non meretur quis vitam aeternam, sed improprie his dicitur aliquis mereri, secundum quod habent similitudinem aliquam cum operatione informata caritate. Et si quidem sit similitudo in substantia actus et in intentione, ut cum aliquis in peccato existens mortali dat eleemosynam propter Deum, dicitur meritum congrui. Si vero sit similitudo in substantia actus et non in intentione, sic dicitur meritum interpretatum, sicut cum quis dat pauperi eleemosynam propter inanem gloriam." The "interpretative" merit which Thomas mentions here is otherwise unknown in the Thomistic corpus. Such a merit had been advanced in some circles in the twelfth century. The description of congruent merit here is rather intriguing. The critical difference between condign and congruent merit clearly is the absence of

Having reviewed the principal features of merit, Thomas concludes the *solutio* by asserting merit of Christ: Christ could merit because Christ fulfilled these three requirements for merit. As human, Christ possessed dominion over his acts, through his freedom of will. Similarly, Christ's acts were manifestly proportioned to God because Christ had complete charity, and so all he did, he performed through the love of God. And, finally, Christ could merit because in this life he was *viator* as well as *comprehensor*. To explain this last point, Thomas notes that the end of human existence, the beatific vision, can be distinguished into two parts. First, there is the *essential* reward of the vision, in which the essential desires of the "higher" part of the human person achieve their fulfillment through union with God. In knowing God who is Truth and Goodness, the soul's deepest urges to know and love are completely satisfied. But the human person is more than simply the soul. The body also is integral to human existence. Thus, in the beatific vision the body too will receive its reward, the secondary rewards of impassibility and immortality. When we speak of Christ as *viator*, we are referring especially to these secondary rewards which are part of the beatific vision. Christ was a *comprehensor* because he always enjoyed the beatific vision which is the essential reward of the soul. But Christ was not always immortal in his body nor impassible. Otherwise, he would not have been able to suffer or die. Thus, with regard to the reward of the body which is granted in the beatific vision, Christ was also a *viator*. Hence, because Christ did not always possess these secondary goods, he could merit them by his action.[85]

grace and charity in the latter and thus the "proportion" between act and reward involved in condign merit. Note that Thomas thinks it possible for the person who lacks charity nevertheless to do an act *propter Deum*; at this stage of his thinking, Thomas does not consistently insist on the transforming power of grace which makes possible new action "for God." For other descriptions of congruent merit as "improperly" or imperfectly merit, see the discussion of *In II* d. XXVII, q. I, a. 4, and note 55 above.

85 The argument offered in the *solutio* is sufficient to dispose of most of the arguments presented in the objections of this article: Objections 1 through 4 are correct in claiming that the *comprehensor* cannot merit, but Christ was a *viator* as well as a *comprehensor* and so could merit. The fifth objection and response are somewhat more intriguing. Objection 5 had rejected the merit of Christ because, it claimed, Christ was unable to choose freely between various courses of action and this freedom is essential to merit. Christ's will was simply determined to the good. In ad 5, Thomas offers two ways of meeting this claim, each of which tells us much about the conditions of meriting in general. First, Thomas allows that Christ's will was determined to the good but says that this was but a "generic" determination. Christ's will was determined to what-is-good in general. But Christ's will was not determined to the numerical good, that is, to this particular good rather than to that. It was up to Christ to do this rather than that, and this decision was in the power of his free choice. Thus, there is place for merit in Christ with respect to human freedom. The second possible answer to the claim of the fifth objection allows for the moment that Christ's will was determined to the

In *In III* d. XVIII, a. 4, Thomas picks up on his comments in the second article about the two facets of the beatific vision, by asking about the rewards which Christ in fact merits for himself.[86] The fourth article is the single longest article of this distinction.[87] Divided into four *quaestiunculae*, the article asks in turn whether Christ merited for himself the *immortality* of the body (qc. I), the *impassibility* of the soul (qc. II), his exaltation before other creatures (qc. III), and the very vision of God (qc. IV). Only the last quaestiuncula is out of place here: Thomas has already maintained that Christ is a *comprehensor* with regard to the essential aspect of the beatific vision, the satisfying of the needs of the soul through union with God, and so this quaestiuncula is superfluous. Indeed, Thomas simply repeats in a. 4, *solutio* IV, that Christ did not merit the beatific vision but always enjoyed it because of the proximity of the divine and human throughout his life.[88] The topics of the first three quaestiunculae of this article are much more interesting. In these articles Thomas fills out the content of the "secondary" rewards involved in the beatific vision by identifying the specific rewards which Christ in fact merited. In enumerating these particular rewards, Thomas is simply following Peter Lombard's lead. In his own treatment of Christ's merit, the Lombard has told us that Christ merited for himself

---

numerical good. Christ "had" to will it. Yet, even if this is the case, Thomas thinks that we can speak of Christ meriting. For Christ was not forced (*coacte*) to will what he willed, he did it willingly and freely (*sponte*). Hence, here too Christ was lord of his acts, and so could merit. The value of this discussion is apparent, for it demonstrates the breadth of Thomas's comments about human freedom as a pre-condition of meriting. At times, he means the ability to choose between various options for the good, and at others, he means our willingness in acting. Both aspects will remain throughout his career. However, his comments about people willing *sponte* will be put on a firmer foundation and given greater significance in the later works, once he has worked out all the implications of his idea about God as transcendent cause. God will move people to their acts but do so in such a way that the integrity of their own causality is respected. That is, God moves them to do willingly and agreeably what God wills them to do. In *In III* d. XVIII, a. 3 ad 2, Thomas will address again the question of Christ willing what God has "determined" him to will; I discuss this text below.

86 I have postponed the discussion of *In III* d. XVIII, a. 3, for the moment, in the interest of describing the flow of Thomas's argument in this distinction more coherently.

87 In the edition of Moos (see the bibliography for full details), the fourth article of this distinction covers eight out of the twenty-seven pages of Thomas's own commentary.

88 See *In III* d. XVIII, a. 4, sol. IV: "Unde ex hoc ipso quod anima Christi erat Deo in persona conjuncta, debebatur sibi fruitionis unio, et non per operationem aliquam est ei facta debita. Et ideo, quia meritum consistit in operatione quae facit nobis aliquid debitum, Christus fruitionem non meruit"; see also ad 3, and especially ad 1: "Christus sibi beatitudinem quae est in fruitione non meruit, non fuit ex insufficientia meriti, sed ex perfectione merentis."

these very rewards, the impassibility and immortality of the body and the soul and the disclosure of the ontological truth of Christ before creatures.[89] As compared to his later discussion of the rewards of Christ's merit for himself, Thomas's discussion here is much more detailed. In no other work has he examined as closely the rewards which Christ's merits have earned for Christ. And yet the present discussion is for this very reason inferior to the later presentations of Christ's merit. The explanation for Christ meriting each of these rewards is always the same, and so the dedication of individual quaestiuncula to each reward is ultimately redundant; Thomas simply repeats his basic analysis in each quaestiuncula of why it is that Christ would have merited such a reward.

The starting point of Thomas's discussion of Christ's merit for himself is the belief that in the incarnation the Son of God has decided to assume what belongs to human nature. Operative in Thomas's description of the incarnation is the distinction he draws between what is owed to the *person* of Jesus Christ and what is owed to the human nature which the Son of God has taken up. If we look at the dignity of the person, then because of the proximity of the divine and human in Christ the body of Christ should have been, or at least could have been, immortal, the soul of Christ could have been impassible, and the dignity of Jesus Christ could have been manifested to all creatures from the very moment of his conception. However, Christ has willed to receive not what is owed to or belongs to his person because of the divinity, but what belongs to people as human. It is natural to people that their bodies dissolve on the removal of the soul. In material things, there is a natural tendency to distintegration.[90] Similarly,

89 At the beginning of Bk III, d. XVIII, Peter Lombard writes that "sibi meruit impassibilitatis et immortalitatis gloriam secundum carnem, sicut ait Apostolus (Phil. II, 8): 'Christus factus est pro nobis obediens usque ad mortem, mortem autem crucis; propter quod et Deus exaltavit illum et dedit illi nomen quod est super omne nomen.' Aperte dicit Apostolus, Christum propterea exaltatum per impassibilitatis gloriam, quia est humiliatus per passionis obedientiam. Humilitas ergo passionis meritum fuit exaltationis, et exaltatio praemium humilitatis."

90 When Thomas speaks of the death of the human person, there are two points which he wishes to make. First, this death is designed by God to be a punishment for sin. If Adam had not sinned, Adam's descendants would have received the immortality in which God created Adam. But, secondly, immortality is a gift which God gave Adam and which God will give to the just in heaven. When this gift is withdrawn, it is natural for the body to die. In this context, Thomas refers to the natural tendency of material things to "pull apart," to dissolve; hence, the body always tends to its demise, and God must sustain its unity. For this latter idea, see *In III* d. XVIII, a. 4, qc. I ad 3: "Christus quamvis non haberet necessitatem moriendi ex peccato, tamen habebat ex principiis naturalibus . . . et ideo naturae humanae in ipso immortalitas non erat debita." By virtue of his sinlessness, Christ need not have died, in the sense of paying his debt to God. But as possessing a corporeal body, he was prone to death, and thus he could merit the reward of bodily immortality.

while the human soul of itself is impassible, in union with the body in the formation of the human person, the soul too undergoes the passions arising from the body and so is passible.[91] Thus, because of Christ's taking up of what belongs to human nature, not what belongs to this unique person,[92] there is a possibility for Christ to merit for himself. Merit means to make owed to oneself what does not belong to oneself.[93] Hence, Christ was able to make owed to himself these different rewards—immortality of the body, impassibility of the soul, and his exaltation before others—which are not owed to human nature, although in a different sense they belong (or could belong) to this person, Jesus Christ. Thus, by his acts as human, Christ obtains the secondary features which normally are associated with the beatific vision: His body is raised to immortality, his soul becomes impassible, and the true glory of Christ is revealed to all.[94]

---

91   For this distinction between the impassibility of the soul in itself and the passibility of the soul as related to the body, see *In III* d. XVIII, a. 4, sol. II, and especially ad 1: "Anima secundum suam naturam est impassibilis, ut pati non possit, quantum ad passiones proprie dictas de quibus loquimur, sine corpore. Est tamen secundum suam naturam passibilis, id est potens pati has passiones in corpore et per corpus." Implicit here is the notion that because of the divinity, the Son of God could have ordained that the soul even in association with the body would have retained its impassibility.

92   For this idea that Christ assumed what was proper to human nature, not what was owed by virtue of the divine nature, see, e.g., *In III* d. XVIII, a. 4, qc. I ad 1: "Quamvis immortalitas et omnia bona quae sunt in potestate Patris, essent in potestate Filii quantum ad divinam personam, non tamen ratione humanae naturae. Unde nos merendo facimus nobis debitum de eo quod non erat debitum neque personae neque naturae. Christus autem fecit merendo debitum naturae de non debito naturae, quamvis esset debitum personae." The case of the third reward merited by Christ, exaltation before other creatures, is basically the same as the others. In the case of immortality and impassibility, Christ has foregone what belongs to him as a unique person and taken up only what belongs to human nature in general. Thus his body died and his soul in conjunction with his body suffered. Similarly, as both God and human, it was Christ's right to be acknowledged as Lord by other creatures. However, Christ at first appeared to other creatures as merely human, and so did not receive this recognition which he deserved. Thus, he was able to merit this exaltation before others through his work in this world and on the cross.

93   Thomas begins *In III* d. XVIII, a. 4, sol. I, as follows: "Meritum secundum se est operatio eius qui justitiam patitur, secundum quam facit suum id quod sibi reddendum est. Non autem datur aliquid alicui qui habet illud eo modo quo habet, nec aliquis facit suum quod suum est eo modo quo suum est." See also note 82 above.

94   For the affirmation that Christ merited for himself the secondary reward of the immortality of the body, see *In III* d. XVIII, a. 4 sol. I: ". . . quatuor requiruntur quantum ad illud quod aliquis mereri dicitur. Primum est quod illud sit de pertinentibus ad beatitudinem. Secundum est quod illud sit non habitum quod per meritum acquiritur reddendum iustitia mediante. Tertium est quod illud sit non debitum quod merendo quis sibi debitum facit. Quartum

Thomas's discussion of the exaltation of Christ is particularly illuminating, for it especially reveals his indebtedness to Peter Lombard. Peter had tied the question of the exaltation of Christ to the Christ hymn in Philippians, in which Christ is said to have received as a result of humility the name which is above every other name.[95] In this way, the Lombard had connected Christ's exaltation to Christ's humility, and so had made the telling point that it is in being humble, in observing the limits of one's dignity and acknowledging the rule of one's superior, that merit especially comes to the fore. Merit is not acting in a superhuman or heroic manner. It means to act as God wills for people and to obey God's will in working out one's destiny. One acknowledges God's lordship and strives to give oneself to God as God wills. Thomas too agrees with this assessment and follows the Lombard in tying merit in general, and that of Christ in particular, to humility.[96] But, secondly, the Lombard had also shown Thomas how to interpret the exaltation of Christ in such a way that the divinity of Christ is not denied or the resurrection made into the crucial and constitutive event in the history of the person of Christ. One problem with Paul's words in Philippians is that they might be construed as suggesting that ontologically Christ was not always the Son of God and that God has given Christ such enhanced dignity only because of what Jesus had done for God on the cross. That is, the Philippians hymn might be read as undercutting the later orthodox claim about the full divinity of Jesus Christ from the moment of his conception. The Lombard, however, has shown later theologians how to interpret this difficult text of scripture benignly: He says that here Paul is using a trope.[97] When Paul says that

est quod illud quod quis mereri dicitur, sequatur ad minus ordine naturae ad ipsum meritum; et ideo gratia quae est principium merendi et alia naturalia quae exiguntur ad meritum, sub merito non cadunt. Haec autem quatuor in Christi immortalitate inveniuntur. Quia est de his quae pertinent ad beatitudinem corporis. Item non fuit ab eo semper habitum, quia a principio mortale corpus assumpsit. Item non fuit sibi debitum ratione naturae, quamvis esset sibi debitum ratione personae. Item immortalitas non exigitur ad merendum. Et propter hoc immortalitatem meruit"; see also ads 1 and 3. For the claim that Christ merited the impassibility of the soul by his acts, see *In III* d. XVIII, a. 4, sol. II. Thomas discusses Christ's merit of his exaltation in *In III* d. XVIII, a. 4, sol. III.

95 See note 89 above. In tying this reward of Christ's merit to the Philippians hymn, the Lombard stands in a long and distinguished line of interpreters. Immediately after the words quoted in note 89 above, he cites Augustine and Ambrose who had emphasized the "merit of humility" in their reading of this text.

96 In *In III* d. XVIII, a. 4, sol. III, Thomas forms his discussion of Christ's merit of exaltation around an exegesis of the Philippians hymn. In the first *sed contra* of this questiuncula, Thomas also cites another "humility/exaltation" text, Luke 14:11, in explaining Christ's exaltation through the merit of humility.

97 Peter Lombard writes in Bk III, d. XVIII: "Secundum tropum illum in Scriptura creberrimum hoc accipiendum est, quo 'dicitur res fieri quando

Christ has now been exalted, he means that the ontological truth of Jesus Christ has now been revealed to all others in the world. The Thomas follows the Lombard in this analysis: The "exaltation" means no more than God's revelation to all of the true nature of Jesus Christ as a reward for Christ's work. Indeed, in offering this interpretation, Thomas uses the very words of Lombard.[98]

In his later discussion of the merit of Christ in the *Summa*, Thomas will repeat that Christ's merit earns for Christ exaltation from God, as well as immortality of the body and impassibility of the soul. However, the later discussion will be somewhat superior because Thomas will make clearer why it is good that Christ in fact has merited these rewards. In the later analysis, Thomas will advance as a truth of his Christology that all perfections should be ascribed to Christ. Thomas tells us in the *Summa* that with regard to some perfections it is better or more perfect to have earned them as a reward than to have received them as a gift, and he says that the "secondary" rewards which he discusses here are in fact such perfections: Christ could have been born with an immortal body, but it was a greater good for him to earn this by his acts. As a consequence, although by virtue of his enjoyment of the beatific vision Christ's body could have received while on earth the immortality of the body associated with the vision, by God's decree the beatitude of the body has been postponed. Thomas had argued that Christ could merit this beatitude of the body by his acts, in this way obtaining the greater perfection associated with meriting such a reward. In the earlier *Scriptum*, however, Thomas really does not "explain" the value of this merit of Christ or why Christ has wanted to merit these secondary perfections rather than possessing them from the first. In one of the objections noted in this article,[99] Thomas does say that it is more glorious to earn something than to have it merely as a gift, and he will repeat this idea in a later distinction.[100] He also alludes to God's

innotescit.' Post resurrectionem vero, quod ante erat, in evidenti positumest, ut scirent homines et daemones. Manifestationem ergo illius nominis donavit ei Deus post resurrectionem; sed illam meruit per obedientiam passionis, qui eo quod obedivit patiendo, exaltatus est resurgendo, et per hoc manifestatum est nomen."

98 See *In III* d. XVIII, a. 4, qc. III ad 1: "Quamvis fuerit exaltatus ab initio suae conceptionis, non tamen sua exaltatio fuit tunc manifesta. Et 'res' in sacra Scriptura 'tunc fieri dicitur, quando innotescit.'"

99 See *In III* d. XVIII, a. 4, qc. IV ob 2: "Gloriosius est habere aliquid per seipsum quam ab alio habere omnia. Sed quod quis meretur, quodammodo habet per seipsum. Cum igitur Christus fruitionem divinam gloriosissime habuerit, videtur quod eam meruerit." As is evident, Thomas refers to this idea in the present distinction only with regard to the essential part of the beatific vision, which of course Christ did *not* merit; he does not refer to this notion when speaking of what Christ did merit for himself.

100 In *In III* d. XX, a. 1, sol. II, Thomas mentions that it is more glorious to obtain something through merit, through one's own efforts, than to have been merely given this thing.

dispensation by which Christ in this world did not enjoy all the rewards normally associated with beatitude, in order that he might merit them.[101] Thomas even knows the Christological "rule" about ascribing all perfections to Christ. He cites it, as we shall see, in the third article of this distinction when he considers the issue of Christ's merit in the first moment of his conception.[102] But in the *Scriptum* he does not combine his ideas about the "glory" of earning rewards and God's dispensation in the case of Christ with the broader Christological rule about the attribution of all perfections to Christ to show why it especially bespeaks Christ's perfection to have merited these secondary rewards. In the *Scriptum*, rather, Thomas is content merely to observe that Christ decided to forego the perfections owed to his person and to take up the deficiencies of human nature, in order to merit their removal by God. He does not explain the significance or the basis of this decision in terms of his general Christology or his reflections about the value of meriting for telling us of the special dignity of the human person. Hence, while the early and the later Thomas will agree on the rewards of Christ for himself, they will differ in explaining the point of such merit. In the *Summa* the merit of Christ for himself will testify to Christ's perfection and Thomas's comments about this merit there will lend new depth to his description of the religious value of meriting in general. In the *Scriptum*, it remains a mystery why Christ should have merited or have decided to acquire these goods by his action. We do not learn from Thomas how meriting discloses in a new way the special dignity of the human person, who is capable of acquiring by his acts such perfections.[103]

In the third article of *In III* d. XVIII, Thomas turns to the problem of the

---

101 Thomas mentions in passing, without explanation, the dispensation of God due to which the secondary rewards of the beatific vision were delayed in the case of Christ in *In III* d. XVIII, a. 4, sol. IV.

102 Thomas articulates this Christological principle in *In III* d. XVIII, a. 3, sol.: "Christo attribuere debemus secundum animam omnem perfectionem spiritualem quae sibi potest attribui."

103 In this case, Peter Lombard too has failed to provide a rationale for such merit on Christ's part. All he says in this regard is that because Christ took up a passible soul and a mortal body, he "had" to merit impassibility and immortality. He does not speculate on why in fact Christ decided to do this or what this means for determining the value of merit. As I have suggested in the text, Thomas in this case has simply followed the tradition's claim that Christ merited without delving into the deeper ramifications of this claim. It is clear that he had the tools at hand to explore the claim. He knows the Christological "principle" regarding perfections. He acknowledges that God must have issued a special ordination in Christ's case to postpone the body's beatitude. And he knows of the "glory" of meriting something for oneself. But he does not exploit these tools to reveal to us the significance of merit, both the merit of Christ and that of others. As he will declare in the *Summa*, for Thomas it testifies to a greater perfection to make an active contribution through one's merit to one's own salvation.

locus of Christ's merit. He asks whether Christ merited in the first moment of his conception. The question, of course, is a school-question and may in fact seem to us somewhat arcane. However, there is considerable value in raising this question, and indeed Thomas will retain the question in *De Veritate* as well as in the later *Summa Theologiae*. By answering this question in the affirmative, Thomas is able to make at least two points about Christ's merit. First, he is able to show the value of Christ's actions before the Passion. Implied in the assertion that Christ merited in the first moment of his conception is the idea that Christ did merit before his death on the cross and that Christians have benefited from these earlier actions.[104] Second, Thomas is able to show the special dignity of Christ. It is beyond our normal experience that people merit from their very first moment of their existence. And yet Thomas is telling us here, it *is* appropriate to proclaim this of Christ. Christ differs from other people because he did merit from the first moment of his conception, and so clearly Christ is superior to others.

The objections to the third article advance an interesting array of arguments against Christ meriting in the first moment of his conception. Thus, the fourth objection draws an analogy with the *devil* to argue against Christ meriting in the first moment. Just as with merit, so sin involves the use of free choice. But the devil did not sin in the first moment of his conception. Otherwise God would have been guilty of creating the devil evil. Rather, God gave the devil being, and then the devil misused his freedom. Similarly, first God gave Christ being, and then Christ used his freedom, in this case for good.[105] The second objection rejects merit in this first moment because merit must cover more than a single moment. This is so because merit entails becoming aware of various courses of action available to the human person, deliberating about these courses of action and then opting for the action which is best for the person. All of this occurs not in a single moment but over a succession of moments, and so it is impossible for Christ to have merited in his conception.[106] The final

---

104 In *In III* d. XVIII, a. 3, Thomas is simply asking whether Christ merited in the first moment of his conception. He is not interested in specifying the beneficiaries of such merit, others or simply Christ alone. However, as we shall see in the sixth article of this distinction, Thomas does think that Christ's meritorious actions before the Passion were of value for others, although it was still necessary for Christ to merit for others by his death on the cross.

105 *In III* d. XVIII, a. 3 ob 4: "Sicut meritum est per liberum arbitrium, ita et peccatum. Sed diabolus non potuit peccare in primo instanti suae creationis. Ergo nec anima Christi in primo instanti suae creationis mereri potuit. Sed primum instans conceptionis fuit primum instans creationis animaea. Ergo in illo instanti mereri non potuit."

106 *In III* d. XVIII, a. 3 ob 2: "Opus meritorium cum deliberatione est, cum sit ex electione liberi arbitrii quae sequitur consilium. Sed deliberatio, cum sit quidam motus, requirit tempus. Ergo in instanti conceptionis mereri non potuit."

objection which must be noted here advances the infirmity of the infant body to dispute such a merit in the first moment. Meriting involves the use of the body both to provide the basic information about the courses of action available to free choice and to accomplish what the will desires. Hence since Christ's body in the first moment of his conception would have been incapable of performing his will or of giving information to the mind, it makes no sense to speak of a merit at the beginning of Christ's being.[107]

Nevertheless, in the *solutio* of this article, Thomas asserts that Christ in fact did merit in the first moment of his conception.[108] Thomas's analysis here falls into two parts. First, he announces the "Christological principle" which makes this affirmation appropriate. We must, Thomas states, attribute to Christ's soul every spiritual perfection which it is possible to ascribe to Christ. Hence, since it is more perfect for Christ to merit in this moment than not to merit, we must conclude that Christ could merit in the first moment of his conception. Secondly, Thomas reviews the various reasons why something might be impossible to an agent in the first moment of its being to show that none of these reasons need apply to Christ. Basically, there are three reasons why something may be impossible for a creature to do in the first moment of its existence. First, a creature may be

107 *In III* d. XVIII, a. 3 ob 5: "Christus quantum ad corpus, in pueritia similis erat aliis pueris. Sed alii pueri propter imbecillitatem organorum corporalium non habent perfectam imaginationem, nec usum liberi arbitrii; per consequens ergo nec Christus. Et ita tunc, ut videtur, mereri non potuit."

108 *In III* d. XVIII, a. 3 sol., reads as follows: "Christo attribuere debemus secundum animam, omnem perfectionem spiritualem quae sibi potest attribui. Unde, cum possibile sit ipsum in primo instanti suae conceptionis actum meritorium perfecisse, dicendum est Christum in primo instanti conceptionis meruisse. Quod enim aliqua res in primo instanti quo est non possit suam actionem habere, non potest contingere nisi tribus modis. Primo, ex hoc quod deest sibi aliqua perfectio quae requiritur ad agendum; sicut catulus in primo instanti suae nativitatis non potest videre, quia non habet organum videndi completum. Alio modo, propter aliquod impediens extrinsecum; sicut aqua generata in aliquo loco, conclusa ut non possit motu proprio moveri. Tertio, ex naturaa operationis quae successionem habet; et tunc in primo instanti quo res est, incipit illam actionem, non tamen illa actio est in illo instanti, sed in tempore; sicut patet quod primum instans in quo ignis est ignis, quod est ultimum instans suae generationis, est primum instans motus sui sursum; sed tamen eius non est in illo instanti, quia motus successivorum est. Constata autem quod in Christo non deficiebat aliqua perfectio ex parte ipsius agentis, quae est necessaria ad meritorium actum. Et iterum nihil erat quod impedire posset. Ipse etiam motus caritatis quo movebatur indivisibilis erat et non successivus; et ideo in ipso instanti mereri potuit." Thomas adds at the end of the *solutio* that an opposing view on this question is that in the first moment of his conception, Christ had merit only *in radice*, meaning that he had all which is necessary for merit (grace, charity, free choice), but did not use his freedom informed by grace in fact to merit until the next moment. Thomas concludes the *solutio* by stating that the first opinion *mihi magis placet* and says that his case against the second opinion will be made in the responses to the objections.

unable to do something because it lacks the perfection which makes such action possible. Hence, a newborn calf cannot see, although it eventually will see, because the calf lacks a completely formed organ of sight. Second, something may be prevented from acting because of an outside force. Thomas's example here is water which is prevented from flowing by being pent up. Third, a thing may be unable to do something because the act requires a number of successive moments. The example which Thomas gives here is a newly lit fire which after its ignition rises upward. When we enumerate these three reasons for the impossibility of an agent doing something in the first moment of its existence, says Thomas, it is clear that Christ could not have been affected by any of these problems. For one thing, in his first moment Christ possessed everything necessary for meriting. Christ was endowed with a will and free choice which were fully operative, and Christ possessed in this moment a fullness of the grace and charity needed to merit before God.[109] Moreover, it is incorrect to suggest that acting follows being if we mean by this a *temporal* succession. Acting does follow being but only in terms of a natural necessity. One must have the power to act, to act.[110] But Christ had the power to act and so could act meritoriously in his first moment. Secondly, Thomas simply rejects the idea that Christ could have been prevented from doing the good in his first moment and so prevented from meriting by something extrinsic, in the way that a dam prevents water from flowing. Thomas dismisses the suggestion here brusquely, saying only that "nihil erat quod impedire posset." Probably implicit here is the idea that all things in this world stand under the dominion of Christ, the Second Adam. And, finally, Thomas rejects the third argument against Christ meriting in the first moment of his being because such merit would require a succession of moments. For Thomas, Christ's charity, the principle of merit, was indivisible, and Christ experienced his love for God immediately in his creation. Hence in his first moment, Christ merited by acting as God wills all people to act, in loving God as his first act.

Thomas experiences little difficulty in meeting the objections originally raised against such merit. For example, he simply rejects the analogy between Christ and the devil. As created, rational beings are set on God. They naturally desire God as the completion of their being. This is the condition in which the devil was originally created. But when the devil came to use

---

109 In addition to the *solutio* Thomas makes this claim in *In III* d. XVIII, a. 3 ad 3: "Illud quod Christus habuit in primo instanti suae conceptionis, scilicet meritum, et ab alio habuit, scilicet inquantum ad meritum exigitur gratia, et a seipso habuit, inquantum meritum procedit ex libero arbitrio. Non enim semper necessarium est ut causa causatum tempore praecedat, sed quandoque sufficit quod praecedat natura." It is because he was conceived in grace and endowed with a fully operative free choice that Christ could merit in the first moment of his conception.

110 Thomas makes this point in *In III* d. XVIII, a. 3 ad 1: "Esse est prius quam agere natura, non tempore de necessitate."

his freedom, he did not act in accordance with this natural desire for God. Rather, he acted for his own ends and so sinned: Natural desire and first act were in discord. This is not the case with Christ, who did not sin—created for God and to will God, when created Christ's first act was to love God, that is, to act in the way appropriate to rational being.[111] While this response focuses on Christ as the perfect human who acts in the way in which all people should act—that is, as God wills them to act, in accordance with the "laws" of their being as established for them by God—his responses to the other two objections which I noted earlier focus rather on the distinctiveness and superiority of Christ as human. To the fifth objection, which had denied merit to Christ in the first moment of his conception because Christ's body could not be of service to the soul, which is required in meriting, Thomas observes the difference between Christ's knowledge and ours. We learn of the courses of action open to us through the evidence initiated by the senses. Thus we can only fully act when the organs of the body come to maturity. Christ's knowledge, on the other hand, was *infused*, given to him apart from the evidence of the senses and the work of the imagination and intellect. Thus, for Christ to merit did not require the help of his body. He could express his love for God without such information.[112] The distinctiveness of Christ also allows Thomas to answer the second objection, which had noted the deliberation and counsel which are normally required for merit: The argument had been that since discovering the various courses of action open to a person, considering them, and then opting for one must occur not in a single moment but over successive moments, we cannot speak of a merit in a "single" moment. In response, Thomas notes that Christ did not have to deliberate or take counsel over various courses of action. By the perfection of his knowledge, Christ was certain about the correct course of action to follow. Thus, knowing what he should do, he simultaneously did it. He loved God and so he merited.[113]

111 *In III* d. XVIII, a. 3 ad 4: "Motus voluntatis in bonum finem, est sibi naturalis; unde in primo instanti creationis suae potest habere motum in bonum finem, quia ad finem naturaliter desideratum appetendum non indigemus deliberatione; et in hoc potest esse meritum. Sed peccatum contingit ex hoc quod voluntas movetur in aliquid quod non competit fini naturaliter desiderato; unde oprtet quod contingat ex falsa collatione illius ad finem. Et ideo requiritur ad peccatum collatio eius quod habet apparentem bonitatem ad id quod est per se bonum naturaliter desideratum."

112 *In III* d. XVIII, a. 3 ad 5: "Christus non habebat acceptam a sensibus scientiam, sed infusam. Et ita habitus scientiae perfectae poterat esse etiam cum infirmitate organorum. Et iterum dictum est quod infirmitas corporis in ipso non refundebatur in mentem, sicut nec gloria mentis corporis infirmitatem tollebat. Et ideo imperfectio organorum corporalium usum mentis non tollebat in ipso."

113 *In III* d. XVIII, a. 3 ad 2: "In Christo non exigebatur deliberatio etiam quantum ad ea quae sunt ad finem, quia de his certus erat." In the first part of this response, Thomas also mentions that Christ was determined to the end of loving God and knew that he should do so *and* in fact did so. Christ

The third article, therefore, establishes that Christ merited before the Passion. While this article thus grants to Christ's earlier works saving significance, it raises in turn a rather serious problem. If Christ has merited for himself by his pre-Passion acts, why did he have to undergo the Passion and thereby merit? Is not the Passion in this way rendered superfluous, at least with regard to Christ's merit for himself? Thomas, of course, is convinced of the necessity of the Passion and thinks that this act adds to the merit of Christ. Thus in the fifth article of *In III* d. XVIII, Thomas takes up the question of the merit of the passion in order to show the value of this merit for Christ himself; in the sixth article, he will continue his discussion of the merit of Christ by showing how the Passion especially works for the salvation of others. The question treated in the fifth article is ultimately of broader application than Christ alone. For Thomas, any act which merits condignly establishes a right to eternal reward. By the one act, absolutely considered, one has a right to heaven and one does not need to acquire a "mass of merits" to storm the gates of heaven. But if one merit absolutely taken merits heaven, why then bother to do additional meritorious actions? What significance can these additional acts have? By answering the question raised by Christ's merit through the Passion, Thomas is thus able to argue for the value of our continuous efforts to do good as God wills and for God's sake.

To show the need for the merit of the Passion for Christ (that is, the need for additional merits by which impassivity, immortality, and exaltation are gained), Thomas again adopts a strategy favored in this distinction. He announces a "definition" of merit and then on this basis shows the added value of the Passion.[114] In the *solutio*, Thomas says that meriting means

truly acted as God wills people to act. For this idea, see also ad 4 of this article, cited in note 111 above, and *In III* d. XVIII, a. 2 ad 5, discussed in note 85 above.

114 *In III* d. XVIII, a. 5 sol., reads as follows: "Mereri, sicut dictum est, est facere aliquid sibi debitum. Hoc autem contingit tribus modis. Uno modo, quando aliquis facit de non debito debitum; sicut aliquis primo motu caritatis meretur vitam aeternam, faciens eam debitam sibi, quae prius ei debita non erat. Alio modo, quod erat minus debitum faciendo sibi magis debitum: quod contingit in eo quod caritas augetur. Tertio modo contingit, quando aliquid quod est uno modo debitum sibi, facit alio modo debitum sibi; sicut puer baptizatus cui debetur vita aeterna ex habitu gratiae in baptismo infusae, quando usum liberi arbitrii habere incipit, facit sibi debitam eam ex actu. Primo igitur modo Christus meruit in primo instanti suae conceptionis claritatem corporis: quae quidem non erat ei debita neque ex conditione naturae in se consideratae, neque consequebatur ex necessitate unionis, sicut gloria fruitionis, ut dictum est. Secundo autem modo Christus mereri non potuit, quia caritas non est augmentata in Christo. Tertio modo meruit in omnibus actibus suis post primum instans suae conceptionis, quia fecit sibi debitum aliquibus actibus quod prius ex aliis actibus debebatur. Actus autem quo quis meretur, est ille cuius agens est dominus, ut dictum est supra, et qui est proportionatus mercedi. Est autem homo dominus suorum actuum per voluntatem, quam

to make something owed to a person which previously was not owed. He adds that there are three ways in which "something which is not owed" is made owed to a person. First, there is the obvious case in which someone who utterly lacks a right to something by his action has acquired a right to that reward. The critical example here is the case of the newly justified person, who establishes a merit deserving of heaven with his first act done in the state of grace. Second, we can speak of the person who has a right to a reward and whose additional action makes him even more deserving of that reward. In the present article, Thomas gives the example of the increase of charity. A person who possesses charity merits more charity by doing acts which dispose him more adequately for his deepened possession of this virtue. Finally, "to make something owed" can be taken to mean that one increases one's right to a particular reward. Hence, Thomas says in the present article, by one act someone obtains the right to heaven or to some other supernatural reward, and by other acts establishes further rights to this same reward. This person is now "owed" heaven on several counts because by several meritorious acts this person has created a number of "claims" to this reward. To apply this to the question posed in this article, the value of Christ's merit for himself in the Passion, it is clear that neither the first nor the second way of "making something owed" pertains to Christ's merit for himself in the Passion. With regard to the first way of making something owed to oneself, Christ has already merited for himself impassivity and immutability from the first moment of his conception, and so the merit of the Passion does not absolutely establish a right to these rewards. But neither can Christ increase his charity and so make something owed to himself in the second way. Because Christ always enjoyed the beatific vision, one aspect of which is perfect charity, it was impossible that he increase his charity by his acts. But the third way of speaking of "making something owed" to himself does apply to Christ. By the merits of his life before the Passion, Christ has established a right to the rewards which Thomas wishes Christ to acquire for himself—immortality, impassivity, and exaltation before others. Yet, by the merit of the Passion, Christ has "increased" his right to these rewards, by doing an additional act out of love—dying for our sins—which adds to his "claims" to these rewards. Thus, with regard to his merit for himself, the Passion is not superfluous, for through it he becomes even more deserving of immortality, impassivity, and exaltation before all.[115]

quia caritas perficit in ordine ad ultimum finem, ideo actum fini proportionatum facit, scilicet beatitudini quae proprie est merces nostrorum meritorum. Et ideo omnis actus voluntarius caritate informatus, meritorius est. Cum igitur Christus passionem suam voluntarie sustinuerit, *oblatus enim est quia voluit*, Is., LIII, 7, et voluntas ista caritate fuerit informata, non est dubium quod per passionem suam meruerit." See also note 82 above for Thomas's assertions in this distinction about the relations between merit and justice and "making something owed" to oneself through one's merits.

115 In addition to the *solutio*, see also *In III* d. XVIII, a. 5 ad 2: "Non oportet quod

Talk about "making something owed" to oneself has a somewhat mercenary ring to it, however, and so Thomas has worked into his discussion of Christ's merit for himself some reflections on the intent of his teaching about merit. The first objection of this article had rejected the merit of the passion for Christ himself precisely because it would seem to be superfluous. The argument here seems to be that it is unnecessary to try to merit after establishing a right to a particular reward. After all, just as a person has once paid the price for a particular item, and so "deserves" it, it is unnecessary and redundant to pay the price again.[116] Thus, since Christ from the first moment of his conception had paid the price for immortality and the other rewards which he merited for himself, he did not have to merit these rewards by the Passion, that is, pay the price again for these rewards. In his response to this objection, Thomas simply rejects the analogy between meriting and purchasing goods in a store. In buying, the purpose of one's action is to obtain the thing which you are buying. In meriting, however, the purpose of the meritorious act is *not* to obtain the reward due this act, but rather to act in accordance with the good of charity (. . . *sed propter bonum caritatis*). Now, charity means to will good for others, and thus one who wills by Christian charity seeks to fulfill the will of God.

faciat sibi magis debitum, quia hoc est secundum intensionem caritatis quae est radix merendi; sed facit sibi pluribus modis debitum."

In one of the responses to objections in this article, Thomas returns to the need for *voluntary* action for merit to occur. The fourth objection had argued that Christ's *passio* could not have been meritorious because a person merits by doing something ("acting"), not by "undergoing" something, by simply suffering it (the literal meaning of *passio*). In ad 4, Thomas makes the point which he had elsewhere made about the sufferings of the saints (see note 20 above). Suffering is meritorious only because it is freely and willingly accepted by the will and done for the sake of God: "Passio, inquantum passio, non est meritoria, quia sic principium eius est extra; sed est meritoria inquantum est acceptata per voluntatem, sic enim est voluntaria, et principium eius est intra." Thomas also makes the observation that Christ had to accept willingly the suffering which he underwent for merit to occur in ad 3: "Quamvis passio sit in corpore, tamen voluntas acceptans passionem fuit in anima."

As I indicated earlier, the present article is of broader application than Christ alone. It tells us why people should continue to do good and thereby increase their merit before God. By their additional acts, they establish new "rights" to the reward of eternal life which their other merits have also deserved. Note, however, that the parallel between Christ and others is not wholly complete. Since Christ's charity was always perfect, his merits did not increase this charity. But given the imperfection of the charity of others, their acts not only increase the right to eternal life, they also merit the increase of charity and grace (in the way indicated in *In II* d. XXVIII, q. I, a. 5 sol.).

116 *In III* d. XVIII, a. 5 ob 1: "Mereri enim est aliquid sibi debitum facere. Sed qui sibi semel aliquid debitum fecit, puta emendo, non ulterius emit illud. Ergo et qui meretur aliquid semel, ulterius non potest mereri illud. Sed Christus ab instanti conceptionis meruit sibi ea quae dicta sunt. Ergo per passionem nihil sibi meruit."

The Christian wants to do what God wills him to do, and this is to act in accordance with God's will for him. Thus, says Thomas in the present article, even if there were no rewards attached to good moral action, the Christian by charity would still act as he does, simply to please God and to pursue God's good. What this means, then, is that even though by one meritorious act the Christian has established a right to a supernatural reward, the Christian will not stop with this one act and rest on his laurels. Since the purpose of Christian acting is not the accruing of merits but the service of God, the Christian will continue to do good in order to serve God, to do God's will. And since by God's promise, God has ordered good actions to their appropriate rewards, by doing God's will the Christian increases his merit before God, even though, as we have seen, this is not the purpose of doing the acts which are meritorious. Hence, in Christ's case, Christ did not stop with the merits of his life before the Passion. In conformity with God's will for him, Christ died on the cross, thereby also enhancing his right to the reward which his earlier works had won for him.[117]

In the final article of this distinction, Thomas seeks to establish the value of the merit of Christ, not for Christ, but for other people. As was the fourth article, the sixth article is divided into a series of quaestiunculae. In the three quaestiunculae of *In III* d. XVIII, a. 6, Thomas asks in turn whether Christ could merit for others (qc. I), whether some obtained heaven apart from Christ's merit for them (qc. II), and whether all of Christ's actions, not just the Passion, were meritorious of heaven for others (qc. III). The question of Christ's merit for others, of course, had been raised earlier in the *Scriptum*. Thus, the present article is designed to complete the teaching about Christ's relation to others first noted in the *ex professo* treatment of merit, *In II* d. XXVII, q. I, a. 6.[118]

---

117 *In III* d. XVIII, a. 5 ad 1: "Emptio principaliter est propter habendam rem quae emitur; et ideo postquam semel empta est, ulterius non emitur. Sed actio qua quis meretur non est principaliter propter praemium consequendum, sed propter bonum caritatis. Unde homo habens caritatem operaretur etiamsi nulla retributio sequeretur; unde etiam postquam meruit aliquid operatur; et id quod primo sibi uno modo debebatur, postea alio modo sibi debetur." See also note 20 above, in which I observe Thomas's conviction about the "selflessness" of charity and the concomitant notion that one does not do merit in order to win heaven; one does the good to please God, in the process also meriting or deserving God as one's reward.

118 *In III* d. XVIII, a. 6, qc. I ob 3, in fact, trades on part of the teaching of *In II* d. XXVII, q. I, a. 6. In the earlier article, Thomas had stated that while Christ could condignly merit for others, ordinary Christians could merit for others congruently. The present objection has conveniently forgotten Thomas's earlier statement about Christ's condign merit for others and focuses on the claim that people can merit for others only congruently: "Christus non meruit secundum quod Deus, sed secundum quod homo habens caritatem. Sed unus homo habens caritatem non meretur alteri nisi e congruo: quod non est per se loquendo meritum." Note again the observation that congruent merit is not "really" merit; on this, see note 55 above.

Thomas's principal goal in the sixth article is to demonstrate both that Christ could merit for others and that the merit of the Passion was especially necessary in this regard. In the first quaestiuncula of the article, the most telling objection against Christ's merit for others would seem to be that such a merit would deny the *personal* quality of merit. Throughout the *Scriptum* and especially in the present distinction, we have seen that merit is a matter between two persons. One person does a good deed which another person, God, rewards. It is because merit involves two persons that Thomas speaks of merit as governed by justice. Justice governs inter-personal relations and requires that there be two partners in a transaction; we do not speak of "justice" in a single person.[119] Now, speaking of Christ's merit for others would seem to offend against this basic idea involved in merit and justice: Rather than God rewarding a person for what that person has done, we would now have to speak of God rewarding a person, not for what he has done, but for what Christ, another person, has done for him.[120] Similarly, the notion of meriting for another would also seem to offend against another important idea in merit, that in rewarding merits God is rewarding what a person has freely and voluntarily done. In this case, the reward would be for something which the person in fact has not done at all, freely or otherwise.[121]

Nevertheless, Thomas does believe that Christ could and did merit for other people.[122] In the *solutio* of the first quaestiuncula, Thomas has

---

119   In a strict sense, we do not speak of justice in a single person. However, Thomas is willing to allow for a "metaphorical" justice in a single person, as when we say that the different "parts" of the soul observe the correct order and hierarchy. Thomas invokes this metaphorical justice when explaining the transformation wrought by God's grace in justification (= making just). Normally, however, justice is between two distinct persons.

120   *In III* d. XVIII, a. 6, qc. I ob 2: "Ezech., XVIII, 4, dicitur: 'Anima quae peccaverit, ipsa morietur.' Ergo eadem ratione anima quae operabitur ipsa praemiabitur; et ita videtur quod Christus nobis mereri non potuit." Again, as in *In III* d. XVIII, a. 3 ob 4, Thomas has drawn an analogy between merit and reward, and sin and punishment. The analogy is frequent throughout the Thomistic corpus.

121   *In III* d. XVIII, a. 6, qc. I ob 1: "Sicut enim laus requirit voluntarium, ita et meritum. Sed propter hoc quod laus requirit voluntarium in laudato, ideo unus non laudatur propter actum alterius. Ergo similiter nec unus alteri mereri potest; et sic Christus nihil nobis meruit."

122   *In III* d. XVIII, a. 6 sol. I, reads as follows: "Sicut dicit Damascenus . . . 'caro Christi et anima erat quasi instrumentum Divinitatis.' Unde quamvis esset alia operatio Dei et hominis, tamen operatio humana habebat in se vim Divinitatis sicut instrumentum agit vi principalis agentis. Et propter hoc dicit Damascenus quod 'ea quae hominis sunt, supra hominem agebat.' Unde et actio Christi meritoria, quamvis esset actio humana, tamen agebat in virtute divina; et ideo erat potens supra totam naturam; quod non poterat esse de aliqua operatione puri hominis quia homo singularis est minus dignus quam natura communis. . . . Inde est quod meritum Christi, quod ad naturam se extendebat, etiam ad singulos se extendere poterat. Et ita aliis mereri potuit."

recourse to the Damascene's description of the humanity of Christ to make his point. The humanity of Christ is the "instrument of the divinity." In the first article of this distinction, Thomas had been concerned to show that in addition to his "divine" action, there is a human action in Christ, and indeed it is on this basis that Thomas is able to argue in the remainder of the distinction for the merit of Christ. Christ could merit because there was an action in Christ which was distinctively human. In the present use of the Damascene's words, Thomas is not retracting this claim about the autonomy of Christ's human action. Rather, he is referring to the peculiar ontological status of Jesus Christ to reveal why Christ's human actions have special value. It is because the humanity of Christ is joined to the divinity and is in perfect harmony with it that the actions of Christ as man have the greatest value. The way that Thomas puts it in the present *solutio* is that by the power of the divinity, the actions of Christ the man have "power over the entire race." Whereas "mere" men can merit only for themselves, Christ as the instrument of the divinity merits not only for his own person but for the entire nature which he has assumed. The greater extent of Christ's merit is the upshot of the incarnation and the intimacy of divine and human in Christ. Since he is who he is, Christ can merit for people what they otherwise would be unable to obtain.[123]

In the second response of this quaestiuncula, Thomas makes some additional comments which help us to grasp why Christ's merits are able to have "power over the entire nature." The second objection had rejected Christ's meriting for others on the grounds that a person should suffer, and benefit, only for what he has himself done. Meriting for others offends against the "personal" quality of merit.[124] In the second response, Thomas agrees with the objection that merit *is* a personal category, but continues by observing how Christ and other people in fact constitute one "person." By virtue of the incarnation, Christ has been designated the head of all humanity and especially of those who are to be saved. Thus, the action of the head of this person, merit before God, can be transferred to the other members of this person.[125] What Thomas has done here is to introduce an

---

123 In addition to the *solutio* of qc. I, see also *In III* d. XVIII, a. 6, qc. I ad 1: "Christum mereri pro alio dicitur dupliciter. Aut ita quod ipse mereatur loco alterius, idest quod pertinet ad aliud ut mereatur; et sic Christus pro aliis non meruit, quia meritum oportet quod procedat ex voluntate merentis. . . . Aut ita quod ipse aliquid alteri mereatur quod sub merito illius non cadit; et sic Christus aliis meruit ea quae ipsi sibi mereri non potuerunt." In the *solutio* to the third quaestiuncula of this article, Thomas will specify what it is that Christ alone could merit for all: the right to enter heaven. For another text which ties the "infinity" of Christ's merit to his divine nature, see *In III* d. XIII, q. I, a. 2, qc. II ad 4.

124 This text is quoted in note 120 above.

125 *In III* d. XVIII, a. 6, qc. I ad 2: "Membra et caput ad eamdem personam pertinent; unde cum Christus fuerit caput nostrum propter Divinitatem et gratiae plenitudinem in alios redundantem, nos autem simus membra eius,

idea which will be further developed and displayed more prominently in
the *Summa*. In the *Summa*, Thomas will speak of Christ having been
ordained by God to be the head of all humanity, the principal means of
salvation. On the basis of this ordination, God has become incarnate in
Christ and granted Christ the habitual grace by whose power Christ's
works can have saving efficacy for all. Although Thomas does not refer in
the *Scriptum* to God's ordination regarding Christ and relate Christ's merit
to it, the other basic elements of the later teaching are nevertheless
present. By the grace of union, God and man are one in Jesus Christ, and
by the habitual grace which accompanies this union, the acts of Jesus
Christ are able to extend to all, for Christ's grace is designed to merit for
others as well. All Thomas will have to do in the *Summa* to complete the
picture of the merit of Christ is to subject these basic elements of his
understanding of the merit of Christ to his mature teaching on the divine
ordination which grounds merit.[126]

Having established in the first quaestiuncula that Christ could merit
for others on the basis of the union with God and Christ's status as the
head of the mystical body, in the second quaestiuncula Thomas asks about
the *extent* of this merit: Did Christ have to merit for others what he merits,
or have some been saved/attained God apart from Christ's merit? In raising
the question, Thomas is thinking especially of the Old Testament patriarchs who seemed to have entered paradise without the benefit of Christ's
merit on their behalf. Since they seemed to have obtained heaven before

---

meritum suum non est extraneum a nobis, sed in nos redundat propter
unitatem corporis mystici." See also the first *sed contra* of this quaestiuncula:
"Christus, secundum quod homo, est caput nostrum. Ergo nobis aliquid
influit. Sed nonnisi meritorie. Ergo Christus nobis aliquid meruit."

126   Indeed, the absence of the *ordinatio* as the ground of merit in the *Scriptum*
is the principal way in which the teaching of the *Scriptum* differs from that
in the *Summa*. With this exception, the details of the two treatments of the
merit of Christ are in fundamental agreement.

Given his statements in this distinction about the "infinite" value of the
merit of Christ because of the intimacy of the divine and human in the person
of Christ and the "perfect" grace of Christ, one might have expected Thomas
to argue here that, whatever the case in the merit of other people, in the case
of Christ's merit *commutative* justice does prevail. Recall that earlier in the
Scriptum, Thomas argued that commutative justice could not be involved in
merit and reward because such a justice entails an equality of quantity
between the merit and reward. As I noted in the first section of this chapter,
in the *Scriptum* Thomas does not envision the grace of the ordinary Christian
establishing such an equality. But one feature of his discussion of Christ is
the insistence on the tremendous value of what Christ does and especially
the power of his grace. It seems to me, therefore, that in the *Scriptum* Thomas
could have read Christ's merit at least in terms of commutative justice. That
he failed to do so is probably to be ascribed to his desire to maintain an
equilibrium between Christ's merit and that of others, as well as to a lapse
in the young systematician. He has simply failed to see the implications of
his claims about the grace of Christ.

Christ merited, this suggests that Christ's merit, while valuable for some, is not necessary for all.[127] In the *solutio* to the second quaestiuncula Thomas frames his answer around the consideration of what it means to say that by merit the "doors of heaven have been opened" so that people can in fact attain God.[128] The gates of heaven were shut to people by sin, by original sin, in the first place, which continues to infect human nature and thereby disqualify the possessors of this nature from heaven, and by actual sin, the sins which each person commits through his own volition. Thus, for the gates of heaven to be opened these two obstacles, original sin and personal sin, must be removed. For Thomas, the obstacle created by personal sin can be "removed" by not sinning. By being firm in the good and refraining from sinning, someone can merit entry into heaven. This, in fact, was the case with the patriarchs.[129] And yet, before Christ, no one, including the patriarchs, could enter the heavenly paradise, because the major obstacle still had to be overcome. Since the nature of all is sullied by original sin, original sin must be removed before people can come to God. Christ alone can remove original sin and establish a right to God on behalf of the entire nature. For, as we have seen, by virtue of the divinity, Christ's acts have power over the entire nature and Christ has been designated the head of all who are saved. Hence it was that only after Christ did his work that anyone could be saved, whatever their personal merits.

The value of this quaestiuncula lies in Thomas's ability to make the case for the centrality of Christ's merit without thereby denying the value of, or

---

127 In *In III* d. XVIII, a. 6, qc. II ob 1, Thomas mentions that Enoch and Elias had entered paradise before Christ and apart from Christ's work; in ob 2, he refers to the *antiqui patres*. Note that Thomas distinguishes in this quaestiuncula between two paradises, an earthly one and a heavenly paradise; see ad 1. He is willing to allow that Enoch and Elias merited entry to the earthly paradise but denies that apart from Christ's merit (for the reason noted shortly in the text) that they could enter the heavenly paradise.

128 *In III* d. XVIII, a. 6 sol. II, reads as folllows: "Sicut clausio ianuae est obstaculum prohibens ab ingressu domus; ita per similitudinem dicitur ianua paradisi clausa, inquantum est aliquod obstaculum prohibens ab introitu paradisi. Obstaculum autem potest esse duplex: unum ex parte personae, quod est per peccatum actuale; aliud ex parte naturae, quod est per peccatum originale. Primum quidem obstaculum non est commune omnibus, sed tantum peccatoribus; sed secundum obstaculum est omnibus commune. Et hoc quidem obstaculum auferri non potuit nisi per eum cuius operatio in totam naturam potuit, scilicet Christum. Et ideo ipse nobis quantum ad hoc apertionem ianuae meruit, quae per peccatum primi hominis toti vitiatae naturae clausa erat." In using the phrase *ianuae apertio*, Thomas is simply following Peter Lombard's own usage; the latter speaks of the "doors of heaven" having been closed to people through sin and reopened through Christ's work.

129 *In III* d. XVIII, a. 6, qc. II ad 2: "Antiqui patres meruerunt introitum paradisi quantum ad id quod personae est, sicut et nos; tamen quod removeretur impedimentum quod erat ex parte naturae, mereri non potuerunt; et ideo semper remanebat eis ianua clausa."

the need for, people meriting for themselves. Quite clearly, Christ's merit stands as the basis of the salvation of all. Only by establishing the right of the entire human nature to a reward from God and by removing original sin do people have the real possibility of coming to God. And yet the establishing of the possibility of salvation for those who possess this nature does not therefore mean that everyone will be saved. Attaining God also involves each person acting correctly and meriting before God. Coming to God means each person acting in such a way that he deserves to come to God, by employing the grace made available to him by God through the actions of Christ, the grace, which enables him to act as God wills him to act. To the right of the *nature* established by Christ before God, the individual must add the right of his *person* before God, through the good acts which he freely does by God's grace.[130]

In the third quaestiuncula of the sixth article, Thomas finally comes to the problem which had been raised in acute form by the earlier assertion (a. 3) that from the first moment of his conception Christ merited. If Christ merited various rewards by his acts before the Passion, was the merit of the Passion superfluous? Or is it the case that Christ's pre-Passion acts were meritorious only for himself, while the Passion merited not for himself but for others. In the earlier discussion of what Christ merited for himself, it was not evident whether Christ's actions before the Passion also availed for others. From what he has written in the first two quaestiunculae of this article, it is not too difficult to grasp why Thomas believes the merit of the Passion to have been crucial for the salvation of others.[131] To come to God,

130 *In III* d. XVIII, a. 6, qc. II ad 3: "Quamvis remotum sit impedimentum quod ex parte naturae est per Christum, tamen oportet quod per actum meritorium efficiatur homini paradisus debitus quantum ad id quod est personae; et ideo oportet quod homo agat ad hoc ut paradisum intrare mereatur." I think that Thomas's analysis of the need for personal merit for those *in* the state of grace is, on the whole, acceptable. I have indicated, however, my profound misgivings about his teaching in the *Scriptum* with regard to the relation of the merit of Christ and the conversion of the sinner in the first section of this chapter; see the discussion of *In II* d. XXVII, q. I, a. 6. The case of the sinner doing good and therefore benefiting from Christ's merit and that of the justified person doing good and therefore "adding" personal merits to the merit of Christ differ because in the latter case, the meritorious acts of the justified *presuppose* the *grace* of Christ—the justified can merit because he has grace—and so merit here testifies to one's indebtedness to God in Christ. In the former case, on the other hand, the good works of the sinner which allow the sinner to benefit from Christ's work testify not to Christ's grace present in the sinner, but to the need for the human person to take the decisive step in human salvation. *Once* this step is taken by one's own initiative, then the rest—God's gift of grace, and more good acts now done in grace and so fully meritorious—will naturally follow. The former case asserts human responsibility, but in the process arguably derogates from the centrality of Christ in salvation.

131 *In III* d. XVIII, a. 6 sol. III, reads as follows: "Obstaculum quod ianuam paradisi claudebat, ut dictum est, fuit peccatum totam naturam inficiens. Et

the impediment of original sin had to be removed. Original sin disqualifies human nature from God's presence, and so it was necessary that Christ, the instrument of the divinity, establish the right to salvation on behalf of the entire nature before God. Moreover, the act by which this right is established for the nature is most fittingly the death of the just man. By original sin, all must die; this is the punishment owed to human nature for original sin. But since Christ did not assume original sin along with his human nature, he stood under no obligation to die. He was truly just. Hence, when Christ freely and without necessity died on the cross, by his act he overcame original sin and established the right of the entire nature to salvation from God. Thus, Christ's death on the cross is meritorious in a way that his earlier acts were not, for it goes to the very heart of the problem facing people who wish to come to God. The passion alone removes the obstacle of original sin and opens the gates of heaven to those who possess human nature. And yet Thomas adds in the conclusion of this quaestiuncula, we must not think that Christ's acts before the Passion were meritorious only for himself and not also for us. In the case of certain rewards which Christ merited earlier for himself such as immortality and impassivity, it is true that they are of benefit for Christ alone. But with regard to the other reward which Christ merits for himself, this also has significance for us. When Christ merited for himself exaltation before other creatures, he merited to be revealed to the world as the principal means by which God saves the world. Thus, Thomas says in the present *solutio*, although by his earlier acts Christ did not merit heaven for others, by these earlier acts Christ did merit "conversion to himself," for through these acts he was declared to be the savior of all. Thus, those who wish to be saved must now turn to Christ in order to embark on the journey to God.

C. Hope and Merit

When compared to the treatment of hope in the *Summa Theologiae* (to be discussed in detail in Chapter 3), the discussion of hope in the *Scriptum* displays significant differences. In the first place, Thomas organizes the discussion of hope differently. In the *Summa Theologiae*, Thomas separates the analysis of the passion of hope from that of the virtue of the same name. The former he treats in the Prima Secundae (I-II 40), in the context of the discussion of the "irascible" passions or emotions of the sensitive soul, the latter he analyzes in the Secunda Secundae, in the course of his examination of the theological virtues (II-II 17–22). In this regard, Thomas works into the discussion of the theological virtue of hope the related questions on the "vices" opposed to this virtue, despair and presumption,

---

ideo quia peccatum per satisfactionem tolllitur, nec satisfactio potuit congrue aliter fieri . . . nisi per passionem Christi; ideo per passionem ipsius tantum aperta est nobis janua et non per alia quae prius operatus est. Tamen per alia quae prius operatus est meruit nobis conversionem ad ipsum, inquantum meruit se nobis manifestari, per quam nos proficimus et non ipse."

as well as the description of the "gift of the Spirit" which perfects this virtue, fear. In the *Scriptum*, on the other hand, Thomas has been content to follow Peter Lombard's order in discussing hope. Thus, he discusses hope where Peter does, in terms of the question of whether *Christ* had hope (*In III* d. XXVI), and treats the passion and the virtue of hope in quick succession (q. I and II, respectively). Correspondingly, as had Peter, Thomas discusses the vices opposed to hope, despair and presumption, in isolation from that of the virtue of hope, at the end of Book II,[132] in the context of the sins against the Holy Spirit and, similarly, delays analysis of the gift of fear until later in Book III (d. XXXIV, q. II). Thus, the discussion of hope in the two works bears a significantly different appearance.

Yet there is a more profound distinction between the analyses of hope in the two works. Not only does Thomas organize the discussion differently, he also depicts the structure of hope somewhat differently in these works. It is safe to say that in the *Summa* and in the *Scriptum* Thomas has provided materially the same definition of hope—hope looks to a *future* good (beatitude, the vision of God) which is *arduous* yet *possible* of attainment.[133] But his understanding of the third aspect of the object of hope, the good as *possible*, has undergone modification in the later work. For Thomas in the *Summa*, beatitude is possible precisely because of the God who is effectively involved in human life—transforming, redirecting, and sustaining human life in its movement to its proper and ultimate end, God. In other words, in the *Summa*, Thomas has discerned a second way in which hope refers to God. First, as in the *Scriptum*, God is the final end of hope, for the vision of God in his essence is the goal to which hope aspires. But second, God is the source of hope, not only in the obvious sense that as a theological virtue, hope is infused by God, but in the more personal sense that hope "knows" God and refers to God as present and active in the existence and actions of the individual, bringing the individual to God. In the treatise on hope in this later work, Thomas has expressed this perception of the ground of hope and the possibility of attaining salvation by asserting that there is in fact a *twofold* object of hope—hope both looks to future beatitude (God as end) and to God who graciously makes possible in contact with the individual the attainment of the first object of hope.

In the *Scriptum*, on the other hand, Thomas has been content to assert only one object of the virtue of hope, God as the future good to which hope tends. In the earlier work, the possibility of hope is established on different

132   In the discussion of despair and presumption at the end of the second book of his commentary, Thomas makes little if any effort to relate despair and presumption to hope. In *In III* d. XXVI, q. II, a. 2 ad 2, Thomas has briefly mentioned in the treatise on hope that despair and presumption are opposed to hope. However, this mention in passing falls rather short of the extensive treatment of these vices in the *Summa*'s treatise on hope.

133   Thomas refers to these "notes" of hope in such texts as *In III* d. XXVI, q. II, a. 2 sol. and ad 2. The *Summa* refers to these aspects of hope in such texts as II-II 17, 1c.

grounds than in the *Summa*. In the *Scriptum*, Thomas does not ascribe the possibility of the possessor of hope reaching the hoped-for end explicitly to the God who is effectively involved in the life of the individual and moving the individual to this end. Rather, "possibility" is discussed in more general, less personal and immediate terms. The future good desired by people transcends human capacity, just as God transcends humanity. Yet hope is based, as it were, on faith, which reveals that God has provided the means to bridge the gap between God and people: We know that by grace it is possible to come to the vision of God. Thus, in this light, when Thomas in the *Scriptum* discusses the possibility of hope, he refers not directly to God actively involved in individual human existence but to the *facultas*, the grace added on to human nature, which God has provided to mankind to allow this attainment of God.[134] Because of this failure to consider "God as

---

134   See, e.g., *In III* d. XXVI, q. II, a. 2 sol.: ". . . quia est aliquod arduum quod excedit facultatem naturae ad quod homo per gratiam potest pervenire, scilicet ipse Deus, inquantum est nostra beatitudo; ideo oportet quod ex aliquo dono gratuito naturae superaddito fiat inclinatio in illud arduum. Et illud donum est habitus spei." Later in this same passage, Thomas calls this grace which gives rise to hope, a *facultas* coming from God. He glosses this *facultas* in two ways. First, it can refer to the gratuitous gift which is habitual grace and the theological virtues, including hope. But, second, it can refer to God's *liberalitas* in general, for it is because God has established a general structure by which salvation is possible that we can attain God and so hope to reach God. For further mention of this *facultas*, see also a. 4, *solutio*: "Quia enim spes supponit facultatem in finem perveniendi quae quidem est ex liberalitate divina et ex meritis, secundum quae omnes virtutes in finem ultimum perveniunt; ideo certitudo spei causatur ex liberalitate divina ordinante nos in finem et etiam ex inclinatione omnium aliarum virtutum et etiam ex inclinatione ipsius habitus; et ideo praeter certitudinem quam habet ut quaedam virtus, includit certitudinem quae est in omnibus aliis virtutibus et ulterius certitudinem divinae ordinationis."

This last text is also of interest for its reference to God "ordaining" people to God. As we shall see in Chapter 3, talk of a divine ordination is most important for Thomas's later teaching on merit, for it is by God's ordination that people have the possibility of meriting God. In the present text, we do not have a foreshadowing of the later teaching on ordination. Rather, Thomas is speaking in general terms of God's "ordaining" people to heaven, in the sense of making them capable of God (see note 12 above), and of God "ordaining" them to heaven by creating habitual grace and the theological virtues that direct their possessors, incline them, to acts leading to heaven. Thomas, however, is not referring here to an ordination of God that also includes God's predestination of some to salvation. This idea, as will become clear in the later discussion, is involved in the later teaching of merit and ordination. Rather, we must read *this* ordination in light of Thomas's discussion elsewhere in the *Scriptum* of how people obtain grace in the first place. By disposing themselves freely for grace, they receive grace and the theological virtues, which God has so devised that they in turn lead their possessors to heaven; see in this regard note 12 above. Thus, the ordination mentioned in the present text should make clearer to us the gulf between the

personal savior" in the discussion of the structure of hope in the *Scriptum*, Thomas has been unable to proceed to the further statement, found in the *Summa*, that there is therefore a second object of the virtue of hope. The difference between the teachings of the two works on the possibility of hope is subtle and yet significant. It is the difference between the acknowledgment of the general possibility of salvation (as if one were to say: "We may hope that we shall be saved for we know of the grace of God which bridges the gap which otherwise separates people from God") and the more personal affirmation and recognition that the God who alone is able to save is in fact working the salvation of the possessor of hope.[135]

This different analysis of hope in the *Scriptum* in turn informs Thomas's understanding of the relation of hope and meritorious actions in this work. For example, Thomas's analysis of the *facultas* which establishes the possibility of hope enables him to interpret in a congenial manner an especially difficult passage in Peter Lombard's discussion of hope. Peter had written of hope that it is the "certain expectation of future beatitude, which arises from the grace of God and from preceding merits."[136] On its

---

       Scriptum and the *Summa* on *possibility* to which I refer in the text. In the *Summa*, the possibility of attaining heaven emerges, and so too hope, because God is directly and effectively involved in bringing the person to God. Hope goes out to this God as the object of trust. In the *Scriptum*, on the other hand, one can hope because in a general way, one is confident that God has provided the means to bridge the gulf between God and people. All one need do is take advantage of this aid which God has offered people, through the correct use of one's capacities.

135   In his study of hope in Aquinas, C.-A. Bernard *Théologie de l'espérance selon saint Thomas d'Aquin* (Paris, 1961) has failed to detect the shift in Thomas's teaching on the possibility of hope, and consequently has not paid adequate attention to the significance of the lack of the affirmation of the second object in the *Scriptum*; Bernard simply assumes that the description of God as help and savior, found in the *Summa*, is present in the *Scriptum* as well. I believe that Bernard's error results from an inattention to chronology. After noting that there is a somewhat different understanding of "virtue" in the two works (in the *Scriptum* virtue is seen as what inclines to action, while in the *Summa*, virtue is defined as the perfection of a power of the soul), Bernard makes no further attempt to discern developments in the depiction of hope itself. On the other hand, V. De Cousenongle, "Le 'Dieu de l'espérance' de saint Thomas d'Aquin," *Studia Theologica Varsaviensis* 12 (1974): 103–20, has detected the change in Thomas's teaching on the possibility of hope. If De Cousenongle's article has a failing in this regard, it is that in the effort to bring Thomas's (later) teaching into dialogue with Moltmann's, he has not paid sufficient attention to delineating Thomas's different analysis of the possibility of hope in the earlier work. J. T. Merkt, "'Sacra Doctrina' and Christian Eschatology" (Ph.D. dissertation, Catholic University of America, 1982), who also is interested in a "dialogue" between Thomas and Moltmann, has failed to note that the divine *auxilium* as the object of hope in the *Summa*'s sense is absent from the *Scriptum*, although he notes (p. 159) that the *auxilium* as object of hope is of only secondary importance in the earlier writing.

136   Peter actually provides two definitions of hope, the second one being the more

own, of course, the statement that hope arises from *grace* would have caused Thomas little difficulty—after all, *theological* virtues by definition are given gratuitously by God along with grace, and thus Peter's statement could have been taken as referring to the fact that the virtue of hope is infused by God. Rather, it is the second part of the couplet, the suggestion that hope arises from *preceding merits* which is the source of the problem for the interpreter of Lombard. After all, what is defined as being gratuitously given (in this case, the particular theological virtue called hope) cannot at the same time be seen as the result of the merits of the recipient (at least it cannot be so seen by one who is faithful to the insight into the gift-nature of the theological virtues). Hence, it is clear, Lombard's words could not be interpreted by Thomas as if they were suggesting that previous good works in addition to grace created in the first place the virtue of hope in the individual.

But given his analysis of the *facultas* of God's grace which constitutes the possibility (as well as his related perception, expressed elsewhere in the *Scriptum*, that grace makes possible the good acts, the merits, which bring a person to God according to the present dispensation), Thomas is enabled to interpret Lombard's words in a benign way. As he says in a number of places in his treatment of hope in the *Scriptum*, the statement that hope "arises from grace and preceding merits" refers not to the virtue, but to the *act* of hope, and the statement becomes fully explicable through the consideration of the general conditions which permit one to hope. We may hope to achieve the beatific vision, as should be clear by now, because we know that despite the transcendence of the goal, God has instituted the means to overcome the gap, grace, which elevates the soul to God's sphere. Hence, hope "arises from grace." But as we saw earlier in discussing the place of merit in Thomas's soteriology, God respects the nature of the possessor of grace, and thus God's grace engages the recipient in the human operations which are suited to the attainment of God. As Thomas says in the present distinction, the end of human existence and activity, God/the beatific vision, is rendered to man as reward for his *merits*.[137] Thus,

significant (and controversial): "Est enim spes certa expectatio futurae beatitudinis, veniens ex Dei gratia et ex praecedentibus meritis." For the sources of Lombard's definition see S. Pinckaers, "Les origines de la definition de l'espérance dans les Sentences de Pierre Lombard," *RTAM* 22 (1955): 306–12 and especially Jacques-Guy Bougerol, *La théologie de l'espérance aux XIIe et XIIIe siècles* (Paris, 1985), vol. 1, ch. 2, pt. 3. Bougerol's study of hope is invaluable for the correct understanding of high medieval teachings on this virtue.

137 See *In III* d. XXVI, q. II, a. 1 ad 3: "Spes multis modis dicitur. Quandoque enim nominat passionem; et sic non est virtus. Quandoque nominat habitum inclinantem ad actum voluntatis similem spei quae est in parte sensitiva, quae est passio; et sic est virtus. Quandoque vero nominat ipsum actum; et sic est actus virtutis. Quandoque vero nominat ipsam rem speratam. . . . Quandoque autem nominat certitudinem quae sequitur spem. . . . Habitus

provided we view merits in their dependance on grace, it is permitted to affirm with Lombard that the act of hope arises not only from grace but from merits as well, in that the expectation of attaining God, the end of our hope, is based on the consideration of the grace and graced actions/merits that God has determined as the way back to God.

The analysis of the *facultas* which creates the possibility of hope also shapes Thomas's treatment of the *certitude* of hope, which as was noted in Chapter 1, is of such importance to Pfürtner. At first glance, as the objections in the article in question suggest, hope cannot be certain. Thus, it is argued, hope cannot be certain because whatever is dependent on contingent factors is uncertain. But the hope of eternal life is based on the merits for which eternal life is rendered, as we have just seen, and merits arise from a most contingent cause, the *liberum arbitrium*.[138] Similarly, it is argued,[139] no one will have eternal life, the end of hope, unless he has grace and charity. But no one can know that he now has these or that at the completion of the present sojourn (*finaliter*) that he will have grace and charity. Thus, there can be no certainty that the end of one's hope will be in fact attained. Yet, for Thomas, once the possibility of hope has been established, there is little difficulty in determining that hope possesses certitude. Hope presupposes the *facultas* of coming to the hoped-for end, whose source in the present article he defines as the *liberalitas divina* (that is, God freely establishing the way by which some will be saved) and the *merita*, arising from grace, according to which all our virtues come to the ultimate end. But what follows from God's will is most certain. Thus, given this *facultas*, there can be no question of the certainty of hope—hope is certain because its basis is certain.[140] Thomas's answer turns on the constant features in the present order of the successful return to God, the

---

ergo spei quae est virtus, ex meritis non procedit, sed objectum, id est ipsa res sperata, pro meritis redditur. Et ideo actus spei in suum objectum tendit ex praesuppositione meritorum; et secundum hoc dicitur ex meritis provenire ratione sui actus;" and *In III* d. XXVI, q. II, a. 3, qc. II ob 1 and ad 1.

138 *In III* d. XXVI, q. II, a. 4 ob 3: "Omne quod dependet ex contingenti non potest habere certitudinem nisi quando iam est. Sed hunc habere vitam aeternam dependet ex meritis quae sunt ex libero arbitrio quod est maxime contingens causa. Ergo non potest esse certitudo de hoc quod iste habeat vitam aeternam. Ergo cum spes sit de hoc, videtur quod spes non habeat certitudinem."

139 *In III* d. XXVI, q. II, a. 4 ob 5: "Nullus habebit vitam aeternam nisi habeat caritatem et gratiam. Sed nullus scit se habere gratiam et caritatem, necdum ut finaliter habeat. Ergo non potest esse in spe certitudo de vita aeterna."

140 *In III* d. XXVI, q. II, a. 4 sol.: "Quia enim spes supponit facultatem in finem perveniendi quae quidem est ex liberalitate divina et ex meritis, secundum quae omnes virtutes in finem ultimum perveniunt; ideo certitudo spei causatur ex liberalitate divina ordinante nos in finem et etiam ex inclinatione omnium aliarum virtutum et etiam ex inclinatione ipsius habitus; et ideo praeter certitudinem quam habet ut quaedam virtus, includit certitudinem quae est in omnibus aliis virtutibus et ulterius certitudinem divinae ordinationis."

grace and good works that make the attainment of the beatific vision possible. Just as we may hope that we shall attain God because of the means established by God to facilitate this, we may be certain in our hope because these means established by God are, as established by God, most certain. Correspondingly, Thomas's determination of the question circumvents the problem of contingency posed in the objections. Hope is certain because its basis is most certain. Contingent factors such as the *liberum arbitrium*, and the actual possession of grace and charity simply do not affect the essential certainty of hope.

Yet it remains the case that this hope which is certain of itself is possessed by agents who are contingent. In the responses to the objections, Thomas supplements the analysis given in the corpus, in order to explain how an agent such as the human person, open to diverse possibilities and susceptible to loss and gain (i.e., of grace now possessed or of good works previously performed), may still be certain in his act of hope. From what we have seen so far, it is clear that hope is not "reflexive," in the sense of being focused on oneself. One does not trust in one's own grace or good deeds. One is confident in the possibility of achieving salvation because the way to salvation is itself sure. But to be saved (that is, to realize the possibility offered by God), one must actually avail oneself of the means provided by God. Thus, says Thomas, while the certainty of hope is not affected by the presence or absence now of the merits which lead to eternal life, and while it is true that we cannot know for certain whether we now have grace or shall have grace at the end of life or that we shall have done sufficient good works to achieve the vision of God, we must accept the way to God provided by God if our hope is to be fulfilled. Hence, Thomas says, the act of hope is certain if the one who hopes intends to make use of the grace and charity, given freely to the human person, and do the good works, by which God wills people to come to God; my act of hope is certain when it is accompanied by the intention to do the good which certainly returns one to God.[141]

The discussion of Peter Lombard's difficult saying about hope and preceding merits, and of the certainty of hope, constitute the principal contexts in which Thomas discusses hope and merit in this distinction. However, there are a few other statements which he makes on this topic in the treatise on hope in the *Scriptum* which warrant comment here. Thus, uncertainty about the relation between hope and the end to which hope tends occasions the suggestion that hope cannot be a virtue because it is too selfish. Virtue, it is said, does good for its own sake (*propter seipsum*). But hope's act, it would seem, is not done for the value attached to hope in itself but rather is performed because of the *reward*, the reward of the

---

141 See the texts mentioned in note 137 above, and *In III* d. XXVI, q. II, a. 4 ad 5: "Licet nesciam utrum finaliter habiturus sim caritatem, tamen scio quod caritas et merita quae in proposito habeo ad vitam aeternam certitudinaliter perducunt."

vision of God, which hope expects. Hence, this objection concludes, hope cannot be a virtue for it is "mercenary" (*mercenarius*), its act tending to the remuneration which is God.[142] In his response to this analysis, Thomas attempts a couple of strategies. First, he argues on the grounds of ordinary usage that it is inappropriate to say that hope is "mercenary," for we use this term only when we talk of action done on account of (*propter*) some *temporal* good, not of action done because of the eternal reward which is God. Second, Thomas offers an alternate suggestion which more success-fully meets the point of the objection, by underscoring the misunderstand-ing of the end for which the act of hope is done on which the objection rests. We may say that something is "mercenary" when it is done because of (*propter*) some end. Thus, hope would be mercenary if it were done because of the reward which is God. But the definition of hope, as we have seen, is that it is the expectation of a future good which is arduous and yet possible of attainment. The notion of "reward" (*merces*) does not enter into the definition of hope, and thus hope is not mercenary. Yet the end of hope, God/the beatific vision is also the reward of the virtuous actions and grace that God provides for the return to God. Thus, Thomas adds, while it is untrue to say that hope is done because of a reward which it might desire (*propter mercedem*), since it expects as its end, not a reward for its own act, but the beatitude which is the reward of human life, all we may allow is that hope is done "regarding" the end which is the reward of our meritorious actions (*circa mercedem*). This, however, does not make hope "merce-nary."[143]

Finally, Thomas turns to the question that in Lombard was the occasion for the analysis of hope in the first place, the uncertainty whether Christ had hope. For St. Thomas, this question is but one in a series of brief quaestiunculae about who is and who is not capable of hope. Thomas asks here whether, in addition to Christ, the angels and the saints in heaven (qc. II), and the damned and the demons (qc. IV), and the fathers in limbo have or had hope (qc. III). The outlines of Thomas's solution is basically the same for each of these quaestiunculae—hope has to do with a *future* and arduous good which is *possible* of attainment; thus, where the attain-ment of the end of hope is no longer possible, as in the case of the damned

---

142 *In III* d. XXVI, q. II, a. 1 ob 5: "Nulla virtus habet actum mercenarium, quia virtus operatur bonum propter seipsum. Sed spes habet actum mercenarium, cum intendat in remunerationem. Ergo spes non est virtus."

143 *In III* d. XXVI, q. II, a. 1 ad 5: "Facere aliquid propter aliquod commodum temporale facit actum mercenarium, non autem facere propter remunerationem aeternam. . . . Vel dicendum quod actus dicitur esse mercenarius qui propter mercedem fit, non autem qui est circa mercedem. Quamvis ergo actus spei sit expectare beatitudinem quae est merces, non tamen eam expectat propter mercedem ipsam, sed ex inclinatione habitus sicut et in aliis virtutibus contingit. Et praeterea. Non expectat eam inquantum est merces, sed inquantum est quoodam summum arduum: habet enim Deum pro principali objecto."

and the demons, or where the end has already been attained and thus is no longer future, as in the case of the angels and the saints in heaven, there is no hope. However, while the case of Christ follows this basic outline, Thomas's answer by necessity is more nuanced. In the discussion of the merit of Christ, we saw that Christ alone is both *comprehensor* and *viator*. He is a *comprehensor* inasmuch as by his nature and by the proximity of the divine and the human in the person of Christ he always was in possession of the vision of God (the goal to which people in this life strive and for which they hope). He is a *viator* in the restricted sense that in regard to certain incidental qualities of the beatific vision, which Thomas calls the "accidental or secondary" reward of the vision of God, he did by his human acts merit, e.g., the glory of the body. Thus, inasmuch as the beatific vision never was *future* with regard to Christ, he never had hope. He possessed as present what others hope to attain in the future. Did Christ then hope to attain the accidental rewards attendant on the essential reward of the vision of God? For Thomas, the answer here must similarly be negative. Only the vision of God, the arduous good which transcends nature and not the circumstances of the body at the vision, is the object of hope. Thus, alone of those in the state of meriting, Christ's merit was not accompanied by the act of hope expecting the end rendered for merit.[144]

Section II. *De Veritate*

Aquinas also briefly discusses merit in *De Veritate,* a collection of disputed questions originating in the first Parisian regency.[145] The final question of *De Veritate* (q. XXIX) examines the grace of Christ, and in the course of this discussion Thomas raises three questions about the merit of Christ: Could Christ merit (q. XXIX, a. 6), could Christ merit for others (q. XXIX, a. 7), and could Christ merit in the first moment of his conception (q. XXIX, a. 8)? In all essentials, Thomas's analysis of Christ's merit in *De Veritate* simply mirrors that in the *Scriptum.*[146] The objections of each of these

144 *In III* d. XXVI, q. II, a. 5 qc. I ad 1: "Spes sumitur ibi [Ps. 30:1, read as said by Christ: "In you, I have hoped"] pro expectatione praemii accidentalis de quo non est proprie spes quae habet Deum pro objecto. Et ideo non sequitur quod Christus proprie spem habuerit."
145 Thomas Aquinas first held the Dominican chair reserved for foreigners at the University of Paris in 1256–59, and the questions published under the title *De Veritate* were originally discussed in disputations over which he presided as regent master. There are twenty-nine questions in this collection, divided into three main groups. The first group (I–IX) discusses truth and the manner in which it is found in the divine and angelic intellects, the second group (X–XX) looks at truth in terms of the human intellect, and the third group of questions (XXI–XXIX) treats of the will and its object, good, as well as the operations of the will. Question XXVII analyzes grace, XXVIII, justification, and XXIX, the grace of Christ. I have used the Leonine edition of *De Veritate.*
146 *De Veritate* q. XXIX, a. 6 (could Christ merit), corresponds to *In Sent.* III d. XVIII, a. 2, combined with a. 4; q. XXIX, a. 7 (could Christ merit for others),

articles, for example, for the most part merely restate the arguments advanced in the corresponding article in the *Scriptum*. When he asks in q. XXIX, a. 6, about the possibility of Christ meriting, therefore, Thomas again focuses on the distinctive feature of Christ's earthly existence, that he was a *comprehensor* throughout his life, and in the objections contemplates how Christ's enjoyment of the beatific vision would seem to make merit impossible.[147]

corresponds to III d. XVIII, a. 6; and q. XXIX, a. 8 (could Christ merit in the first moment of his conception), corresponds to III d. XVIII, a. 3. Given the essential similarity between the teachings of De Veritate and the Scriptum on the merit of Christ, it would be unduly repetitious to recount in the text De Veritate's analysis of the merit of Christ. The discussion of Christ's merit in the text is meant simply to illuminate this basic identity in teaching and is not designed to be exhaustive. The following notes, however, substantiate the claim about the fundamental identity of these two discussions.

147   The difficulty posed by Christ's earthly enjoyment of the beatific vision is alleged in various ways in the objections of De Veritate q. XXIX, a. 6. See, for example, ob 2, which observes that one can only merit what one lacks, and ob 6, which notes that Christ in this life possessed the fullness of charity that characterizes beatitude. In De Veritate, Thomas does not offer the extensive consideration of the precise rewards merited by Christ found in the Scriptum (III d. XVIII, a. 4); he simply lists these rewards (impassibility and incorruptibility) in the corpus without additional comment. However, the third objection of the article does refer briefly to these specific rewards and states that they could not be merited because they were already owed to Christ as to one who was beatified, and what is already owed to one cannot be merited. There is one argument against Christ's merit in the Scriptum which does not reappear in De Veritate. The sole focus of De Veritate is on the difficulty created by Christ's enjoyment of the beatific vision. In the corresponding article of the Scriptum, Thomas pursues an additional line of inquiry: He also asks how Christ's divinity might preclude speaking of Christ meriting some reward for himself. In the discussion of this approach to the problem earlier in the chapter, I have indicated that this is not a compelling objection to the merit of Christ and Thomas omits it in the present work.

The other articles on the merit of Christ in De Veritate similarly more or less merely rehearse the insights and difficulties posed by the objections in the Scriptum. The quaestiunculae of In Sent. III d. XVIII, a. 6, had argued against Christ's merit for others on a number of grounds. First, merit for another is rejected because it offends against the notion that one is rewarded, or punished, only for what one oneself does freely; see In III d. XVIII, a. 6, qc. I ob 1 and 2. Second, a person's acts can have religious value only for himself. Since Christ merited as a human being, his acts were similarly of value only for himself; see In III d. XVIII, a. 6, qc. I ob 3. Third, In III d. XVIII, a. 6, had argued against Christ's merit for others because such a merit would seem to be superfluous. There seems to have been people (the patriarchs) who had entered heaven before Christ and so did not need his merit (qc. II ob 2). Moreover, to enter heaven Christians are required to perform their own meritorious acts, and so Christ's merit, at the least, does not suffice for salvation (qc. II ob 3). Finally, the objections of In III d. XVIII, a. 6, had also focused specifically on the merit of the *Passion* of Christ and had said that at least this merit could not be "for others." Christ had merited by all his earlier acts. So, if these acts had merited salvation "for others," a merit of the Passion

Similarly, in the corpus of each article in *De Veritate* treating the merit of Christ, Thomas repeats the basic analysis offered in the earlier *Scriptum*. The argument for the possibility of Christ meriting in question XXIX, a. 6, for example, turns on the consideration of the requirements of merit and on demonstrating that Christ met these requirements. In merit, says Thomas in this article, two things are necessary. First, one must be in the correct state: One must be a *viator*, a person on the way, who lacks some reward which can be acquired through good moral action. But Christ was a *viator* as well as a *comprehensor*, for in his earthly existence he lacked some of the factors associated with the beatific vision—impassibility of the soul and glory of the body—and so could merit these rewards by his acts. Second, merit presupposes the *ability* to merit, which includes both dominion over one's acts and the grace which proportions these acts to a supernatural end.[148] But says Thomas in the present article, Christ fully pos-

---

"for others" would be redundant; see *In III* d. XVIII, a. 6, qc. III obs 1 and 2. The thirteen objections to the merit of Christ for others in *De Veritate* for the most part follow one or another of these approaches to the question. For the rejection of merit for another on the grounds that one should be rewarded only for what one does, see for example q. XXIX, a. 7 obs 2 and 11; for the humanity of Christ as precluding merit for others, see q. XXIX, a. 7 obs 1 and 3; for the notion that Christ's merit would be superfluous, see q. XXIX, a. 7 obs 7, 8, and 9; and for the claim that at the least the merit of the Passion must be for Christ alone, see q. XXIX, a. 7 ob 6.

Again, the objections to q. XXIX, a. 8, on the merit of Christ in the first moment of his conception, repeat those in *In Sent.* III, d. XVIII, a. 3. For example, the second objection of q. XXIX, a. 8, attempts to draw the parallel first suggested in *In Sent.* III d. XVIII, a. 3 ob 4, between the sin of the devil and the first moral act of Christ; q. XXIX, a. 8 obs 1, 6, 8, and 9, oppose the notion of a merit in the "first" moment because the meritorious action falls into different parts and so must occur over a succession of moments, an observation made earlier in *In Sent.* III d. XVIII, a. 3 ob 2; and the tenth objection of q. XXIX, a. 8 points, as did *In Sent.* III d. XVIII, a. 3 ob 5, to the feebleness of the infant body, which would have been unable to carry out the meritorious act at this moment, as proof of the impossibility of Christ meriting at the beginning of his existence.

148 In the only article in *De Veritate* in which he contemplates in any detail the merit of ordinary Christians, Thomas reiterates that for merit to be possible the act must lie within the power of the person as well as be informed by grace. *De Veritate* q. XXVI, a. 6, broaches the intriguing question whether one can merit by one's "passions." The basic argument against merit in this regard has to do with the involuntary character of the passions: They are what their possessors literally "suffer" or "undergo." But the meritorious act must be a voluntary act, which lies within the powers of the person's will and which is performed by him; see, for example, sed contra 1. In the corpus of this article, Thomas agrees that only the voluntary act is meritorious and, moreover, adds that only the voluntary act done in grace is fully meritorious. Grace and charity (through which grace is most directly active) are required for merit because they orient the act to the supernatural end which is God and give the performer of the act and the act itself a pleasing aspect before God. "Cum

sessed this ability: As human, he was master of his activity, and he was endowed with the full power of the grace which elevates the human person and his acts to the supernatural level. Thus, concludes Thomas in the sixth article of this question, Christ could and did merit.[149]

enim mereri respectu mercedis dicatur, proprie mereri est aliquid sibi acquirere pro mercede: quod quidem non fit nisi cum aliquid damus quod est condignum ei quod mereri dicimur; dare autem non possumus nisi id quod nostrum est, cuius domini sumus. Sumus autem domini nostrorum actuum per voluntatem, non solum illorum qui immediate ex voluntate eliciuntur, ut diligere et velle, sed eorum etiam qui a voluntate imperantur per alias potentias eliciti, ut ambulare, loqui et huiusmodi. Isti autem actus non sunt condignum quasi pretium respectu vitae aeternae, nisi secundum quod sunt gratia et caritate informati. Unde ad hoc quod aliquis actus sit per se meritorius, oportet quod sit actus voluntatis vel imperantis vel elicientis, et iterum quod sit caritate informatus. Quia vero principium actus est et habitus et potentia et etiam ipsum obiectum, ideo quasi secundario dicimur mereri et habitibus et potentiis et obiectis; sed illud primo et per se est meritorium, est voluntarius actus gratia informatus." Having reminded the reader of these requirements of merit, Thomas then adds that a passion can be "meritorious" only to the extent that it is related to the will in some appropriate way. Now, passions are neither commanded nor elicited by the will and so do not fall directly under the will. But the passions can still come into contact with the will in a variety of other, indirect ways and therefore be meritorious. First, the passion can be the object of the will, as when the passion experienced by a person is accepted and loved by the will; in this case merit arises from the free, loving acceptance by the will. Second, a passion comes into contact with the will when it is the occasion of its exercise. For example, one might experience some concupiscence, some burning over some illicit object. The voluntary resistance to this concupiscence in grace and charity brings merit to the person. The final way in which passion and the will may come into contact is when the movement of the will is so strong that it occasions the appropriate passion. Hence, when one actively detests sin and concomitantly experiences shame over sin, this passion of shame is itself, according to Thomas, meritorious. Throughout this account of the "indirect" merit of the passions, then, runs Thomas's insistence that merit occurs only when the person acts voluntarily, aided by grace.

149 *De Veritate* q. XXIX, a. 6c: "Christus meruit ante passionem, quando erat viator et comprehensor; quod sic patet. Ad meritum enim duo requiruntur, scilicet status merentis et facultas merendi. Ad statum quidem merentis requiritur quod desit sibi id quod mereri dicitur. . . . Facultas vero merendi requiritur ex parte naturae et ex parte gratiae. Ex parte naturae quidem, quia per actum proprium quis mereri non potest nisi sit dominus sui actus, sic enim suum actum quasi pretium pro praemio dare potest; est quis dominus sui actus per liberum arbitrium; unde naturalis facultas liberi arbitrii requiritur ad merendum. Ex parte vero gratiae, quia cum praemium beatitudinis facultatem humanae naturae excedat, per naturalia pura ad illud merendum homo non potest sufficere, et ideo requiritur gratia per quam mereri possit. Haec autem omnia in Christo fuerunt; defuit tantum aliquid eorum quae ad beatitudinem perfectam requiruntur, scilicet impassibilitas animae et gloria corporis, ratione cuius viator erat. Fuit etiam in eo facultas naturae ratione voluntatis creatae et facultas gratiae propter plenitudinem

While the analysis of the merit of Christ in *De Veritate* thus proceeds along the same lines as that in the *Scriptum*, there is an added nuance in *De Veritate*'s discussion which should be noted. In establishing the possibility of Christ meriting in the sixth article of question XXIX, Thomas has inserted a lengthy discussion which is not found in the corresponding article in the *Scriptum*. After he had observed that merit presupposes that the person be in the correct state, for one must lack the reward that one hopes to acquire through one's acts, Thomas acknowledges that some

gratiarum, et ideo mereri potuit."

De Veritate q. XXIX, a. 7c, similarly establishes that Christ could merit for others along the lines outlined in the corresponding article in the *Scriptum*, III d. XVIII, a. 6. Again, Thomas points to the peculiar ontological status of Jesus Christ to make the case for Christ's merit for others. Christ is both divine and human, and the humanity of Christ serves, in the words of the Damascene which are quoted in the present text, as the "instrument of the divinity." Because the divinity works through the humanity of Christ, the effects of Christ's action can have universal application: As Thomas puts it here, because of its proximity to the divinity, the humanity of Christ is able to "exercise a spiritual influence upon other men" (*Christus secundum suam humanitatem spiritualiter influere potuit in alios homines*). Thus, what Christ does—his merits—can be applied to all others who share his human nature and who accept him as their head (on this latter point, see ad 3).

De Veritate q. XXIX, a. 8c, on the merit of Christ in the first moment of his conception, similarly mirrors its counterpart in the *Scriptum*, III d. XVIII, a. 3. First, Thomas refers in the two passages to a basic principle which informs his thinking about Christ, that all spiritual perfections which possibly can be should be attributed to Christ. Then, in both works, he asserts that this particular perfection should be ascribed to Christ and *can be*, inasmuch as it can be shown that there is no compelling reason why Christ could not have so merited. In the present discussion, Thomas notes that the meritorious act is impossible at a given instant for one of two reasons: either because there is a deficiency in the agent of the act, or because there is some problem posed by the act itself which makes action is a single moment impossible. Meriting requires full dominion over one's acts, as well as the grace which elevates the person and the act to the supernatural level. Thus, when either grace or dominion is absent in an agent, the agent will be unable to merit. But Christ lacked neither grace nor dominion over his acts from the first moment of his existence. He possessed the fullness of grace at this first moment and, moreover, as a *comprehensor* he had to have been able to exercise his will. Hence, as an agent possessed with complete freedom and the fullness of grace, Christ was able to merit in his first moment. Similarly, it might be impossible to do an act in a single moment, as when the completion of the act entails a succession of moments. For example, a complete action requires both the willing of the end and the choice of the means to the end, and normally the doing of the entire act covers a series of moments. But meriting for Christ did not require a succession of moments. Christ was always determined to the one good which is God. Christ naturally willed God as end. And Christ in that moment was also able to choose the means leading to this end. Hence, since all perfections should be affirmed of Christ, we must posit, says Thomas, that in fact Christ did so merit in the first moment of his existence.

(*quidam*) have argued that it is possible to merit what one already possesses. The example given by these unnamed authors is that of the blessed angels who by their subsequent actions on behalf of humans merit the beatitude which they already possess. Thomas, however, rejects the argument, and insists that we can only speak of meriting a reward that is lacked. Thomas offers two arguments for his position. The first rests on the authority of Augustine. The "Pelagians" wished to make the infusion of the first grace the result of meritorious activity. Against them, Augustine argued that if the reception of this grace were dependent on the good moral activity of the human person, no one would receive grace—since people without grace must sin, and the just deserts of sin is punishment and not grace, grace would never be granted. Thomas then attempts to apply the Augustinian argument to the case at hand. In his opponents' view, one can merit what one already has, and so, says Thomas, they would conceivably be affirming anew the Pelagian position rejected by Augustine: In their analysis, the good acts done after the reception of the first grace would have "retroactive" significance and would thus merit the reward of this grace.[150]

The second argument advanced by Aquinas in this article is more important because it illuminates well his understanding of the nature of meritorious causality. If Thomas's opponents were correct, the meritorious act would be the final cause of the reward, for the reward would be given for the sake of the merit which would then "deserve" this (earlier) reward. But states Thomas, it is the other way around: The reward is the final cause of the merit. And, more significantly, meritorious activity should be reduced, not to final, but to efficient, causality. In merit, notes Thomas, a person is made worthy of a reward and is disposed for it, and the reward is given as the consequence of the act. Thomas adds that in efficient causality, the cause must be prior in time to that of which it is the cause. Hence, he concludes, it is impossible for a person to merit what he already has. In merit and reward, therefore, first one merits and then one receives the reward of this act.[151]

<hr>

150   *De Veritate* q. XXIX, a. 6c: "Sed hoc non videtur esse verum propter duo; primo, quia contrariatur probationi Augustini, per quam contra Pelagianos probat gratiam sub merito cadere non posse, quia ante gratiam nulla sunt merita nisi mala, cum ante gratiam homo sit impius, et 'meritis impii non gratia, sed poena debetur'; posset enim dici quod gratiam quis meretur per opera quae post acceptam gratiam facit." When Thomas rejects with Augustine the "merit" of the first grace, he is thinking of merit in the fullest sense, condign merit. See the discussion of Thomas's position in the *Scriptum* on the possibility of "meriting" justifying grace. I shall argue shortly in the text that Thomas's retention of the *facere quod in se est* in *De Veritate* in the sense advanced by the *Scriptum* makes it most probable that he considers in *De Veritate* the autonomous action of the sinner done to please God *congruently* meritorious.

151   *De Veritate* q. XXIX, a. 6c: "Secundo, quia est contra rationem meriti, nam meritum est causa praemii, non quidem per modum causae finalis, sic enim magis praemium est causa meriti, sed magis secundum reductionem ad

The in-depth discussion of merit in *De Veritate* revolves around the merit of Christ and fails to consider the basic problems associated with the merit of the average Christian. There is no enumeration in *De Veritate*, for example, of the rewards to which the Christian's merit extends. Nevertheless, in this work Thomas does examine grace in general as well as the relation of human freedom to grace, especially at the beginning of the spiritual life, and what he writes on these related matters allows us to conclude that his understanding of the merit of Christians has also remained the same. In particular, like the *Scriptum De Veritate* probably allows for the congruent merit of the first grace. The crucial text is question XXIV, a. 15, in which Thomas asks whether a person can prepare himself to have grace without the aid of grace. Some theologians have argued that grace is necessary to prepare for grace, understanding by this necessary grace a habitual grace which disposes one for grace.[152] But, says Thomas, at least two arguments can be raised against this supposition. First, the positing of this preliminary grace fails to explain why some people receive justifying grace while others do not. When theologians speak of the preparation for grace, they are referring to a reason on the part of the human person why the person has received justifying grace: The person has readied himself for the reception of a perfective form. If the preliminary grace is given to all people, then all people would receive justifying grace, for they all would have been disposed for this grace by the earlier grace. But if this preliminary grace is given only to some, since it is itself a habitual grace these people would have to be prepared for *its* reception by an additional grace, which in turn would require a disposition caused by some other grace granted to the person for the reception of that grace, and so on to infinity. It is better, Thomas concludes, to abandon the notion of such a preliminary habitual grace that disposes the person for justifying grace and posit some other reason that distinguishes the recipient of justifying grace from those who do not receive it.

Second, Thomas argues against a preceding habitual grace that prepares one for justifying habitual grace because this would undermine the notion of human freedom and responsibility. When theologians speak of "preparing" for grace, they are simply referring to doing what one is capable of, to performing what lies in one's power. But it lies within the power of free choice to do good. Thus, by his natural power, a person must be able to prepare himself for grace, and, Thomas adds, theologians commonly say

causam efficientem, in quantum meritum facit dignum praemio et per hoc ad praemium disponit. Id autem quod est causa per modum efficientis, nullo modo potest esse posterius tempore eo cuius est causa; unde non potest esse quod aliquis mereatur quod iam habet."

152 Thomas is referring here to the analysis of such contemporary Franciscans as Bonaventure. Bonaventure posited a habitual grace, which he terms a *gratia gratis data*, which is necessary to prepare a person for the reception of justifying grace. For more on this position, see R. C. Dhont, *Le probleme de la préparation à la grâce* (Paris, 1946).

that to those who do their best God does not deny grace.[153] In other words, to explain why one person rather than another receives justifying grace, Thomas has recourse to the *facere quod in se est*. The gift of grace is the divine response to the correct exercise of human freedom, and this exercise lies within the powers of the human person. This understanding of the *facere quod in se est* in terms of the autonomous, freely performed action of the human person opens the door, at the least, to a congruent merit of the first grace.[154]

---

153 *De Veritate* q. XXIV, a. 15c: "Quidam dicunt quod homo non potest se praeparare ad gratiam habendam nisi per aliquam gratiam gratis datam: quod quidem non videtur esse verum, si per gratiam gratis datam intelligant aliquod habituale gratiae donum, duplici ratione: primo quidem quia propter hoc ponitur praeparatio ad gratiam necessaria, ut ostendatur aliqualis ratio ex parte nostra, ex qua quibuisdam detur gratia gratum faciens et quibusdam non. Si autem nec ipsa praeparatio gratiae sine aliqua gratia habituali esse non potest, aut ista gratia datura omnibus aut non: si omnibus datur, non videtur aliud esse quam aliquod naturale donum, nam in nullo inveniuntur omnes homines convenire nisi in aliquo naturali; ipsa autem naturalia gratiae dici possunt in quantum nullis praecedentibus meritis homini a Deo dantur; si autem non omnibus datur, oportebit iterum ad praeparationem redire, et eadem ratione aliquam aliam gratiam ponere, et sic in infinitum, et ita melius est ut stetur in primo. Secundo quia praeparare ad gratiam alio modo dicitur facere quod in se est, sicut est consuetum dici quod si homo facit quod in se est, Deus dat ei gratiam. Hoc autem dicitur in aliquo esse, quod est in potestate eius: unde si homo per liberum arbitrium non potest se ad gratiam praeparare, facere quod in se est non erit praeparare se ad gratiam."

154 In the remainder of the corpus of q. XXIV, a. 15, Thomas considers another possible definition of the term 'grace,' and his discussion tells us a good deal about his understanding of providence and predestination and in general the role of God in human salvation in *De Veritate*. After the words quoted in the previous note, Thomas adds that rather than define 'grace' as a habitual gift, it is possible to equate it with divine providence. Thus, to the question about the possibility of preparing for justifying grace without grace, one must respond that without preceding grace (= divine providence) it is in fact impossible to dispose oneself for grace. God must mercifully direct one in such a way that one will prepare for grace and so receive it. Thomas continues: "Quod quidem patet duplici ratione. Primo quidem, quia impossibile est hominem incipere aliquid velle de novo nisi sit aliquid quod ipsum moveat; sicut patet per Philosophum in VIII Physicorum, quod motus animalium post quietem necesse est praecedere alios motus quibus anima excitatur ad agendum. Et sic, cum homo se ad gratiam incipit praeparare de novo volunatatem suam convertendo ad Deum, oportet quod ad hoc inducatur aliquibus exterioribus occasionibus, utpote exterior admonitione aut corporali aegritudine aut aliquo huiusmodi; vel aliquo interiori instinctu, secundum quod Deus in mentibus hominum operatur; vel etiam utroque modo. Haec autem omnia ex divina misericordia homini providentur; et sic ex divina misericordia contingit quod homo se ad gratiam praeparet. Secundo quia non qualiscumque motus voluntatis est sufficiens praeparatio ad gratiam, sicut nec qualiscumque dolor sufficit ad remissionem peccati, sed oportet esse aliquem determinatum modum. Qui quidem homini notus esse

While *De Veritate*'s discussion of Christ's merit, and of the beginning of the spiritual life merely reasserts the positions taken in the *Scriptum*, there is at least one significant advance in Thomas's teaching on grace in *De Veritate* which will be of immense importance for Thomas's mature teaching on merit. The *Scriptum* conceives grace exclusively as "habitual": Grace is a perfection added to the soul which makes it pleasing to God and

non potest, cum etiam ipsum donum gratiae cognitionem hominis excedat; non enim potest sciri modus praeparationis ad formam nisi forma ipsa cognoscatur. Quandocumque autem ad aliquid faciendum requiritur aliquis certus modus operationis ignotus operanti, operans indiget gubernante et dirigente. Unde patet quod liberum arbitrium non potest se ad gratiam praeparare nisi ad hoc divinitus dirigatur." By saying that God's providence must precede and direct the individual's first movement to God, Thomas is asserting God's control over the salvific process: Things will turn out as God wants, and so when God desires someone to turn to God, God directs the person to this end. Lacking this direction, there will be no conversion. As was observed earlier in this chapter, the *Scriptum* occasionally makes similar claims about the need for providential direction in conversion. *De Veritate* has simply inserted this insight into its *ex professo* discussion of the *facere quod in se est*: When someone without grace takes the first step toward God, ultimately this "first step" must be seen as a freely performed response to God's offer of salvation. However, in neither the *Scriptum* nor *De Veritate* is this really the same as the teaching of the *Summa Contra Gentiles* and the *Summa Theologiae*, that God works the conversion of the sinner by inwardly moving the sinner away from sin and to God. In the latter works, the *facere quod in se est* is radically reinterpreted so that God Himself is responsible for the *facere*. In *De Veritate*, on the other hand, Thomas says that grace (= divine providence) prevenes *either* inwardly or outwardly. Thomas is not yet convinced that the renunciation of sin requires anything more than God's adroit manipulation of the external circumstances of the person's life. In this sense, the teaching on providence in *De Veritate* is identical with that in the *Scriptum*.

However, finally, there *is* a difference between the teachings on providence in the *Scriptum* and in *De Veritate*. Apart from the relatively few comments in the *Scriptum* about providence evoking the *facere* in the person, there is little sense in this writing of the *causal* character of providence. In *De Veritate*, as the fifth question of this collection demonstrates, Thomas is more conscious of the causal quality of providence. God wants certain things to occur—for example, the salvation of the individual—and sees that they do. But Thomas has not yet attained his mature understanding of providence (and predestination). In the *Summa Theologiae*, Thomas insists on the causality of providence and states that this extends to every event in the world. What God wants to happen, happens and does so as God wants it to happen. In *De Veritate*, God's providential causality extends only to general effects, not to individual events. Thus, if God wills the salvation of a person, this eventually will occur, as will the conversion required for salvation. But that conversion happens at this particular time rather than another falls outside the scope of divine providence. Naturally, the restriction of the causal certitude of providence to general effects leaves a great latitude to human freedom: The person is free to reject the offer of conversion at any given moment, and when the person does respond correctly (= *facere quod in se est*), the person does so freely, albeit in accordance with the divine will.

enhances its power. By the end of his career, Thomas will offer a subtler view of grace. In the *Summa Theologiae*, Thomas retains habitual grace but adds a distinctive type of grace, the grace of *auxilium*, and depicts it in much more dynamic terms. In addition, in the *Summa* Thomas divides this *auxilium* into two parts, the operative *auxilium* that inwardly works conversion and grants every good thought as well as perseverance in grace, and the cooperative *auxilium* that confirms the person in the good and strengthens the person in moral activity. This cooperative *auxilium* will be prominent in Thomas's treatment of meritorious activity.[155] The discussion of grace in *De Veritate* marks an intermediary stage between the *Scriptum* and the *Summa*. Thomas continues to view grace, as he did in the *Scriptum*, as primarily habitual[156] but it is in *De Veritate* that he also introduces the notion of a second grace, a cooperative *auxilium*.[157] As was observed in Chapter 1 in the review of Lonergan's study of operative grace, there are difficulties with this initial presentation of the grace of *auxilium*. First, Thomas does not assert in this writing an operative *auxilium* to parallel the cooperative *auxilium*. Second, in describing the functions of this cooperative *auxilium* in *De Veritate*, he in effect confuses it with what he will later call 'operative' *auxilium*, for he ascribes to cooperative *auxilium* activity more appropriate to the operative mode of this grace. Hence, in addition to confirming a person in the good, Thomas says in this writing that cooperative *auxilium* also works perseverance and grants good thought. Thomas's initial approach to *auxilium* thus stands in need of refinement. But as his thought on this grace deepens, Thomas will come to possess in the fully developed notion of the grace of *auxilium*, operative and cooperative, a valuable tool for the precise description of the respective roles of God and human freedom in meritorious activity. Despite its general closeness in tone to the teaching of the *Scriptum*, then, *De Veritate* points forward to Thomas's mature teaching on grace and merit.

---

155 Thomas's division of both habitual grace and *auxilium* into operative and cooperative is found in *Summa Theologiae* III 111, 2c, which I discuss at length in the next chapter.
156 In the text, I am most interested in Thomas's introduction in *De Veritate* of a grace of *auxilium*. It is this grace that marks the true innovation in *De Veritate*. However, in *De Veritate* Thomas has as well introduced some modifications to the description of habitual grace found in the *Scriptum*. For these, see the discussion of Lonergan in Chapter 1.
157 See *De Veritate* q. XXVII, a. 5 ad 3, in which Thomas mentions the need for a divine help in addition to habitual grace and says that this "help" takes the form of cooperative grace. Ad 1 in this article should also be consulted. Here, Thomas refers to a "cooperative" grace that causes the movement of free choice, removes obstacles to the execution of the external act and gives perseverance, in all of which, he adds, free choice as well has its role to play.

Chapter Three

The Mature Teaching on Merit

THIS CHAPTER studies the teaching about merit in Thomas's mature period, focusing on his masterpiece, the *Summa Theologiae*, written between 1266 and 1273.[1] Thomas conceived of the *Summa* as a replacement for current textbooks of theology. It is likely that he had particularly in mind Peter Lombard's *Sententiae*, by Thomas's time second only to the Bible as the basic textbook of Christian theology, as well as commentaries by scholastics on the Lombard. In the prologue to the *Summa Theologiae*, Thomas states that contemporary textbooks of theology are unnecessarily repetitious, obscure,and verbose in their teaching, and confused in their planning. Alert to these deficiencies,[2] Thomas intended his own work to be a straightforward, systematic introduction to *sacra doctrina*. To provide a

---

1   According to Weisheipl, *Friar Thomas d'Aquino,* p. 360. Weisheipl (p. 361) states that the Prima Pars was completed in 1268, the Prima Secundae toward the end of 1270, and the Secunda Secundae by the spring of 1272. The Tertia Pars was left incomplete due to Thomas's ill health. I have used the bilingual (Latin-English) Blackfriars edition of the *Summa Theologiae*; see the bibliography for full details. In citing the *Summa*, the number in Roman numerals refers to the Part of the *Summa*, the next number to the question in the Part, and the following number to the article; the information provided after the article number refers to the part of the article which is cited—*ob* refers to an objection; *ad* to a response to an objection; and *corpus* to the body of the article; *sed contra* refers to the part of the article in which Thomas cites an authority from tradition or Scripture that offers a perspective different from that offered in the objections. Hence, e.g., "I 19, 5c" means Part I, question 19, article 5, the corpus of the article.

2   "Consideravimus namque huius doctrinae novitios in his quae a diversis scripta sunt plurimum impediri, partim quidem propter multiplicationem inutilium quaestionum, articulorum, et argumentorum, partim etiam quia ea quae sunt necessaria talibus ad sciendum non traduntur secundum ordinem disciplinae, sed secundum quod requirebat librorum expositio, vel secundum quod se praebebat occasio disputandi, partim quidem quia frequens eorumdem repetitio et fastidium et confusionem generabat in animis auditorum." For a different proposal about the occasion of the *Summa*, one that has gained currency among scholars of Thomas, see Leonard E. Boyle, "The Setting of the *Summa theologiae* of Saint Thomas," The Etienne Gilson Series 5 (Toronto, 1982). For Boyle, the *Summa* is Thomas's most "Dominican" work (p. 30). Thomas shared with his brethren a concern for moral matters but felt that earlier Dominican moral and pastoral writings had been insufficiently theological. Hence, in the *Summa* Thomas has

more satisfactory review of the truths of the Christian faith which are considered in theology, Thomas organized the *Summa* in three basic parts. The first part (Prima Pars = I) is concerned with God, both in God's essence and as the cause of all that is other than God. The Second Part (Secunda Pars = II) is itself divided into two sections, the Prima Secundae (= I-II), and the Secunda Secundae (= II-II). The topic of the Secunda Pars is the return of the rational creature to God, both in general terms (I-II) and in specific (II-II);[3] it is at the end of the Prima Secundae (q. 114) that Thomas offers his *ex professo* treatment of merit in this work. Finally, in the Tertia Pars (= III) Thomas discusses the actual means by which God achieves the return of the rational creature to God, looking at Christ in qq. 1–59 and in qq. 60–90 at the sacraments, the means instituted by God to convey the effects of Christ's work to other people. While it was left unfinished, the *Summa* provides ample testimony to Thomas's genius as a systematician. Thomas has incorporated into this work in a brilliant and comprehensive way the fruits of his lifelong reflection on the Christian faith.

When compared to the *Scriptum* on the *Sentences* of Peter Lombard, it is a rather different teaching about merit found in the *Summa Theologiae*. As I shall argue, the differences in Thomas's teaching about merit must be attributed primarily to two factors: the evolution in his understanding of grace, and his recognition that merit can only be correctly understood when

---

attempted to locate the discussion of ethical questions in a more secure and explicit theological framework: He has connected the ethical material of the Secunda Pars (I-II and II-II) to reflection on God and the procession of all creatures from God (the Prima Pars) and Christ (the Tertia). While intriguing, this proposal arguably pays insufficient attention to the "scholastic" dimension of the *Summa*. Scholastic authors, Thomas included, were concerned to find the most effective way of organizing the presentation of the truths of the Christian faith. Most of the "extra-Dominican" material of the *Summa* is found in other scholastic systematic treatises. Hence, it is probably preferable to see the *Summa* as yet another attempt by Thomas, along with his *Scriptum* and the *Summa Contra Gentiles* (to name but the leading examples), to find a satisfactory way of teaching Christian theology.

3   It would not be quite correct to say that in the Prima Pars, God as creator is seen especially or exclusively as efficient cause, while in the Secunda, God is seen especially or exclusively as the final cause of things and especially of the rational creature. The description of God as efficient cause may in fact predominate in the Prima Pars, and the view of God as final cause may be the main focus in the Secunda. But Thomas is able in the *Summa* to offer consistently a more nuanced and complete analysis of the relation of the world to God, and hence is reluctant to portray in any part of his treatment this relation exclusively in terms of one kind of causality. Hence, in the Prima Pars, as will become clear in the first section of this chapter, God as Creator is described not only as efficient cause but also as the ultimate final cause. God brings all into existence efficiently, for the purpose of manifesting the divine goodness outside of God. Similarly, efficient causality has its place in the Secunda Pars as well: It is through God's efficient causality expressed in grace that the attainment of God by the rational creature is made possible.

related to the plan of God in creating and redeeming the world. Before turning directly to his discussion of merit (and hope) in the *Summa*, it is first necessary to examine the background to his teaching about merit in this work, i.e., his analyses of God's creation of the world in accordance with the divine wisdom and God's salvation of humanity through grace.

Section I. The Background to the Discussion of Merit

A. *God's Creative and Redemptive Plan*

In the *Summa Theologiae*, the starting point of Thomas's theology is the affirmation of God as the creator of all that is: In large measure, Thomas's theology, including his discussion of grace, is designed to explicate and portray the various implications of this affirmation about God.[4] For Aquinas, God's act of creating is utterly free.[5] God's sovereignty and freedom mean that God is not necessitated or forced to do anything, including create the world. Similarly, God's perfection precludes creating for the purpose of obtaining some additional perfection for God's being. The world does not "make a difference to God," at least in this sense of contributing to God's

---

4   The following is based on the opening forty-five questions of the *Summa Theologiae*, drawing especially from I 19–26, I 44–45, and I 5–6. For a competent orientation, see W. J. Hankey, *God in Himself: Aquinas' Doctrine of God as Expounded in the Summa theologiae* (Oxford, 1987). The discussion of the role of wisdom in Thomas's vision of reality has been anticipated by John H. Wright, *The Order of the Universe in the Theology of St. Thomas Aquinas* (Rome, 1957); the value of this work as a study of the *Summa* is undermined by its indiscriminate sampling of the various works of Aquinas. In two essays published in Scott MacDonald (ed.), *Being and Goodness: The Concept of the Good in Metaphysics and Philosophical Theology* (Ithaca, N.Y., 1991), Norman Kretzmann has identified from a philosophical perspective difficulties in Thomas's account of creation; see "A General Problem of Creation: Why Would God Create Anything at All?" and "A Particular Problem of Creation: Why Would God Create This World?" pp. 208ff. See, however, the review of the book, including these essays, by David Burrell, in *Faith and Philosophy* 9(1992): 538–43, especially pp. 540–42. My own recognition of the centrality of creation for Aquinas has been stimulated and confirmed by such works of Burrell as *Aquinas, God and Action* (Notre Dame, 1979) and *Knowing the Unknowable God: Ibn-Sina, Maimonides, Aquinas* (Notre Dame, 1986). In a later note in this chapter, I will compare Burrell's reading of Aquinas with my own.

5   Thomas insists that God's creative act is free and unnecessitated in a number of places. See, e.g., I 19, 3c, where Thomas states that God wills only God's goodness (= Himself) "from necessity" but wills other things only as they are ordained to God's goodness. Thomas also observes in this text that God stands in no need of these other things and does not will them into existence by any necessity of supplementing the divine being. See in the same vein I 19, 3 ad 2 and ad 3, and I 19, 4. For Thomas, the creative act is a freely chosen act by God accomplished by the divine knowledge and will; see I 14, 8c, in this regard.

improvement or self-realization. Rather, that God creates is due solely to God's free determination to do so.

Yet, although creating is not required by God to complete God's being, creating is not without motive or devoid of meaning. When he seeks to display the reasonableness of God's free decision to create, Thomas often asserts that God does have a purpose in creating and says that this purpose is the manifestation of the goodness of God.[6] In Aquinas, the 'good' or 'goodness' bears a number of connotations. It refers to what is *perfect* and *desirable,* and *self-communicative.*[7] In the first place, goodness suggests perfection (in the sense of completeness), and here the 'good' is viewed as more or less convertible with being. What is actually or really something is more perfect or complete than what is only potentially so, and so is more "good." Thus, for example, every being in the world possesses a nature that constitutes its potential for a certain kind of existence. The more a creature realizes the potential of its nature, the more it shares in the quality of the good. But as Thomas has shown elsewhere[8] in his analysis of God as pure act of being, in whom there is no potency, God is being itself (*esse*, the act of being), and thus God possesses most fully the quality of goodness. Indeed, God is goodness.[9]

Secondly, the good adds to being the further note of desirability. The good is what all things desire, for each nature desires (seeks) its own perfection (fullest actualization). As goodness itself, God too shares this general feature of things. God desires or wills God's own goodness. But, Thomas stresses, there is a crucial difference between God's desire of the divine goodness and the desire of creatures for the good proper to themselves. In the creature, desire reaches out to the good as to a goal not yet

---

6   Thomas makes this point well in I 19, 2c. Here, he notes that natural things tend to pass on their goodness to their like. He then draws the parallel with God, absolute goodness, to whom it is appropriate (*condecet*) to diffuse God's own good to God's "like," that is, to the creation. Thomas repeats the point in I 19, 2 ad 2. In addition, see the texts listed below in notes 11, 12, and 14, in which Thomas asserts that God creates to diffuse the divine goodness in accordance with the plan of the divine wisdom.

7   Thomas provides a fine summary of the various "notes" associated with the 'good' in I 5, 1c. In this text he says that "to be good" is really the same as "to exist," although the words have different meanings. Citing *Ethics* I, 1, he says that the goodness of a thing consists in its being *desirable*. He continues that desirability is consequent upon *perfection*, for things always desire their perfection, and the perfection of a thing depends on how far it has achieved *actuality*. It is clear, he concludes, that a thing is good inasmuch as it exists—for; it is by existing that everything achieves actuality. The word 'good,' then, differs from 'exist' by adding to being the notion of desirability. See also I 5, 1 ad 1, and I 5, 3c, for the same analysis; and I 4, 1c, for further reflections on the relation between 'perfection' and 'actuality.'

8   I 3 in its entirety is germane to this discussion. See in particular I 3, 4c, where Thomas considers the identity of essence and existence in God.

9   See I 6, 3.

possessed. For God, on the other hand, the divine goodness is fully possessed.[10] To be more precise, given the divine simplicity and the identity of God's essence and existence, the disjunction between God's will or desire of the divine goodness and the divine goodness is, in God, merely notional: God's will is God's goodness. Thus, in God, desire refers not to a tendency toward a good but rather to a resting in or delighting in a goodness which is already possessed and which is identical with the willing of it.

Third, referring to the Pseudo-Dionysius, Thomas observes that the good tends to "diffuse" itself.[11] The basic idea here is that that which is perfect or complete is inclined to communicate its perfection to its like (*simile*). For example, the more mature he becomes and realizes the potential of his nature, the more a man tends to (and is capable of) producing his like, by fathering a child: Here, the male passes on to another the form (the perfection) which makes him human. Given his belief that God's act of creating is free and intentional, Thomas naturally rejects the necessitarian and emanationist overtones of the Pseudo-Dionysius's original discussion of this trait of goodness. Rather, Thomas simply uses this idea about the good to show that creating is not incompatible with the nature of God. Since God is complete goodness and is fully actual, it is not inappropriate for God to produce God's like; in the free act of creation, God establishes the world that reflects the goodness that is God.

The world, however, is not God, and the goodness which is manifested in the world is not identical with the goodness that is God. In God, the divine essence and existence are identical, and all the perfections (goods) that exist in God exist not only in a preeminent way but also in a simple way, as one and as identical with each other. But in everything other than God, essence and existence are not identical. Whatever exists exists because God has called it into existence, that is, because it has received its existence from God. By definition, the creature cannot receive the divine goodness as it exists in God, as simple and as identical with the divine existence. Hence, the realization of the purpose of creating, the manifestation of God's goodness outside of God, requires the communication of God's goodness in a way appropriate to what is not God. Here, Thomas refers to God creating "according to the plan of the divine wisdom."[12] In Aquinas,

---

10   Thomas makes this comment in I 19, 1 ad 2: "Voluntas in nobis pertinet ad appetitivam partem; quae, licet ab appetendo nominetur, non tamen hunc solum habet actum ut appetat quae non habet, sed etiam ut amet quod habet et delectetur in illo. Et quantum ad hoc voluntas in Deo ponitur, quae semper habet bonum quod est eius objectum, cum sit indifferens ab eo secundum essentiam."

11   Thomas characterizes creating as God's diffusion of God's goodness outside of God in I 19, 2c, to which reference has been made in note 6 above. Pseudo-Dionysius is cited as the authority for this idea in, e.g., I 5, 4 ob 2 and ad 2.

12   Thomas speaks of creation in accordance with the divine wisdom for the manifestation of the divine goodness in any number of places. In I 44, 4c,

wisdom refers to the contemplation of the highest cause and the ordering (*ordinare*) of other causes in this light.[13] Thus, creation according to wisdom refers to God creating in accordance with a plan "formulated" and adopted by the divine wisdom to manifest the divine goodness outside of God. The result of this formulation is the creation as we know it. God creates a multitude of things, endowing each with its own nature, for the purpose of proclaiming the divine goodness outside of God. Every creature is designed (ordained, disposed) to proclaim the divine goodness in the manner appropriate to it. By its nature, the creature recalls some aspect of the divine nature. Human nature, with its capacity for thinking and willing, for example, imitates the divine intelligence and will, although clearly falling short of the divine nature. Taken together, the multiplicity and variety of natures disclose the divine goodness and being as much as is possible by what is not God.[14]

Thomas asserts that God is the final cause of all things and states that God does not create because God needs to be "completed" or perfected by what God creates, but only to communicate God's own completeness, which is God's goodness, to others. In the article immediately preceding (3c), Thomas has made clear that God is the first exemplar cause of all things and states that each creature may be traced back to its model in the divine wisdom. In I 9, 1 ad 2, Thomas states that nothing can exist except as it is a sort of reflection deriving from the wisdom of God as from its first efficient and formal cause. He adds in this text that higher creatures share this likeness to the divine wisdom most, lower things less. See also I 21, 4 ad 4, where Thomas asserts that creation "convenit divinae sapientiae et bonitati," and I 47, 1c, which is reviewed at length in note 14 below.

13   Recall in this connection Aristotle's definition of the wise man: "It belongs to the wise man to govern (*ordinare*) and not to be governed." Thomas cites this text from the *Metaphysics* (I, 2) in I 1, 6 ob 2, in the context of asking whether *sacra doctrina* is a *sapientia*. He also refers to it in the corpus of this article. When we speak of God's wisdom, then, we refer to God considering how best to convey God's goodness outside of God and creating in this light.

14   Thomas addresses the need for a variety of creatures to display the divine goodness in a number of places. In such texts as I 14, 1 ad 2, and I 13 4c, he draws our attention to the very fact that what pre-exists in God in a simple and unified way is divided among creatures as many and varied perfections. In I 47, 1c, he devotes the entire article to showing why God's will must be the cause of the variety of things. In the corpus, Thomas states that God brought things into existence so that the divine goodness might be communicated to creatures and re-enacted through them. And because one single creature was not enough to do this, God produced many and diverse creatures so that what was wanting in one expression of the divine goodness might be supplied by another—for goodness, which in God is single and unified, in creatures is multiple and scattered. Hence the whole universe more perfectly shares and represents the divine goodness than any one creature. Thomas concludes the corpus by reminding the reader that the divine wisdom is the source of this variety in things. In I 47, 2c, Thomas adds that the divine wisdom is the cause of the inequality in things, to facilitate the more adequate representation of God's goodness outside of God. Finally,

The divine plan for the manifestation of the divine goodness outside of God, however, extends beyond the mere institution of creaturely natures. It involves their characteristic activity and the attainment of the ends of their natures determined for them by God in creating. Thomas uses the term 'providence' to refer to the part of the divine plan that establishes the role of each creature's activity in the manifestation of the divine goodness. By the divine providence, God ordains each creature to its end and directs each creature to this appointed end.[15] The activity of the creature in reaching its end is designed to reflect some aspect of divine activity and goodness. In discussing providence in the *Summa*, Thomas makes a number of points that are relevant to this book. First, the divine providence is all-inclusive. Every creature in the world, including the human person, and every event which occurs in the world, falls under divine providence. Everything is ordained to the manifestation of God's goodness.[16] Second,

for other statements of how individual kinds of creatures manifest the divine goodness outside of God in accordance with the divine wisdom, see such texts as I 50, 1c, in which Thomas discusses the existence of angels in this perspective, and I 65, 2, where he states that corporeal things too were made on account of God's goodness. Note that in this last text, Thomas rebuts the position of Origen who had claimed that spiritual substances were united to grosser or more subtle bodies in accordance with their merits as separate substances. The "heresy" of Origen is mentioned and rejected by Thomas throughout his career.

15 Thomas discusses providence in I 22. He defines providence as the *ratio* of the *ordo* in things to their ultimate end (the divine goodness) that exists in the divine mind in, e.g., I 22, 1c, and I 22 3c. He uses the verb *ordinare* of divine providence in such texts as I 22, 4c (it pertains, he says here, to providence *ordinare res in finem*), and I 23, 1c (all creatures *ordinantur ad suos fines* by the divine providence). Thomas draws a distinction between 'providence' and 'government': Technically, 'providence' refers to the *ratio* established by God and which is in the divine mind; 'government' refers to the execution in the world of this plan; see I 22, 1 ad 2. However, in practice Thomas uses 'providence' to cover both *ratio* and the execution of the plan for creatures established in the divine mind.

16 The objections to I 22, 2, suggest possible cases which escape the rule of divine providence: the fortuitous (ob 1), evil (ob 2), the necessary (ob 3), human beings who are endowed with freedom (ob 4), and dumb animals (ob 5). Thomas's basic position is that all that happens accords with divine providence and that God is able to achieve God's will through secondary causes. In the case of evil (ad 2), Thomas notes that evil taken in isolation is a defection from the divine plan, but that God is able to turn evil to some larger good, which promotes the prosecution of God's plan. In ad 4, he states that human freedom is not endangered by divine providence. Freedom entails the capacity to opt for different courses of action; people, says Thomas, are able freely to move in this direction or another, and yet what they do is used by God in the service of God's plan. Finally, in ad 5 Thomas notes how God's providence applies to people and to dumb animals differently. Dumb animals are set by nature to one course of action alone. People, however, are free; they can act in this way or that. To be concrete, they are freely and voluntarily

the execution of the divine providence (that is, the realization of the divine plan) is infallible. What God wills to occur, does occur, and so the divine purpose in creating and governing is attained through creatures and their acts.[17]

But, third, the infallibility of divine providence is not destructive of the causality proper to the different creatures in the world. Thomas makes this point in I 22, 4, when he asks whether everything that occurs occurs necessarily. In the corpus, Thomas notes that there are different kinds of causes in the world, e.g., necessary causes and contingent causes. When God achieves the divine will through necessary causes, the effect is necessary, for it pertains to necessary causes that their effects follow necessarily. When God achieves the divine will through contingent causes, the effect follows infallibly but not with necessity; it does occur as God plans but it occurs contingently, in keeping with the nature of the secondary cause.[18] Thomas here is expressing his conviction that God is a transcendent cause.[19] As the cause of everything who exists above all things, God is able

---

able to follow the path set for human beings by God. Given this freedom, Thomas here argues that God as ruler of the universe imputes to people blame (*culpa*) or merit, according to how they respond to God's will for human beings.

17   For this point and the one discussed below in the text, see I 19, 8c: "Cum igitur voluntas divina sit efficacissima, non solum sequitur quod fiant ea quae Deus vult fieri, sed et quod eo modo fiant quo Deus ea fieri vult. Vult autem quaedam fieri Deus necessario, quaedam contingenter, ut sit ordo in rebus ad complementum universi. Et ideo quibusdam effectibus aptavit causas necessarias quae deficere non possunt, ex quibus effectus de necessitate proveniunt; quibusdam autem aptavit causas contingentes defectibiles ex quibus effectus contingenter eveniunt. Non igitur propterea effectus voliti a Deo eveniunt contingenter quia causae proximae sunt contingentes, sed propterea quia Deus voluit eos contingenter evenire contingentes causas ad eos praeparavit." See also I 19, 8 ad 2. In I 22, 3c and 4c, Thomas observes specifically with reference to the working out of divine providence that God achieves God's will infallibly but that this efficacy respects the causality proper to the secondary causes employed by God.

18   I 22, 4c: "Providentia divina quibusdam rebus necessitatem imponit, non autem omnibus, ut quidam crediderunt. Ad providentiam enim pertinet ordinare res in finem. Post bonitatem autem divinam, quae est finis a rebus seperatus, principale bonum in ipsis rebus existens est perfectio universi; quae quidem non esset si non omnes gradus essendi invenirentur in rebus. Unde ad divinam providentiam pertinet omnes gradus entium producere. Et ideo quibusdam effectibus praeparavit causas necessarias ut necessario evenirent; quibusdam vero causas contingentes ut evenirent contingenter, secundum conditionem proximarum causarum."

19   B. McGinn, "The Development of the Thought of Thomas Aquinas on the Reconciliation of Divine Providence and Contingent Action," *The Thomist* 39 (1975): 741–52, provides a fine discussion of God as the transcendent cause able to apply all secondary causes to their acts in a way which preserves their proper causality. McGinn examines the development in Thomas's ability to perceive the implications of the transcendence of God for the portrayal of

to move secondary causes infallibly to their action in a way congenial to their natures. Since the human person is a contingent cause, what the human person does/effects does not have to occur, and it does not have to occur in the way it does. By divine ordination, the human person is not restricted to a single course of action, in the way that a non-rational creature is limited to what pleases it instinctively. Through reason and will, the human person is able to discover and contemplate various courses of action to attain the fulfillment of his being. God respects this freedom and leaves human contingency intact. Nevertheless, while the human person retains dominion over his acts, his activity falls under the divine providence employed by God for the achievement of God's plan.[20] Fourth, Thomas points to this use by God of secondary causes as testimony to the divine greatness. God does not treat creatures as mere "puppets" that contribute nothing of their own to the realization of God's plan. Rather, creatures possess their own causality as granted to them by God (they participate in the causality proper to God), and God uses these creatures in their characteristic activity for the achievement of God's will: God does not work "in spite of" the causality of creatures, but *through* it, including through the freedom of the human person.[21]

Thomas's general reflections on the creation and governing of the world according to the divine wisdom for the purpose of manifesting the divine goodness are critical to the study of his thought on merit. In the *Summa,* Thomas has worked out his basic understanding of human salvation (including as we shall see, of merit before God) in terms of the divine goodness and wisdom. As has been noted, God institutes the natures of creatures, grants them their characteristic activity, and appoints for individual creatures their appropriate destiny, all for the purpose of proclaiming the divine goodness outside of God. Each thing in the world by its being and doing manifests the divine goodness as best as it can, and taken together the universe of beings with their activities constitutes a faithful proclamation of the goodness of God, in accordance with the plan of the divine

---

God's causal action in the world. McGinn's article is intended as a supplement to the reflections of Lonergan on the development of Thomas's teaching about operative grace discussed in Chapter 1.

20   See, e.g., I 22, 2 ad 4, discussed in note 16 above.

21   In I 22, 3c, Thomas looks at both the *ratio* that exists in the divine mind and the execution of this *ratio* in considering whether God immediately provides for all things. With regard to the *ratio*, God does provide directly for the purpose of each thing. But as for the execution of the plan, divine providence works through intermediaries or secondary causes. For Thomas, that God so acts is evidence of God's greatness: "Ad secundum, sunt aliqua media divinae providentiae, quia inferiora gubernat per superiora, non propter defectum suae virtutis sed propter abundantiam suae bonitatis, ut dignitatem causalitatis etiam creaturis communicet." Similarly, he writes in I 22, 3 ad 2: "Per hoc quod Deus habet immediate providentiam de rebus omnibus, non excluduntur causae secundae, quae sunt executrices huius ordinis."

wisdom. The human person too falls under this plan of the divine wisdom. The human person suggests the knowledge of God, thus contributing in his own way to the fulfillment of God's purpose in creating the world.

Yet, Thomas continues, God has determined to manifest the divine goodness in a special way. It is this special determination by God that provides the basis for Thomas's discussion of human salvation.[22] To manifest the divine goodness in a pre-eminent way, God has decided to share God's own life with certain rational creatures (including some human beings), allowing them to attain to the highest possible destiny, the immediate vision of God which is naturally enjoyed by God. Hence, Thomas says, in accordance with the divine wisdom, God wills that certain rational creatures will become "like God," knowing and loving God as God knows and loves Himself (to the extent that creatures can experience such activity), and then moves these creatures to the attainment of this goal. This willing and electing of certain rational creatures to rise to God's level is God's *predestination* of the individual. As Thomas says in explaining the relation of predestination to God's general plan of wisdom for manifesting the divine goodness, predestination is that part of the divine providence by which God determines that a certain rational creature will surpass the limits of his natural existence and enter into the intimacy of the divine

---

22   For a good summary statement of Thomas's position, see I 23, 5 ad 3. In this text, he is seeking to show how both the predestination of some to salvation and the reprobation of others accord with the divine purpose of manifesting the divine goodness: "Ex ipsa bonitate divina ratio sumi potest praedestinationis aliquorum et reprobationis aliquorum. Sic enim Deus dicitur omnia propter suam bonitatem fecisse, ut in rebus divina bonitas repraesentetur. Necesse est autem quod divina bonitas, quae in se est una et simplex multiformiter repraesentetur in rebus; propter hoc quod res creatae ad simplicitatem divinam attingere non possunt. Et inde est quod ad completionem universi requiruntur diversi gradus rerum, quarum quaedam altum et quaedam infimum locum teneant in universo. Et ut multiformitas graddum conservetur in rebus, Deus permittit aliqua mala fieri, ne multa bona impediantur. . . . Sic igitur consideremus totum genus humanum sicut totam rerum universitatem. Voluit igitur Deus in hominibus quantum ad aliquos, quos praedestinat, suam repraesentare bonitatem per modum misericordiae parcendo, et quantum ad aliquos, quos reprobat, per modum justitiae puniendo. Et haec est ratio quare Deus quosdam eligit, et quosdam reprobat." Thomas completes this part of his response by citing Romans 9:22 and II Timothy 2:20 in support of his analysis.

After these paragraphs, Thomas continues the discussion by stating that it is impossible to give a reason why God has chosen this person rather than that to be a vessel of righteousness. God's willing, he says, is the sole ground of the disparity among people. Nor does this make God unjust. God could justly have left all people to the consequences of their sin. That God saves anyone at all, concludes Thomas, must be acknowledged as God's free, merciful gift. In so arguing, Thomas shows himself the true heir of the later Augustine. I shall return to Thomas's indebtedness to St. Augustine later in this chapter and in detail in Chapter 4.

life.[23] By predestination, God decides to elect a person to God's own life and then grants that person all that is needed,including grace, to attain this special end to which he is ordained through God's decision.[24] Just as is creation, so too God's predestinating will is absolutely free, not determined by anything outside of God. There is no dignity or merit in the person that would "cause" God to choose that person for eternal life. Indeed, that there comes to be a special dignity or worth in the one predestined by God is itself due to God's decision to manifest the divine goodness through the election of this person to salvation.[25]

Thus, as a result of predestination, Thomas can speak of these rational creatures being ordained and directed to a twofold good. First, they are directed to the end that is proportionate to their natural powers and which can be reached through these natural powers. Second, they are ordained to the higher good that is God's own life. In reaching this end, they are enabled to achieve an even greater approximation of the good.[26]

---

23 In I 23, 2c, Thomas offers this definition of predestination: "Quaedam ratio ordinis aliquorum in salutem aeternam in mente divina existentem." For the relation between providence and predestination, see I 23, 1c, and especially I 23, 3c, which also considers reprobation: "Sicut praedestinatio est pars providentiae respectu eorum qui divinitus ordinantur in aeternam salutem, ita reprobatio est pars providentiae respectu illorum qui ab hoc fine decidunt."

24 Thomas considers the *electio* which is the basis of predestination in I 23, 4c, and adds that this *electio* itself presupposes *dilectio*. As he writes here: "Praedestinatio . . . est pars providentiae. Providentia autem . . . est ratio in intellectu existens praeceptiva ordinationis aliquorum in finem. . . . Non autem praecipitur aliquid ordinandum in finem nisi praeexistente voluntate finis. Unde praedestinatio aliquorum in salutem aeternam praesupponit secundum rationem quod Deus illorum velit salutem, ad quod pertinet electio et dilectio. Dilectio quidem, inquantum vult eis hoc bonum salutis aeternae; nam diligere est velle alicui bonum. . . . Electio autem, inquantum hoc bonum aliquibus prae aliis vult, cum quosdam reprobat."

25 Thomas devotes I 23, 5, to establishing that God's foreknowledge of merits is not the cause of predestination. In I 23, 4c, after the words quoted in note 24, Thomas refers to the causal character of God's love; it is because God loves a person in this special way that this person possesses an enhanced dignity. I shall return to Thomas's remarks about the causal character of God's love and the way in which God's love differs from human love later in this section.

26 For Thomas's affirmation of the twofold ordination, see I 23, 1c: "Ad providentiam autem pertinet res in finem ordinare. . . . Finis autem ad quem res creatae ordinantur a Deo, est duplex. Unus, qui excedit proportionem naturae creatae et facultatem; et hic finis est vita aeterna, quae in divina visione consistit; quae est supra naturam cuiuslibet creaturae. . . . Alius autem finis est naturae creatae proportionatus, quem scilicet res creata potest attingere secundum virtutem suae naturae. Ad illud autem ad quod non potest aliquid virtute suae naturae pervenire oportet quod ab alio transmittatur, sicut sagitta a sagittante mittitur ad signum. Unde, proprie loquendo, rationalis creatura, quae est capax vitae aeternae, perducitur in ipsam quasi a Deo transmissa. Cuius quidem transmissionis ratio in Deo praeexistit, sicut et in eo est ratio ordinis omnium in finem, quam diximus

esse providentiam. Ratio autem alicuius fiendi in mente actoris existens est quaedam praeexistentia rei fiendae in eo. Unde ratio praedictae transmissionis creaturae rationalis in finem vitae aeternae praedestinatio nominatur; nam destinare est mittere. Et sic patet quod praedestinatio, quantum ad objecta, est quaedam pars providentiae."

It may be objected that my description of the twofold ordination in the text has restricted the ordination in an unacceptable manner. There are Thomists who would argue that just as all people *qua* human are ordained to their natural end, so too all are ordained to the supernatural end of seeing God. There *is* a sense in which it is correct to say that all people are ordained to eternal life. After all, Thomas does sometimes say that "man" is ordained to a twofold end, and this "man" is meant to be all-inclusive. However, I think there is a way to read such statements that will give them their full due and yet preserve the point made in the text, that God has predetermined certain people actually to attain God and then has moved them to this end. When Thomas generalizes about the universal scope of the ordination to eternal life, he is saying that all people as rational are "capable" of coming to this end, "capable" in the sense of possessing rational capacities that make rising to the direct intellectual knowledge a real possibility. In this regard, such texts as the following are relevant. In III 9, 2c, in discussing whether Christ was a *comprehensor*, Thomas notes: "Homo autem est in potentia ad scientiam beatorum, quae in visione Dei consistit, et ad eam ordinatur sicut ad finem; est enim creatura rationalis capax illius beatae cognitionis, inquantum est ad imaginem Dei." Similarly, he writes in III 9, 2 ad 3: "Visio seu scientia beata est quodammodo supra naturam animae rationalis, inquantum scilicet propria virtute ad eam pervenire non potest. Alio vero modo est secundum naturam ipsius, inquantum scilicet per naturam suam est capax eius, prout scilicet ad imaginem Dei facta est." Conversely, those creatures that are not rational (or, as these texts put it, not "made in the image of God") are not "capable" of the beatific vision and so are not "ordained" to this second end: In I 23, 1 ad 2, Thomas writes "creaturae irrationales non sunt capaces illius finis qui facultatem humanae naturae excedit," which in the corpus Thomas has stated is the special end to which rational creatures are ordained, life with God. Thus, in texts such as III 9, 2c, I agree that "ordained" to the beatific vision means simply what the terms *"capax Dei"* and *"capax gratiae"* mean, no more and no less.

But if we ask how it is that people make the move, as it were, from the merely natural to the supernatural level, the answer cannot be that they have exploited their potential for so rising or that God has "ordained" them to such a move by making them what they are. No, the answer is found in the predestinating will of God, who decides whom God will save and acts accordingly. God does not first create essences and then form a plan and then manipulate these essences in accordance with this plan. Rather, God creates individual creatures for specific purposes, and in creating them endows them or determines to endow them at some time with all they need to attain the end set for them. Thus, at this point, it is necessary to insist that "ordination" also has a deeper, more exclusive sense, one which is exclusively concerned with the destiny of the elect. Here, when Thomas is thinking of God's predestination and the actual realization of the highest end, 'ordination' is synonymous with 'predestination,' and this predestination is directed to specific individuals who have a determined role in the divine plan for creation

The Mature Teaching on Merit

and redemption. For an example of Thomas referring to the predestination of chosen people to salvation in terms of "ordaining," see I 23, 3c, which is quoted in note 23 above. Thomas makes the point that "predestination," this special ordination, involves "some" rational creatures, not all, in this same text, as well as in I 23, 2c (also quoted in note 23 above), and I 23, 4c, quoted in note 24 above. In addition, see III 24, 1 ad 2, in which Thomas observes that predestination has to do with the person, not with the nature of the person. Given the different connotations of "ordination" in Thomas, care must be given to grasping correctly the scope of the reference indicated by any particular use of the word. Sometimes *ordinatio* simply means that all people are capable of eternal life because they are created as rational. At other times, it means the same as *praedestinatio* and indicates that God has so created and disposed certain people that they will in fact attain God in this highest fashion. Later in the chapter, when discussing *ordinatio* as the ground of merit, I will show that it is in this narrower sense that we must read the *ordinatio* of merit.

The Thomist teaching about predestination, however, has also been open to divergent interpretations. For a rather different reading of predestination and the significance of human action for determining one's destiny, see J.-P. Arfeuil, "Le dessein sauveur de Dieu: La doctrine de la prédestination selon Saint Thomas d'Aquin," *Revue Thomiste* 7 (1974): 591–641. To explain predestination, Arfeuil concentrates on the distinction between the antecedent and consequent will of God inherited by Thomas from John of Damascus; Thomas discusses this distinction in I 19, 6 ad 1. The antecedent will of God is God's ordaining of all people to salvation and offer of all that is needed for them to come to God. This is the will to which I Timothy 2:4 ("God wills all people to be saved") refers. Yet not all people are saved, for some sin and so reject God's offer of salvation. In light of this rejection, God's consequent will comes into play. It would be inappropriate for God to will sinners to be saved. By their sin they have rejected God. Hence, God's consequent will takes note of the circumstances of each person, and only those who have responded correctly to the offer of grace receive the reward of heaven from God. Arfeuil adds (e.g., p. 610) that God's antecedent and consequent wills correspond to God's providence and predestination. Arfeuil believes that this view of the relation of God's antecedent and consequent will and human action holds throughout Thomas's career. Note that it is on this basis that he quotes texts from early and later in Thomas's career indiscriminately and sees no development in Thomas's thought. If Arfeuil's view of providence and predestination is at all accurate, it is accurate only for the early Thomas, in the *Scriptum* and *De Veritate*. From the 1260s on, however, Thomas has brought his thought on predestination more closely in line with that of the later Augustine, and it is impossible to see in the later Thomas God's willing of salvation in predestination being so "reactive" to or dependent on human works. There is no need to offer here a detailed rebuttal of Arfeuil's account of predestination. Such a rebuttal would unnecessarily repeat what is written in this chapter about predestination and, especially, about the operative graces of conversion and perseverance which issue from predestination and which are so significant in the later Thomas. That someone is saved in the later Thomas is due to God's decision to save that person; God's predestination and effective involvement in the life of the person are the reason for the person's salvation and for all the good which

In his discussion of God as the creator and governor of the world who
seeks to express the divine goodness in the world, Thomas makes a number
of additional points directly relevant to this study of merit. First, the act
of creation that occurs in accordance with the divine wisdom is characterized by Thomas as an act of *love*. The same act of love by which God
rests in the divine goodness as in its object stands as the cause, in God's
free decision to create, of all that comes into existence. A favorite strategy
of Thomas to underline the causal nature of the divine love is to distinguish
human and divine loves. Both loves are related to the good. Human love,
however, is evoked or caused by the good that exists in things. Divine love,
on the other hand, is not evoked by existing good in things but instead
causes these things themselves, that is, causes these goods.[27] For Thomas,
the causal power of divine love explains too the variety of things. While it
is the one and same act of love which is directed to the divine goodness and
to the creation, there are varying degrees of this love for what exists outside
of God and so varying goods/things issue from the divine love. Thomas
makes this point in an article in which he establishes that God loves the
better more. It is not, he says, because the better thing, that is, the
possessor of a greater good, incites God to a greater love for it. Rather, that
it possesses more good is due to God's greater love for it in the first
place—God has loved it more and therefore it possesses more good.[28] To
apply this to Thomas's teaching on predestination: All humans have been
equal recipients or beneficiaries of God's love to the extent that God's love
creates them with the same nature and capabilities by which they are
capable of the good natural to their beings. Yet those whom God loves more,
those whom God ordains to a greater destiny (life with God), have received
an even greater good. God's special love for them infuses in them the grace,
the effect of this love, which makes it possible for them to attain this special
good.[29] Thomas's basic point, then, is that at the basis of all which exists

that person does, including the correct response to God's offer of salvation.
Arfeuil can make a case for his reading of predestination in the *Summa* only
by ignoring or suppressing all the texts in the *Summa* in which Thomas
makes clear that God prevenes and is sovereign in the process of salvation.
For my part, such texts provide the correct starting point for the
interpretation of predestination and merit in Thomas. It should also be noted
that Arfeuil shows no grasp of God as transcendent cause in Thomas and so,
to preserve human freedom and contingency, must speak in generalities
about a free acceptance or rejection by the person of the offer of salvation and
grace.

27   Thomas draws this contrast in I 20, 2c.
28   See I 20, 4c, which supplements the teaching of the third article of this
     question. In the corpus of the fourth article, Thomas writes: "Deus magis
     diligat meliora. Dictum est enim (3c) quod Deum diligere magis aliquid nihil
     aliud est quam ei maius bonum velle; voluntas enim Dei est causa bonitatis
     in rebus; et sic ex hoc sunt aliqua meliora quod Deus eis majus bonum vult.
     Unde sequitur quod meliora plus amet."
29   Thomas observes that grace follows upon predestination as an effect follows

and all which creatures, including those rational creatures called to be with God, achieve, is God's creative love.

Second, God's relations to the creature are characterized not only by love but also by justice. For Thomas, justice means to render what is owed (*debitum*) to another.[30] On the basis of the divine goodness and wisdom, there is a twofold *debitum* in things. In the first place, there is the *debitum* owed to God. All creatures "owe" to God that they fulfill the part assigned to them by the divine wisdom for the manifestation of God's goodness. Second, there is the *debitum* owed by God to creatures. God ought to render to each creature what it needs to fulfill its role in the divine plan. Thus, if God decides to create a human being, God owes to that creature that it be endowed with all that pertains to human nature. As is clear, this second *debitum* ultimately is reducible to the first. Only because God has assigned a specific role to a creature in the divine plan is there anything "owing" to that creature. Indeed, Thomas adds, because of the divine ordination it is really more correct to say that this second *debitum* is owed not so much to the creature as to God Himself. Thus, as he will do in the discussion of merit (which entails the requital of a *debitum*) in I-II 114, 1, Thomas here denies that God is in fact a debtor to anyone other than to God. In rendering what is "owed" to the creature, God is ultimately remitting a debt owed to God on account of the determination of the divine wisdom.[31]

---

on its cause in I 23, 2 ad 4. In I-II 110, 1c, Thomas completes his discussion of God's creative love begun in I 20. In I-II 110, 1c, he also draws the contrast between human and divine love first made in I 20, 2c, and argues that the good of grace is established in the soul because of God's special love for the individual.

30   See, e.g., I 21, 1 ob 3, in which the subject is the justice of God: "Actus iustitiae est reddere debitum."

31   The discussion in the text reports Thomas's teaching in I 21, 1 ad 3: "Unicuique debetur quod suum est. Dicitur autem esse suum alicuius quod ad ipsum ordinatur, sicut est servus domini, et non e converso; nam liberum est quod sui causa est. In nomine ergo debiti importatur quidam ordo exigentiae vel necessitatis alicuius ad quod ordinatur. Est autem duplex ordo considerandus in rebus. Unus, quo aliquid creatum ordinatur ad aliud creatum, sicut partes ordinantur ad totum, et accidentia ad substantias, et unaquaeque res ad suum finem. Alius ordo, quo omnia creata ordinantur in Deum. Sic igitur et debitum attendi potest dupliciter in operatione divina, aut secundum quod aliquid debetur Deo, aut secundum quod aliquid debetur rei creatae; et utroque modo Deus debitum reddit. Debitum enim est Deo ut impleatur in rebus id quod eius sapientia et voluntas habet, et quod suam bonitatem manifestat; et secundum hoc iustitia Dei respicit decentiam ipsius secundum quam reddit sibi quod sibi debetur. Debitum etiam est alicui rei creatae quod habeat id quod ad ipsam, ordinatur, sicut homini quod habeat manus, et quod ei alia animalia serviant; et sic etiam Deus operatur iustitiam quando dat unicuique quod ei debetur secundum rationem suae naturae et conditionis. Sed hoc debitum dependet ex primo, quia hoc unicuique debetur quod est ordinatum ad ipsum secundum ordinem divinae sapientiae. Et licet Deus hoc modo debitum alicui det, non tamen ipse est debitor, quia ipse ad

While Thomas is only incidentally concerned with merit in the present text, his reflections here about the twofold *debitum* in things are of great interest for the correct understanding of Thomas's merit for they suggest how Thomas conceives the "debt" established by merit. Extrapolating from his teaching in the present text, Thomas will argue that by the first *debitum*, a human being owes to God the service for which he was created. The person is meant to manifest the goodness of God and does this when he fulfills God's will for him as delineated in God's law (natural and divine) that has been given to him. When the person acts as God wishes and so offers to God the service and honor for which God has created him, the second *debitum* comes into play. By performing the acts required by God that allow him to attain the end set for him by God, this person becomes qualified to receive as a reward from God the end ordained for him. His good acts constitute the second *debitum*, the "debt" of merit. Conversely, this teaching about the twofold *debitum* also permits us to see how Thomas can speak of punishment as owed for the debt of sin. The human person possesses dominion over his acts. This basic freedom makes it possible for the person to defect from the rule established by God to guide human beings to their appropriate end. When the person misuses his freedom in this way, the person fails to offer to God the requisite service (fails to requite the *debitum* owed by all creatures to their Creator) and so fails to establish the *debitum* of reward from God. Rather, the sinner by his defection from the standard set for him by God becomes liable to the punishment deserved by those who fail to honor God. Through sin, he merits to be deprived of the possibility of attaining to the vision of God.[32]

alia non ordinatur, sed potius alia in ipsum. Et ideo iustitia quandoque dicitur in Deo condecentia suae bonitatis, quandoque vero retribution pro meritis. Et utrumque modum tangit Anselmus dicens, Cum punis malos justum est, quia illorum meritis convenit; sum vero parcis malis justum est, quia bonitati tuae condecens est."

32 As texts such as I 23, 5 ad 3 (quoted in note 22 above), make clear, when God gives to the sinner the just reward of his sin, this punishment also contributes to the manifestation of the divine goodness, although in a different way than is the case for the predestination of a rational creature to life with God. By punishing the sinner, God reveals God's justice, which itself is a good.

   Thomas himself has discussed merit before God in terms of the twofold *debitum* of I 21, 1 ad 3, in I-II 21, 4c, in which he offers basically the same analysis given in the text. I-II 21, 4c, however, along with I-II 21, 3, offers special difficulties to the interpreter of Aquinas, for Thomas speaks of merit and demerit before God here without explicit references to the need for grace and charity for merit or of the special ordination which, according to I-II 114, 1c, makes merit possible. The difficulties in I-II 21, 3–4 have led some Thomists to suggest that Thomas in these articles is speaking not of "theological" merit, which is the topic of this book, but of a "natural" merit, which applies to all moral acts, including those done by the natural powers alone of the person, that is, those acts which are not performed in grace. Arguably, this is what T. Deman, *Der Neue Bund und die Gnade* (Heidelberg, 1955), p. 417, is suggesting. Hence, naturally good acts would deserve an

As Thomas makes clear in his discussion of the justice of God in the *Summa*, he finds no incompatibility in his dual affirmation of love and justice regulating the relations of God and the world. In the first place, from what has already been said, it is clear that justice is secondary to the love of God and presupposes God's love for the world and the human person. Unless God first loved the person, establishing the person as a creature of this type and, most crucially, as called to a certain destiny, there would be no need to speak of justice according to Aquinas. That there is a *debitum* to be requited by God in justice is itself due to God's decision to accord this creature this particular role in the divine scheme to manifest the divine goodness outside of God.[33] Second, even in God's act of justice toward the individual God's love is present and governs God in rendering for the *debitum*, a point Thomas adds in the question on God's justice. As Thomas says, when God is acting justly toward the individual, God does more than justice requires, for by God's love, God always grants more to the person than the person's *debitum* demands.[34] Thus, while justice is present in the

---

appropriate reward from God, although not a supernatural reward from God. For my part, I do not think that there is such a species of merit in Aquinas. I think that I-II 21, 3–4 can be squared with Thomas's teaching about merit elsewhere in the *Summa* as long as we acknowledge that these articles cannot be read on their own and that they do not constitute Thomas's major discussion of merit; this discussion is found in I-II 114, 1–10. What Thomas wishes to establish in these earlier articles of I-II 21 is the simple point that all our acts, good or bad, as moral actions deserve and elicit a reward or punishment from God; Thomas does not want to spell out all the conditions which must be observed for merit to occur. Later in this chapter, I return to I-II 21, 3–4, showing how its teaching supports Thomas's insight, expressed in I-II 114, that merit presupposes a community existing between God and the recipients of God's favor.

33   See I 21, 4c: "Opus autem divinae iustitiae semper praesupponit opus misericordiae, et in eo fundatur. Creaturae enim non debetur aliquid nisi propter aliquid in ea praeexistens vel praeconsideratum. Et rursus si illud creaturae debetur, hoc erit propter aliquid prius. Et cum non sit procedere in infinitum, oportet devenire ad aliquid quod ex sola bonitate divinae voluntatis dependeat, quae est ultimus finis: utpote si dicamus quod habere manus debitum est homini propter animam rationalem, animam vero rationalem habere ad hoc quod sit homo, hominem vero esse propter divinam bonitatem." Note that Thomas speaks of 'mercy' here. For Aquinas, 'mercy' means "removing some defect" and can be used as a synonym for 'love.' In I 21, 4 ad 4, Thomas describes the creative work of God as 'mercy,' for in creation God brings a thing out of non-being into being, that is, removes the defect of non-being by mercifully granting being. In this regard, the texts listed in notes 27 and 28 above, in which Thomas underscores the causal nature of the divine love, should be recalled. In I 21, 4 ad 4, Thomas also mentions the quality of *justice* involved in creating, for the reason mentioned earlier in this chapter—for creation "convenit divinae sapientiae et bonitati." I shall return to the importance of God's prevenient love in merit in detail later in the chapter, in the course of analysing the teaching of I-II 114, 1–4.

34   Thomas makes this point in I 21, 4c, where he states that it is characteristic

relations of God and the human person, justice plays a secondary role in Thomas's theology. It is subordinate to, and completed by, the love of God that is expressed by God principally for Himself and secondly for the creation as manifested in God's free decision to create the world.

With this review of Thomas's teaching about God's creation and redemption for the purpose of manifesting the divine goodness outside of God, the general context of Thomas's teaching about merit in the *Summa Theologiae* has been outlined; as we shall see, in this work Thomas understands and explains merit in terms of this plan for the manifestation of the goodness of God formulated in accordance with the divine wisdom. However, before turning to Aquinas's discussion of merit in the *Summa*, it is first necessary to examine his teaching in this work about grace, the immediate context of his reflections on merit.

B. Grace

Three basic distinctions inform Thomas's discussion of grace in the *Summa Theologiae*.[35] First, Thomas draws our attention to the difference between the supernatural and natural orders of existence,[36] and uses this

of divine goodness to share itself more than it has to, that is, more than strict justice requires. What this means in terms of the *debitum* of merit is that because God makes possible meritorious acts (as we shall see in the next section of this chapter), God owes a reward in justice for these works (as we shall see in the second part, in the discussion of merit). But in requiting these acts, God will give an even greater reward (that is, more of the reward) than is strictly deserved, for God is characteristically generous in all that God does.

35   The present discussion of Thomas's teaching about grace in the *Summa* makes no claim to exhaustiveness. Rather, the focus is on the features of Thomas's description of grace which figure prominently in his analysis of merit. Bouillard and Lonergan (see Chapter 1) have located the *Summa*'s treatise on grace in the general development of Thomas's understanding of grace. The present discussion of the *Summa* on grace has benefited greatly from their studies. In addition, the book by J.-M. Laporte, *Les structures dynamiques de la grace* (Montreal, 1973) and the commentary by T. Deman on the treatise on grace, *Der Neue Bund und die Gnade*, have also proved helpful.

36   This distinction between the two orders of existence has already been introduced in the discussion in the previous section on the twofold ordination of people. In this section, I am concerned with the two orders of existence inasmuch as they figure in Thomas's discussion of grace. As should be evident by this point, the distinction between the natural and supernatural orders is acknowledged throughout Thomas's career and always constitutes the background of Thomas's discussion of merit. Yet, as is clear from the reflections on predestination in the previous section, Thomas's teaching about how the "move" by the human person from the natural level of existence to the supernatural is negotiated is not the same in his various works. In the *Summa Theologiae,* as in the *Summa Contra Gentiles* (but not in the *Scriptum*), Thomas insists that God predestines and thereby effects this move by a person so that the person receives the grace which issues from predestination and then acts, under the guidance of grace, in the way which

distinction to portray the various ways in which grace can be said to be necessary.[37] The word 'natural' has a number of meanings in Aquinas. In the present context, 'natural' refers to what is appropriate and possible for a being endowed with a given nature—the "natural" is what conforms to its nature.[38] Every being possesses a nature, and thus what is natural for

will lead with certainty to the special supernatural end determined for this person by God. In other words, entry to life on the supernatural level which is accomplished by grace as well as the remaining stages of supernatural life in this world are clearly subordinated by the later Thomas to God's causally effective predestination of individuals to supernatural life. Given the different nuances of the later Thomas's understanding of the role of predestination (and therefore of grace, the effect of predestination), it is not redundant or out of place here to consider anew the significance of the distinction between the natural and the supernatural orders for Thomas's teaching on grace in the *Summa*.

37   Thomas considers the need for grace in ten articles in I-II 109. As will become clear in this section as well as in the discussion of the *ex professo* treatment of merit, I-II 109 is very important for determining Thomas's understanding of merit in the *Summa*, for it often provides valuable and illuminating parallel discussions of issues examined in the articles on merit.

38   Thomas refers to the good which is 'natural' for a person *qua* human in a number of articles in the treatise on grace. In many of the articles of I-II 109, Thomas wishes to stress that the Fall has introduced a new need for grace, for sin not only caused the first people to lose the opportunity to act supernaturally, it also disrupted the original harmony of the soul and so has made difficult the doing even of the good which is natural to people. Hence, in these articles, Thomas states that there is a good natural to people, and then evaluates how near people could come to this good before and after sin. In I-II 109, 2c, for example, he states that in the state of integral nature, a person could *per sua naturalia* will and do the good proportionate to his nature ("velle et operari bonum suae naturae proportionatum"), and identifies this as the good of acquired virtue (on the notion of "virtue," and for the difference between "acquired" and "infused" virtue, see below in the text), but notes that after the corruption of sin, "deficit homo ab hoc quod secundum suam naturam potest, ut non possit totum huiusmodi bonum implere per sua naturalia." Thomas adds here that the corruption of nature by sin has not been total, and so even in the state of sin a person without grace can do some particular acts by the power of his nature which accord with his natural end, such as "build houses, plant vines, and other things of this sort"; nevertheless, the sinner cannot do "totum bonum sibi connaturale, ita quod in nullo deficiat." For a similar list of acts natural to the human person and still possible for the sinner, see I-II 109, 5c; Thomas believed he was deriving this list from an authentic work by Augustine, but as the editor of the Blackfriars edition notes (p. 86, n. 8), the *Hypognosticon* is the work of a follower of Augustine, Marius Mercator. For other texts in which Thomas speaks of the good "connatural" to the person as human, see I-II 109, 3c, where he explains in what sense the love of God above all things is *connaturale homini*, and I-II 109, 7 ad 3, where Thomas says that grace is needed to restore to the sinner the *bonum sibi connaturale*. Other instances of Thomas speaking of what is natural to the person will be listed in the course of the analysis of the functions of grace.

one being differs from what is natural for a different kind of being. It is "natural" for the stone to come to rest; it is "natural" for the plant to vegetate; it is "natural" for the human person to come to abstract knowledge through the information first gathered by the senses. God too "has" a nature. It is proper to God to be engaged in constant self-contemplation and love,[39] although it should be immediately added that in God, just as God's nature is God's existence, so too the subject and object of this contemplation are completely identical and can be distinguished only for the purposes of discussion. Correspondingly, as the word suggests, the "supernatural" refers to what is above (*super*) a nature of a given type. In the treatise on grace, the "supernatural" refers to God's own life of self-love and knowledge which transcends the capacities of natural human existence. While it is natural for God to know and love God directly, this is not natural for the human being.[40]

Yet, as has already been noted, God calls certain people to share in God's own existence, to become, as it were, God. God's call issues in grace, which for Thomas elevates (*gratia elevans*) the person to the supernatural level of existence, to the level of God's own activity.[41] For Thomas, grace is the participation in God's own nature,[42] which makes it possible for the person

39 Thomas uses the language of connaturality of God in a number of places. See, e.g., I 12, 4c: "Relinquitur . . . quod cognoscere ipsum esse subsistens sit connaturale soli intellectui divino, et quod sit supra facultatem naturalem cuiuslibet intellectus creatae"; and I-II 5, 7c: "Habere autem perfectum bonum sine motu convenit ei quod naturaliter habet illud. Habere autem beatitudinem naturaliter est solius Dei."

40 Thomas speaks of the supernatural good which surpasses the natural capacities of human being in, e.g., I-II 109, 2c, where he says it is a *bonum supernaturale* and a *bonum superexcedens*, and is the good of infused virtue. See also I-II 109, 7 ad 3, where Thomas contrasts the good *connaturale* to human being and the *bonum supernaturalis iustitiae*.

41 For grace as "elevating," see I-II 109, 9c, where Thomas says that grace elevates restored human nature to perform the works meritorious of eternal life, which exceeds the proportion of nature (". . . et etiam sanata elevetur ad operanda opera meritoria vitae aeternae, quae excedunt proportionem naturae"). For the description of grace as "supernatural," see I-II 110, 1c, where Thomas identifies grace with the special love of God for the predestined: "Alia . . . dilectio est specialis, secundum quam trahit creaturam rationalem supra conditionem naturae ad participationem divini boni. . . . Sic igitur per hoc quod dicitur homo gratiam Dei habere, significatur quiddam supernaturale in homine a Deo proveniens." See also I-II 110, 2c.

42 The words in the text are meant to echo II Peter 1:4, which is cited by Thomas in I-II 110, 3c: He writes here that the infused virtues dispose a person in a higher way than do the acquired virtues, "and in view of a higher end; and also, it follows, with reference to some higher nature. Now this in fact is the divine nature as possessed by participation, as II Peter says, 'He has given us most great and precious promises, that by these you may be made partakers [*consortes*] of the divine nature.'" A little later in the corpus, Thomas adds that the light of grace "est participatio divinae naturae." II Peter 1:4 is also quoted in I-II 62, 1c, in which Thomas is discussing the theological

to act "like" God. Now, the purpose of God's call is to bring the individual to the direct vision of God in the next life, and grace by its nature is oriented to the beatific vision. It "moves" the human person on the path to God and prepares the person for the vision of God. Yet, in this life, the human person remains separated from God and is incapable of the direct vision of God. Rather, the individual is capable, through grace, only of acts which "anticipate" in a way appropriate to human nature the final vision of and union with God. Thus, whereas in the next life the person will know God directly in the way that God knows Himself, in this life, the person "knows" God only indirectly, by the faith instilled in him by grace.[43]

In the light of this distinction between the natural and the supernatural, Thomas can provide a highly nuanced analysis of the need for grace. In *Summa Theologiae* I-II 109, Thomas asks a series of questions about the extent of the need for grace, and his answers in large measure trade on the difference between the natural and the supernatural. In article 1, for example, he asks whether a person can know any truth without grace. In the corpus, Thomas notes that there is natural and supernatural truth. Natural truth is the truth which lies within the normal scope of the human powers of knowing. Since by birth a person has the natural endowments which allow him to know such truths, Thomas states here that grace is not needed to know natural truth. All that is required is the correct use of one's natural powers to know. Supernatural truth, on the other hand, is the truth which only God knows naturally. Hence, since such truth transcends the natural powers of the human person for knowing, the human person can know such truths only when the person is empowered to act like God. Since it is grace that makes possible such action (in ways to be specified shortly), Thomas argues here that grace is needed for the knowledge of supernatural truth.[44]

---

virtues.

43 In Thomas's extended treatment of the theological virtues, he offers his reflections on the way in which each of these virtues anticipates different facets of the beatific vision. Thus, in this world the Christian holds by faith certain truths about God, without grasping their full content or holding them with the certainty associated with demonstrative knowledge. Similarly, the Christian hopes to be joined to God as to his end, without being immediately joined to God at present as he will be, at the beatific vision. An important part of Thomas's teaching about the theological virtues is that faith will give way to the direct knowledge which is the heart of beatification. And that hope will be replaced by "comprehension," the direct attachment to God. Only charity remains fundamentally the same in this life and the next, although in direct contact with the good, charity will become even more intense than it is in the present life. For this teaching about the provisional nature of the theological virtues, see, e.g., I-II 67, 3–6.

44 See I-II 109, 1c: "Unaquaeque autem forma indita rebus creatis a Deo habet efficaciam respectu alicuius actus determinati, in quem potest secundum suam proprietatem; ultra autem non potest nisi per aliquam formam superadditam, sicut aqua non potest calefacere nisi calefacta ab igne. Sic

The second distinction shaping Thomas's analysis of grace is the one that he draws between habitual grace and the *auxilium* of God.[45] In the philosophy of Aquinas, action of any type presupposes the potency to act in that way. Hence, for example, it would be inappropriate to demand thinking from a stone, since the stone lacks the basic power required for thought, the mind. Yet the human being possesses a mind and so is able to think. Thomas states that the same requirement holds for action on the supernatural level. Supernatural action presupposes a basic structure that makes such action possible. It is at this point that Thomas introduces the

---

igitur intellectus humanus habet aliquam formam, scilicet ipsum intelligibile lumen quod est de se sufficiens ad quaedam intelligibilia cogniscenda, ad ea scilicet in quorum notitiam per sensibilia possumus devenire. Altiora vero intelligibilia intellectus humana cognoscere non potest, nisi fortiori lumine perficiatur, sicut lumine fidei vel prophetiae, quod dicitur *lumen gratiae*, inquantum est naturae superadditum." Similarly, the distinction between the natural and the supernatural permits Thomas to offer a careful analysis of the extent of the need for grace in I-II 109, 2c, in which, asking whether grace is needed to will and do good, Thomas notes that there are two goods, the natural and the supernatural, and that the reason for the need of grace for the attainment of each differs.

45   As we saw in Chapter 1, Bouillard and Lonergan disagree whether habitual grace and *auxilium* are two separate graces (Lonergan) or two ways of conceiving the same grace (Bouillard). Bouillard based his case especially on the claim that Thomas does not know of any divinely caused action which does not realize a potential for action of that type. Hence, when Thomas speaks of *auxilium* working the conversion of the sinner, he implies that included in this *auxilium* is the habitual grace which establishes the potential (see below in the text) for God-directed action. Lonergan, on the other hand, has enumerated instances where Bouillard's claim is disproved. Thomas does know of God working acts of willing or acting which do not presuppose the potential in the person for such motion. For our purposes, it is not necessary to take a stand on this issue. While I think that Lonergan makes the better case, it does not materially affect this study of merit whether Thomas means two distinct graces or simply the same grace seen in two different ways, that is, as habitual grace and as the "motion" or dynamic contribution of God. What *is* important is that we be aware of the different nuances in Thomas's thought about grace. Hence, for example, in I-II 114, 9c, when Thomas speaks of our inability to merit the grace of preserverance, he speaks of the *motio* of grace; although he does not tell us explicitly, from the parallel discussion in I-II 109, 9c, he is thinking here especially of the *auxilium* of grace conceived along Augustinian lines, as the dynamic involvement of God in all the good which people do—in I-II 114, 9, he is not thinking of grace as "habitual." Yet I-II 109, 9c, alerts us to a vexing feature of Thomas's language about grace. In note 52 below, I will cite passages which disclose the principal function and meaning of *auxilium*, God's application of people to their acts. But as I-II 109, 9c, and similar texts show, Thomas can at times use the term *auxilium* also to refer to *habitual* grace. Thomas's relaxed terminology does not, of itself, make Bouillard's argument. But it does warn us to be careful to determine in every use of the term whether Thomas is using *auxilium* in a narrow or broad sense.

concept of "habitual grace." For Thomas, a habit is a steady disposition for action of a certain type. It is a perfection of the soul or of a power of the soul that makes possible action of a certain type.[46] On the natural level, Thomas speaks of *acquired habits*. These are habits acquired through repeated action of a type. Once one acquires through one's action such a habit, he will tend by this habit to produce such action when occasion demands it. Supernatural habits, however, cannot be acquired since we do not naturally do what transcends our capabilities. Rather, these habits are infused by God, who elevates the recipient of God's love to God's own level.[47] In discussing habits on the supernatural level, Thomas refers to the difference between the grace that is habitual and the theological virtues accompanying this grace. This difference mirrors Thomas's psychology, in which the essence of the soul is distinguished from the powers of the soul

---

46   For Thomas's working definition of 'habit,' see, e.g., I-II 49, 4c: "Habitus importat dispositionem quamdam in ordine ad naturam rei, et ad operationem vel finem eius, secundum quam bene vel male aliquid ad hoc disponitur." Good habits—that is, habits which make possible repeated action in keeping with the laws and end of human nature—are called by Thomas 'virtues'; see, e.g., I-II 55, 3c. Conversely, 'vices' are bad habits, that is, they dispose to acts which do not contribute to the fulfillment of human being.

47   As mentioned in notes 38 and 40, in I-II 109, 2c, Thomas says that the good connatural to the human being is the good of acquired virtue, while the good to which people are divinely ordained by God and which exceeds their natural powers is the good of infused virtue. For a general discussion of the different ways in which the virtues can originate, see I-II 51; Thomas discusses the origin of the infused virtues in I-II 51, 4. In the discussion of I-II 114, 5, and parallel texts, I shall examine Thomas's teaching in the *Summa* about the "preparation" required for the infusion of habitual grace and why this "preparation" is not meritorious. In I-II 110, 2c, Thomas draws a parallel with the requirement of creatures for natural action to make the case for the need for the formal perfection of habitual grace and the theological virtues. After noting the need for God's *auxilium* to apply people to their acts (see below in the text), Thomas writes: "Alio modo adiuvatur homo ex gratuita Dei voluntate, secundum quod aliquod habituale donum a Deo animae infunditur; et hoc ideo quia non est conveniens quod Deus minus provideat his quos diligit ad supernaturale bonum habendum quam creaturis quas diligit ad bonum naturale habendum. Creaturis autem naturalibus sic providet, ut non solum moveat eas ad actus naturales, sed etiam largiatur eis formas et virtutes quasdam, quae sunt principia actuum, ut secundum seipsas inclinentur ad huiusmodi motus. Et sic motus quibus a Deo moventur fiunt creaturis connaturales et faciles, secundum illud *Sap., Et disponit omnia suaviter*. Multo igitur magis illis quos movet ad consequendum bonum supernaturale aeternum infundit aliquas formas, seu qualitates supernaturales, secundum quas suaviter et prompte ab ipso moveantur ad bonum aeternum consequendum; et sic donum gratiae qualitas quaedam est." In I-II 110, 3c, Thomas writes that "sicut . . . virtutes acquisitae perficiunt ad ambulandum secundum quod congruit lumini naturali rationis, ita virtutes infusae perficiunt hominem ad ambulandum secundum quod congruit lumini gratiae."

flowing out from the essence. Hence, habitual grace, which grants the human person the basic capacity for action on the supernatural level, is rooted in and perfects the essence of the soul, while the theological virtues that "flow out" from habitual grace perfect the powers of the soul that arise from the soul's essence—faith perfects the intellect; love and hope, the will.[48] At any rate, habitual grace and the theological virtues constitute for Aquinas the basic structure necessary for action on the supernatural level.

In the *Summa*, Thomas completes his reflections about habitual grace by noting a second function of this grace. Habitual grace is not only *elevans*; it is also *sanans*.[49] For Aquinas, *rectitudo* is a matter of right relationship and correct order. As originally created, the human person existed in the right order to God: Human reason was absolutely subject to the divine will, and offered to God the obedience asked of it by God. Similarly, in the human person himself, there existed a correct ordering between the different levels of the soul. The lower powers of the soul were utterly subordinate to the command of reason, just as reason was subordinate to God. Sin, however, has disrupted this pristine order: Just as human sin has withdrawn the reason from its subjection to God, so too by sin the lower powers of the soul no longer are amenable to the rule of reason. Hence, in place of the original harmony of the soul, in the sinner reason no longer holds sway and each part of the soul seeks its own end without concern for the true good of the human person.[50] In light of this analysis of the disruption caused by sin,

---

48   I-II 110, 4, is crucial for this distinction between habitual grace and the theological virtues. In ad 1, Thomas writes: "Sicut ab essentia animae effluunt eius potentiae, quae sunt operum principia, ita etiam ab ipsa gratia effluunt virtutes in potentias animae, per quas potentiae moventur ad actus." See also the corpus: "Unde relinquitur quod gratia, sicut est prius virtute, ita habeat subjectum prius potentiis animae; ita scilicet quod sit in essentia animae. Sicut enim per potentiam intellectivam homo participat cognitionem divinam per virtutem fidei, et secundum potentiam voluntatis amorem divinum per virtutem caritatis, ita etiam per naturam animae participat secundum quamdam similitudinem naturam divinam per quamdam regenerationem, sive recreationem"; and I-II 110, 3 ad 3: Grace is not "idem quod virtus, sed habitudo quaedam quae praesupponitur virtutibus infusis, sicut earum principium et radix."

49   Thomas refers to the healing function of grace in, e.g., I-II 109, 3c, 4c, and 8c. Grace is described as both elevating and healing in such articles as I-II 109, 9c; he says here that a person needs God's habitual grace (*aliquod habituale donum*), "per quod natura humana corrupta sanetur, et etiam sanata elevetur ad operanda opera meritoria vitae aeternae, quae excedunt proportionem naturae."

50   For a brief description of the *rectitudo* proper to human beings, see I-II 113, 1c, in which Thomas indicates that one meaning which 'justice' can have is that it "importat rectitudinem quamdam ordinis in ipsa interiori dispositione hominis, prout scilicet supremum hominis subditur Deo, et inferiores vires animae subduntur supremae, scilicet rationi." For the disruption caused by original sin in the soul, see I-II 85, 3c, and for the rectitude of the human being in the original state, see I 94, 1c.

when he speaks of habitual grace Thomas adds that this grace is designed by God to restore the rectitude lost by sin. Not only does habitual grace re-orient the person to God and raise the person to the supernatural level, it also heals the person of the disorder caused by sin, restoring in the soul the proper subordination of the lower parts of the soul to the reason and thus making possible the consistent pursuit of the good. However, while order in the soul is restored for the most part by habitual grace, this reparation is never complete in this world. As the aftereffect of the disruption of sin, the lower parts remain prone to further rejection of the rule of reason and hence are open to more sin. The consummation of the healing work of habitual grace, then, must await the next life, when the soul will enjoy the direct vision of God and rest perfectly in this union with the good.[51]

Thomas's description of the other grace involved in supernatural action, the *auxilium* of God,[52] employs notions derived from both Aristotle and Augustine. In the first place, following Aristotle, Thomas asserts that what is in potency to act is reduced to act only by what is already in act. What is in potency to act does not move itself. In the *Summa Theologiae* it is God,

---

51 Thomas asserts the provisional and incomplete healing accomplished by habitual grace in I-II 109, 9c. In this article, he says that human nature is healed as far as the *mens* is concerned, but that it continues to be corrupted and infected with regard to the flesh. Moreover, the understanding itself remains plagued by a kind of ignorance, which hinders the effort to ascertain with certainty where the good truly lies. For these reasons, as will be stated shortly in the text, Thomas affirms the need for God's future involvement in the mode of *auxilium gratiae*, to help the justified person to will and do the good. In I-II 109, 8c, Thomas says that habitual grace heals the mind, and adds that fleshly desires are not yet wholly (*nondum totaliter*) repaired by grace. This is why, he adds, the justified can refrain completely (with the aid of grace) from mortal sin, which is an affair of reason, but not from venial sin, which arises in the flesh.

52 As I observed in note 45 above, *auxilium* can have both a narrower and a broader significance. In its specialized sense, Thomas means by the term something at least conceptually distinct from habitual grace: This is God applying or moving the rational creature perfected by habitual grace and the theological virtues to its act, or even God's first moving of the sinful soul back to God; in the discussion of I-II 111, 2c, below in the text, the different meanings of this "application" will be clarified. For *auxilium* in this sense, see such texts as I-II 109, 1c, where he calls it *divinum auxilium*, I-II 109, 2c (*divinum auxilium*), I-II 109, 3c (*auxilium Dei moventis, auxilium Dei*), I-II 109, 4c (*auxilium Dei moventis*), I-II 109, 5 ad 3 (*auxilium gratiae*), and I-II 109, 6c (*auxilium gratuitum Dei interius animam moventis*). On the other hand, Thomas also uses *auxilium* to refer to both this meaning of the term and to habitual grace—see, e.g., I-II 109, 6c, where he says that we need the *auxilium divinum* understood both as habitual grace, which is involved in meritorious acts, and as God's moving of people to God; I-II 109, 7c, where he uses *auxilium* to refer to the *habituale donum* and to the *interior Dei motio*; and I-II 109, 9c, where again *auxilium* covers both *habituale donum* and the interior moving by God of the soul.

Pure Act, who moves the individual to action, by reducing the theological virtue that inclines the individual to a certain action to this act. Hence, grace is responsible not only for the possibility of doing on the supernatual level, but as *auxilium* also in a radical way for the doing itself.[53] But, secondly, *auxilium* in Thomas is not simply affirmed because of his adoption of Aristotelian physics. Thomas also uses *auxilium* to express distinctively Augustinian ideas. In his discussion of perseverance, Thomas acknowledges that justification entails the transformation of the individual, conquering the sin and tendency to sin that characterizes the sinner before the reception of grace and making it possible for the individual to perform the acts of grace and justice that God desires of the human person. Yet, Thomas adds, the transformation entailed in justification is never so complete in this life that the individual can no longer sin; indeed, left to himself, the justified individual would be drawn back to sin by the inclination to and temptations of sin remaining in him after justification. Because of the continued presence of sin, Thomas concludes, it is constantly necessary for God to direct and move the justified person to the good acts which truly fulfill his being—only by God's contribution to human action does the human person in fact do the good. Thus, in the *Summa*, *auxilium* refers not only to God causing human action but indeed to God causing *correct* human action.[54]

---

53   Throughout I-II 109, Thomas refers to the *auxilium* of God moving the person to supernatural acts; see, e.g., I-II 109, 2c: "Secundum . . . utrumque statum natura humana indiget auxilio divino ad faciendum vel volendum quodcumque bonum, sicut primo movente." In I-II 109, 1c, Thomas cites Aristotle (*De Anima* III, 4) as the source of his teaching. Note that Thomas insists that God's involvement is required not only for supernatural activity but also for action on the natural level, for the same reason. What is in potency to act is reduced to act only by what is already in act, God. Thus, e.g., in I-II 109, 1c, Thomas says that God must move the soul to know natural truths as well. For the purpose of clarity, when I refer to *auxilium* as grace, I mean only God's action vis-à-vis the rational creature in the supernatural order of existence. With regard to the *auxilium* on the natural level, it is perhaps better not to call this grace, but rather to refer to it as God's "general concursus." It should be noted that this "natural" *auxilium does* figure at one point in Thomas's teaching about merit; see the discussion of I-II 114, 10, where he analyzes whether temporal goods fall under theological merit.

54   See I-II 109, 9c, where Thomas is asking whether the justified person needs the further aid of grace. As to habitual grace, he says that once this is received, there is no need for a new infusion of habitual grace. But when we look at the other mode of the aid of grace, God's motion or application, then we have to assert the need for the further gift of such grace, "ut scilicet a Deo moveatur ad recte agendum." Later in this chapter, I shall return to this operative grace of perseverance, in the discussion of Thomas's teaching of the impossibility of meriting this grace. As I will suggest there, and argue at greater length in the final chapter, Thomas's incorporation of this form of the *auxilium* of God into his teaching on merit evinces the significance of the later Augustine's insights into grace for the formulation of Thomas's teaching about grace and

The final distinction important to Thomas's discussion of grace in the *Summa* is that between operative and cooperative grace, articulated in *ST* I-II 111, 2. Here, Thomas asserts that his understanding of grace as habitual and as divine *auxilium* can be expressed in these traditional Augustinian terms.[55] Reflecting his greater interest in the *Summa* in grace as *auxilium* that moves us to act, in the corpus Thomas discusses how *auxilium* is both operative and cooperative first and in fact devotes much more space in this article to the discussion of *auxilium* than to that of habitual grace.[56] In treating *auxilium* in terms of these Augustinian categories, Thomas first offers a definition of 'operative' and 'cooperative.' 'Operative' refers to that effect in which the mind is moved and does not move itself. God alone is the mover. 'Cooperative,' on the other hand, refers to that effect in which the mind is not only moved by God, but also is a mover ("In illo ergo effectu in quo mens nostra est mota et non movens,

---

merit in the *Summa*.

55 For the significance of I-II 111, 2, see the discussion of Lonergan's study of operative grace in Aquinas in Chapter 1. In the present discussion of this article, I have no intention of rehearsing Lonergan's analysis. Rather, it is necessary to look at I-II 111, 2c, in detail because, as I note toward the end of this section, in this text Thomas offers his most comprehensive treatment of the respective contributions of God and the human person to the meritorious act. I have also discussed this passage in my articles "'Perseverance' in 13th-Century Theology: The Augustinian Contribution," *Augustinian Studies* 22 (1991): 125–40, and "On the Purpose of 'Merit' in the Theology of Thomas Aquinas," *Medieval Philosophy and Theology* 2 (1992): 97–116.

56 The first part of I-II 111, 2c, reads as follows: "Gratia dupliciter potest intelligi: uno modo divinum auxilium, quo nos movet ad bene volendum et agendum; alio modo habituale donum nobis divinitus inditum. Utroque autem modo gratia dicta convenienter dividitur per operantem et cooperantem. Operatio enim alicuius effectus non attribuitur mobili, sed moventi. In illo ergo effectu in quo mens nostra est mota et non movens, solus autem Deus movens, operatio Deo attribuitur; et secundum hoc dicitur *gratia operans*. In illo autem effectu in quo mens nostra et movet et movetur, operatio non solum attribuitur Deo, sed etiam animae; et secundum hoc dicitur *gratia cooperans*. Est autem in nobis duplex actus. Primus quidem interior voluntatis; et quantum ad istum actum voluntas se habet ut mota, Deus autem ut movens, et praesertim cum voluntas incipit bonum velle, quae prius malum volebat: et ideo, secundum quod Deus movet humanam mentem ad hunc actum, dicitur *gratia operans*. Alius actus est exterior, qui cum a voluntate imperetur . . . consequens est quod ad hunc actum operatio attribuatur voluntati. Et quia etiam ad hunc actum Deus nos adiuvat, et interius confirmando voluntatem, ut ad actum perveniat, et exterius facultatem operandi praebendo, respectu huius actus dicitur *gratia cooperans*. Unde post praemissa verba [in the *sed contra*] subdit Augustinus: *Ut autem velimus, operatur; cum autem volumus, ut perficiamus, nobis cooperatur*. Sic igitur, si gratia accipiatur pro gratuita Dei motione, qua movet nos ad bonum meritorium, convenienter dividitur gratia per *operantem* et *cooperantem*."

solus autem Deus movens, operatio Deo attribuitur; et secundum hoc dicitur *gratia operans*. In illo autem effectu in quo mens nostra et movet et movetur, operatio non solum attribuitur Deo, sed etiam animae; et secundum hoc dicitur *gratia cooperans*"). Thomas then applies these basic definitions to his analysis of human action. In the present article, he affirms that in us, there are two kinds of activity. The first is the interior act of the will. Here, the will is moved and God is the mover, and Thomas adds that this is *especially* (*praesertim*) so when the will that previously had willed evil begins to will the good. Hence, when God moves the will to will good, we speak of *auxilium* in terms of operative grace ("Primus [actus] quidem interior voluntatis; et quantum ad istum actum voluntas se habet ut mota, Deus autem ut movens, et praesertim cum voluntas incipit bonum velle, quae prius malum volebat: et ideo, secundum quod Deus movet humanam mentem ad hunc actum, dicitur *gratia operans*"). There is also the exterior act of the will, that is, the act commanded (*imperetur*) by the will. For Thomas, in this act too God helps the human person, both by confirming the will within so that it might achieve its act and by providing the means of action without ("etiam ad hunc actum Deus nos adiuvat, et interius confirmando voluntatem, ut ad actum perveniat, et exterius facultatem operandi praebendo"). When we refer to this *auxilium* of God, says Thomas, we call this 'cooperative grace.' Thus, he concludes this part of the discussion, when we speak of grace as God's gratuitous motion by which God moves us to the meritorious good, grace is satisfactorily divided into operative and cooperative grace.

There are at least two basic problems confronting the interpreter of Thomas's teaching to this point. First, the division of human action into two parts in the present article does not easily square with the analysis of the human act offered by Thomas earlier in the Prima Secundae.[57] According to Thomas, there are three fundamental parts to the human act: the conceiving and willing of the *end*; the deliberation about and choice of the *means* to the end; and the *execution* of the act. It is clear enough that the "interior activity" of I-II 111, 2c, is the willing of the end, while the "exterior activity" corresponds, in part at least, to the previously described execution of the act. The difficulty here is what to do with the choice of the means, the middle stage of the human action. Does it fall under the interior activity of the will or under the exterior? The significance of this question is great. Since merit is the effect of cooperative grace,[58] when we ask whether the

---

57   For the more detailed analysis of human action in the *Summa*, see I-II 8–17. In the text, I refer to three basic "parts" of action; as the more detailed discussion in I-II 8–17 discloses, each of these main parts can again be broken down into a number of steps. Alan Donagan, "Thomas Aquinas on human action," in *The Cambridge History of Later Medieval Philosophy,* ed. N. Kretzmann et al. (Cambridge, 1982), p. 642ff., provides a good introduction to Aquinas's analysis of action and its dependence on Aristotle. S. A. Edwards, *Interior Acts* (New York, 1986), ch. 5, may also be consulted with profit.

58   See the prologue of I-II 113: Merit "est effectus gratiae cooperantis." In the

choice of means is the effect of operative *auxilium* or of cooperative *auxilium*, we are in effect defining the limits of human merit. If we say that the choice of the means is, like the willing of the end, moved by God alone, then merit is restricted to the mere execution of the act. On the other hand, if we say that the choice of the means is, like the execution of the act, due to the will as moved by God *and* as mover, we are providing a somewhat greater scope to merit. In the latter case, God would operate the willing of the end, and we would, with the cooperation of God, choose the means to the end and execute the act, in both ways meriting. The question is difficult, but the second appears to me to be more likely. In the *Summa*, Thomas often describes the distinctiveness of the human person in terms of the *liberum arbitrium* which the person possesses. And when Thomas describes the choice of the means to the end, he states that it is the act of the *liberum arbitrium*. Thus, it would fit in well with Thomas's preference for citing *liberum arbitrium* as the distinguishing feature of human being if in the present article he understands the part of the human act in which the person also moves himself to include this characteristic activity.[59]

The second problem in *ST* I-II 111, 2c, is raised by the word *praesertim* in the description of the operative *auxilium*. As we have seen, Thomas offers the example of the conversion of the sinner for such *auxilium*: The will is moved, and God is mover especially when a will which before had willed evil begins to will the good. Is conversion the only example of operative *auxilium*? Such a surmise receives some support from Thomas's own discussion. In the present article, conversion is the only example that he offers. More important, when in I-II 113 he turns to the more detailed discussion of the "effect of operative grace,"[60] his only example again is the justification of the impious, that is, conversion. Thus, it may be that *praesertim* in the present article really means "only": The only time God moves the will to will good is when God effects the fundamental re-orientation of the will away from sin and toward God which is called conversion. This, however, would entail quite a linguistic stretch of the word *praesertim*. Moreover, from I-II 109, 9c, and its parallel in I-II 114, 9c, we do know of yet another instance of operative *auxilium* in the *Summa Theologiae*, the grace of perseverance.[61] Thus, rather than restrict operative *auxilium*

---

opening sentence of I-II 114, Thomas repeats the assertion.

59   For the choice of the means as the act of the *liberum arbitrium*, see I 83, 3c, and I-II 13, 1c. For the *liberum arbirtium* as the distinguishing mark of human being, see I-II 114, 1c and 3c. Lonergan, *Grace and Freedom*, 135–36, also describes the choice as the effect of cooperative grace. Lonergan observes that when Thomas speaks of this cooperative *auxilium*, he says that it not only "provides the means of action without," it "confirms the will within," and takes this to refer to the execution of the plan, by adopting the appropriate strategy, to achieve the end willed through operative *auxilium*.

60   See the prologue of I-II 113: "Et primo, de iustificatione impii, quae est effectus gratiae operantis."

61   For this second operative *auxilium*, see note 54 above.

to the one case of conversion, it would be better to take *praesertim* as signifying that conversion is the most outstanding instance of operative *auxilium* but by no means the only case. Any time the will conceives and wills an end which is appropriate to maintaining the spiritual dignity of the justified soul, and thereby perseveres in the state of grace, this willing of the end is moved by God. This analysis again has tremendous implications for Thomas's teaching about merit. For Thomas, action follows knowledge. One only chooses means and executes an act on the basis of the preceding decision in favor of an end. When Thomas suggests, in the present article, that God operates every willing of the end, he is telling us that before each of our meritorious acts (of choosing the means and executing) stands the initiative of God moving the will to an end whose attainment will be meritorious.

Thomas concludes I-II 111, 2c, by stating that habitual grace also may be divided into operative and cooperative grace. Thomas's discussion here is somewhat truncated and obscure. He writes:

> Si vero accipiatur gratia pro habituali dono, sic etiam duplex est gratiae effectus, sicut et cuiuslibet alterius formae; quorum primus est esse, secundus est operatio: sicut caloris operatio est facere calidum, et exterior calefactio. Sic igitur habitualis gratia, inquantum animam sanat vel iustificat sive gratam Deo facit, dicitur *gratia operans*; inquantum vero est principium operis meritorii, quod etiam ex libero arbitrio procedit, dicitur *cooperans*.

His analysis here seems to trade on two features of "habit." First, that it establishes a *structure* by which action is possible. And, second, that it *inclines* the possessor of the habit to that action. Hence, when we consider what habitual grace establishes in its possessor, we speak of its establishing new possibilities for acting (*primus est esse*). It overcomes sin in the individual (*animam sanat vel iustificat*), restoring at least in principle the harmony of the soul and the correct subordination of the lower parts to the reason. It reorients the individual to God (*iustificat*) and "raises" the individual to the supernatural level, making possible acts which are pleasing to God (*sive gratam Deo facit*). This, Thomas adds, is all due to operative habitual grace. If, on the other hand, we refer to the tendency created in us by habit to action of a certain type, when we speak of habitual grace we may also note that it *inclines* us to action consonant with the nature of grace. Here, Thomas states, we call habitual grace "cooperative," and in this mode it is the *principium operis meritorii*, the *principium*, that is, in the sense that it makes its possessor prone to the appropriate choice of means and execution of the meritorious act. By the time of the *Summa*, however, the mere possession of habitual grace was not viewed by Thomas as sufficient to guarantee the actual use of this grace or issuing of this grace in correct action. Habitual grace merely inclines the soul to such action, but the free choice retains its freedom before this inclination. It can act on it or ignore it. Hence, Thomas stipulates in the present article, cooperative habitual grace is the *principium* of meritorious action, but this meritorious action indeed proceeds from the free choice as well (*inquantum vero est principium operis meritorii, quod etiam ex libero arbitrio procedit, dicitur cooperans*).

ST I-II 111, 2c, constitutes an important contribution to Thomas's teaching on merit in his mature period. Despite the difficulties posed for interpreters of Aquinas, this article provides us with Thomas's most detailed discussion in the *Summa* of the respective "contributions" of grace and the human agent in good, meritorious action. Considered as "operative," the divine *auxilium* moves the will to the willing of the end in every good act. As "cooperative," *auxilium* strengthens and confirms the human person in the correct choice of the means leading to the end and the execution of the act, the two parts of human action that serve as the locus of merit for Aquinas. Similarly, considered as "operative," habitual grace works the transformation of the individual and elimination of sinfulness, and elevates the individual to God's own level, thus making possible the supernatural activity that brings one to God. As "cooperative," habitual grace makes one inclined to act correctly, without necessitating the free choice to act in that way. The discussion of the respective roles of grace and human freedom in the present article frees Thomas from having to consider this question when he comes to examine merit explicitly in the *Summa*. In the *ex professo* treatment of merit of his later career, *ST* I-II 114, Thomas is free to concentrate on other problems; it is to this question that we now turn.

Section II. Merit in the *Summa*: I-II 114 (and related texts)

Thomas's discussion of merit in q. 114 is divided into ten articles. The basic organization of the question is not immediately evident. However, Thomas most likely meant the question to be seen as falling into two unequal parts.[62] In the first article, he establishes the very possibility of merit by locating merit in the broader context of God's predestination of individuals to salvation. Once he establishes in this article the possibility of meriting, in the remaining articles he shows what exactly may (and may not) be merited by the individual from God. Thomas considers four objects or rewards of merit: In articles 2 to 4, he asks whether eternal life may be

---

62 T. Deman, *Der Neue Bund*, p. 418, also divides the question in this way. Deman's commentary helps us grasp the main points in Thomas's treatment of merit. However, his discussion of I-II 114 seldom penetrates to the major insights guiding Thomas's analysis. For example, he offers the reader little in the way of exploring the meanings of the divine ordination which constitutes the ground of merit. Rather, he is satisfied to refer (p. 420) merely to God's ordering of human action to a supernatural reward. As will become evident later in this part of the chapter, Thomas's understanding of *ordinatio* is much richer, and his use of this term connects his reflections on merit directly to his reflections on the divine wisdom and goodness which are revealed in creation and redemption.

merited from God; in articles 5 to 7, he contemplates the meriting of the
first entry onto the path to God; in articles 8 and 9, he looks at the increase
of grace as the effect of merit, treating grace first as habitual (a. 8) and
then as *auxilium* (a. 9);[63] and finally, in the tenth article, he considers
whether temporal benefits fall under meritorious action. The achievement
of I-II 114, is that Thomas offers in this question a comprehensive discussion of merit in the Christian life which fits coherently with the insights
into grace and the motive of creation and redemption which shape the
theology of the *Summa*.

In the first article of his *ex professo* treatment of merit in the *Summa
Theologiae*, Thomas Aquinas raises the problem of the *possibility* of merit
before God. Is it possible, he asks, for a person through good acts to
establish a right to a reward from God?[64] If it is possible, why precisely is
God "obligated" to reward the good that people do? Thomas's demonstration
of the possibility of merit in the first article is of obvious importance for his
teaching on merit in the rest of the question: Unless Thomas can show why
merit is possible and portray convincingly the nature of the obligation
created by merit for God's rewarding of good acts, the rest of the discussion
in the *Summa* becomes pointless.

As shown in the first article, Thomas is acutely aware of the difficulties
involved in affirming merit before God. Thomas directs our attention to
these difficulties by first considering merit in a "non-theological" setting:
He asks what is involved when one person is said to "merit" remuneration
(not from God but) from another person. Aquinas observes that merit and
reward in a purely human setting are governed by justice. When someone
rewards a good work, he is acting justly, for he has recognized the value of
this work and is rendering what is due for the work.[65] Since merit and
reward fall under justice, a number of conditions associated with justice
must obtain for there to be merit and reward in a purely human setting.
The basic meaning of justice is "equality,"[66] and so in merit and reward

---

63   That the focus of I-II 114, 8, is *habitual* grace and of a. 9, divine *auxilium* or
motio conceived as God's dynamic involvement in human life, is a conclusion
that will be defended in the appropriate place. In aa. 8 and 9 of this question,
Thomas refers simply to "grace," without specifying which kind or modality
of grace he is thinking.

64   As we saw in Chapter 1, although some Thomists earlier in the century
argued that the basic meaning of merit is "disposing a person for a reward,"
Lynn, *Christ's Redemptive Merit*, by a careful examination of the pertinent
texts has shown that for Aquinas, merit basically means "creating a right to
a reward;" see, e.g., p. 6ff.

65   I-II 114, 1c: "Meritum et merces ad idem referuntur. Id enim merces dicitur,
quod alicui recompensatur pro retributione operis vel laboris, quasi quoddam
pretium ipsius. Unde sicut reddere justum pretium pro re accepta ab aliquo
est actus iustitiae, ita etiam recompensare mercedem operis vel laboris, est
actus iustitiae."

66   I-II 114, 1c: "Iustitia autem aequalitas quaedam est." Thomas here cites
Aristotle, *Ethics* V, 2, as the source of the definition. The definition reappears

there must be a basic equality between the two. This means, in the first instance, that the reward must be equal in value to the meritorious act; there must be a fair payment here.[67] But, secondly, it also means that there must be equality between the *person* who merits and the one who rewards. As Thomas's reference in the corpus to the inability of slaves to merit, in a straightforward way, from their masters, or sons from fathers, suggests, only equals in rank or social prestige can merit, in a straightforward way (*simpliciter*), from each other.[68] The objections to the present article note an additional requirement for merit in everyday relationships. "Meriting" basically means establishing a right or claim to a reward from another. The establishment of the claim may itself occur in a variety of ways. For example, the one who merits may give to the other something of value that the other does not possess (ob 1),[69] and so in merit and reward there can be a simple exchange of goods. Or the one who merits places the other in his debt by doing him a favor, by giving a benefit to the other through his action which occasions the reward (ob 2).[70] In any event, the objections note, meriting normally involves meeting some deficiency or need in the one who rewards the good act. One obtains a reward only from a person helped in some fashion by the meritorious deed.

Once the conditions of merit in everyday life are established, the objections to the affirmation of merit *before God* become easier to grasp. First, the basic problem with "theological" merit is that it threatens the divine transcendence by implying an equality between people and God that simply does not exist. People cannot merit from God because God infinitely transcends the world, and there is no correspondence in worth between our action (merits) and God's (reward).[71] Similarly, since meriting means the establishment of a claim in justice on another, the affirmation of theological merit would again threaten the divine transcendence by suggesting that it is possible through our acts to "manipulate" God. If our action were meritorious before God, God would be placed by our acts in our debt, and thus be necessitated by justice to requite our deeds; since God is debtor to no person, there clearly cannot be merit before God (ob 3).[72] Finally, merit

in the discussion of "right" in II-II 57, 1 ad 3: ". . . quia iustitia aequalitatem importat . . ."

67 See the lines quoted in note 65 above.
68 I-II 114, 1c: ". . . eorum vero quorum non est simpliciter aequalitas non est simpliciter iustitia."
69 This is implicit in I-II 114, 1 ob 1; this objection asks what a person has which has not been first received from God and expresses doubt that a person can render even this adequately to God.
70 I-II 114, 1 ob 2: "Homo bene operando sibi proficit, vel alteri homini, non autem Deo." The objection goes on to quote Job 35: "If you have done justly, what do you give him, or what does he receive from your hand?"
71 I-II 114, 1c: "Manifestum est autem quod inter Deum et hominem est maxima inaequalitas (in infinitum enim distant), et totum quod est hominis bonum est a Deo."
72 I-II 114, 1 ob 3: "Quicumque apud aliquem aliquid meretur constituit eum

before God is impossible because such merit would imply imperfection in God. But what can people do that would benefit or help God in any way? Indeed, there is no good in people—their nature, gifts, indeed their actions—which does not come to them from God. Thus, in doing the good, which is purportedly meritorious, people are not giving to God something which God needs or lacks; they are simply returning to God what they have received from God in the first place (obs 1 and 2).[73]

In I-II 114, 1c, Thomas acknowledges the legitimate insights of the arguments against merit and concedes in their light that there is no merit, at least simply taken (*simpliciter*), of people before God. "It is clear," he says, "that there is the greatest inequality between God and man; they are infinitely far from each other, and man's whole good is from God. Thus there can be no justice between man and God in the sense of absolute equality."[74] But although there is no **simple** relation of merit between people and God, Thomas nevertheless thinks that there is yet a meritorious relation between them in a restricted sense (*secundum quid*). It is at this point that Thomas introduces the notion of the *divina ordinatio* as the basis of this merit in a "restricted" sense. By the divine ordination, he asserts, it becomes possible to say that people do merit from God without concomitantly impugning God's transcendence and perfection. After he writes that there can be no justice between people and God in the sense of absolute equality, Thomas adds that there can be a justice

> secundum proportionem quamdam, inquantum scilicet uterque operatur secundum modum suum. Modus autem et mensura humanae virtutis homini est a Deo. Et ideo meritum hominis apud Deum esse non potest nisi secundum praesuppositionem divinae ordinationis: ita scilicet ut id homo consequatur a Deo per suam operationem, quasi mercedem, ad quod Deus ei virtutem operandi deputavit; sicut etiam res naturales hoc consequuntur per proprios motus et operationes ad quod a Deo sunt ordinatae. Differenter tamen, quia creatura rationalis seipsam movet ad agendum per liberum arbitrium, unde sua actio habet rationem meriti; quod non est in aliis creaturis.

What Thomas is saying here is that the affirmation of merit before God does not require making people or their acts equal to God: The distance between God and people remains, but God's ordination regarding people makes it possible to evaluate human actions as leading "meritoriously" to

---

sibi debitorem: debitum enim est ut aliquis merenti mercedem rependat. Sed Deus nulli est debitor; unde dicitur *Rom.*, 'Quis prior dedit illi, et retribuetur ei?' Ergo nullus a Deo potest aliquid mereri."
73   The text summarizes the objections made in I-II 114, 1 obs 1 and 2.
74   I-II 114, 1c: "Manifestum est autem quod inter Deum et hominem est maxima inaequalitas (in infinitum enim distant), et totum quod est hominis bonum est a Deo. Unde non potest hominis ad Deum est iustitia secundum absolutam aequalitatem." The translation in the text is by C. Ernst, the editor and translator of the Blackfriars edition of the treatise on grace (volume 30).

God's reward. The "divine ordination" similarly dispels the concerns articulated in the objections. It is true that merit creates a debt. After all, merit means the establishing of a right in justice to a reward. But the debt involved here is not that of God to the person who does good. God, Thomas agrees, is debtor to no person. Rather, in rewarding merit, God is simply being faithful to the divine ordination which lies at the basis of merit. To the extent that we may speak of a debt in merit, then, the debt is only that of God *to* God (ad 3).[75] The divine ordination, finally, also enables us to see why the affirmation of merit need not suggest imperfection or deficiency in God. God has no "need" for good human action in the sense that such acts would add anything to God or benefit God in some fashion. God is perfect. Rather, the benefit derived from merit belongs solely to the human person. God "has allotted to the person a power of action." The person has the freedom to fulfill the law of human being, as set for the person by God. When the person does act as God wishes, that is, in accordance with the law of human nature,[76] the end of human life as established by God, participation in the life of God through the direct vision of God, is given to the person as reward, for the divine ordination has established the necessary link between good human action and the reward of God.[77]

The importance of the divine *ordinatio* for Thomas's teaching about merit, then, is evident. For Aquinas, it is the divine ordination which makes merit before God possible. Yet, although the importance of the *ordinatio* for Thomas's description of merit is clear, a serious difficulty still confronts the student of Aquinas. It is not immediately clear what exactly Thomas means by the divine ordination in this article on the possibility of merit. As was noted in Chapter 1, the uncertainty about Thomas's meaning is revealed by the rather different interpretations of the *ordinatio* offered in the literature on merit in Aquinas.[78] Hamm, for example, views the

---

75   I-II 114, 1 ad 3: "Quia actio nostra non habet rationem meriti nisi ex praesuppositione divinae ordinationis, non sequitur quod Deus efficiatur simpliciter debitor nobis, sed sibi ipsi, inquantum debitum est ut ordinatio impleatur."

76   I-II 114, 1 ad 1: "Homo inquantum propria voluntate facit illud qoud debet meretur."

77   As Thomas notes in the first paragraph of the corpus, even in a purely human setting there is merit between unequals. Thus, to return to the example of the father and son, the son lacks equality with the father and so cannot merit *simpliciter*; but the son can merit from the father in a restricted sense, on the basis of some presupposition or condition which preserves in some fashion the *ratio iustitiae* and *meriti*.

78   The first chapter examined at some length the interpretations of the divine *ordinatio* offered by such scholars as Auer, Pesch, Lynn, and Hamm. As indicated in Chapter 1, Lynn's approach to the *ordinatio* is the most acceptable, for he correctly relates the ordination which grounds merit to Thomas's discussion of the wisdom of God. Yet, as also stated in the first chapter, Lynn's discussion of the ordination leaves a great deal to be desired. The ordination does not constitute the focal point of his treatment of merit,

ordination in terms of the inner finality of the grace which is given to the individual by God, while Pesch likens the divine *ordinatio* to the Scotist *acceptatio*, although he adds that God's determination to accept good works done in grace as meritorious cannot be viewed apart from the intrinsic quality of grace.

But in light of the discussion in the first section of this chapter, it is evident that the divine *ordinatio* which makes merit possible has a primarily "sapiential" reference. It refers to the wisdom of God that formulates a plan for manifesting the goodness of God in the creation.[79] The "ordination" to which Thomas refers in the first article on merit recalls to us, in the first place, the discussion in the Prima Pars about God's providence and predestination. God's providence is the plan formulated in accordance with the divine wisdom by which every creature is ordained to a specific end and given all that is required to come to this end; the execution of the plan for creatures also comes under the ordination of the divine providence. In the *Summa*, predestination refers to that part of providence dealing with the special destiny of certain rational creatures: By predestination, God ordains certain rational creatures to the highest good, life with God, and in accordance with predestination, God grants this rational creature all that

---

and thus he does not accord it the significance which it deserves in Thomas's entire teaching about merit. Similarly, his comments about the ordination are made in passing and are scattered throughout the first part of his book, and so his position has to be "reconstructed" by the careful reader. Finally, Lynn does not look at all of the texts that are relevant to an understanding of the exact content of the divine *ordinatio*.

79   In the text, a detailed attempt is made to relate the "ordination" language of I-II 114, 1c, to such language as used explicitly of the divine wisdom. It should be noted, however, that in I-II 114, 1c, there are some clues to the primarily sapiential reference of the divine ordination on which merit is based. Thus, for example, Thomas says here that God sets for the human person the "mode and measure" of human capacity; this mention of "mode and measure" recalls the activity of the divine wisdom, which sets the measure and limit of all things—see, e.g., III 7, 12c, in which Thomas states that a suitable measure (*mensura*) is set for every form, including grace, by the wisdom of God and quotes in support Wisdom 11:21: "Omnia in numero, pondere et mensura disposuisti." Thomas adds that the "measure" of each form is established in view of its purpose. See also I 45, 7c, where Thomas is considering whether a trace of the Trinity is perceptible in creatures; he affirms that there is and cites this text from Wisdom in support. Similarly, the use of "measure and mode" in I-II 114, 1c, recalls to us Thomas's teaching that the reason that one person has more grace than another is to be found in the divine will, for God accomplishes the divine plan in creating and redeeming by establishing various degrees among created things. In I-II 112, 4c, Thomas makes this point, and quotes in support Ephesians 4:7, "Unicuique data est gratia secundum mensuram donationis Christi," for the perfecting of the saints and the building up of the Body of Christ. Later in the text, I shall refer to I-II 114, 1 ad 2, in which Thomas explicitly works his thought about merit into his discussion of the divine wisdom and goodness.

is necessary (i.e., grace and the theological virtues) for coming to this end. Thus, when Thomas affirms in I-II 114, 1c, that merit is possible on the basis of the divine ordination, he is situating his affirmation of merit in the context of the divine predestination of certain rational creatures to God's own life. Merit is possible because God has chosen the person to attain God and in this light moves the person through grace to God,[80] all for the purpose of manifesting the goodness of God in a special way through the salvation of the individual. Indeed, in I-II 114, 1 ad 2, Thomas explicitly makes this point about the place of salvation "through" merit in the divine plan. The second objection of this article had argued against the possibility of merit before God because, it assumed, meriting entails being of benefit to the person for whom the meritorious act is done. Yet, the objection continued, our acts cannot help God, for God requires no completion through the acts of God's creatures. Rather, if anyone derives any benefit from morally good action, it will be the doer of the act himself.[81] In response, Thomas grants that God derives no benefit from our meritorious acts and that indeed we are the "beneficiaries" of merit in the sense discussed in the second objection, for by our meritorious acts we are enabled to attain the ultimate perfection of life with God. Yet, Thomas insists in this response, talk about merit is acceptable for the Christian, for merits contribute to the divine plan that guides all that God seeks to accomplish through the creation. As Thomas writes here, "what God seeks from our good works is not profit but glory, that is, the manifestation of his own goodness, which is also what God seeks from God's own works too."[82]

By the "divine ordination" which is the basis of merit, however, Thomas

---

80   As observed in note 29 above, grace and predestination are not identical. Rather, predestination is the *ratio* in the divine mind and is the cause of grace, which facilitates the accomplishment of the divine plan with regard to the elect. In I-II 114, the equivalence of the *ordinatio* which grounds merit with "predestination" means that in aa. 2ff., when Thomas speaks of the "movement of grace," he is not referring to the ordination itself, but to what follows on the ordination as its effect. Once God ordains a person to come to eternal life through his merits, God gives the grace which makes it possible to attain the eternal life, and the degree of eternal life which God desires for the person, ordained for the person by God. Hence, as I observed in the first chapter, those such as Hamm who simply identify *ordinatio* and grace are incorrect.

81   I-II 114, 1 ob 2: "Ex eo quod aliquis sibi proficit, nihil videtur mereri apud eum cui nihil proficit. Sed homo bene operando sibi proficit, vel alteri homini, non autem Deo; dicitur *Job, Si juste egeris, quid donabis ei? aut quid de manu tua accipiet?* Ergo homo non potest aliquid a Deo mereri."

82   I-II 114, 1 ad 2: "Quod Deus ex bonis nostris non quaerit utilitatem, sed gloriam, idest manifestationem suae bonitatis; quod etiam ex suis operibus quaerit. Ex hoc autem quod eum colimus, nihil accrescit, sed nobis; et ideo meremur aliquid a Deo, non quasi ex nostris operibus aliquid et accrescat, sed inquantum propter eius gloriam operamur." The translation in the text is by C. Ernst.

means more than simply God's predestination of people to salvation. In Aquinas, the ordination does denote that a person has been predestined to attain God. But the ordination also is meant to "explain" why the rational creature comes to God precisely through his activity, through his merits. As Thomas writes in I-II 114, 1c, "man can only merit before God on the presupposition of a divine ordination, of such a kind that by his work and action man is to obtain from God as a sort of reward that for which God has allotted him a power of action."[83] In other articles of the *Summa*, Thomas has attempted to show in what sense good works are necessary for eternal life, and his argument elsewhere helps us to grasp more adequately the full content of the ordination which lies behind merit. In I-II 5, 7, Thomas asks whether good works are required for the person to obtain beatitude. In the corpus, he observes that in beatitude, the human person will be perfectly directed to God. The various parts of the person will be in complete harmony, with the lower powers obeying the reason, and the reason itself being perfectly subject to God. Rectitude of the person, therefore, will characterize the beatific vision and is necessary if the person is to view God as God is. In this way, the "matter" of the person will be perfectly disposed for the reception of the form by which the vision is possible. The task of the person to whom beatitude is promised, in this analysis, is to become perfectly righteous so as to facilitate the vision of God. And, says Thomas, this is what the person does by doing good. By avoiding sin and pursuing good, one achieves harmony in one's being and approaches to God, through the doing of what God wills one to do.

Yet, Thomas adds in the present article, it is not absolutely necessary that people obtain beatitude through their acts. They do have to be righteous to enjoy the vision, and righteousness means being properly disposed for the vision, but God could make a person whose will was at once rightly set on its end *and* already possessing it, as sometimes God simultaneously disposes matter and produces its form ("posset enim Deus simul facere voluntatem recte tendentem in finem, et finem consequentem; sicut quandoque simul materiam disponit et inducit formam"). In other words, it falls within the divine power to make a rational creature for beatitude and to dispose it completely for beatitude, without requiring the person to contribute to the disposition for eternal life.[84] But, Thomas says,

---

83   The translation in the text is by Ernst. The Latin was quoted above in the text.

84   Thomas's teaching here that God could so arrange that merits are not required for salvation is in keeping with his general understanding of the power and wisdom of God. The divine wisdom formulates a plan to manifest the divine goodness as best as possible outside of God. Yet the goodness found in creation is not identical with the divine goodness, for the reasons noted above in the text. Creatureliness requires a diffusion and fragmentation of the divine goodness and a re-arrangement of this goodness which the divine wisdom accomplishes. In his discussion of the power of God in the Prima Pars, Thomas observes that it certainly falls within the divine power to have

arranged the creation in a way different from the actual order so that the divine goodness would be manifested in a different way. In this regard, see I 25, 5c: "Cum autem potentia Dei, quae est eius essentia, non sit aliud quam Dei sapientia, convenienter quidem dici potest quod nihil sit in Dei potentia quod non sit in ordine divinae sapientiae, nam divina sapientia totum posse potentiae comprehendit. Sed tamen ordo a divina sapientia rebus inditis . . . non adaequat divinam sapientiam, ut sic divina sapientia limitetur ad hunc ordinem. Manifestum est autem quod tota ratio ordinis quem sapiens rebus a se factis imponit a fine sumitur. Quando igitur finis est proportionatus rebus propter finem factis, sapientia facientis limitatur ad aliquem determinatum ordinem. Sed divina bonitas est finis improportionabiliter excedens res creatas. Unde divina sapientia non determinatur ad aliquem ordinem rerum, ut non possit alius cursus rerum affluere ab ipsa. Unde dicendum est simpliciter quod Deus potest alia facere quam quae facit." See also I 25, 5 ad 3, and I 105, 6c. This different arrangement, while not better than the present order, could have been as effective as the present order in disclosing the divine goodness. The basic idea here is that nothing apart from God fully exhausts or matches the divine goodness; hence, alternate ways of showing forth the divine goodness could have been devised and implemented by the divine mind. For a more extensive discussion of the possibility of other orders, see M. A. Pernoud, "The Theory of the Potentia Dei according to Aquinas, Scotus and Ockham," *Antonianum* 47 (1972): 69–95. Thomas's reflections on different possible orderings of the world constitute a thirteenth-century anticipation of the later medieval discussion of the ordained and absolute powers of God. Note, however, that Thomas does not wield the distinction of the two powers as a tool to "solve" every theological problem. He notes the possibility of different orders, but then passes on to what he perceives as the real task of the theologian, the contemplation of the actual and the effort to "read" the world in its ordering in its dependence on God.

In a number of his studies, David Burrell has drawn an interesting distinction between Thomas and Duns Scotus. As Burrell notes, Scotus roots the contingency of things in the possibility that conditions could have been otherwise, in accordance with a different disposition by the divine will. In Aquinas, on the other hand, contingency is rooted in his reflections on *esse*. Creatures derive their being from God, and that they exist at all is due to the divine decision to create these creatures by imparting *esse* to them. See David Burrell, "Creation, Will and Knowledge in Aquinas and Duns Scotus," in *Pragmatik,* ed. H. Stachowiak (Hamburg, 1985), 1: 247, and *Knowing the Unknowable God* (Notre Dame, Ind., 1986), 108. In his works on creation in Aquinas, Burrell seldom considers the role of divine wisdom in the act of creation, and accordingly does not refer to Thomas's speculations about other possible arrangements of the world. Nevertheless, there is no incompatibility between my presentation of Aquinas, which stresses the sapiential features of God's free acts of creation and redemption, and Burrell's analysis. In a private conversation, Burrell has acknowledged the presence in Thomas's thought of the "sapiential" element to which I have repeatedly referred in this chapter and has told me that his own contrast of Aquinas and Scotus is not meant to deny the presence of this element in Aquinas's teaching about creation. Rather, Burrell has been concerned to point out in broad terms the different orientations of the thought of Aquinas and Scotus and to insist that

God does not as a rule act in this way. Rather, there is an order (*ordo*) in things which has been established by the divine wisdom, and God observes this order in the salvation of rational creatures. Hence, as Thomas says in one of the responses, that people must come to God through their actions is not due to any deficiency in the divine power, but rather that the order found in things be maintained.[85] As we have already seen, this *ordo* in things is freely established by God in order to manifest the divine goodness outside of God in as adequate a way as possible in God's free act of creation. Thus, as Thomas continues in the present corpus, that people do come to God through their activity is due to the divine determination, according to the divine wisdom, that this occur. God wills that what is natural to God, the vision of God, be obtained by certain rational creatures and be obtained by them through their acts. Just as their vision of God manifests the goodness of God in a special way, so too that they come to this vision by their acts follows on the determination of the divine wisdom. This way of salvation also contributes to the realization of the divine plan to display God's goodness outside of God.[86]

Thomas locates contingency in the act of creating itself. I agree with Burrell's diagnosis of the principal divergence between Scotus and Aquinas, while adding that for a complete account of creation in Thomas it is necessary to refer to the ordering role of wisdom. I am also convinced of the importance of Burrell's studies of creation in Aquinas. Burrell has re-focused our attention on what I think is the most important insight informing Thomas's theology, that God is the Creator of all that is. It would be a worthwhile enterprise to apply Burrell's work to a more historical study of all of Thomas's writings. My own impression is that such a study would reveal that Thomas progressively succeeded in organizing his theology more and more in the light of his convictions about the creator God. As I hope will become clear, this is certainly the case with his teaching about merit. By the time of the *Summa*, Thomas has perceived that an adequate presentation of merit demands examining it in terms of God's creative plan.

85 See I-II 5, 7 ad 1: "Operatio hominis non praeexigitur ad consecutionem beatitudinis propter insufficientiam divinae virtutis beatificantis, sed ut servetur ordo in rebus."

86 In the corpus, Thomas adds that God has ordained that one kind of rational creature, angels, is able to attain the vision through one act alone. The next section of the chapter discusses the merit of angels, as well as of Christ, in terms of the divine ordination. The entire corpus of I-II 5, 7, reads as follows: "Rectitudo voluntatis . . . requiritur ad beatitudinem, cum nihil aliud sit quam debitus ordo voluntatis ad ultimum finem; quae ita exigitur ad consecutionem ultimi finis, sicut debita dispositio materiae ad consecutionem formae. Sed ex hoc non ostenditur quod aliqua operatio hominis debeat praecedere eius beatitudinem: Posset enim Deus simul facere voluntatem recte tendentem in finem, et finem consequentem; sicut quandoque simul materiam disponit, et inducit formam. Sed ordo divinae sapientiae exigit ne hoc fiat: ut enim dicitur in II *de Caelo, eorum quae nata sunt habere bonum perfectum, aliquid habet ipsum sine motu, aliquid uno motu, aliquid pluribus.* Habere autem perfectum bonum sine motu convenit ei quod naturaliter habet illud. Habere autem beatitudinem naturaliter est solius Dei. Unde solius Dei proprium est

The teaching of I-II 5, 7, about the divine ordination is also affirmed in the Prima Pars, in one of the articles on predestination. In I 23, 5, Thomas wishes to show that predestination of a person to salvation is not dependent on God's foreknowledge of the good works that a person who might be given grace would do. Rather, as should be abundantly clear from the previous discussions of Thomas's teaching about the causal nature of divine love, that there is any dignity or worth in a person is due to the divine love. God's love is not evoked by the good in things but creates the good in them, including the good works that the elect do. Thus, predestination is not occasioned by anything on our part, but prevenes not only our actions but our very existence.[87] Yet, while Thomas is able in this way to resolve the principal problem of this article, he is also concerned here to offer a more general consideration of the place of good works in human salvation. It is

---

quod ad beatitudinem non moveatur per aliquam operationem praecedentem. Cum autem beatitudo excedat omnem naturam creatam, nulla pura creatura convenienter beatitudinem consequitur absque motu operationis per quam tendit in ipsam. Sed angelus, qui est superior ordine naturae quam homo, consecutus est eam, ex ordine divinae sapientiae, uno motu operationis meritoriae. . . . Homines autem consequuntur ipsam multis motibus operationum, qui merita dicuntur. Unde etiam, secundum Philosophum, beatitudo est praemium virtuosarum operationum." Note that in the corpus, Thomas wishes to show that the affirmation of meritorious activity is in keeping with good Aristotelian philosophy. The final chapter argues that Thomas's teaching about merit is meant to explain certain *biblical* data and thus is not an incorporation of purely philosophical insights into a Christian theology. The present text really does not disprove this claim in advance. Rather, Thomas refers to Aristotle's observations about reality as it is to support his own analysis of the need for human activity to come to heaven. Yet Thomas transforms Aristotle by suggesting here the radical contingency of the present state of affairs which calls for merit. That merits are needed is due to God's ordination that they be required. Yet, as he says, God could have created a different order of things in order to achieve God's plan in which there would have been no need for merits.

87   In I 23, 5c, Thomas comments on some earlier errors in Christian thought concerning the relation of predestination and merits. First, he mentions the error of Origen, who postulated that souls were attached to bodies of different types in accordance with their merits as separated substances; for another discussion in the *Summa* of Origen's error, see I 65, 2c, mentioned in note 14 above. In I 23, 5c, Thomas also refers to the error of the "Pelagians" about merits and predestination; from his description of this error ("The Pelagians thought that the first steps in well-doing come from us, while the finishing comes from God"), he is thinking of what since the sixteenth century has been called "semi-Pelagianism." Against the Pelagians, Thomas cites II Corinthians 3:5 ("We are not sufficient of ourselves to think anything as of ourselves") and, noting that thought marks the beginning in human action, concludes that we cannot occasion predestination by anything we do. This argument, of course, fits in well with Thomas's teaching in I-II 111, 2c, about God working the conception and willing of the end of human action by operative *auxilium*.

clear that a person does not receive the grace essential for the attainment of God as a result of good works. Thomas has just made the observation that entry into grace is the result of God's free predestination of the individual. Nor does God's ordination of the individual to the end of eternal life fall under human merit: There is no "motive" for this ordination in the person. That a person is ordained to life with God is due to the free determination of the divine will that decides to employ this person in this way for the special manifestation of the divine goodness. But, Thomas adds here, while good works do not cause the initial entry into the supernatural life nor the divine ordination of the individual to the end of supernatural existence, there is a sense in which merits can be viewed as a "cause" of coming to salvation. The entire spiritual process of grace and glory falls under God's predestinating will. This process itself can be divided into "parts" or "stages"; and, while each of these parts is itself subject to the predestinating will of God, when seen in their relation to each other, one part of the spiritual life can be seen as the "cause" of another. Hence, Thomas states in this article, glory can be said to be the "cause" of grace, as its final cause. Most significant, Thomas states here that good works can also be seen as the "cause" of glory because they are its "meritorious cause." If we ask the further question why one part of the process should be viewed as the cause of another, Thomas offers here an answer familiar to us from I-II 5, 7c: It is because God has *ordained* that one effect of God's predestinating will will itself be the cause in some way of another. Thus, he writes in I 23, 5c, to explain the place of merits in the general scheme of salvation, "we may say that God pre-ordains (*praeordinavit*) that God will give glory because of merit, and also pre-ordains that God will g i v e grace to a person in order to merit glory."[88]

From I-II 5, 7c, and I 23 5c, then, it is possible to draw at least two conclusions. First, when he speaks of the divine ordination not only as the

---

88   The translation in the text is by T. Gilby, the editor and translator of volume 5 (I 19–26) of the Blackfriars edition. The pertinent part of I 23, 5c, reads as follows: "Effectum praedestinationis considerare possumus dupliciter. Uno modo in particulari; et sic nihil prohibet aliquem effectum praedestinationis esse causam et rationem alterius; posteriorem quidem prioris secundum rationem causae finalis, priorem vero posterioris secundum rationem causae meritoriae, quae reducitur ad dispositionem materiae. Sicut si dicamus quod Deus praeordinavit se daturum alicui gloriam ex meritis, et quod praeordinavit se daturum alicui gratiam ut mereretur gloriam. Alio modo potest considerari praedestinationis effectus in communi; et sic impossibile est quod totus praedestationis effectus in communi habeat aliquam causam ex parte nostra; quia quidquid est in homine ordinans ipsum in salutem comprehenditur totum sub effectu praedestinationis, etiam ipsa praeparatio ad gratiam. Neque enim hoc fit nisi per auxilium divinum, secundum illud *Thren., Converte nos, Domine, ad te, et convertemur.* Habet tamen hoc modo praedestinatio ex parte effectus pro ratione divinam bonitatem, ad quam totus effectus praedestinationis ordinatur ut in finem, et ex qua procedit sicut ex principio primo movente."

predestination of a person to salvation but indeed as the ordaining of this person to come to God through meritorious acts, Thomas does not appear to be affirming the exact equivalent of the Scotist *acceptatio*. In Scotus, God decides freely to treat certain acts done under certain conditions (that is, in grace and charity) as meritorious. This promise to reward such acts binds God, by God's will, to this course of action. God need not have promised to reward merits, and God's promise of salvation could have taken some other form. In Thomas, on the other hand, the *ordinatio* is not a determination extrinsic to the created order of things by which God promises to follow a particular economy of salvation, to reward people when, possessing grace, they do what God wills them to do. Second, the divine ordination that grounds merit in Aquinas refers to God's decision, formulated in the divine wisdom, to fashion a rational creature whose repeated morally good and graced actions permit it to come meritoriously to God. In the light of this decision to make a creature whose acts can have salvific significance, God then grants to the object of God's special love everything necessary to attain this transcendent end, that is, the grace and charity that cause the acts that orient the elect rational creature to God and draw him to God. Thus, on the basis of I-II 5, 7c, and I 23, 5c, it is necessary to dissent from Pesch's argument that the Thomist *ordinatio* and the Scotist *acceptatio* are essentially the same. Thomas proposes a teaching of merit that, like Scotus, insists on the divine freedom with respect to merit. For Thomas, God need not have created a creature who can attain God and attain God by acts. But, unlike Scotus, Thomas does not preserve the divine freedom by asserting a merely extrinsic determination on God's part to provide for merit. Thomas's teaching about the divine ordination as the basis of merit is the result of his insight that we can speak intelligently about merit only when we pay sufficient attention to the ultimate reason for God's creation and redemption of human beings. Just as creation is designed to manifest the divine goodness outside of God, so too the salvation of human beings and their meriting of the end-term of salvation contribute in their own way to the accomplishment of the divine plan for the manifestation of the divine goodness.[89]

---

89 In his 1991 doctoral dissertation ("Divine Self-Expression Through Human Merit According to Thomas Aquinas," University of Toronto), Michael Arges explores one facet of the mature teaching on merit. Well into his project, Arges learned of my 1988 Yale University doctoral dissertation, on which the present book is based; after supplying him with a copy (he subsequently returned the favor), he incorporated the results of my research into his own study. On the whole, Arges is favorably impressed by my dissertation, saying that his own work confirms and builds on mine. Understandably concerned to distinguish his own approach, he has, however, enumerated what he considers flaws in my analysis. For one thing, Arges argues that I have assimilated Thomas's *ordinatio* too closely to the Scotist *acceptatio*; see, e.g., p. 357, n. 20, where he writes, "Wawrykow's analysis appears to suggest that Thomas's *ordinatio* is like Scotus's *acceptio* [sic] with an aspect of divine

In the second article of I-II 114, Thomas begins the consideration of the rewards that the human person can merit from God as a result of the divine ordination, by asking whether an individual can merit from God eternal life, the ultimate end to which he is ordained by God. The exact form of the question considered in this article is whether the human person can merit this end without grace (*sine gratia*). Earlier in the treatise on grace, Thomas had already raised this question. In I-II 109, 5c, Thomas had argued for the necessity of grace on the basis of the human's supernatural end. Only that which is proportioned to an end is able to attain it; what lacks essential capacities will fail to reach the end. But life with God in God's self-contemplation and love is an end natural only to God. It transcends the natural capacities of the human person. Thus, if the human person is to reach this supernatural end, God must grant the person the basic capacity that makes this end a possibility. God must give to the person chosen by God to reach God as end the grace that raises him to God's level and endows him with the power to act in the manner leading to God.[90]

---

wisdom superadded." This, however, is to ignore the full range of my criticisms of Pesch (see the first chapter) and my comments throughout about the contribution of grace to the working out of human salvation in accordance with the divine will and purpose. I would emphasize, yet again, the close connection between ordination and grace. While not identical, grace issues from the divine ordination, which is itself closely tied to God's causally efficacious love, making possible the acts that are "meritorious." By virtue of the mature teaching on grace and the ordination that grounds grace, Thomas is thus able to create a space for the human contribution to salvation while preserving his insights, expressed in the teaching on ordination, about the divine purpose and sovereignty in the salvific process. This differs markedly from Scotus, who seems not to have championed an "actual" grace, similar to Thomas's grace of *auxilium*, that is due to a divine "ordination" and that is required for morally good, meritorious action. A second objection to my analysis advanced by Arges can be more summarily dismissed, that I have made too much about the enhanced "sapiential" dimension of the mature teaching on merit (see, e.g., p. 313). Arges ignores the context of this claim, that it is dealing not with some other thirteenth-century thinkers at whom Arges glances, but with Thomas himself, charting one of the principal ways in which the teaching of the *Summa* differs from that of the *Scriptum*. Since he himself looks at the *Scriptum* only on an *ad hoc* basis, Arges is hardly in position to evaluate my claim. I turn to the final objection raised by Arges to my analysis in a note later in this chapter.

90   I-II 109, 5c: "Actus perducentes ad finem oportet esse fini proportionatos. Nullus autem actus excedit proportionem principii activi; et ideo videmus in rebus naturalibus quod nulla res potest perficere effectum per suam operationem, qui excedat virtutem activam; sed solum potest producere per operationem suam effectum suae virtuti proportionatum. Vita autem aeterna est finis excedens proportionem naturae humanae . . . et ideo homo per sua naturalia non potest producere opera meritoria proportionata vitae aeternae; sed ad hoc exigitur altior virtus, quae est virtus gratiae. Et ideo sine gratia homo non potest mereri vitam aeternam; potest tamen facere opera perducentia ad bonum aliquod homini connaturale, sicut laborare in agro,

In I-II 114, 2c, Thomas repeats this basic analysis. Merit of eternal life requires grace, for it is grace that makes possible supernatural acts and makes the person's acts proportionate to God as the end of life.[91] However, Thomas has deepened the earlier analysis of this need for grace by situating the discussion in a more "historical" context. Here, Thomas notes the additional need for grace created by the sin of the first human.[92] Humanity has always required grace to merit eternal life for the reason outlined above: God as end transcends the human's natural capacities. For the realization of this end, grace is required to "raise" the person to God's level and to facilitate supernatural acts. But sin introduces a second need for grace for the merit of eternal life. Sin involves offense against God. When God rewards an act, God is looking kindly upon the deed of the person. But God does not look kindly upon sin, nor at the doer of sin. Hence, before God will reward with eternal life the actions of the individual, it is necessary that the offense against God, the sin of the person, be removed. God does this by the gift of grace that covers the sin and makes the individual pleasing to God. Thus, in the present article, Thomas argues the necessity of grace for the merit of eternal life not only because of the need for the "elevating" function of grace but also because of the need for grace to heal and to remove the disfigurement in the individual caused by sin. Only when sin is removed and the individual is brought into God's favor can that person receive from God eternal life as the reward for his acts.[93]

---

bibere, manducare, et habere amicum, et alia huiusmodi, ut Augustinus dicit."

91 I-II 114, 2c: "Vita autem aeterna est quoddam bonum excedens proportionem naturae creatae. . . . Et inde est quod nulla natura creata est sufficiens principium actus meritorii vitae aeternae, nisi superadditur aliquod supernaturale donum, quod *gratia* dicitur."

92 The additional need for grace created by the Fall is mentioned in a number of articles in I-II 109; see, e.g., 2c, where the topic is the willing and doing of good; 3c, in which Thomas considers the love of God above all things; 4c, where he looks at the fulfilling of the law; and 8c, where he talks about the possibility of refraining from sin. However, in I-II 109, 5c, which is the passage parallel to I-II 114, 2c, Thomas does not insert into his analysis a "historical" dimension, that is, a consideration of the human being before and after the intrusion of sin.

93 I-II 114, 2c: "Hominis sine gratia duplex status considerari potest. . . . Unus quidem naturae integrae, qualis fuit in Adam ante peccatum; alius autem naturae corruptae, sicut est in nobis ante reparationem gratiae. Si ergo loquamur de homine quantum ad primum statum, sic una ratione non potest homo mereri absque gratia vitam aeternam per pura naturalia, quia scilicet meritum hominis dependet ex praeordinatione divina. Actus autem cuiuscumque rei non ordinatur divinitus ad aliquid excedens proportionem virtutis quae est principium actus: hoc enim est ex institutione divinae providentiae, ut nihil agat ultra suam virtutem. Vita autem aeterna est quoddam bonum excedens proportionem naturae creatae; quia etiam excedit cognitionem et desiderium eius, secundum illud I ad *Cor.*, *Nec oculis vidit, nec auris audivit, nec in cor hominis ascendit*. Et inde quod nulla natura

The introduction of this second need for grace, in turn, helps us to perceive an additional dimension to Thomas's discussion of the "distance" between God and the human person in the first article of this question. In the first article, it is fairly clear that the distance to which Thomas refers has as its principal meaning the ontological disparity between God and the human person. People are not God, and their acts apart from the divine ordination do not measure up to God. But in the light of this second article, in which Thomas asserts the need for grace after the Fall to overcome sin and make merit possible, it can be suggested that there is a secondary dimension to the "distance" separating God from the human person. Not only does the distance refer to the ontological difference between the two but also to a "moral" distance. God has set a standard that the individual should observe. When he observes this order, the individual serves the purpose for which the person has been created and so manifests the divine goodness. By his acts and by his reaching the end of his acts, the person proclaims in the way appropriate to him the meaning of God's goodness. In terms of the significance of morally good action, by his acts the person conforms himself ever more perfectly to the divine will and so readies himself for the ultimate vision. Another way of putting this "preparation" for the vision of God is to say that through meritorious action, the person approaches or draws near to God. By becoming more and more as God wills him to be, this servant of God becomes ever more "like" God, imitating in the way conformable to human nature the perfection of divine activity. On the other hand, sin marks a defection from the order set for humanity by God. Sin disrupts the order of the human being to God and mars and sullies the image of God that naturally exists in the human being, making the person increasingly "unlike" God. Hence, sin separates the individual from God in a moral sense,[94] and so the grace attendant to the divine ordination

---

creata est sufficiens principium actus meritorii vitae aeternae, nisi superaddatur aliquod supernaturale donum, quod *gratia* dicitur. Si vero loquamur de homine sub peccato existente, additur cum hoc secunda ratio, propter impedimentum peccati. Cum enim peccatum sit quaedam Dei offensa excludens a vita aeterna . . . nullus in statu peccati existens potest vitam aeternam mereri, nisi prius Deo reconcilietur dimisso peccato, quod fit per gratiam. Peccatori enim non debetur vita, sed mors, secundum illud *Rom., Stipendia peccati mors.* In I-II 114, 2 ad 3, Thomas repeats that before people can merit from God, their sin against God must be forgiven gratuitously by God. In this respect, he adds, merits before God and before people are similar. As Thomas says, we also cannot merit from a person whom we have offended, until satisfaction is made for the previous sin. See also I-II 112, 2 ad 1, in which Thomas says that only one justified by grace can merit from God; this seems to be an implicit reference to Thomas's argument in I-II 114, 2c, that sin must be removed before merit can occur.

94   While "distance" language on the whole is commonly used by Thomas to suggest the ontological disparity between God and creatures (see, e.g., I 115, 1 ad 4), there are texts in the *Summa* which adopt this spatial metaphor to refer to the disjunction caused by sin between God and the human person.

not only must remove the ontological distance between God and the human person, it must also draw the person closer to God by repairing the damage inflicted by sin and making the person more capable of acting as God wills. If this surmise about an additional dimension to the "distance" bridged by the divine ordination (and the grace of God that is effected by predestination) is correct, what we may have here is Thomas's attempt to work into his teaching on merit the traditional Augustinian-Bernardian notion of the *regio dissimilitudinis*, which has as its principal point of reference the separation and exile of the person from God created by sin and the person's fascination with sin.[95]

Once he has argued on these grounds for the need for grace to merit eternal life, in the third article Thomas considers whether human acts merit eternal life "condignly" (*ex condigno*) or, as the Blackfriars translator felicitiously puts it, whether these acts merit this reward "in strict equivalence." The question here posed may be stated in the terms familiar to us from the first article. Given that merit involves payment for a work, Thomas is now asking whether meritorious actions are equal in value to the reward God grants them, or is it that God in fact gives the meriting person more than that person strictly deserves? The first objection in this article advances biblical evidence that would seem to rule out condign merit of eternal life. The term 'condign merit' itself is of course post-biblical. But the apostle Paul seems to be referring to the notion suggested by the term when he considers, in Romans 8:18, the suffering of the saints. Yet Paul states here that the sufferings of the saints are not equal (*condignae*) to the glory they shall receive in heaven: "Non sunt condignae passiones huius temporis ad futuram gloriam quae revelabitur in nobis." Thus, since the works of the saints would seem to be most meritorious, the first objection concludes that no human merit can be equal in value to the reward of eternal life.[96]

Thomas nevertheless affirms in I-II 114, 3c, the condign merit of eternal life. In the earlier discussion of operative and cooperative grace in the

---

See in this regard I-II 113, 1 ob 3, where the statement is made that through sin, one becomes distant from God. The response to this objection does not question this statement and notes that in justification that God "moves" a person "away" from sin. Indeed, I-II 113 in its entirety trades on the notion of justification "moving" a person closer to God. Justification means a person "turning away" from sin and "toward" God, suggesting that by justification, a person is re-oriented to God, turned in the right direction so that he will not continue to stray away from God through sin.

95   For Bernard's use of the *regio dissimilitudinis*, see Etienne Gilson, *The Mystical Theology of Saint Bernard*, trans. A. H. C. Downes (New York, 1940), chapter 2, especially p. 45ff.

96   I-II 114, 3 ob 1: "homo in gratia constitutus non possit mereri vitam aeternam ex condigno; dicit enim Apostolus, ad *Rom.*, *Non sunt condignae passiones huius temporis ad futuram gloriam quae revelabitur in nobis*. Sed inter alia opera meritoria maxime videntur esse meritoriae sanctorum passiones. Ergo nulla opera hominum sunt meritoria vitae aeternae ex condigno."

Summa,[97] it had been observed that in every good act, it is necessary to discern both the divine and the human roles in working the action. In terms of the cooperative grace that is involved in meritorious action, as habitual grace it establishes the possibility for such action and inclines the person to it. As *auxilium*, cooperative grace confirms the will in the choice of the means and execution of the good act and, as operative, initiates the act by proposing to the will the end which it moves the will to pursue. In the present article, Thomas refers to the contributions of grace and the human person to meritorious activity in order to show why it is that our merits can be "equal" to the reward that they incur. Thomas looks at each, grace and the human contribution, in isolation, though he by no means wants to suggest that, say, the human person is able to perform meritorious acts without grace. This is merely a speculative move.[98] If we look at what the will in isolation from grace "does," then there is no way that our acts are "equal" to the reward of eternal life or deserving of it "by strict equivalence." There is, after all, an infinite distance between God and the human person considered as human, and there is, accordingly, a similar gap between their respective works.[99] But if we look at the grace involved in meritorious actions, it *is* possible to say that our acts are condignly deserving of eternal life. In the corpus, Thomas offers a few reflections on the nature and meaning of grace that suggest why merits can be equal to this reward. First, grace connotes the work of the *Holy Spirit* in people, moving them to good. Hence, grace elevates people to the Spirit's own level and orients them to the Spirit's own end, God. What belongs "naturally" to the Spirit comes into the purview of those possessed and directed by the Spirit.[100]

---

97 See the review of I-II 111, 2c, at the end of the first section of this chapter, as well as the discussion of Lonergan's study of operative grace in Aquinas in Chapter 1.

98 There have been Thomists who in the past have diluted Thomas's theology of grace by muffling his insistence that God is involved effectively in human life in order to move people to meritorious acts. Rather, they speak of God making by grace supernatural acts "facile," or easier to do. The implication is that without, say, the divine *auxilium*, people could still do these acts, only with more difficulty. I hope that my own position on this matter has become abundantly clear in the course of this chapter. Grace not only makes such acts "easier," it makes people do these acts. That people act correctly is due to God's application of them to the acts appropriate to the human being. Thomas's theology is very much formulated in the light of the insight into the respective roles of primary and secondary causes and the need for God to be involved intimately in all action for action to occur.

99 In I-II 114, 3c, Thomas refers to the "great inequality" (*maxima inaequalitas*) which separates the actions of God and of the human person.

100 In I-II 114, 3c, Thomas refers to the "virtus Spiritus Sancti moventis nos in vitam aeternam." In I-II 114, Thomas seldom explicitly refers to the different kinds or modalities of grace which he has described so carefully in the earlier questions of the treatise on grace. Thus, in q. 114, he does not state that he is thinking especially of habitual grace or of *auxilium* in any given passage. Rather, he assumes our familiarity with the different nuances of grace

Similarly, grace as habitual endows the individual with new being. It transforms the person and makes him, in the words of II Peter, a sharer in the divine nature,[101] so that what is "owed" to and enjoyed by God likewise becomes "owed" to those who have been endowed with God's "nature." To put it another way, through grace people have been adopted as "sons of God" to whom the inheritance of God, God Himself, is owed by the very right of adoption. As Romans 8:17 says, "If sons, then also heirs."[102] Hence,

---

obtained through a close study of the earlier questions and hence relies on our ability to detect of which kind or modality of grace he is thinking in a given passage in the question on merit. The reference to the Holy Spirit "moving" a person to meritorious action should make us think that Thomas is referring here especially to the grace of *auxilium* which moves or applies people to their act.

101 Thomas does not explicitly cite II Peter 1:4 in this article, but his statement that by grace, a person is *consors factus divinae naturae* certainly brings this text to mind. For Thomas's earlier, explicit use of II Peter in the treatise on grace, see I-II 110, 3c, mentioned in note 42 above. In the earlier use of this scriptural text, Thomas was discussing whether grace viewed as habitual is a "virtue"; in I-II 114, 3c, when he says that a person by grace is made a "sharer in the divine nature," it is likely that he is also thinking of habitual grace, which elevates the person to God's level.

102 Thomas's talk about "sonship" in the present article is meant, in the first instance, to remind us of the discussion in the first article about the possibility of merit. In that place, Thomas noted that in a non-theological setting, it is possible to speak of a merit between unequals. For, as he noted, although they are unequals, a son can merit from his father, according to a restricted sense. In I-II 114, 1c, Thomas went on to explain why the human person can merit from God, although he is not equal to God. God has so ordained that this can occur, and so there can be justice in this case in a restricted sense. In I-II 114, 3c, Thomas completes, as it were, his reflections in this vein, by casting talk about sonship and merit in a theological key. In 3c, he is saying that God's ordination/predestination means that people are given the grace consequent upon the ordination which makes them the children of God. Hence, just as natural children can have a right to a reward from their father in a restricted sense, so too by the ordination and grace of God, people are made the children of God and so can merit a reward from their spiritual Father.

Language about sonship in the context of merit, however, has further implications. In the first place, the act of adopting, through which a person establishes an intimate relation between parent and child, is free. Thus, when Thomas speaks here of people being made the adopted children of God, he is suggesting anew God's freedom in bringing a person to eternal life. As observed in note 87 above, God's predestination of a person to share in the divine life presupposes no dignity in the person but is due to God's decision to employ this person as the vessel of God's mercy. Thomas returns to this idea when he considers the impossibility of meriting the first grace in I-II 114, 5. Secondly, adoption also grants to the child new rights. The child now has the right to, or is owed (*debitur*), what belongs to the parent. The adopted child becomes the parent's heir. Thus, in terms of merit, God's free act of love by which the person is chosen to eternal life creates for the recipient of God's

when they act in accordance with grace, since their acts are now "god-like," grace grants their works the value by which they come to deserve the end freely appointed for them by God, God's own life of eternal beatitude.[103]

Coupled with the introduction of the technical term *meritum ex condigno* to express this condign right to eternal life, Thomas makes use in the present article of the other technical term already familiar to us, merit *ex congruo*, "congruent merit." When he analyzes the meritorious act in terms of the contribution of human freedom, he stresses, as we have seen, the great gulf between the human person and God that makes impossible condign merit on this score. But, he continues, the correct exercise of human freedom creates its own right, albeit a secondary and less strict one, to eternal life, on the basis of a certain fittingness (*congruitas*). Thomas draws our attention here to a proportion which can exist between what we do as human and what God does. To a person who works in the degree of his own power, it is fitting that God recognize the person's effort and make return to that person according to the excellence of God's own person. In place of the equality between work and reward created by the grace in condign merit, in congruent merit there is a looser, proportional equality, in which God rewards a work in proportion to the effort of the person in producing it.[104]

---

love new rights—rights, that is, to inherit the goal to which God has called him. What we have here, then, is a further instance of Thomas's reflections about the intimate relation which exists between justice and love in God's dealings with the world. As observed in the first section of the chapter, the justice involved in merit presupposes the love which God shows for people. Later in this chapter, the general discussion of I-II 114, 2–4, offers further reflections on love and justice in Thomas's teaching about merit.

103 I-II 114, 3c: "Si autem loquamur de opere meritorio secundum quod procedit ex gratia Spiritus sancti, sic est meritorium vitae aeternae ex condigno. Sic enim valor meriti attenditur secundum virtutem Spiritus sancti moventis nos in vitam aeternam, secundum illud *Joan.*, *Fiet in eo fons aquae salientis in vitam aeternam.* Attenditur etiam pretium operis secundum dignitatem gratiae, per quam homo consors factus divinae naturae adoptatur in filium Dei, cui debetur haereditas ex ipso iure adoptionis, secundum illud *Rom.*, *Si filii, et haeredes.*" In I-II 114, 3 ad 3, Thomas offers a slight qualification of his description in the corpus of the equality of grace and the reward given for works performed under the guidance of grace. Here, he says that grace and glory are not equal as to actuality (*in actu*). Nevertheless, there is an equality between the two, for grace is equal to glory "in power" (*in virtute*), and the impulse of grace is oriented to its flowering in the full actuality of glory. In this regard, Thomas draws a parallel with the seed and the tree. The tree is "greater" than the seed because it is more actual. But the seed is also equal to the tree because it is potentially a tree and the tree arises from it. Recall the significance of this text for Hamm, whose book, *Promissio,* was discussed in Chapter 1. Although Hamm has confused grace and the ordination which lies behind grace as its cause, his comments about the inner finality of grace are acceptable as long as they are taken as referring only to the nature of grace.

In the light of the entire corpus, then, the argument of the first objection against condign merit loses its force. In short, when in Romans 8:18 Paul denies the condignity of the acts of the saints to the eternal reward, he is not thinking of condign merit. Paul simply leaves this notion out of consideration in the passage.[105] Rather, in Romans 8:18 Paul is looking at the works of saints in terms simply of the contribution of the free choice in the doing of the act. Hence, since God's action transcends that of the creature, Paul is making the limited point that as to their substance, the acts of the human being are not in fact equal to the reward that God will grant them for their good acts performed under the guidance of grace.[106]

---

104 I-II 114, 3c: "Opus meritorium hominis dupliciter considerari potest: uno modo, secundum quod procedit ex libero arbitrio; alio modo, secundum quod procedit ex gratia Spiritus sancti. Si consideretur secundum substantiam operis, et secundum quod procedit ex libero arbitrio, sic non potest ibi esse condignitas propter maximam inaequalitatem; sed est ibi congruitas propter quamdam aequalitatem proportionis. Videtur enim congruum ut homini operanti secundum suam virtutem Deus recompenset secundum excellentiam suae virtutis."

105 Yet, Thomas would insist, in other passages Paul speaks in a way which makes clear his own belief that good works are condignly equal to the reward of human life. In this regard, Thomas refers to texts in Paul and elsewhere in Scripture which affirm a just judgment by God of human beings, which in Thomas's reading would seem to imply a reward strictly equivalent to the act. See, e.g., the *sed contra* of the present article, in which Thomas cites II Timothy 4:8 ("As to the rest, there is laid up for me a crown of justice, which the Lord, the just judge, will render to me on that day"). The final chapter considers Thomas's use of Scripture in his teaching on merit. There, it is noted that Thomas tends to quote texts such as II Timothy 4:8 to make the case for merit. Thomas's faithfulness to the biblical witness in this usage will also be evaluated.

106 I-II 114, 3 ad 1: "Apostolus loquitur de passionibus sanctorum secundum eorum substantiam." The mention in this response, as well as in the corpus, of the substance of human acts recalls the discussion in I-II 109, 4, where Thomas asks if the precepts of the law can be fulfilled *per sua naturalia* without grace. In the corpus, Thomas notes that there is a difference between the act itself (= the substance of the act), which can be a just or brave act, and the way in which the act is performed. With regard to the latter, the manner of performance has been determined by the "lawgiver," by God, who wishes these virtuous acts to be done out of love for God. Having made this distinction, Thomas then considers natural capabilities "historically," that is, before and after sin (for this historical dimension in Thomas's thought about grace, see note 92 above). Before the Fall, the person could fulfill all the commandments as to the substance of the acts. But after the Fall, the person cannot do all the acts required by the commandments. As for the manner in which the commandments are to be done, Thomas states in I-II 109, 4c, that both before and after the Fall grace and charity are required so that the person will act in the way that God requires. Now, in I-II 114, 3, Thomas mentions, as we have seen, the "substance" of the act, but leaves out of account the "manner of performance" of the act, that is, by grace and charity. Nor does Thomas refer explicitly to this feature of the doing of the act in a. 4 of this

As it stands now, however, the present article's teaching on congruent merit is perhaps open to serious misunderstanding. What Thomas wants to say in I-II 114, 3c, is that by their acts people achieve a twofold right to the reward of eternal life. When we look at the grace informing the act, they possess a strict or condign right to this reward. When we look at the human effort arising from the use of the will, there is, for the same act, a secondary, less strict right to the reward of eternal life, a congruent merit that seems to rest as much on God's willingness to acknowledge such effort as on the requirements of justice. The present teaching about congruent merit is meant to apply only to the meriting of eternal life. But Thomas's words about congruent merit conceivably could be taken to apply as well to the actions of those who exist outside of grace, that is, to the congruent meriting of the first grace. To those who lack grace but "do their best," God in this view would give the grace that leads to eternal life. Is there a congruent merit of the first grace even in the *Summa*? We shall turn shortly to Thomas's discussion of the (im)possibility of meriting the first grace. For the most part, in the later discussion of the merit of first grace, Thomas is preoccupied with demonstrating the impossibility of *condign* merit of the first grace. Yet he says enough in the later article to show that he wishes to discuss a congruent right to a reward only in the context of the relationship to God established by grace. He does not want to speculate about, or affirm, a congruent merit outside this graced relationship between God and the human person. In the sixth article, Thomas is discussing the possibility of one person meriting the first grace for someone else. He says that apart from Christ, no one can condignly merit the first grace for another. But, he adds, a person can *congruently* merit the first grace for another, because of, as he puts it, the "proportion of friendship" (*amicitiae proportio*) existing between God and the human person as a result of grace. Since the human person through God's gracious initiative now exists in a state of friendship with God, when that person endeavors to do God's will, for the sake of the salvation of another, God looks with favor upon the request of God's friend and fulfills the friend's request, provided there is no impediment of sin in the designated beneficiary of the friend's act.[107] In the light of I-II 114, 6c, then, it is clear that the "proportionate equality" of I-II 114, 3c, which enables the individual to merit congruently eternal life, presupposes and

question, where he contemplates the need for charity for merit. However, given the earlier analysis, it is likely that Thomas means for us to recall the discussion in I-II 109, 4c, and so to see that grace (3c) and charity (4c) are required for condign merit of eternal life because they cause the person to do God's will in the manner God wishes.

107   I-II 114, 6c: "Sed merito congrui potest aliquis alteri mereri primam gratiam: quia enim homo in gratia constitutus implet Dei voluntatem, congruum est secundum amicitiae proportionem ut Deus impleat hominis voluntatem in salvatione alterius, licet quandoque possit habere impedimentum ex parte illius cuius aliquis sanctus iustificationem desiderat." Later in this chapter, I shall provide a more detailed analysis of this article.

is based on the friendship established by God between God and the human person. This proportion is the "proportion of friendship" to which the sixth article refers. *Once* this friendship exists because of grace, then the individual can congruently merit eternal life for himself (3c) and congruently merit the first grace for someone else (6c). But since this friendship and proportion presuppose grace, when this grace is absent, as it is in the unjustified, there can be no congruent merit of the first grace. In this case, there is lacking the proportion demanded by Aquinas when he refers to a merit of God's reward of eternal life created by human effort considered *in abstracto*.

Thomas completes his analysis of the merit of eternal life by asking in the fourth article whether grace is the principle of merit more especially (*principalius*) through charity than through the other theological virtues. For Thomas, the difference between grace and the theological virtues mirrors the distinction he draws between the essence of the soul and its powers. Just as the powers of the soul are rooted in the essence of the soul and derive their being from it but are not identical with the essence of the soul, so too the theological virtues of faith, hope, and charity flow from habitual grace, perfecting the powers of the soul, and are not identical with this grace.[108] Thus, in the present article, having shown that grace is necessary for the merit of eternal life by making possible good works equal to and deserving of God, Thomas now seeks to specify which of the theological virtues is most involved in this meriting of eternal life.

As he had done in the third article, Thomas here distinguishes two elements in merit to facilitate this analysis. However, Thomas is in fact concerned in these two articles with different features of merit. In the third article, he is concerned directly with meritorious activity, and so answered the question about the condign meriting of eternal life by noting that there are two aspects or constituents of such meritorious action, grace and free choice. In the fourth article, his attention is focused not on the action but rather on the meritorious quality of these good actions, the *ratio meriti*, and so his two elements are not the grace and freedom involved in meritorious action but the two elements which make it possible for us to speak of merit in the first place: the divine ordination of a person to eternal beatitude, which is the cause of the grace that moves the person to heaven; and the freedom proper to the human person, which distinguishes the person from non-rational creatures and which makes it possible to apply himself freely in his acts to the due order established for him by God and so to merit. When we consider these two aspects of the *ratio meriti*, says Aquinas, it becomes evident that it is principally through the virtue of charity that grace works in the meriting of eternal life. By the divine ordination, the person is destined by God to the enjoyment of God as his ultimate end and good. Of the theological virtues, it is clear that charity is

---

108   For the distinctions between the essence of the soul and its powers, and between habitual grace and the theological virtues, see note 48 above.

most intimately concerned with God as the good of human life. While by faith one holds certain truths about God on the authority of God's word, and by hope one hopes to achieve God as one's end through God's help, by charity one is united directly to God through the affection of love. And one wills, as God wills, the good of God as the end and motive of one's existence and acts. By charity one wills the good which is God.[109] Because charity is concerned with God as the end of our acts and unites the lover to God as to the lover's good, charity holds the principal role in human meritorious action. As I noted earlier in the chapter, in the discussion of I-II 111, 2c, there are three chief "parts" of a human act: First, there is the willing of the end; then, the choice of the means to the end; and, finally, the actual execution of the act. Thus, by directing us to God as the end of our every action, charity insures that every deed we do is referred to God as our end and so places our deeds in the context of bringing us to God.[110]

---

109   There are, of course, different kinds of love in Aquinas. For example, he knows of an *amor concupiscentiae*, a love which seeks and desires the good for its own benefit. When he is speaking of the theological virtue of charity, however, he is thinking rather of the *amor amicitiae*, the love of friendship. In the *amor amicitiae*, the lover wills the good of the beloved; see II-II 23, 1c: The love of friendship is the love which goes along "cum benevolentia, quando scilicet sic amamus aliquem ut ei bonum velimus." Now, in the *Summa*, Thomas insists that the creation arises in order to manifest the goodness of God: All things are ordained to disclose the divine goodness in the ways appropriate to them. When Thomas speaks of charity as the love of friendship which wills the good of the beloved, he is attempting to work charity into the general framework of his discussion of the motive of creation and redemption: By charity, people seek God's good and refer and ordain their acts to God in the manner God wills them to, and so fulfill by charity the role they are ordained to perform in the divine plan.

110   Modern Thomists have shown a great deal of interest in the place of charity in Thomas's teaching on merit. Much of the latter part of De Letter's book on merit in Aquinas (*De ratione meriti*) is devoted to demonstrating the significance of charity in Thomas's reflections about merit. De Letter's discussion of charity is relatively accurate and helpful. As he correctly notes, the virtue of charity is created and instilled in the creature by God's love for the recipient and this charity brings the recipient back to God. For other discussions of charity in the context of merit, see A. J. Falanga, *Charity: The Form of the Virtues according to Saint Thomas* (Washington, D.C., 1948), chs. 2 and 3; A. Zychlinski, "De caritatis influxu in actus meritorios iuxta S. Thomam," *ETL* 14 (1937): 651–56; and V. Cathrein, "Gottesliebe und Verdienst nach der Lehre des h. Thomas von Aquin," *Geist und Leben* 6 (1931): 15–32. Falanga, Zychlinski, and Cathrein are all concerned with a problem which seems to have enjoyed a certain prominence among Thomists but which Thomas does not discuss in the question on merit: What kind of influx of charity is required for meriting? In modern (pre-Vatican II) Catholic theology, a number of positions on this question have been sketched, and attempts have been made to portray Thomas as the father of each of these positions. Some state that an *act* of charity is required for merit to arise. When this act is missing, there is no merit, regardless of the moral goodness of the

act. Others suggest that only the *habit* of charity is required. This is infused freely by God and orients all the works done by the possessor of this habit to God, without requiring an act of this habit. Finally, others speak of a "virtual" influx of charity; by this is meant that at some point, the person makes an act of charity by which he intends that all he does will be referred to God and done for God's sake. As long as mortal sin does not intervene, this one act is enough to direct all subsequent acts to God, and so to merit. There is no need, however, to be consciously intending one's work for God once this act of charity is made. Charity exercises rather a "virtual" influence over subsequent acts. Thus, for example, someone may intend to give ten alms. He gives the first for the love of God and then ceases to think consciously of the love of God. As long as he does not sin mortally, the subsequent giving of alms will be influenced by charity and so will be meritorious. Cathrein notes (p. 19) that while Bonaventure speaks explicitly of a "virtual" influx of charity, Thomas does not, and so Cathrein argues that Thomas must be thinking of a habitual reference of charity which makes acts meritorious. Thomas tells us elsewhere that an act of charity is not required every time a person merits by a virtuous act. If it were, this would place an intolerable burden on the individual (see II-II 24, 8c). But it is doubtful if he would recognize a habit of charity which does not issue in acts, as Cathrein seems to affirm. In the first place, in justification God not only infuses the habit of charity, God moves the individual to an act of charity, by which the person is re-directed to God as to his end; see I-II 113, 4 ad 1. Hence, at the very beginning of the spiritual life, there is an act of charity moving the person to God. Similarly, while acts of charity are not always required of the person because of the frailty of human existence, this does not mean that the person is not required to love God in actuality. Thomas does think that the habit of charity in fact issues in acts of charity. Hence, we can eliminate Cathrein's suggestion of a merely habitual orientation of charity for meriting, as well as the suggestion that acts of charity are always required in meritorious acts. At times (see below), it suffices that acts of a virtue simply be infused by the habit of charity. This leaves the so-called "virtual" orientation of charity as the sole requirement for merit. With Falanga (p. 194), we can say that acts of charity are not required in every meritorious act. Rather, subsequent acts of virtue can be informed virtually by the act emerging from the habit of charity which stands at the beginning of the series.

There are, however, some further observations which must be made about the literature on this question. First, there is something "un-Thomistic" in the pre-occupation shown by such Thomists with this question. Cathrein and the others seem to want to spell out "minimum" requirements for the occurence of merit, and such a minimalism, which boarders on the legalistic, seems foreign to Thomas's own concerns when speaking of merit. Second, these discussions are all hindered by inadequate views of grace in Thomas, especially as he treats grace in the *Summa Theologiae*. Little if any mention is made of the *auxilium* of grace by which the Holy Spirit moves people to meritorious acts done in and by charity. Hence, in establishing the minimum requirements of meriting, they tend to think of grace merely as habitual and to contemplate the *liberum arbitrium* in its relation solely to this grace. They ignore the work of the Holy Spirit moving human freedom to act in accordance with the inclinations of habitual grace and the theological virtues. Finally, the literature on this question as a rule fails to pay sufficient attention to the

In scholastic language, when we contemplate the divine ordination that directs us to God, charity is the most important theological virtue in merit because it is the "form" of the virtues. It "forms" or shapes our acts by directing them to God as their end.[111]

The other feature of the *ratio meriti* is the human freedom to take up the path to which God directs a person and to do willingly the good that leads to God. When Thomas examines this feature of merit, he again argues that charity is the principal virtue in meriting. In a way not quite paralleled in his other discussions of merit, Thomas here draws upon the *experience* of the Christian to make his point. Acts are deserving of reward because they are willingly done by the individual. Yet, Thomas notes, we most willingly do that which we love. Hence, because it adds a note of spontaneity and willingness to our acts, here too charity is the principal virtue in merit.[112]

There are a number of features of Thomas's argument in these articles that require further comment. First, Thomas's choice of scripture to support his argument here is revealing. The final chapter will examine in some detail Thomas's use of scripture in his teaching on merit. Without preempting that discussion, one should note that Thomas favors biblical passages that speak of God's just judgment of human acts and reward for

developments in Thomas's analysis of willing. By the time of the *Summa*, Thomas is well able to distinguish willing the end and the choice of the means. In the willing of the end, the will is simply moved by God, while in the choice of the means, the will also moves itself. In light of this differentiation of the tasks of the will, it is not too difficult to see that the act and habit of charity are involved principally in the willing of the end. The Holy Spirit moves the will informed by charity to actually will the end of God or an end ordained to God; and then human freedom aided by habitual grace and the *auxilium* of God devises the means to accomplish this end, in this latter way establishing merit before God. In the choice and execution of the means, the earlier act of love of God in willing the end will continue to exercise its influence, and so the acts done by the free will aided by grace will be meritorious.

111   I-II 114, 4c: "Primo enim considerandum est quod vita aeterna in Dei fruitione consistit. Motus autem humanae mentis ad fruitionem divini boni est proprius actus caritatis, per quem omnes actus aliarum virtutum ordinantur in hunc finem, secundum quod aliae virtutes imperantur a caritate. Et ideo meritum vitae aeternae primo pertinet ad caritatem, ad alias virtutes secundario secundum quod earum actus a caritate imperantur." Thomas also discusses charity as the *forma virtutum* in II-II 23, 8c: "In moralibus forma actus attenditur principaliter ex parte finis, cuius ratio est quia principium moralium actuum est voluntas, cuius objectum et quasi forma est finis. Semper autem forma actus consequitur formam agentis. Unde oportet quod in moralibus id quod dat actui ordinem ad finem det ei et formam. Manifestum est autem . . . quod per caritatem ordinantur actus omnium aliarum virtutum ad ultimum finem. Et secundum hoc ipsa dat formam actibus omnium aliarum virtutum. Et pro tanto dicitur esse forma virtutum, nam et ipsae virtutes dicuntur in ordine ad actus formatos."

112   I-II 114, 4c: "Similiter etiam manifestum est quod id quod ex amore facimus, maxime voluntarie facimus. Unde etiam secundum quod ad rationem meriti requiritur quod sit voluntarium, principaliter meritum caritati attribuitur."

these acts to support his teaching on merit. To a large extent, Thomas's tendency to cite such texts is present in these articles. In the *sed contra* of the second article, which is concerned to show that grace is required to merit eternal life, Thomas however refers to a rather different kind of text. He quotes Romans 6:23: "The grace of God is eternal life." Conditioned as we are by the Reformation critiques of merit, at first reading this particular text in an argument in favor of merit is rather jarring. The entire passage in Romans seems to contrast what people as sinners deserve (that is, death) with what they freely receive from God (eternal life). Hence, our initial tendency is to regard Thomas's use of this text as unfortunate and indeed as ultimately destructive of a teaching on merit. On the basis of what we have seen in this chapter, however, it is possible to grasp what Thomas intends in his use of this text. If we read 'grace' in Romans 6:23 as referring to the *cause* of grace, the text is relevant in that a person comes to eternal life only because God freely decides to ordain this person to this end. Again, eternal life is "grace" and yet not opposed to merit because it is by God's free ordination that good acts do deserve eternal life, although for the purpose of disclosing the divine goodness. Or, if we take 'grace' in this text as the effect of predestination and preordination, Thomas's use of the text is apposite, inasmuch as one reaches eternal life, one merits it, only as moved to these meritorious acts by grace (in the ways specified earlier in the chapter). At any rate, the use of Romans 6:23 has the value of recalling to us that while merit and reward are governed by justice, this justice is itself located in the broader context of God's gracious action toward people. As Augustine would put it, when God rewards our merits (in justice), God is in fact crowning God's own gracious gifts.[113]

Second, Thomas's teaching about merit in the *Summa* is clearly "juridical": He explains merit to be a quality of an act by which one deserves, in justice, a reward from God.[114] Yet Thomas's "juridicism" is highly nuanced, and he is careful to focus our attention on the context in which justice can govern divine-human relations. Most important, he argues that this justice

113 See in this respect I-II 114, 3 ad 2. In ob 2, the objection had denied the condign merit of eternal life on the basis of the Gloss on Romans 6:23; as the Gloss states, the word 'grace' in this text from Romans is meant to disclose that the attainment of eternal life is due to God's mercy, not to our merits and hence eternal life is not owed to us in justice. In his response, Thomas argues that the Gloss is pointing (correctly) to the primary cause of coming to eternal life, the mercy of God. But, he adds, while God is the primary cause of attaining heaven, human merit still has a role, as the secondary cause of reaching the good of human existence: "Verbum illius Glossae intelligendum est quantum ad primam causam perveniendi ad vitam aeternam, quae est miseratio Dei. Meritum autem nostrum est causa subsequens."

114 See the comments in Chapter 1 about Thomas's "juridicism." While I appreciate the sentiments, those such as Catão, Hamm, and Pesch who deny the juridical features of merit go too far. However, as was also asserted in Chapter 1, that merit entails a right to a reward in justice does not mean that Thomas's teaching on merit is "legalistic."

only holds sway when there exists a special community between God and the human person, and this community is itself created by the gift of God. The "communal" basis of justice is disclosed by Thomas's description of grace in terms of sonship. By grace, God freely elevates people to God's own level, treating them as "sons" to whom what belongs to the Father can also belong. As the term "sonship" suggests, the community which lies behind merit is itself Christ-centered. It is through the action of the Son of God that others are enabled to be adopted as God's children.[115] The communal aspect of merit is similarly suggested by the importance of charity for Thomas's teaching on merit. The basic thrust of charity is that by it one wills the good of a friend. But also involved in charity is mutual love. As Thomas says in the treatise on charity,[116] we only love with the love of friendship those who love us in return. Yet there is mutual love only where two people share something in common. But there is, as Thomas stresses in the first article, the greatest distance between God and all which God creates. God bridges this gulf when God allows certain rational creatures to rise to God's own level. Hence, as Thomas states clearly in the treatise on charity, there can be a mutual love between God and people because God has freely decided to share God's own beatitude with them, thus establishing the common ground that God and people may share. On the basis of God's prevenient love, in other words, there can arise in the person through God's gift the charity that orients all the person's acts to God as to one's ultimate end. It is on this basis, then, that Thomas can go on to speak of merit and reward between people and God. Because God and people exist in the same community through God's love and God and people can love each other, the good which people do because of God and through God can be reckoned, in justice, as merit.[117]

---

115   See the discussion of I-II 114, 3c, above, and note 102 above. Thomas offers further reflections on God's adoption of people to eternal life in III 23. See especially III 23, 1c, in which Thomas neatly works his thought about God's adoption of people into his general reflections about the divine goodness as the motive of all which God does vis-à-vis the creation. In III 24, 3c, Thomas refers God's adoption of certain rational creatures to God's predestination of Christ to be the Son of God by nature. Later in the chapter, in the discussion of Christ as the "Head" of all those who are saved, the centrality of Christ for Thomas's thought about human salvation will become more evident.

116   In II-II 23, 1c, after stating that good will alone is not sufficient for the love of friendship, Thomas adds: "Sed requiritur quaedam mutua amatio, quia amicus est amico amicus. Talis autem mutua benevolentia fundatur super aliqua communicatione. Cum igitur sit aliqua communicatio hominis ad Deum secundum quod nobis suam beatitudinem communicat, super hac communicatione oportet aliquam amicitiam fundari. De qua quidem communicatione dicitur I Cor., *Fidelis Deus per quem vocati estis in societatem Filii eius.* Amor autem super hac communicatione fundatus est caritas. Unde manifestum est quod caritas amicitia quaedam est hominis ad Deum."

117   See also the reflections about the relation of justice and love in God's dealings

Finally, the initial articles of I-II 114 raise the question of the possibility of development in Thomas's teaching on merit even within the *Summa* itself. The first chapter noted that a significant feature of Thomas's *ex professo* treatment of merit in the earlier *Scriptum* was its interest in determining the kind of justice involved in merit. In that work, he argued that it is *distributive* justice that God observes in rewarding the good works people do. Coupled with this identification of distributive justice was Thomas's clear statement that commutative justice simply cannot apply to God and God's relations to the world. A favorite biblical text that Thomas cites in this regard is Romans 11:35: "Who has first given to him and recompense shall be made to him?" meaning that the kind of justice

---

with creation at the end of the first section of this chapter. For further comments about the "community" existing between God and people which merit presupposes, see I-II 21, especially article 4. As was mentioned in note 32 above, although not insurmountable, certain problems are posed by this article for the interpreter of Aquinas on merit. For example, Thomas does not here explicitly mention the need for grace and charity. Nevertheless, I-II 21, 4c, does support the analysis offered in the text about the communal context of merit in Aquinas. In this article, Thomas says that all moral actions are meritorious or demeritorious to the extent that they work for the benefit or harm of another. This "other" can refer either to an individual, in this case God, or to the community as a whole to which one belongs. In both cases, our acts set up the debt of merit or demerit before God. They do so with regard to God, for God is the final end of human existence, and our acts are supposed to serve God. To the extent that people maintain the order set for them by God, they serve God and so merit a reward from God. But to the extent that they fail to observe this order—as is the case when they sin—they fail to offer God the service God seeks from people. Similarly, moral acts add to or detract from the goodness of the community to which people belong, all for the purpose of glorifying God. Since God is the ruler of this community, it falls to God to reward those who serve the community—by manifesting the divine goodness in the manner required of them by God—and to punish those who detract from the splendor of the community by sinning. As remarked in note 32, care must be taken when reading this article. In particular we must recall that Thomas insists that "service to God" (and hence meriting) involves doing the good in the way which God requires. This requires charity—see note 106 above. Similarly, the "community" of those who in fact merit eternal life form God is not simply the "community of the entire universe" or of "rational creatures in general" (as I-II 21, 4c, at first glance would lead one to think) but the community of the elect, who have been chosen by God to come to God and who belong by God's election to the community of the elect centered in Jesus Christ. Thus, God rewards with eternal life those who persevere in grace to the end of their lives. For all other rational creatures, who belong as created to the "broader" community of God's creation, they receive the just punishment of their demerit. Yet, once we read I-II 21, 4c, in the light of the later, more detailed discussions of merit and the conditions of merit, we are able to apply this text to the determination of Thomas's teaching about merit, in this case by stressing on the basis of I-II 21, 4c, that God does reward the good which people do and rewards them as the ruler of the special community to which God has summoned them to live.

involved in buying and selling or trading simply cannot enter into human-
divine relations. Thomas's position on the impossibility of commutative
justice between God and the human person is re-affirmed throughout his
career. Hence, in the *Summa Contra Gentiles*,[118] Thomas repeats that it is
distributive justice that holds between God and the human person. Thomas
also makes this point in the Prima Pars of the *Summa Theologiae*. In I 21,
1c, he repeats that only distributive justice can govern the relations of God
and the world, and in the corpus he again cites this favorite text from
Romans.[119] But in the *ex professo* treatment of merit in the *Summa*,
Thomas's earlier interest in identifying the species of justice in merit has
vanished. While he makes it clear that there is justice involved in merit,
he makes no attempt to determine the kind of justice here involved. Yet,
although he is no longer preoccupied with identifying the species of justice
in merit, it is plain enough that when he speaks of justice in merit he is
thinking more in terms of *commutative* justice. In the corpus of the first
article of I-II 114, for example, he speaks of buying and selling as the model
of justice, and in the third article, where he argues for the equality of
reward and merit because of grace, he seems to be thinking of commutative
justice. Moreover, later in the *Summa*, in the treatise on the virtue of
justice, Thomas explicitly notes in passing that in merit it is in fact
commutative justice governing the relation of God and the human person.[120] The question, then, is whether in the later parts of the *Summa*
Thomas has abandoned his position on distributive and commutative
justice that he held throughout his career and has repeated in the Prima
Pars.

The question is difficult, and a number of possible answers can be
suggested. First, the most obvious suggestion is that Thomas has in fact
changed his mind about the kind of justice which can govern the relations

118   See *Summa Contra Gentiles* Bk. III, ch. 142, #2, and also Bk. II, ch. 28, #6,
in which Romans 11:35–36 is quoted in the context of the discussion of the
justice involved in creation. Note that in the *Summa Theologiae* this text from
Romans is cited in I-II 114, 1 ob 3, as an argument against merit itself; see
note 72 above.

119   *ST* I 21, 1c: "Duplex est species iustitiae. Una quae consistit in mutua datione
et acceptione, ut puta quae consistit in emptione et venditione, et aliis
huiusmodi communicationibus vel commutationibus; et haec dicitur a
Philosopho, 'iustitia commutativa,' vel directiva commutationum sive
communicationum. Et haec non competit Deo, quia, ut dicit Apostolus, *Rom.*,
Quis prior dedit illi, et retribuetur ei? Alia quae consistit in distribuendo, et
dicitur 'distributiva iustitia,' secundum quod aliquis gubernator vel
dispensator dat unicuique secundum suam dignitatem. Sicut igitur ordo
congruus familiae vel cuiuscumque multitudinis gubernatae demonstrat
huiusmodi iustitiam in gubernante; ita ordo universi, qui apparet tam in
rebus naturalibus quam in rebus voluntariis, demonstrat Dei iustitiam."

120   In II-II 61, 4 ad 1, Thomas asserts that divine judgment follows the form of
commutative justice, "prout scilicet recompensat praemia meritis et supplicia
peccatis."

between God and the human person. Thus, just as the *Scriptum* and the *Summa* are differentiated by their approach to the question of the species of justice, so too the Prima Pars and the Prima Secundae differ in their analyses of this question. Further, the different answer given in the Prima Secundae can be explained by referring to Thomas's increased attention, by the time of the composition of the treatise on grace, to the intrinsic qualities of grace which permit him to allow for commutative justice in merit. This is indeed possible, although it might be suggested that if Thomas had come to reject the *Summa*'s earlier analysis, one might have expected him to have drawn our attention to his change of mind, as he has occasionally done with regard to other questions. A second possible explanation of the difference between I 21, 1c, and I-II 114 is to say that in the first part of the *Summa* he has simply ignored the question of our good works done in grace and concentrated on the general rule governing the relations between God and the world. Now, as Thomas says in the very beginning of the *Summa*, the *Summa* was designed to provide newcomers to theology with a basic, straightforward introduction to the discipline. As Weisheipl has noted,[121] it is especially in the Prima Pars that Thomas has kept to his original intention. While from the Prima Secundae on the *Summa* becomes more and more a work of high theological sophistication, in the Prima Pars Thomas wishes to keep the analysis simple, for the benefit of his principal audience. Thus, in this view, in the earlier part of the *Summa*, Thomas focuses only on what is of general application—he tells us that at the foundation of things lies God's gifts which are dispensed equitably in accordance with the condition and nature of each thing as these have been determined by God according to the divine wisdom. He is not concerned to draw our attention to the "exception," as it were, to the rule, namely, that once God has ordained a rational creature to the destiny of life with God and has given accordingly the grace needed to reach this goal, it then becomes possible, due to the nature of grace, to do good works that God rewards according to commutative justice; Thomas assigns this particular instance of God-human relations to its appropriate place, to the discussion of merit in the Prima Secundae.

A third possible answer to the seeming discrepancy between the Prima Pars and the Prima Secundae is a variant on this second approach. Here, it can be stressed that ultimately the analyses of the Prima Pars and the Prima Secundae need not be seen in opposition to each other. Rather, they are complementary, for they deal with different "moments" in the relation of the rational creature to God. Thomas never abandons the principal insight of the statement in the Prima Pars about distributive justice. God renders to each (in distributive justice) in accordance with the plan of the divine wisdom for the manifestation of the divine goodness. The stress on distributive justice in the establishment of things is meant to show that creatures receive and "deserve" to receive only on the presupposition of

---

121 Weisheipl, *Friar Thomas d'Aquino*, p. 362.

God's prior decision to make creatures of different types and to give each type of creature everything pertaining to its existence. Correspondingly, the rejection of commutative justice in the Prima Pars is designed to reinforce this point about the justice involved in the establishment of things. Creatures would have a right to the fair payment from God entailed in commutative justice at this "moment" of God-human relations only if they existed independently of God and did not arise through God's creative act. They then would be able to offer something to God that God would repay according to commutative justice. But this is not the case: Things exist and have a right to receive what they are "owed" by God in the first place only because God has decided to create them and to make them of a certain type. Yet, given the existence of the rational creature and the summons to life with God that is accomplished by the grace that elevates the rational creature to God's own level, it then does become possible to move to the next "moment" in God-human relations, to the good deeds that people do to bring them closer to God and that God repays by granting eternal life. At this point, within the divine ordination to life with God and after the distribution of God's spiritual goods to the rational creature because of the ordination, it becomes possible to describe the relation of merit and the reward of eternal life in terms of a commutative justice that is observed by God. In this reading, then, the text from Romans to which Thomas often refers in making the case against commutative justice continues to apply but is seen as pertaining to God's establishment of things and construction of a plan regarding each creature in the world. It does not support the complete rejection of commutative justice governing the relations of God and God's elect in the case of merit and reward.

And yet, while it is thus arguable that there is no development in Thomas's position within the *Summa* but only refinement, it remains true that there has been a development on this question between Thomas's earlier and later works. The basic difference between the *Scriptum* and the *Summa Theologiae* in this regard lies in Thomas's inability in the earlier work to recognize the special case created by grace of our good works before God. With the single exception of the passage noted in Chapter 2, Thomas does not recognize in the *Scriptum* that due to the intrinsic qualities of the grace granted freely to its recipient the good works of the justified can be treated by God according to commutative justice. He views the institution of things and the rewarding of the justified as falling under the same rule. Hence, the materially identical statements in the *Scriptum* and in the Prima Pars of the *Summa* affirming that only distributive justice, not commutative, apply to God-human relations do not argue against development in this regard between the earlier and later stages of Thomas's career. In the later work, Thomas makes this statement as the general rule applying to the creation of all things but then in the Prima Secundae notes the "modification" of this rule in the special case of the rewarding of the good done by those called to spiritual fellowship with God. This is the departure from the analysis of the *Scriptum*.[122]

Thus the goal to which God freely and graciously ordains the human person can be merited, and be merited condignly by that person. In the next set of articles in q. 114 (aa. 5–7), Thomas turns his attention to the beginning of the spiritual life on earth, at least as far as the human individual is concerned,[123] and asks whether it is possible of a person to merit the first grace. Again, as with the question of the merit of eternal life, Thomas had earlier in the treatise on grace considered the question of the merit of first grace. Indeed, I-II 112, 1–4, can be viewed as an extended meditation on this question. The topic of q. 112 is the cause of grace, and Thomas wishes in this question to stress that God is the cause of grace in the individual. So, in the first article, Thomas argues in terms sufficiently familiar to us from the preceding discussions, that only God can cause grace. Since grace is a participation in the divine nature, and an effect only proceeds from an agent who is capable of producing that effect, only God can produce this effect by which the recipient is endowed with divine being.[124] But he continues in the next article, while God alone causes or creates grace and infuses it in the person, there is a secondary sense in

122 M. Arges, "Divine Self-Expression," thinks it mistaken to conclude that in the *Summa* it is commutative, not distributive, justice that governs merit, suggesting that I have granted too much weight to II-II 61, 4 ad 1 (e.g., p. 308, n. 159). Arges's remarks, however, are somewhat disingenuous, for he allows (p. 308) that his own reading of the *Summa*'s teaching about justice in merit is close to the third answer that I give in the text. In light of the marked decrease in attention between the *Scriptum* and the *Summa* given by Thomas himself to the question of the kind of justice here involved, Arges's preoccupation with the kind of justice in merit in the *Summa* seems wrongheaded as well. Yet, to the extent that Thomas bothers with the question—and recall that II-II 61 comes well after the *ex professo* treatment of merit, and Thomas speaks only in passing on the matter—there does appear to have been a change in Thomas's analysis, one that incorporates the developments in his teaching on grace. Arges would probably also have benefited from taking more seriously the divine transcendence. God does not fit nicely into our categories; thus, neither distributive nor commutative justice would be fully appropriate in speaking of God's relations with human beings. But because of Thomas's teaching in the *Summa* in his reflections on merit about the power and value of grace, and by virtue of the passing comment in II-II 61, if we need to specify the justice involved in merit, we should speak of a kind of commutative justice that here obtains.

123 That is, Thomas is concerned in these articles with the elect's entry into the state of grace, not with God's predestination from eternity of the individual to eternal life. As we have already seen (e.g., in notes 22 and 87 above), in the *Summa*, when Thomas speaks of predestination he insists that God's decision to save this person rather than that one is a mystery, comprehensible only by the divine mind and in accordance with the determination of the divine will. There is nothing in people which could prevene this determination and occasion it.

124 I-II 112, 1c: "Nulla res potest agere ultra suam speciem, quia semper oportet

which the recipient of grace is also a "cause" of grace or, at least, a cause
of its reception. In the corpus of the second article, Thomas recalls his
distinction between the two kinds of grace, habitual grace and *auxilium*,
and asks whether the recipient of grace need prepare himself for the
reception of these two graces. As far as *auxilium* is concerned, Thomas
says, there is no need for the individual to prepare for grace, and indeed
this is impossible. *Auxilium* is God's reduction of a potency for action to
this act, and God does this freely, in accordance with God's will for the
person. But as for habitual grace, we can speak of a preparation for grace
on the part of the recipient that must precede the granting of this grace.
To make his meaning clear, Thomas draws on an analogy from Aristotelian
physics. In any generation of form in matter, the matter must be prepared
or disposed for that form. The form will be received to the extent that the
matter has been prepared for it. The infusion of habitual grace, Thomas
notes, proceeds along these lines. Habitual grace is a formal perfection of
the soul, and the soul, the "matter" in this case, must be readied for the
infusion of this form. Along with other medieval thinkers, for Thomas this
preparation for grace is constituted by morally good acts that ready the
soul for grace. Thus, in the second article, Thomas argues that human
causality is required for the reception of grace; in this way, the soul becomes
"worthy" of this grace.[125]

Thomas, however, has not here descended into a new semi-Pelagianism.
He qualifies the "doing of what is in one" with some further comments in
the present article and in the next. It is true, he says in the present article,
that there is need for a preparation for habitual grace on the part of the
human person. But, he adds, this preparation for grace must ultimately be
ascribed not to some free and autonomous individual who first decides on
his own to prepare for grace and then does so. Rather, he stresses, this very
preparation for grace is the result of grace. One disposes oneself for the

quod causa potior sit effectu. Donum autem gratiae excedit omnem
facultatem naturae creatae, cum nihil aliud sit quam quaedam participatio
divinae naturae, quae excedit omnem aliam naturam. Et ideo impossibile est
quod aliqua creatura gratiam causet. Sic enim necesse est quod solus Deus
deificet, communicando consortium divinae naturae per quamdam
similitudinis participationem, sicut impossibile est quod aliquid igniat nisi
solus ignis." Again, as in I-II 114, 3c (mentioned in note 101 above), without
explicitly telling us Thomas refers here to II Peter 1:4, a favorite text for
describing (habitual) grace: Grace establishes a "participation" in the divine
nature.
125 I-II 112, 2c: "Gratia dicitur dupliciter: quandoque quidem ipsum habituale
donum Dei; quandoque autem auxilium Dei moventis animam ad bonum.
Primo igitur modo accipiendo gratiam, praeexigitur ad gratiam aliqua gratiae
praeparatio; quia nulla forma potest esse nisi in materia disposita. Sed si
loquamur de gratia secundum quod significat auxilium Dei moventis ad
bonum, sic nulla praeparatio requiritur ex parte hominis quasi praeveniens
divinum auxilium; sed potius quaecumque praeparatio in homine esse potest,
est ex auxilio Dei moventis animam ad bonum."

infusion of habitual grace as *moved* by God's *auxilium* to the acts by which one is prepared for grace.[126] In the light, then, of his deeper readings in Augustine in the 1260s as well as of his more theoretical considerations of the need for God to reduce human potential to action, Thomas has re-read the *facere quod in se est* in such a way that he can argue for the human responsibility to prepare for grace without endangering the basic insight into God's free decision to save the individual as the source and origin of that person's salvation.

Thomas reinforces this insight that it is due to God, through *auxilium*, that the human soul becomes readied for the infusion of habitual grace, in the third article of q. 112 by asking whether the infusion of grace must follow the preparation of the human soul for grace. In the corpus, he says that we may look at this question from two angles. First, the preparation for grace may be viewed as a human accomplishment, that is, as the deeds of this particular person. In this perspective, there is no necessity that the infusion of grace follow the preparation for grace. Just as God transcends the human person, so the acts of the person *qua* human fall short of any divine effect.[127] But, secondly, the preparation is principally the work of God, and God does nothing idly or to no good purpose. Hence, if God reduces free choice to act and so prepares the individual for the reception of habitual grace, it must be because God wills that this person receive habitual grace. Thus, since God infallibly realizes God's will, from this perspective there is a necessary connection between the preparation for grace and its infusion. What God has begun through the causality of God's *auxilium* is perfected by God through the infusion of the formal perfection that transforms and elevates the being of the human person.[128]

126 After the words quoted in note 125, Thomas adds in I-II 112, 2c: "Et secundum hoc ipse bonus motus liberi arbitrii, quo quis praeparatur ad donum gratiae suscipiendum, est actus liberi arbitrii moti a Deo. Et quantum ad hoc dicitur homo se praeparare, secundum illud *Prov., Hominis est praeparare animum*, et est principaliter a Deo movente liberum arbitrium. Et secundum hoc dicitur *a Deo voluntas hominis praeparari* [Proverbs 8:35], et *a Domino gressus hominis dirigi*." See also I-II 112, 2 ad 3: "Agens infinitae virtutis non exigit materiam vel dispositionem materiae quasi praesuppositam ex alterius causae actione, sed tamen oportet quod secundum conditionem rei causandae in ipsa re causet et materiam et dispositionem debitam ad formam; et similiter ad hoc quod Deus gratiam infundat animae, nulla praeparatio exigitur quam ipse non faciat"; and I-II 112, 3 ad 3: "Etiam in rebus naturalibus dispositio materiae non ex necessitate consequitur formam, nisi per virtutem agentis, qui dispositionem causat."

127 I-II 112, 3c: "Praeparatio hominis ad gratiam est a Deo sicut a movente; a libero autem arbitrio sicut a moto. Potest igitur praeparatio dupliciter considerari. Uno quidem modo, secundum quod est a libero arbitrio; et secundum hoc nullam necessitatem habet ad gratiae consecutionem, quia donum gratiae excedit omnem praeparationem virtutis humanae."

128 I-II 112, 3c: "Alio modo potest considerari secundum quod est a Deo movente; et tunc habet necessitatem ad id ad quod ordinatur a Deo, non quidem

Finally, in I-II 112, 4c, Thomas completes these reflections on the reception of first grace by discussing why it is that one person "has" more grace than another. When we speak of a habit being greater in one than in another, what we are referring to is that the habit is more perfectly rooted in the soul of one than in that of another. This is due to the greater preparation of the one for this perfection. To apply this to the question of habitual grace, one person has more habitual grace because this person has prepared his soul more perfectly for this grace. And yet, as has just been stated, the preparation of the soul is itself worked by God. God's *auxilium* moves the free choice in such a way that it becomes capable of attaining grace. Thus, one's greater possession of habitual grace is due to the greater preparation for this grace wrought by *auxilium*. In the fourth article of q. 112, Thomas makes explicit reference to God's purpose in creating and redeeming to make more understandable the disparity in the workings of God's *auxilium*. God wills to manifest the divine goodness outside of God in accordance with the plan of the divine wisdom. In this plan, God has assigned different roles to different people for the manifestation of God's goodness. In broad terms, God has ordained some people to salvation to disclose the divine goodness in a special way. Others God leaves to their just fate. Within the group of the elect, God designates one to a greater reward, another to a lesser, all for the purpose of attaining the variety in the world needed to disclose the divine goodness outside of God. Thus, that God's *auxilium* prepares this elect person more than that one, and so a greater degree of habitual grace is infused into that person, follows from God's eternal plan to manifest the divine goodness in the most appropriate way. Since God loves this person more in accordance with the divine plan, the effect of God's love, grace (and ultimately the reward that follows on grace), is greater in this person, all for the purpose of achieving the divine plan in creating and redeeming.[129]

---

coactionis, sed infallibilitatis, quia intentio Dei deficere non potest, secundum quod Augustinus dicit quod *per beneficia Dei certissime liberantur quicumque liberantur.* Unde si ex intentione Dei moventis est quod homo, cuius cor movet, gratiam consequatur, infallibiliter ipsam consequitur, secundum illud *Joan., Omnis qui audivit a Patre, et didicit, venit ad me.*" Note that the passage from Augustine quoted here is from *De Dono Perseverantiae* (14). Recall the importance which this work, along with *De Praedestinatione Sanctorum*, had for the formulation of Bouillard's thesis, discussed in Chapter 1.

129 I-II 112, 4c: "Cuius diversitatis ratio quidem est aliqua ex parte praeparantis se ad gratiam; qui enim magis se ad gratiam praeparat pleniorem gratiam accipit. Sed ex hac parte non potest accipi prima ratio huius diversitatis, quia praeparatio ad gratiam non est hominis, nisi inquantum liberum arbitrium eius praeparatur a Deo. Unde prima causa huius diversitatis accipienda est ex parte ipsius Dei, qui diversimode suae gratiae dona dispensat ad hoc quod ex diversis gradibus pulchritudo et perfectio Ecclesiae consurgat; sicut etiam diversos gradus rerum instituit ut esset universum perfectum." See also I-II 112, 4 ad 2, in which Thomas reminds us that while all the elect are called to

In I-II 114, 5, Thomas takes up the precise problem of the *merit* of first grace and asks whether a person can merit the first grace *for himself.* He denies the possibility of such merit, and his argument repeats the analysis of q. 112 while incorporating other insights expressed elsewhere in the treatise on grace and in the question on merit. In the present article, Thomas's analysis is divided into two main parts. First, he examines the properties of grace and advances two reasons why grace cannot be merited through the acts of the non-justified. The first reason is familiar to us from I-II 112. Grace is supernatural and transcends our natural capacities. Thus none of our acts done without grace can bring us to the level of grace.[130] Along the same lines, in one of the responses to this article, Thomas admits that acts done outside of grace serve as a preparation for first grace, by disposing the soul for its infusion. But as he had done in I-II 112, 2 ad 3, in this response he immediately stipulates that this preparation is itself worked by grace. When God wills to infuse grace, God prepares the soul by reducing it to the acts which ready it and make it worthy for grace.[131] The implication is that God's operation in *auxilium* here makes it impossible to speak of merit of the first grace;[132] in such preparatory acts, the will is

the same end (i.e., the vision of God), the degree of the participation in this end differs from case to case, in accordance with the grace received from God: "Non enim gratia secundum hoc major esse quod ad majus bonum ordinet, sed ex eo quod magis vel minus ordinat ad idem bonum magis vel minus participandum. Potest enim esse diversitas intensionis et remissionis secundum participationem subjecti, et in ipsa gratia et in finali gloria." The present discussion reflects Thomas's basic conviction about the causal nature of God's love; for Thomas, God's love is responsible for the very existence of things and for the diversity of goods in creation. In this regard, see notes 27 and 28 above. The third part of this chapter will consider the merit of angels. As we shall see there, the granting of grace and glory to elect angels is in accordance with their diverse natural capacities. In that place some reflections will be offered on the way in which the determination of the degree of salvation to which humans, and angels, arrive differs in the two cases.

130 I-II 114, 5c: "Alio modo potest considerari secundum naturam ipsius rei quae donatur; et sic etiam non potest cadere sub merito non habentis gratiam . . . quia excedit proportionem naturae . . ."

131 I-II 114, 5 ad 2: "Deus non dat gratiam nisi dignis; non tamen ita quod prius digni fuerint, sed quia ipse per gratiam eos facit dignos, *qui solus potest facere mundum de immundo conceptum semine, Job* [14:4]."

132 Thomas's discussion of operative and cooperative grace in I-II 111, 2c, makes it possible for him to reject in the *Summa* unequivocally any merit of the first grace, even by a congruous merit. In I-II 111, 2c, Thomas makes clear that conversion is worked by an operative *auxilium* grace; in operative grace, the will is simply moved and does not move itself. Thomas also states in this text and elsewhere (see note 58 above for these other texts) that merit is the effect of cooperative grace, and in I-II 111, 2c, Thomas stresses that in cooperative grace, the will is moved and moves itself. In I-II 114, 3c, Thomas has found room for a congruent merit for one who is already in the state of grace: His acts done in grace are condignly meritorious, because of the grace, and congruently meritorious, because of the contribution of the *liberum*

simply moved and hence makes no contribution of its own by which it may merit this grace.

Reflection about the properties of grace yields a second reason why first grace cannot be merited by someone outside of grace. For Aquinas, to be "outside of grace" means to exist in the state of sin, and this sin creates an impediment to the merit of grace.[133] In this article, Thomas is somewhat abrupt; he clearly means for us to refer to his earlier discussions of the antipathy between sin and grace. Indeed, as we saw, in the second article of q. 114, one of the reasons which Thomas advanced against the merit of eternal life without grace is this same "impediment of sin" (*impedimentum peccati*). There, he described sin as an offense against God that puts the sinner at odds with God. For God and sinner to be reconciled, grace must intervene.[134] Therefore, in the fifth article, Thomas simply assumes that we will recall the earlier discussion of sin as an impediment to merit. The merit of eternal life presupposes the community with God established by the removal of sin through grace. Where the community with God is lacking, so too is the opportunity to receive any reward from God for our acts; and this is precisely the case with those existing in sin.[135]

Coupled with these reflections on the intrinsic qualities of grace, Thomas advances a rather different kind of reason for saying that there

---

arbitrium. Since in conversion the free choice is simply moved, there is no possibility of speaking of a sinner's congruent merit at the beginning of the spiritual life, for the will does not "contribute" in the way which I-II 114, 3c, says is needed for congruent merit. In addition, the proportionate equality of friendship on which congruent merit rests is likewise lacking between the sinner and God.

133 After the words quoted in note 130 above, to the effect that grace cannot be merited by one who lacks grace because of the transcendence of grace, Thomas adds in I-II 114, 5c, this second reason why grace cannot be merited: "... tum etiam quia ante gratiam in statu peccati homo habet impedimentum promerendi gratiam, scilicet ipsum peccatum."

134 See the texts mentioned in note 93 above.

135 In I-II 114, 5c, Thomas adds that once first grace is received, the actions which issue from this grace cannot "retroactively" merit this grace. In meriting, one merits a reward from another and, thus, is given something which he does not have. In this analysis, there is a temporal as well as a natural order: First one merits and then one receives the appropriate reward. If one were to merit something which one already has, this correct order would be upset. Moreover, the acts which issue from grace are not simply "facilitated" by grace; grace makes them possible—without grace, the acts which are meritorious through grace would not only not be meritorious, they would also not occur. Thomas makes this additional point in I-II 114, 5c, when he writes: "Gratia vero est principium cuiuslibet boni operis in nobis, ut supra dicitur est"; the reference here is to I-II 109 which has enumerated the many ways in which grace is "necessary." See also I-II 114, 5 ad 3, for this position. Thomas also rejects the "retroactive" meriting of the grace necessary to establish one in the supernatural order when he discusses the merit of angels; see I 62, 4c.

can be no merit of the first grace. The very word 'grace' denotes that it is gratuitously given and so cannot be given as a reward for merit.[136] Thomas supports with scripture this argument based on the meaning of the word 'grace.'[137] In the corpus, immediately after saying that 'grace' means to be given "gratuitously," Thomas cites Romans 11:6: "If it is by works, it is no longer by grace." Similarly, in the *sed contra*, Thomas quotes another text from Romans (4:4) to make this point: "To one who works, his reward is reckoned not as a grace but as his due." Now, as we shortly see, Thomas thinks it possible for one who is already in the state of grace to merit further grace, at least when grace is viewed as habitual grace. For him, these texts from Romans pose no opposition to the meriting of additional grace: Indeed, in Thomas's reading, Romans 4:4 confirms that once in grace a person can merit more grace. They simply disallow the merit of grace in the first place—this entry into grace is always the gift of God and our works before grace in no way influence God's decision to give us grace.[138] Rather, as we have seen, God's decision to give someone grace moves that person to the acts dispositive to grace. In the restriction of these and other such texts to the question of first grace, Thomas is consistent in his various writings. For him, these texts refer simply to the beginning of the spiritual life and are designed to show that God's free gift starts the sinner on the path to God.[139] But once established in grace, with God's cooperation the justified

---

136 I-II 114, 5c: "Donum gratiae considerari potest dupliciter. Uno modo secundum rationem gratuiti doni; et sic manifestum est quod omne meritum repugnat gratiae."

137 For this notion of 'grace' as a "gratuitous gift," see also I-II 110, 1c, in which Thomas mentions this as one of the three basic meanings of the word *gratia*.

138 See the earlier discussion of God's freedom in predestining people to salvation and Thomas's rejection of any suggestion that God predestines people to salvation because of some pre-existing good in them; consult notes 22, 87, and 123 above. See also Thomas's statement in I-II 110, 1c, where he refers to the "grace of predestination": "Quandoque tamen gratia Dei dicitur ipsa aeterna Dei dilectio, secundum quod dicitur etiam gratia praedestinationis, inquantum Deus gratuito et non ex meritis aliquos praedestinavit sive elegit: dicitur enim ad *Eph., Praedestinavit nos in adoptionem filiorum, in laudem gloriae gratiae suae.*"

139 Thomas refers to both Romans 11:6 and 4:4 earlier in the treatise on grace, in I-II 111, 1. In I-II 111, 1 ad 2, he notes the debt (*debitum*) involved in merit, and observes that a person can perform meritorious actions which bring reward from God; after citing Romans 4:4 in support of this observation, he adds that the (first) supernatural gift of grace cannot be owed in this sense of merit—it is freely given. He cites 11:6 in the *sed contra* of this article, to confirm the point that grace is "freely given." In I-II 112, 2, in which Thomas is asking whether a person has to prepare for the bestowal of grace (see the discussion of I-II 112, 2 and 3, and notes 125 and 126 above), the first objection also cites Romans 4:4, to make the case that no preparation on the part of the human person is required for grace, for such preparation would have to be through a "working" on man's part. In his response, Thomas argues that the bestowal of first grace is in no way merited. But, he adds, the person's

person is able to merit rewards from God, including the increase of his grace. Presumably, Thomas feels that his insistence on the role of grace in the "mechanics" of the meritorious act, as well as his oft-expressed conviction that the meriting of reward is in accordance with God's free ordination, permit him to speak of a merit of "more" of the grace which one has received from God and to conclude that Romans means to exclude the merit of first grace alone.

In I-II 114, 6, Thomas asks the question about the meriting of the first grace in a somewhat different context: If a person is unable to merit the first grace for himself, can that person merit the first grace for *someone else*? While he does not explicitly state so, in this article Thomas is clearly thinking of a person who is already in the state of grace meriting entry into grace for a sinner. Thomas offers a highly nuanced answer building on what he had said earlier in this question about the divine ordination that establishes the possibility of merit, the motion of grace consequent upon the divine ordination that moves God's people to meritorious acts, as well as the human freedom to apply oneself to the path prescribed by God that is essential to the occurrence of merit. In the corpus of the sixth article, there are three parts to Thomas's argument. First, he wishes to show why there is no condign merit of the first grace for another, with the single exception of Christ. Secondly, he suggests why Christ can condignly merit the first grace for other people. And third, he allows for the Christian's congruent merit of the first grace for another, at least in certain circumstances.

The first two parts of Thomas's argument can be taken together. He wants to claim that while Christians cannot condignly merit the first grace for another, Christ can. After having recalled the teaching of I-II 114, 3c, about condign merit of eternal life on the basis of the power of grace, Thomas addresses merit for another and writes in the present corpus:

> Ex quo patet quod merito condigni nullus potest mereri alteri primam gratiam, nisi solus Christus, quia unusquisque nostrum movetur a Deo per donum gratiae, ut ipse ad vitam aeternam perveniat; et ideo meritum condigni ultra hanc motionem non se extendit. Sed anima Christi mota est a Deo per gratiam, non solum ut ipse perveniret ad gloriam vitae aeternae, sed etiam ut alios in eam adduceret, inquantum est caput Ecclesiae et auctor salutis humanae, secundum illud ad *Heb.*, *Qui multos filios in gloriam adduxerat, auctorem salutis* etc.

As it stands now, this answer is somewhat puzzling: Why does the motion of grace for the average Christian extend only to condign merit of eternal life for oneself, while the motion of grace has greater scope for Christ?

reception of grace can, in a way, be meritorious, although not of the grace which he receives freely from God. Rather, once the act of reception is informed by grace, the act can then be meritorious of eternal life.

Again, Thomas assumes that we are familiar with his earlier teaching about merit, and in particular with his understanding of the relation between the motion of grace involved in meriting and the divine ordination standing at the basis of merit. There is an intimate relation between ordination and the motion of grace. The motion of God extends to the end for which a person is ordained by God. Hence, in the present text, what we have is an important insight into the precise content of the divine ordination that makes merit possible. What Thomas is telling us here is that in the normal state of affairs—that is, with regard to all the elect other than Christ—the divine ordination that establishes their role in the divine plan to manifest the goodness of God has to do with their personal salvation. It ordains them to eternal life and by the motion of grace, guarantees that they will obtain this end by their acts. But, Thomas tells us, Christ has been ordained to a greater role. Christ has been chosen by God to be the savior of all, through whose acts the possibility of salvation is achieved. Thus, in accordance with *this* ordination, the motion of the grace given to Christ is greater. It deals not so much with Christ's personal salvation but with the ability of Christ's work to be extended to others.[140] Thus, Christ alone can merit condignly for others because God has ordained Christ and Christ's acts to do this.

But as we have also seen, there is a secondary kind of merit in Aquinas, merit *ex congruo*, which has to do with the meritorious act as it proceeds from the free choice. In this kind of merit, there is a fittingness that God should make return, in proportion to the excellence of his power, to a man who works in the degree of his own power.[141] As I have already noted earlier in the chapter,[142] in the present article Thomas specifies that the "proportionate equality" making congruent merit possible presupposes grace and the community of friendship that grace establishes. It is fitting for God to reward good acts on this basis in the way that it is fitting for a friend to look favorably on the efforts of a friend. Thus, Thomas continues in the corpus of the sixth article, while there can be no condign merit by the

---

140   In the next section of this chapter, I shall return to the merit of Christ and offer a more thorough examination of the scope of Christ's merit according to Aquinas. I shall be especially interested in how Thomas "distinguishes" the ordinations which ground the merit of Christ, and of angels, from that which constitutes the basis of human merit.

141   I-II 114, 6c: "Alio modo habet rationem meriti, secundum quod procedit ex libero arbitrio, inquantum voluntarie aliquid facimus; et ex hac parte est meritum congrui, quia congruum est ut dum homo bene utitur sua virtute, Deus secundum superexcellentem virtutem excellentius operetur." See also I-II 114, 3c: "Si consideretur secundum substantiam operis, et secundum quod procedit ex libero arbitrio, sic non potest ibi esse condignitas propter maximam inaequalitatem; sed est ibi congruitas propter quamdam aequalitatem proportionis. Videtur enim congruum ut homini operanti secundum suam virtutem Deus recompenset secundum excellentiam suae virtutis."

142   See the discussion of congruent merit in I-II 114, 3c, above.

Christian of the first grace for another, if we consider the meritorious acts of the believer in terms of congruent merit, we may indeed say that the works of one may merit congruently first grace for another. Here, God is reacting favorably to the entreaty of a friend.

Thomas, however, immediately adds an important qualification to this teaching. God will react favorably to the congruent merit of one person for another, provided that there is in this other no impediment to the fulfillment of the will of the one who is meriting for him.[143] On the face of it, this qualification would seem to have the effect of *eliminating* all congruent merit for another. After all, the *impedimentum* to which Thomas must be referring is the impediment of sin,[144] and everyone who is not in the state of grace possesses this impediment. This includes the one for whom the friend of God merits congruently. Despite his affirmation in this article, is Thomas, then, really excluding every merit for another, including congruent merit? I do not think so. His present teaching becomes understandable when we place it in the broader context of his teaching on divine providence developed in the Prima Pars. As has been repeatedly stated, there is a divine plan which governs the world, and the execution of this plan is infallible. But in executing this plan, God employs secondary causes, using them in such a way that these secondary causes retain their proper causality and yet contribute in the way designed for them by God to the achievement of God's plan. Now, the end of each creature is set by this divine plan, as are the circumstances by which the plan is realized in their case.[145] To apply this to the present article, God may have ordained that this sinner will be converted through the meritorious intervention of this friend of God. When the friend of God merits congruently the conversion of the sinner, this will occur, *provided* that God has determined to use this merit as the occasion and reason of the sinner's conversion. Hence, in the present article, when Thomas says that congruent merit can fail to attain its desired effect because of an impediment, what he means is that God has not decided to free the sinner of his sin and hence has not ordained the merit of God's friend to this end. God simply leaves the sinner to his sin, despite the meritorious entreaty of God's friend, and allows him to suffer the consequence of his offense against God. The consequence of the pre-

---

143   I-II 114, 6c: "Sed merito congrui potest aliquis mereri primam gratiam: quia enim homo in gratia constitutus implet Dei voluntatem, congruum est secundum amicitiae proportionem ut Deus impleat hominis voluntatem in salvatione alterius, licet quandoque possit habere impedimentum ex parte illius cuius aliquis sanctus justificationem desiderat."

144   Thomas specifies that the "impediment" opposed to merit is the *impedimentum peccati* in, e.g., I-II 114, 2c and 5c.

145   In this regard, see such texts as I 22, 4 ad 2 and ad 3; here, Thomas insists that God provides that, e.g., contingent effects will occur through the contingent causes which God has prepared for them. For a more complete treatment of this point, see the discussion in the first sub-section of the first section of this chapter, and the texts listed in notes 17 to 21 above.

sent article is to underscore the value of our work—it may be the "means" by which God converts another—while acknowledging the sovereignty and freedom of God; God does not react to our works or change God's mind because of them, but employs them in the achievement of God's will.[146]

In I-II 114, 7, Thomas concludes his discussion of the merit of the first grace by returning to the merit of this grace for oneself: He asks the additional question, is it possible to merit restoration for oneself after falling? Thomas's language in this article is somewhat oblique, and it is conceivable that someone would read him as asking whether someone who had been in the state of grace but who had fallen from it through sin could then merit restoration from God. This, however, is not Thomas's question. That question would be the same as asking whether it is possible to merit

---

146 What Thomas says here of congruent merit for another holds, with one difference, also of our prayer for the conversion of others. In I 23, 8c, Thomas is evaluating the value of prayer. He says that God of Himself determines whom God will predestine to salvation. Hence, the prayers of the saints do not influence this decision of God. But, Thomas adds, we should still pray, for God may have ordained to achieve the conversion of another through our prayer or some good work done for another. Hence, the divine providence in this case will have determined to use the secondary cause of human prayer for the furtherance of divine providence. The pertinent part of I 23, 8c, reads as follows: "In praedestinatione duo sunt consideranda, scilicet ipsa praeordinatio divina et effectus eius. Quantum igitur ad primum, nullo modo praedestinatio iuvatur precibus sanctorum. Non enim precibus sanctorum fit quod aliquis praedestinetur a Deo. Quantum vero ad secundum dicitur praedestinatio iuvari precibus sanctorum, et aliis bonis operibus, quia providentia, cuius praedestinatio est pars, non subtrahit causa secundas; sed sic providet effectus, ut etiam ordo causarum secundarum subjaceat providentiae. Sicut igitur sic providentur naturales effectus ut etiam causa naturales ad illos naturales effectus ordinentur, sine quibus illi effectus non provenirent; ita praedestinatur a Deo salus alicuius ut etiam sub ordine praedestinationis cadat quidquid hominem promovet in salutem, vel orationes propriae vel aliorum vel alia bona vel quidquid huiusmodi, sine quibus aliquis salutem non consequitur. Unde praedestinatis conandum est ad bene operandum et orandum; quia per huiusmodi praedestinationis effectus certitudinaliter impletur." In I-II 114, 6 ad 2, Thomas alludes to the essential difference between prayer and congruent merit for another: He tells us that in prayer, the "response" of God to the request is due solely to the mercy of God: "Impetratio orationis innititur misericordiae." On the other hand, while congruent merit is not governed by the strict justice found in condign merit, where grace makes the meritorious act equal to the reward of God, as "merit" congruent merit nevertheless falls under God's justice, although as we have seen congruent merit is very much dependent on the context of love and friendship created through God's initiative to take effect. In this sense, congruent merit comes, as it were, halfway between the mercy involved in God's response to prayer, and the strict justice entailed by condign merit. Later in this section of the chapter, in the discussion of the grace of perseverance which cannot be merited, we shall note that the Christian must also pray for his own continuance in grace.

the first grace, and Thomas has already answered this question in the fifth article of the present question.[147] Rather, the situation to which Thomas refers is that of the person who, while in the state of grace, wishes to so merit that if he should fall, he would receive restoration to grace from God because of his previous merits. Thomas's answer to this question is that it is impossible to merit future restoration, condignly or congruently. As we have seen in the third article, condign merit arises from the motion and dignity of grace. We merit condignly that to which we are moved by grace. This includes the end to which the possessor of grace is ordained, eternal life, as well as the growth of one's grace. But as we have also seen in the fifth article of this question, the merit of the first grace does not fall under the motion of grace. Rather, God freely grants this grace in accordance with the ordination of God's predestining will and then, once possessed, its recipient can condignly merit. When sin intervenes, the motion of grace is interrupted. The loss of grace entails the loss of the ability to merit. Hence, if the fallen is to be restored to grace, this cannot be due to a previous merit, for the motion of grace has been interrupted, but will be the result of God's free determination to restore the sinner to grace. In other words, the first grace, whether first absolutely in the life of the sinner or first relatively (that is, in relation to a sin after the initial reception of grace), will always be a gift of God, not merited in any way by its recipient.[148]

Nor will a subsequent first grace fall under the congruent merit of the one who possesses grace. Thomas's reason for so arguing is completely in accord with his analysis of the congruent merit for another in the previous article. One may congruently merit grace for another as long as there is no impediment of sin in the other. In the present case, there will be an impediment to congruent merit of restoration for oneself—the very sin by which the one who merits has fallen from the state of grace. Hence, even with regard to the lesser claim to God's reward established by congruent merit, it is impossible to merit restoration to grace after sinning.[149]

---

147   Thomas has also discussed the person's arising anew from sin in I-II 109, 7c, where he offers a number of reasons having to do with the nature of sin why it is God who must move the person away from the new sin, and the debt and disfigurement created by this sin, which has caused the person to defect from God.

148   I-II 114, 7c: "Nullus potest sibi mereri reparationem post lapsum futurum, neque merito condigni neque merito congrui. Merito quidem condigni hoc sibi mereri non potest, quia ratio huius meriti dependet ex motione divinae gratiae; quae quidem motio interrumpitur per sequens peccatum. Unde omnia beneficia quae postmodum aliquis a Deo consequitur, quibus reparatur, non cadunt sub merito, tanquam motione prioris gratiae usque ad hoc non se extendente."

149   I-II 114, 7c: "Meritum etiam congrui, quo quis alteri primam gratiam meretur, impeditur ne consequatur effectum propter impedimenttum peccati in eo cui quis meretur. Multo igitur magis impeditur talis meriti efficacia per impedimentum quod est et in eo qui meretur, et in eo cui meretur: hic enim utrumque in unam personam concurrit. Et ideo nullo modo aliquis potest sibi

There is a related question about the merit of one who subsequently falls into sin, but is restored, which Thomas addresses not in I-II 114, but later in the third part of the *Summa* (III 89, 4–5) in the treatise on penance. Do the merits of this person performed before he sinned count before God after the restoration to grace? Thomas argues that they do. Restoration to grace entails the revival of the merits performed before the fall into sin, and so the person does receive the reward due to these earlier meritorious acts. According to Aquinas, the meritorious act establishes a right to a reward from God. The act as transient itself passes away, but the effect of the act remains. It remains, says Thomas, in the *acceptatio Dei*,[150] meaning by this that God accepts them as deserving of the reward of eternal life and will so treat them in future. When the person sins and falls from grace, the previous meritorious acts remain in the *acceptatio Dei*. But the claim to God's reward can no longer be applied to the performer of these acts: Sin creates an *impediment* that blocks, as it were, the bestowal of the reward on the sinner.[151] However, the repentance worked by God's operative *auxilium* removes the impediment of sin, and so the effect of the previously performed meritorious acts that has remained in the *acceptatio Dei* can now be applied to the performer of these acts. These merits are "revived," to use the scholastic terminology, and because of them, as well as because of the meritorious acts performed in future after the restoration to grace, the doer of these acts will receive his just reward in heaven.[152] Thus, sin

---

mereri reparationem post lapsum."
150   See III 89, 4 ad 1: "Sicut opera peccatorum transeunt actu, et manent reatu, ita opera in charitate facta, postquam transeunt actu, manent merito in Dei acceptatione; et secundum hoc mortificantur, inquantum impeditur homo ne consequatur suam mercedem." Thomas also refers to meritorious works abiding *in acceptatione divina* in III 89, 5c. This *acceptatio Dei* should not be confused with the *acceptatio Dei* in Scotus. See the discussion earlier in this section of the chapter in which the Thomist *ordinatio* and the Scotist *acceptatio* are differentiated. In Scotus, the *acceptatio* grounds merit and denotes that God has freely bound God to treat certain acts done in given circumstances as meritorious. In Aquinas, the *acceptatio* refers not to the ground of merit (which is provided by the *ordinatio*) but to God's recognition and acceptance of the meritorious force of the good works done under the influence of grace.
151   See I-II 114, 7 ad 2: "Aliquis potest alteri mereri ex congruo primam gratiam; quia non est ibi impedimentum, saltem ex parte merentis, quod invenitur dum aliquis post meritum gratiae a iustitia recedit."
152   III 89, 5c: "Sed quod isti qui ea fecit, non sint efficacia ad ducendum in vitam aeternam, provenit ex impedimento peccati supervenientis, per quod ipse redditus est indignus vita aeterna. Hoc autem impedimetum tollitur per poenitentiam, inquantum per eam remittuntur peccata. Unde restat quod opera prius mortificata, per poenitentiam recuperant efficaciam perducendi eum quo fecit ea in vitam aeternam, quod est ea reviviscere. Et ita patet quod opera mortificata per poenitentiam reviviscunt." In III 89, 6c, Thomas adds that works performed in sin (*opera mortua*) do not receive meritorious power when the sinner converts. For merit, works must be done in grace. Thus, although the

disturbs the progress to God that is achieved by merit. But once sin is removed freely by God, sin does not destroy the earlier good by which the justified has approached God. God "recalls" the good the justified had done and rewards him accordingly.[153]

subsequent works of the justified person will be meritorious of eternal life, his earlier good acts done before grace cannot contribute to his salvation.

153   In his article, "La reviviscenza dei meriti secondo la dottrina del dottore Angelico," *Gregorianum* 13 (1932): 75–108, R. Marino has examined a curiosity in Thomas's teaching about the revival of merits. Thomas's teaching is that sin blocks the effect of our merit so that while God continues to regard the claim to the reward of eternal life established by these acts, God does not apply this reward to the sinner. With repentance, however, the removal of sin allows the application of previous merits to the penitent. The problem in Thomas's teaching arises in the case of penitents who rise to a *lower* form of charity and grace than they had before their fall. What if they were to die in this lower state of charity? Would they obtain the degree of beatitude owed their previous merits, done in a higher state of charity, or would they enjoy the lower beatitude owed to their later merits? In III 89, 5 ad 3, Thomas has advanced an answer which has puzzled later Thomists: As for the essential reward (the vision of God), it is the degree of charity at the time of death which is determinative. If this degree of charity is less than that held before the fall from grace, then the revived merits will have no effect on beatitude, at least in terms of the degree of the essential reward received. Rather, they will apply only to the "accidental" reward, the created good associated with the beatific vision. Hence, in accordance with the revived merits, the participant in the vision will have a greater amount of joy over these works than over the works done in the lesser state of charity.

Thomists, it seems, have worried that this analysis somehow contradicts the analysis offered in the corpus of this article. Marino notes three basic ways Thomists have tried to coordinate the corpus and ad 3, and he himself attempts a reconciliation. In these attempts to show the compatibility of the corpus and ad 3, for example, there has been some effort to show that Thomas does not mean what he says in ad 3. Hence, some have said that not only the right to the reward of eternal life but also the previous grace is restored when merits are revived. Thus, one would get the essential reward in heaven which earlier merits deserved because the grace which had disposed and readied one for a high degree of the beatific vision would have been completely restored. There is no need to examine Marino's approach. He does not pay sufficient attention to the fact that the re-conversion of the sinner is in accordance with God's predestining will. He says that the degree of repentance will be due to the intensity of the human free response to God, disposing oneself to God's grace, an analysis which in the light of the treatise on grace in the *Summa* sounds rather suspect. Moreover, he ascribes repentance to the earlier-done merits (102ff) which flies in the face of I-II 114, 7, which incidentally he does not discuss. I think Thomas's analysis of the revival of merits in the corpus and in ad 3 need not cause us any problem. What he is saying in this article is that earlier works do have a value. When the sinner returns to the friendship with God created by grace, these earlier merits again give their possessor the right to eternal life. But as we shall see, merits also have the secondary right to the increase of habitual grace which occurs in this life during the movement to God. The grace which follows on

To this point in the discussion of merit, Thomas has been concerned with the beginning and end of the spiritual life. He has argued that the good to which God ordains certain rational creatures, eternal beatitude, falls under merit, both condign and congruent. He has also consistently denied the merit of the first grace. First grace always remains the gift of God, being given to the individual in accordance with God's predestinating will. In the remainder of I-II 114, Thomas turns to the "middle" of the spiritual life, as it were, to the part of the journey from the state of sin to eternal beatitude that comes after the reception of first grace but before the entry into heaven. In articles 8 and 9, he is concerned with the "spiritual" goods belonging to this stage of the journey to God; in article 10, he asks whether temporal prosperity comes under theological merit. The value of these remaining articles is that they allow Thomas to provide a thorough analysis of the question of merit at every stage of the spiritual life.

In the eighth and ninth articles of I-II 114, Thomas asks whether the person who has received grace can then merit by his actions growth (a. 8) and perseverance (a. 9) in grace. Thomas does not use the technical terms familiar to us from the earlier questions on grace, *auxilium* and 'habitual grace.'[154] Rather, in these articles, he continues to refer simply to 'grace' or to the 'motion of grace.' Nevertheless, in the light of his earlier descriptions of each of these two kinds or modalities of grace, it is usually easy enough in I-II 114 to recognize from the context whether he is thinking more especially of grace as *auxilium* or as habitual. This is true also in I-II 114, 9, for it is clear that when he denies that perseverance in grace can be merited he is thinking of grace primarily as the *auxilium* by which God works the perseverance of the justified in the state of grace. In I-II 114, 8, however, it is not immediately evident which of the two graces Thomas is thinking of. With the exception of a single remark in this article (to be noted

---

meritorious acts is destroyed by sin, and since God has already given *this* reward, when sin is later removed this habitual grace does not return—having been granted, it has been removed and no longer exists. Rather, the grace now possessed by the restored person is in accordance with God's motion. And as ob 3 and ad 3 recognize, this grace can be less than what was previously held. This is God's will, and if the person dies in this lesser grace, the essential reward will be in accordance with this lesser grace. The merits done before the fall will establish in an absolute sense the right to this essential reward, but since sin has destroyed the grace which accompanies these earlier merits and which disposes the individual for the form of glory, these merits will not determine the degree to which beatitude is enjoyed, for the earlier grace is not restored and no longer exists. And as for the accidental reward entailed in beatitude, the person will recall all the good which he has done and revel in it, but this has nothing to do with grace, restored or not. Because the earlier deeds were more godlike, this person will take a greater pleasure in these acts than in the acts he did after his restoration, that is, than in the acts which have in fact disposed him for the vision and determined the precise degree of the beatific vision to which this person will attain.

154   This point has been made in note 100 above.

below) he does not indicate to us whether he is asking here whether we can merit growth in habitual grace, or *auxilium*, or both. Rather, in the corpus of the present article he simply argues in somewhat general terms that good acts do merit the increase of grace and charity. In the corpus, he refers yet again to the favorite designation in this question of the grace that follows the divine ordination. Grace is a *motion* by which its recipient is guided and moved to the end set for him by God.[155] By contemplating this "motion" of grace, it is possible to see why increase of grace can be merited. In any movement, we have the two terms of the motion, its starting point and its destination. But we also have the "path," as it were, between these two points, and this also falls under the movement of the journey. Now, in the movement of grace to eternal life, the path between the two terms is the life and action by which the possessor of grace readies himself for the beatific vision and approaches more nearly to this end. To express this notion more theologically, the middle ground of the life of grace is a growth in grace and the theological virtues, by which these theological habits become more firmly rooted in their possessor and the possessor becomes more apt for the vision of God. Hence, Thomas concludes, the motion of grace, which provides by our acts for the merit of eternal life (aa. 2 and 3) also extends to the growth in grace and charity by which we are readied for the ultimate vision of God.[156]

Nevertheless, although Thomas does not explicitly tell us, from his other discussions in the *Summa* of the increase of grace and of the theological virtues, it is plain that he is thinking in article 8 especially of the increase of *habitual* grace and of the habit of charity. In his discussions elsewhere of the increase or growth of the theological habits, Thomas has drawn our attention to the special circumstances that attend such an increase. For example, in the treatise on charity in the Secunda Secundae, Thomas explains how the growth of a theological virtue differs from that of an acquired virtue. In the case of an acquired virtue, the virtue is acquired in the first place through repeated acts of a certain kind. By acting repeatedly in a certain way, one becomes prone to act in that way in the future, whenever such activity is called for. Moreover, once the habit to act in that way is attained, further action of that type makes one even more prone to

---

155 I-II 114, 8c: "Illud cadit sub merito condigni ad quod motio gratiae se extendit." Thomas refers frequently in this question to the "motion of grace," and to God "moving" people "through grace": see, e.g., 3c ("virtus Spiritus sancti moventis nos in vitam aeternam"); 6c ("vis motionis divinae"; Christ's soul was *mota* by God *per gratiam*); 7c (*motio divinae gratiae*); and 9c (free choice is directed by God *movens*).

156 I-II 114, 8c: "Illud cadit sub merito condigni ad quod motio gratiae se extendit. Motio autem alicuius moventis non solum se extendit ad ultimum terminum motus, sed etiam ad totum progressum in motu. Terminus autem motus gratiae est vita aeterna. Progressus autem in hoc motu est secundum augmentum caritatis vel gratiae. . . . Sic igitur augmentum gratiae cadit sub merito condigni."

act in that way. In this case, we talk of a deepening or increase of the habit in its possessor.[157] The attainment of a theological virtue and of habitual grace, however, is rather different. Non-graced acts cannot produce such habits in an individual. No agent produces effects beyond its capacities. Rather, the theological virtues and habitual grace are freely infused in the recipient by God, and any disposition of the recipient for the reception of these formal perfections is itself worked by God, as has already been stressed in the discussion of article 5 of this question. But once habitual grace and the theological virtues are infused by God, can we then speak of an increase in them occurring in the same way as the acquired virtues are increased, that is, as due to the correct and repeated use of these habits? In this case, growth in charity would be effected directly and solely by our charitable acts. However, Thomas denies the parallel. The growth of a theological virtue is more complex, and account must be taken of the roles of both the possessor of the virtue in its growth *and* of God. "To grow" in any virtue means that the virtue is rooted more perfectly in its subject. In the case of acquired virtues, this deeper "rooting" occurs as the direct consequence of action. The action disposes the "matter" in which the formal perfection is rooted for an increase of the habit, and the act effects the more perfect rooting of the habit in the disposed matter. Growth in a theological virtue similarly requires disposition of the subject of the virtue for this growth. This disposition is achieved by the use of the virtue through the guidance of the grace of God. Yet the use of the theological virtue does not directly effect the growth of the virtue, as is the case with acquired virtue. The act of the theological virtue does not create more of the virtue. As supernatural, it is caused and created only by God. Rather, under the influence of God the possessor of the virtue simply disposes himself for more of the virtue. The actual increase of the virtue, the granting of a more intense possession of it, remains the work of God. Hence, in the case of habitual grace and the theological virtues, the human person aided by grace disposes himself for more of these habits. God in response to this disposition grants the increase.[158]

In his description of the disposition for the increase of habitual grace and the theological virtues, Thomas speaks of 'merit.' As done under the influence of grace and charity, these dispositive acts are also meritorious.[159] In Chapter 1, in the discussion of Lynn and De Letter, it was observed that Thomas is able to speak of 'merit' in two ways: first, as a right to a reward; and second, as a disposition for a perfection. For the most

157   Thomas discusses the origination of the acquired virtues in I-II 51, 2–3, and I-II 63, 2, and their increase in I-II 52 *passim.*

158   Thomas considers the origination of the theological virtues in general in I-II 51, 4. For his detailed discussion of the infusion and subsequent growth of the theological virtue of charity, see II-II 24, 2–10. Thomas makes the point that it is God who causes the growth of charity in II-II 24, 8c.

159   For the assertion that every act of charity merits eternal life and the increase of charity, see II-II 24, 6 ad 1.

part, in Aquinas the two ways of speaking of merit coincide. By one's acts one disposes oneself for a greater perfection, including ultimately the perfection of the light of glory. By one's acts one likewise creates a right to the reward of eternal life and of the growth in grace and charity that leads to eternal life. In his discussion of the increase of a theological virtue, however, Thomas notes the crucial instance in which disposition and right to a reward do not exactly coincide. In a charitable act, there can be greater or lesser fervor, and not every act of charity disposes the doer sufficiently for the increase of charity. Rather, in the case of "remiss" acts of charity, the increase of charity does not immediately follow but awaits a sufficient number of such acts to dispose the doer sufficiently for more charity. A fervent act of charity, on the other hand, sufficiently disposes the doer so that God's granting of more charity immediately follows. Yet every act of charity, remiss or fervent, establishes thereby a right to the reward of eternal life, as well as establishes a right to the reward of the growth in grace and charity. But the actual bestowal of this latter reward only occurs when the possessor of the habit is sufficiently disposed for its increase. Hence, there is a disparity in this case between disposition and right to a reward—while every graced and charitable act deserves its reward (eternal life and the increase of grace and charity), not every graced act disposes its doer sufficiently for the increase of the habit. Thomas makes this point in the treatise on charity, in the discussion of the problem of less fervent acts of charity.[160] But he also makes the point in one of the objections and responses to the article in q. 114 that deals with the growth of charity and of grace. And it is this reference which is the one clear indication that Thomas in I-II 114, 8, is speaking of the growth precisely of habitual grace and the theological virtue of charity.[161]

---

160 II-II 24, 6c: "Augmentum spirituale caritatis quodammodo simile est augmento corporali. Augmentum autem corporale in animalibus et plantis non est motus continuus, ita scilicet quod, si aliquid tantum augetur in tanto tempore, necesse sit quod proportionaliter in qualibet parte illius temporis aliquid augeatur, sicut contingit in motu locali: sed per aliquod tempus natura disponens ad augmentum et nihil augens actu, et postmodum producit in effectum id ad quod disposuerat, augendo animal vel plantam in actu. Ita etiam non quolibet actu caritatis caritas actu augetur, sed quilibet actus caritatis disponit ad caritatis augmentum, inquantum ex uno actu caritatis homo redditur promptior iterum ad agendum secundum caritatem; et, habilitate crescente, homo prorumpit in actum ferventiorem dilectionis, quo conetur ad caritatis profectum; et tunc caritas augetur in actu." See also II-II 24, 6 ad 1, mentioned in the previous note. Lynn, *Christ's Redemptive Merit*, pp. 54–60, observes that every act of charity, including remiss acts, merits eternal life and the increase of charity, although not every act of charity disposes its possessor sufficiently for the increase of charity. In this regard, Lynn affirms that there is a development between the *Scriptum* and the *Summa*, for in the *Scriptum* Thomas had not been as willing to state that even the remiss act of charity merits eternal life and the increase of charity.

161 I-II 114, 8 ad 3: "Quolibet actu meritorio meretur homo augmentum gratiae,

In I-II 114, 9, Thomas asks whether the person in the state of grace can merit perseverance in this state. As with many of the issues treated in q. 114, Thomas had discussed this question earlier in the treatise on grace. In the earlier discussion,[162] Thomas had observed that "perseverance" means the ability to refrain from actions that could cause the loss of grace (i.e., sin) and the actual doing of the good compatible with the graced life. Now, it is clear that justification entails the transformation of the sinner so that the disruption caused by original and actual sins is rectified. Through the infusion of habitual grace, the lower powers of the soul had been restored to their appropriate subordination to the reason, just as the reason itself had been restored to its correct subordination to God. Yet, Thomas added, this restoration of the hierarchy within the soul is never complete in this life. While grace does improve the soul, making the lower parts more willingly amenable to the rational will's command, the effects of sin are never totally overcome in this life. There remains a "residual" tendency to further sin, which the individual must constantly strive to overcome. It is in this context that Thomas had affirmed the necessity of an additional grace that would enable the individual to overcome the temptations of sin and to remain in the state in which he had been placed by God. For Aquinas, this grace of perseverance is an operative *auxilium*, by which God reduces the individual to acts in keeping with his status as the child of God. Through this grace, the individual resists the temptation to sin and freely does the good.

In I-II 114, 9c, Thomas recalls this earlier analysis of the grace of perseverance and affirms that such a grace cannot be merited. This grace is simply given freely by God in accordance with the divine ordination for the moving of this individual to the vision of God.[163] In effect, what Thomas

---

    sicut et gratiae consummationem, quae est vita aeterna. Sed sicut vita aeterna non statim redditur, sed suo tempore, ita nec gratia statim augetur, sed suo tempore, cum scilicet aliquis sufficienter fuerit dispositus ad gratiae augmentum."

162 Thomas's teaching about the *auxilium* of perseverance is discussed in the second sub-section of the first section of this chapter. It was noted that *auxilium* incorporates both Aristotelian and Augustinian notions; see notes 45, 51, and especially 54 above.

163 I-II 114, 9c: "Perseverantia ... viae non cadit sub merito; quia dependet solum ex motione divina, quae est principium omnis meriti. Sed Deus gratis perseverantiae bonum largitur cuicumque illud largitur." In the corpus of the ninth article, Thomas refers to a second kind of perseverance, the perseverance in glory. This refers to the final state of the human being, in which the person will remain forever in the vision of God to which he has attained. With regard to this kind of perseverance, Thomas says, it does fall under merit, for, as aa. 2 and 3 have made clear, by their acts people do merit the end to which they are ordained by God; and part of this end is that it is everlasting. Incidentally, one of the reasons that Thomas criticizes Origen is that Origen had suggested that the beatific vision is not everlasting and that the beatified could fall from this state and re-enter the world; see I-II 5, 4c.

has done in this ninth article is to complete the analysis begun in the fifth article about the role of operative *auxilium* in the movement of the individual to God. In that article, Thomas denied that the operative grace of conversion could be merited, for this grace is given by God solely at God's discretion in accordance with God's plan for this person. In the present article, Thomas asserts a similar operative grace of perseverance, thereby showing that the success of the person's attempt to come to God is ultimately dependent not so much on the good effort of that person as on the pleasure of God, by which God keeps the individual in the state of grace by moving the individual to the good acts that permit the person to increase his grace and hence on the correct path to God. The beginning of the spiritual life *and* its continuance both rest on God's free and purposeful involvement in the life of the individual moving this person to God.[164] We cannot merit either of these operative *auxilia*. All we can do is hope in God's mercy and pray for the granting of these necessary graces by which salvation becomes a reality.[165] By asserting this second operative grace, Thomas succeeds in underscoring in the heart of the question on merit that salvation is indeed the gift of God.

Finally, Thomas concludes his *ex professo* treatment of merit in the *Summa* by asking in the tenth article of q. 114 whether *temporal* goods fall under merit. The question comes as something of a surprise. The contemplation of the relation between theological merit and temporal goods would seem to mark a significant departure from the consideration up to this point of the meriting of spiritual goods such as glory and grace.[166] The

For Thomas's general criticism of Origen on the question of merit, see note 87 above.

164 Thomas's insistence on the impossibility of meriting these two operative *auxilia* marks a real advance on the teaching on merit offered in the *Scriptum*. In the final chapter, I shall suggest that Thomas's incorporation of a discussion of these operative graces into his account of merit reflects his greater familiarity with the later anti-Pelagian writings of Saint Augustine, in which these graces are affirmed, and Thomas's desire to bring his teaching on merit more closely into line with that of the great church father.

165 See I-II 114, 9 ad 1, in which Thomas notes that we can receive the grace of perseverance only by prayer: "Etiam ea quae non meremur orando impetramus: nam et peccatore Deus audit peccatorum veniam petentes, quam non merentur. . . . Et similiter perseverantiae donum aliquis petendo a Deo impetrat vel sibi vel alii, quanmvis sub merito non cadat." Note 146 above briefly delineates the value of prayer according to Aquinas, and the difference between the impetration of prayer and congruent merit. The fourth section of this chapter examines Thomas's teaching on hope as this complements his understanding of merit.

166 De Margerie, "La sécurité temporelle du juste," discusses the tenth article at some length. The discussion is not particularly illuminating, and while de Margerie has drawn on other parts of the *Summa* for help in interpreting the article, he makes no reference to the *Commentary on Job*, which, as I suggest in the text, marks the closest parallel to this article. Nor does he really attempt to read this article in the light of the previous articles on merit.

closest parallel in the Thomistic corpus to the present article is probably his *Commentary on Job* from the early 1260s, but even here the resemblance is not complete. In the *Commentary on Job*, Thomas has pursued a significant and yet relatively modest goal. In discussing the suffering of the just man, he wishes to show that although divine providence governs all which occurs and insures that every act will receive its just reward, retribution for evil need not come in the present life. The evil will receive their full punishment in the next world. Concomitantly, he argues that the evil that the just now endures need have no relation to punishment for previous sin. God may impose want and suffering on the just in order to give that person occasion for the exercise of the appropriate virtue. In any case, Job makes no attempt to articulate a fully thought-out teaching on merit or to incorporate more closely the rewards and punishments of the present life into such a teaching. Such an effort is made by Thomas only in the present article.

In *ST* I-II 114, 10c, Thomas affirms that temporal benefits and conditions do fall under merit but adds that they can fall under merit in two ways. They may be owed to merit "simply" (*simpliciter*), or may be merited only in a restricted sense (*secundum quid*).[167] The basis of the distinction between these ways of meriting, says Thomas, is the distinction between the two goods possible to people in human life. The first good is that with which Thomas has been concerned in the entire discussion of grace and merit, God as the beatific end. This is the good in an unqualified sense, for it is in God alone that the human person can find the true and complete fulfillment of his desire for perfection. Included in the good taken in this absolute sense are all the lesser goods that are ordained to God as the end of human life and that lead to God.[168] Hence, in terms of the discussion of merit to this point, habitual grace and the theological virtues are goods in an absolute sense, for they are oriented to the attainment of God as the end of life. But Thomas stresses in the present article, temporal goods can

---

167 Care should be taken not to confuse the teaching of the first article of this question and that of the tenth. In the first article, Thomas acknowledges that there cannot be justice *simpliciter* between those who are unequal but that there can be justice in a restricted sense, *secundum quid*. As we saw, the divine ordination provides for this justice *secundum quid*, and hence for merit of the end to which God has ordained people, the absolute good, God Himself. In the tenth article, Thomas is distinguishing between the *good* in an unqualified sense (*simpliciter*) and that which is good only in a restricted sense (*secundum quid*). Hence, the good in an unqualified sense (*simpliciter*) in the tenth article is that which people merit, through the divine ordination, according to justice *secundum quid* in the first article.

168 I-II 114, 10c: "Illud quod sub merito cadit, est praemium vel merces, quod habet rationem alicuius boni. Bonum autem hominis est duplex: unum simpliciter, aliud secundum quid. Bonum hominis simpliciter est ultimus finis eius, secundum illud *Psalm., Mihi autem adhaerere Deo bonum est* [Ps. 72:28]; et per consequens omnia illa quae ordinantur ut ducentia ad hunc finem, et talia simpliciter cadunt sub merito."

also lead to the attainment of God: They can be useful for the virtuous action by which a person comes to eternal life, and so they too, as referred to God, are good in an unqualified sense. As we have seen, the spiritual goods leading to God such as grace and charity fall under the motion of grace and their increase can be merited through human acts. So too, then, can the temporal goods likewise ordained to God be merited in this unqualified sense. Actually, in the present article he argues this point more subtly, reflecting here his awareness that the just do not always enjoy prosperity in this life. After he says that temporal goods fall under merit directly and simply (*directe et simpliciter*) to the extent that they bring the person to God, he adds that "God gives just men so much in the way of temporal goods, and evils too (*et etiam de malis*), as will profit them on the way to reaching eternal life."[169] The addition of this reference to the evil that may fall under merit in an absolute sense is significant, for it undermines any simple equation between doing the moral good and enjoying temporal prosperity. Someone may do the good and suffer want in this life. This want will be given as the desert for these previous good acts and will ultimately be seen as beneficial, for it will lead to further good, by providing the opportunity for the exercise of the virtues, guided by charity, that bring the actor to the true good of human life, to God.

The other good found in human life is good only in a restricted sense (*secundum quid*).[170] What Thomas means by this is that temporal goods in themselves are good in the sense that they offer some (albeit partial) satisfaction for the human desire for perfection and "mirror" in their being the absolute good, God. But they do not fully satisfy the desire for fulfillment, and if they are not placed in reference to God, they are good only in a limited and partial sense (*secundum quid*). They reflect God and so are good but do not lead to God and so are only good in a limited way. Because these goods are viewed as the ultimate end of human action, they do not fall under the direct and simple merit of those who are ordained and moved by God to the true good of eternal life. Nevertheless, they do come under merit, the merit *secundum quid* which has to do with goods which are good *secundum quid* because they are seen only in isolation from God: Thomas

---

169 I-II 114, 10c: "Secundum hoc ergo dicendum est quod si temporalia bona considerentur prout sunt utilia ad opera virtutum, quibus perducimur in vitam aeternam, secundum hoc directe et simpliciter cadunt sub merito, sicut et augmentum gratiae, et omnia illa quibus homo adjuvatur ad perveniendum in beatitudinem post primam gratiam. Tanturm enim dat Deus viris justis de bonis temporalibus, et etiam de malis, quantum eis expedit ad perveniendum ad vitam aeternam; et intantum sunt simpliciter bona huiusmodi temporalia." The translation in the text is by C. Ernst, the editor and translator of the treatise on grace in the Blackfriars edition.

170 I-II 114, 10c: "Bonum autem secundum quid et non simpliciter hominis est quod est bonum ei ut nunc, vel quod ei est secundum ali, quid bonum; et huiusmodi non cadunt sub merito simpliciter, sed secundum quid."

here states that God grants these goods as the just consequence of human action.[171]

While these goods do not promote personal salvation (for they do not come under the divine ordination to the good that is God), Thomas adds in article 10 that the acts leading to these rewards are nevertheless caused by a "divine motion." At first glance, the reference to a divine motion in regard to acts that are not ultimately meritorious of eternal life is somewhat perplexing. After all, in I-II 114, Thomas has hitherto discussed the divine "motion" only in terms of the grace given in accordance with the divine ordination to bring an individual to eternal life. Thus, based on the knowledge of the divine motion available from this single question, it is not immediately clear what Thomas means in speaking of a divine motion that is involved in the mere merit *secundum quid* of temporal goods. But Thomas's teaching about the divine motion involved in this merit in the present article is explicable when placed against the broader background of Thomas's teaching found elsewhere in the *Summa* about divine providence and God's involvement in all activity in the universe. The divine providence encompasses more than the ordination of individuals to life with God. It covers all that happens in the world and directs all events to the manifestation of God's goodness in the universe. Moreover, everything that occurs, occurs due to God's causality. We have already seen that God's aid is required for every good act which is done on the supernatural level. This is the grace of *auxilium* by which God reduces human potential for supernatural activity to act. But Thomas also says in I-II 109 that such *auxilium* is also needed on the purely natural level. Unless God as Pure Act reduces natural beings to their acts, there will be no action.[172] Hence, in I-II 114, 10c, in his teaching about merit *secundum quid* Thomas is referring to his general teaching on providence and to the need for God's involvement even at the natural level for activity to occur. Merits in this restricted sense follow on acts moved by God at the non-supernatural level that have their place in the plan of the divine providence.[173] Since the

171 I-II 114, 10c: "Si autem considerentur huiusmodi temporalia bona secundum se, sic non sunt simpliciter bona hominis, sed secundum quid. Et ita non simpliciter cadunt sub merito, sed secundum quid, inquantum scilicet homines moventur a Deo ad aliqua temporaliter agenda, in quibus suum propositum consequuntur Deo favente. Ut sicut vita aeterna est simpliciter praemium operum justitiae per relationem ad motionem divinam . . . ita temporalia bona in se considerata habeant rationem mercedis, habito respectu ad motionem divinam, qua voluntates hominum moventur ad haec prosequenda; licet interdum in his non habeant homines rectam intentionem." In ad 3 of this article, Thomas adds that just as for the good, so too to the wicked God grants evil in return for their sinful acts. However, for the good, their punishment serves for their amendment (or, for the opportunity to exercise the appropriate virtue), while for the wicked, it is simply an evil.

172 For this "natural" *auxilium*, see note 53 above.

173 In his article, "Naturale meritum ad Deum," *Angelicum* 19 (1942): 139–78,

performance of these acts is not ordained by God to the special end of human life, the vision of God, they are not meritorious *simpliciter*. They do not lead to the attainment of God because, lacking this ordination, they are not done in the grace and charity consequent on the divine ordination that refers these acts, and the temporal goods attendent on these acts, to God. But they do merit the temporal goods for which they are done. God applies the person to this act in accordance with the divine providence, and the person receives the desired temporal good as a reward, all for the purpose of realizing in this way the divine plan to manifest God's goodness outside of God.

When compared to the earlier *ex professo* treatment of merit in the *Scriptum*, the teaching of I-II 114 appears markedly different. First, Thomas has incorporated into the later teaching on merit a more developed and subtle teaching on grace. The speculation on grace during the years separating the *Scriptum* and the *Summa* has manifested itself in the later teaching on merit in both "negative" and "positive" ways. Negatively, his reflections on the need to posit a grace of *auxilium* as well as habitual grace have led Thomas to incorporate into his question on merit a discussion of the spiritual goods which *cannot* be merited. Hence, he tells us here explicitly that it is impossible to merit the first grace, which is an operative *auxilium* grace of conversion. Similarly, the human person cannot merit the grace of perseverance, which is an additional instance of operative *auxilium*. More positively, more extended contemplation of the nature of grace has caused Thomas to change his mind about the kind of justice present in merit. In place of the distributive justice that receives such great attention in the *Scriptum*, in the *Summa* Thomas argues that the grace that causes meritorious action is intrinsically "equal" to the reward merited by human acts, eternal life, and so these acts merit their reward according to a kind of commutative justice. Second, Thomas's teaching about merit in the *Summa* marks a considerable advance because it is more coherently integrated into his general soteriology. In the *Scriptum*, Thomas offers a

---

Lumbreras has also recognized that Thomas is referring to the involvement of God's *auxilium* at the natural level in this part of I-II 114, 10c; see p. 156. As I have already indicated elsewhere, I am reluctant to speak of a "natural" merit in Aquinas. Certainly, Thomas is much less concerned with such a merit (if it exists) than is Lumbreras, who develops an extended analysis of such a merit by analogy with Thomas's statements about theological merit. For my part, "natural" merit should not be the focus of speculation in its own right. It should be considered only in relation to "theological" merit, merit in the true sense. In this light it would be revealed clearly as but an imperfect reflection of the merit about which Thomas really wishes to speak, for it marks a failure to evince the conditions needed for authentic merit before God. As we have seen, Thomas's teaching about merit is designed to display the manner in which human acts are useful in the attainment of God and must be seen as they contribute in a special way to the realization of God's plan in creating and redeeming. A merit which does not bring one to God in this viewpoint can only be of secondary interest and importance.

teaching about merit that focuses on merit in isolation from other relevant features of his understanding of God's relation to the world and of human salvation in general. In the *Summa,* on the other hand, Thomas grounds the possibility of merit in the divine ordination and in this way immediately situates his reflections on merit in his broader "sapiential" theology. He discusses merit in this work as a special instance of the divine plan formulated in the divine wisdom for the manifestation of the divine goodness outside of God. Thomas's greater attention to grace and to the divine wisdom results in a more adequate teaching about merit that can ascribe value to human action without undercutting Thomas's fundamental insight that human salvation is ultimately the gift and work of God.[174]

Section III. The Merit of Angels, and of Christ

To this point, I have been exclusively concerned with Thomas's teaching about the merit of ordinary human beings before God. In the *Summa,* however, as elsewhere in the Thomistic corpus, Thomas also discusses the merit of other rational beings, a discussion that sheds additional light on his understanding of merit and the ordination which constitutes the basis of merit. Hence, this review of merit in the *Summa* will conclude by examining Thomas's teaching in this work about the merit of angels and of Jesus Christ.

Earlier, this chapter, referred to I-II 5, 7c, as an aid in explicating the meaning of *ordinatio* in I-II 114, 1c. It was observed that in I-II 5, 7c, Thomas explicitly relates the *ordinatio* which accounts for the possibility of merit to the divine plan, formulated in the divine wisdom, for the manifestation of the goodness of God *ad extra*. In this text, Thomas says that people come to eternal life by their acts because God has decreed that they will contribute in this way to the proclamation of God's goodness outside of God. In I-II 5, 7c, however, Thomas has not been content to discuss only the place of human meriting in the divine plan. He offers a more exhaustive summary of merit in the divine dispensation by considering also the merit of angels and its role in God's plan. Hence, he observes that knowing God immediately and directly is natural only to God. God exists from eternity in timeless self-contemplation. But according to the divine plan, God has admitted others to God's own life of self-love and contemplation. Thus, as we have seen, God has designed the human being to come to this life through a series of acts. In these acts of love and faith, the human person mirrors God's own acts of knowledge and love, and most important, by the divine ordination, through these acts comes to possess

---

174 The final chapter returns to the question of development in Thomas's teaching about merit, asking to what extent Thomas's greater familiarity with the later writings of Augustine have contributed to the changes in his teaching about merit. That chapter suggests that with regard to both grace and the divine purpose, the development in Thomas's teaching about merit reflects the increasing "Augustinianism" of Thomas's later theology.

God. But, adds Thomas, there is also a "middle" level between God's immediate and natural possession of God and the human person's coming to God through the meritorious acts made possible by the grace of God. In this regard, Thomas refers to the angels and asserts that angels have been so designed by God that they too can merit the supernatural knowledge of God, not by a series of acts but by a single meritorious act.[175] Thus, just as human merits in their way contribute to the manifestation of the divine goodness, so too the single act of merit required by angels to be saved also proclaims the goodness of God, in accordance with the plan of the divine wisdom.

This text from the Prima Secundae provides a fair summary of the more detailed discussion of angelic merit found in the Prima Pars. Angels merit God by a single act of love (made possible by grace), and they too contribute in this way to the realization of the divine plan.[176] In the earlier discussion of angels in the Prima Pars, Thomas provided a rather exhaustive description of the numerous ways in which angelic merit both parallels and deviates from human merit before God. In the first place, just as are human beings, so too the angels are ordained to a twofold end—one that is consonant with their natural capacities and obtained by their natural powers (i.e., natural knowledge through species) and another which transcends their natural capacities. This latter end is supernatural life with God, in which rational creatures are able to see God as God sees Himself.[177] Secondly, for angels as for humans, elevation to the supernatural level is beyond natural capacities. To rise to God's own level the one who naturally possesses such life, God, must move the creature to will God as God wills God. Hence, just as Thomas speaks of the need of an operative *auxilium*

---

175   I-II 5, 7c: "Sed angelus, qui est superior ordine naturae quam homo, consecutus est eam, ex ordine divinae sapientiae, uno motu operationis meritoriae."

176   Thomas discusses the attainment by angels of their supernatural end by a single meritorious act in I 62, 5c; I shall return to this article shortly in the text. For the role which angels play in the divine plan for manifesting the divine goodness, see I 50, 1c, and for the importance of their salvation in this regard, I 62, 6c.

177   I 62, 1c: "Ultima autem perfectio rationalis seu intellectualis naturae est duplex; una quidem quam potest assequi virtute suae naturae; et haec quodam modo beatitudo vel felicitas dicitur. Unde et Aristoteles perfectissimam hominis contemplationem, qua optimum intelligibile, quod est Deus, contemplari potest in hac vita, dicit esse ultimam hominis felicitatem. Sed super hanc felicitatem est alia felicitas, quam in futuro expectamus, qua *videbimus Deum sicuti est*, quod quidem est supra cuiuslibet intellectus creati naturam. . . . Sic igitur dicendum est quantum ad primam beatitudinem, quam angelus assequi virtute suae naturae potuit, fuit creatus beatus. . . . Sed ultimam beatitudinem, quae facultatem naturae excedit, angeli non statim in principio suae creationis habuerunt; quia haec beatitudo non est aliquid naturae, sed naturae finis. Et ideo non statim eam a principio debuerunt habere."

to convert the human person to God, so too in I 62, 2c, he refers to the *auxilium gratiae* by which the angel is directed to God as to his super-natural end.[178] At this point, however, there emerges a difference between angels and people. In his discussion of the need for an operative *auxilium* to effect the conversion of people after the Fall, Thomas noted two grounds on which this grace is needed: the transcendent quality of supernatural life; and the disorder of the will caused by sin, through which the will is directed away from God. In the case of angels, however, the second reason is inapplicable: Thomas thinks it most probable that angels were created in a sanctifying grace[179] and that they merit heaven or hell by their first act of will after creation. Hence, there is no "moment" between creation and first action in which sin could intervene. Thus, angels need to be converted by grace to God for only the first reason, that they be enabled to rise to God's own level,[180] and in this, the case of angels parallels the situation in which the first person found himself before the Fall.[181]

---

178 I 62, 2c: "Angeli indiguerunt gratia ad hoc quod converterentur in Deum prout est objectum beatitudinis . . . naturalis motus voluntatis est principium omnium eorum quae volumus: naturalis autem inclinatio voluntatis est ad id quod est conveniens secundum naturam. Et ideo si aliquid sit supra naturam, voluntas in id ferri non potest, nisi ab aliquo alio supernaturali principio adjuta; sicut patet quod ignis habet naturalem inclinationem ad calefaciendum et ad generandum ignem. Sed generare carnem est supra naturalem virtutem ignis, unde ignis ad hoc nullam inclinationem habet, nisi secundum quod movetur ut instrumentum ab anima nutriva. Ostensum est autem supra, cum de De cognitione ageretur, quod videre Deum per essentiam, in quo ultima beatitudo rationalis creaturae consistit, est supra naturam cuiuslibet intellectus creati. Unde nulla creatura rationalis potest habere motum voluntatis ordinatum ad illam beatitudinem, nisi mota a supernaturali agente; et hoc dicimus auxilium gratiae. Et ideo dicendum est quod angelus in illam beatitudinem voluntate converti non potuit nisi per auxilium gratiae."

179 In I 62, 3c, Thomas notes that some thought the angels were created in a natural condition only, while others thought that they were created in the state of grace. He terms the latter view *probabilius*, and ascribes it to the church fathers.

180 In I 62, 2 ad 3, Thomas offers an interesting reflection on the different senses which the word 'conversion' can bear. First, 'conversion' can refer to the perfect turning to God which is found in the beatific vision. Here one rests perfectly in God. Second, there is the "conversion" of those who have received grace and merit God by their acts. For this "conversion," habitual grace is required, for habitual grace is the principle of merit (. . . *habitualis gratia, quae est merendi principium*). Finally, there is the first conversion, by which those who were turned away from God are turned back again, by the grace of God.

181 In the *sed contra* of I 62, 2, Thomas cites Romans 6:23 ("The grace of God is eternal life") to support his contention that angels need to be converted to God by grace. Otherwise, bliss would be obtained by purely natural means, and this would contradict the Apostle's teaching. Recall the use of Romans 6:23 in I-II 114, 2, sed contra; there, this text is also cited to show why merit

While angels and human beings share a twofold ordination as well as the need for grace to merit and to be saved, in the remaining articles of I 62 Thomas is concerned more to outline the principal differences between angelic and human merit. The major difference has already been noted. While people come to God through many merits, angels merit beatitude by a single act.[182] To make this difference more transparent, in I 62, 5c, Thomas refers to the nature of angels, according to which God has designed them to know intuitively through species, in a single act. Human beings, on the other hand, do not know intuitively. Rather, by the divine dispensation, people know discursively, reflecting the divine knowing in this particular way.[183] Now, as Thomists are wont to say, grace does not destroy nature but perfects it, completing it in the way appropriate to it. Hence, argues Thomas here, that human beings come to their supernatural end by the power of grace through a series of meritorious acts is in keeping with human nature, which comes to its natural end discursively, or step by step. The same principle holds for angels. It is appropriate for angels to merit God by a single act, just as they attain their natural end through a single act of knowledge.[184] Thus, the difference between human and angelic merit follows on the difference between human and angelic nature. And as has been repeatedly stressed, the difference between natures is in accordance with the divine creative will, which establishes different kinds of things to manifest more adequately the abundance of the divine goodness.

Thomas makes one further point in this question which underscores the

---

presupposes grace; see the general comments on I-II 114, 2–4, in part two of this chapter and note 113 above.

182   In I 62, 5c, Thomas qualifies this point slightly. It is absolutely true that God has designed angels to come to God by one meritorious act, and people by many. But as we saw in the discussion of I-II 114, 7, and related texts on the claim established by merit to eternal life which remains in God's *acceptatio* even after sin, each act done in charity merits eternal life. Hence, as Thomas suggests here, if a person does one such act and then dies, that person will have earned eternal life. However, the point made in the text remains valid: People are meant to come to God through several meritorious acts.

183   Thomas contrasts human and angelic knowledge in I 62, 1c: "Quia perfectionem huiusmodi angelus non acquirit per aliquem motum discursivum, sicut homo, sed statim ei adest propter suae naturae dignitatem."

184   I 62, 5c: "Angelus post primum actum charitatis, quo beatitudinem meruit, statim beatus fuit. Cuius ratio est quia gratia perficit naturam secundum modum naturae, sicut et omnis perfectio recipitur in perfectibili secundum modum eius. Est autem hoc proprium naturae angelicae quod naturalem perfectionem non per discursum acquirat, sed statim per naturam habeat. . . . Sicut autem ex sua natura angelus habet ordinem ad perfectionem naturalem, ita ex merito habet ordinem ad gloriam; et ita statim post meritum, in angelo fuit beatitudo consecuta." See also I 62, 5 ad 3: "De natura angeli est quod statim suam perfectionem consequatur, ad quam ordinatur. Et ideo non requiritur nisi unus actus meritorius, qui ea ratione medium dici potest, quia secundum ipsum angelus ad beatitudinem ordinatur."

way in which angelic meriting is unlike human. There is one human nature, and all humans are members of the same species. Angels too share the same nature but do not belong to the same species. Rather, each angel constitutes its own species, and that there are as many species of angels as there are angels and that these angels exist in a hierarchy in which there are nobler and less noble angels are again due to the divine plan in creating. This diversity is required to achieve the divine desire to display the divine goodness as completely as possible. Now, in I 62, 6, Thomas asks a question which at first glance seems puzzling, considering the stress in the *Summa* on grace and predestination to salvation in accordance with God's will. He asks whether angels are given grace and glory in accordance with their natural capacities. If asked of human beings, an affirmative answer would be evidence of a form of Pelagianism, in which the supernatural would be achieved through merely natural acts. All human beings by their natural capacities are "capable of God" (*capax Dei*) in the sense that as rational there is nothing in their nature dissonant from being raised to God's own level and knowing God directly. Indeed, as was mentioned earlier in this chapter,[185] Thomas will even say that in their very institution as rational, human beings are "ordained" to God. But that this person rather than that human actually attains God is due to God's predestination, by which God ordains this being to come in actuality to the vision of God. Now, all those human beings who are predestined, are predestined to the same reward, the vision of God. But not every one of the elect attains to the same perfection of vision. Rather, in accordance with the different will of God in the case of different people, people attain to varying levels of the beatific vision. God predestines them to different levels of vision and, in accordance with this predestination, gives them the grace needed to do the meritorious acts by which they will each attain the limit set for them by God. Thus, in the case of human beings, by nature each equally stands open to the beatific vision. It is God's predestination alone, however, which realizes the possibility and determines the degree of this enjoyment of God.

But as asked of angels, the affirmative answer to the question of whether angels receive grace and glory in accordance with their natural capacities need not imply Pelagianism or suggest that God's predestination plays no role in the granting of grace and glory to angels. Each angel possesses angelic nature to the degree appropriate to its species, and its species has been set for it by God, to display the divine goodness in its own way. Moreover, as rational, each angel is *capax Dei* in the sense that as rational it is capable of being raised to the highest intellectual activity of knowing God directly. And just as there is a hierarchy of angels according to species, so each angel is capable of enjoying the vision of God to a greater or lesser degree, in accordance with the measure of its species. Hence, if God were to realize the potential of an angel for the vision of God and so manifest

---

185   See the earlier discussion of "ordination" in the sense of the rational creature's "capacity" for the vision of God in note 26 above.

the divine goodness through this creature in a special way, by moving this angel by grace to the merit of God, the angel would achieve the degree of the vision of God appropriate to its species. And the degree of vision attained by this angel as compared to that would differ, according to the different places in the angelic hierarchy originally occupied by each. Hence, as compared to human nature and the predestination of human beings to eternal life, there is a greater symmetry between the institution of angelic species and the predestination of angels to eternal life. In the case of angels, their very institution is designed to reflect different degrees of divine goodness: God has designed the nobler angel to reflect in a greater way God's goodness. So too the predestination of angels to eternal life respects the differences in species established by God. When God freely decides to move an angel to eternal life, God moves it to the measure of eternal life corresponding to the species of angelic being as set up originally by God. In this way, in the case of angels who actually attain the vision of God, creation and predestination more neatly mesh than is the case for the human elect. For human beings, the degree of their participation in eternal life is due exclusively to the divine predestination and is not due to disparity in their possession of human nature (for there is no such disparity). For angels, on the other hand, God makes them specifically different, and when God freely decides to save them, God predestines them to a greater or lesser degree of the beatific vision. This degree corresponds to their original institution as determined by the divine wisdom.[186]

Thomas's discussion of the merit of Christ is scattered throughout the

186   I 62, 6c: "Secundum gradum naturalium angelis data sint dona gratiarum, et perfectio beatitudinis. Cuius quidem ratio ex duobus accipi potest. Primo quidem ex parte ipsius Dei, qui per ordinem suae sapientiae, diversos gradus in angelica natura constituit. Sicut autem natura angelica facta est a Deo ad gratiam et beatitudinem consequendam; ita etiam gradus naturae angelicae ad diversos gradus gratiae et gloriae ordinari videntur; ut puta, si aedificator lapides polit ad constituendum domum, ex hoc ipso quod aliqous pulchrius et decentius aptat, videtur eos ad honorationem partem domus ordinare. Sic igitur quod Deus angelos altioris naturae fecit, ad majora gratiarum dona et ampliorem beatitudinem ordinaverit." See also I 62, 6 ad 1: "Sicut gratia est ex mera Dei voluntate, ita etiam et natura angeli. Et sicut naturam Dei voluntas ordinavit ad gratiam, ita et gradus naturae ad gradus gratiae." In the corpus, Thomas mentions a second reason why grace and glory are given according to the natural capacities of the angel. Each angel is a single nature and not a compound of two natures. The human person is "composed," as it were, of two natures. Now, those things which are composite do not act with the utter singleness of purpose and energy with which the thing of a single nature acts. In the human person, the intellectual part is often at odds with his sensual nature. But the angel is able to devote its entire energy to the attainment of the end of its unified nature. Thus, given this difference between angels and humans, "rationabile est quod angeli qui meliorem naturam habuerunt, etiam fortius et efficacius ad Deum sint conversi," and that God would give more grace to the higher angelic nature able to act more intensely.

Tertia Pars,[187] and has two main parts. Thomas delineates the extent of Christ's merit *for himself*; and he establishes why it is that Christ merited *for others*. On the face of it, a good case can be made against any merit by Christ for himself. Merit is ordained to the attainment of eternal life as well as of all which leads to eternal life, i.e., the increase of habitual grace and the theological virtues. But Thomas has argued in the Tertia Pars, Christ was a *comprehensor* and in his lifetime enjoyed the direct vision of God: Since the humanity of Jesus Christ existed in personal union with the Son of God, the historical Jesus throughout his life experienced the direct vision of God that other people hope to achieve in the next world.[188] Now, it is a constant feature of Thomas's teaching about merit that a person merits only what he does not have. Hence, since Jesus Christ already experienced the beatific vision, Thomas insists that Christ did not merit for himself the vision of God. For the same reason, Thomas adds that Christ did not merit an increase in the habitual grace that is designed to dispose the ordinary Christian more perfectly for eternal life.[189]

But Christ was not only a *comprehensor*; Thomas also asserts that in his lifetime Christ was in a sense also a *viator*,[190] and so it is possible to

187 For our purposes, the principal texts are III 19, 3, in which Thomas asks whether Christ merited for himself; III 19, 4, where he asks whether Christ could merit for others; and III 48, 1, where the question is whether Christ achieved our salvation *per modum meriti*. Other pertinent texts are: III 2, 11, where Thomas argues that no merits of Jesus Christ preceded the incarnation; III 34, 3, in which Thomas considers whether in the first instant of his conception Christ could merit; and III 49, 6, where the topic is Christ's merit of his exaltation through the passion.

188 For the affirmation that Christ in his lifetime was a *comprehensor*, see III 9, 2c: "Illud quod est in potentia reducitur in actum per id quod est actu: oportet enim esse calidum id per quod alia calefiunt. Homo autem est in potentia ad scientiam beatorum, quae in visione Dei consistit, et ad eam ordinatur sicut ad finem; est enim creatura rationalis capax illius beatae cognnitionis, inquantum est ad imaginem Dei. Ad hunc autem finem beatitudinis homines reducuntur per Christi humanitatem. . . . Et ideo oportuit quod cognitio ipsa in Dei visione consistens excellentissime Christo homini conveniret; quia semper causam oportet esse potiorem causato." In addition, in III 15, 10c, Thomas writes: "Christus . . . ante passionem, secundum mentem plene videbat Deum: et sic habebat beatitudinem quantum ad id quod est proprium animae."

189 III 19, 3c: "Unde nec gratiam, nec scientiam, nec beatitudinem animae, nec divinitatem meruit: quia cum meritum non sit nisi eius quod nondum habetur, oportet quod Christus aliquando istis caruisset," and Thomas adds, this would be to the detriment of Christ's dignity.

190 III 15, 10, specifies in which sense Christ was both *viator* and *comprehensor*. In the corpus, Thomas distinguishes between the principal part of beatitude, which has to do with the perfection of the soul in vision, and secondary aspects of it, having to do with the beatitude of the body. He then asserts that in his lifetime, Christ always enjoyed the beatitude of the soul, but that his body obtained the perfection appropriate to it, such as impassivity, only after the resurrection. Thus, he concludes, with respect to the beatitude of the body,

speak of a merit of Christ for himself. In the beatific vision, the deepest desire of the rational soul, its yearning for knowledge, is satisfied. Yet, given his Aristotelian psychology with its stress on the intimacy and need of both soul and body in the human person, it is not surprising that Thomas does not restrict the glory of heaven to the soul. Just as the human person in this life is not the soul alone, but the soul acting through body, so the body too receives its share of glory in heaven. As Thomas puts it, God has so ordained that the glory of the soul will overflow to the body, in accordance with the merits that the human person (soul and body) had earned on earth.[191] Now, in the single case of Christ, the attendant features normally associated with the vision of God did not occur or at least did not immediately follow on the vision. Although Christ did enjoy the beatific vision while in this world, God so ordained that the glorification of the body that ordinarily accompanies the vision of God would not occur until after Christ's resurrection after the Passion.[192] Thus, since Christ did not possess these rewards in this world, by his meritorious acts he was able to

in his lifetime Christ was a *viator*: "Aliquis dicitur viator ex eo quod tendit in beatitudinem, comprehensor autem dicitur ex hoc quod iam beatitudinem obtinet. . . . Hominis autem beatitudo perfecta consistit in anima et corpore . . . in anima quidem, quantum ad id quod est ei proprium, secundum quod mens videt et fruitur Deo; in corpore vero, secundum quod corpus *resurget spirituale, et in virtute et in gloria et in incorruptione,* ut dicitur in I *Cor* [15:42]. Christus autem, ante passionem, secundum mentem plene videbat Deum: et sic habebat beatitudinem quantum ad id quod est proprium animae. Sed quantum ad alia deerat ei beatitudo; quia et anima eius erat passabilis, et corpus passabile et mortale. . . . Et ideo simul erat comprehensor, inquantum habebat beatitudinem animae propriam; et simul viator, inquantum tendebat in beatitudinem secundum id quod ei de beatitudine deerat."

191 III 19, 3 ad 3: "Redundantia gloriae ex anima ad corpus est ex divina ordinatione, secundum congruentiam humanorum meritorum; ut scilicet, sicut homo meretur per actum animae quem exercet in corpore, ita etiam remuneretur per gloriam animae redundantem ad corpus. Et propter hoc non solum gloria animae, sed etiam gloria corporis cadit sub merito, secundum illud *Rom., Vivificabit mortalia corpora nostra propter inhabitantem Spiritum eius in nobis* [8:11]. Et ita potuit cadere sub merito Christi." See also III 15, 10 ad 2, in which Thomas refers to the perfection of the body in a secondary way in the beatific vision: "Beatitudo principaliter et proprie consistit in anima secundum mentem; secundario tamen, et quasi instrumentaliter, requiruntur ad beatitudinem corporis bona; sicut Philosophus dicit [Ethics I, 8] quod exteriora bona organice deserviunt beatitudini."

192 For the divine ordination to postpone the beatitude of Christ's body, see III 49, 6 ad 3: "Dispensatione quadam factum est in Christo ut gloria animae ante passionem non redundaret ad corpus, ad hoc quod gloriam corporis honorabilius obtineret, quando eam per passionem meruisset. Gloriam autem animae differri non conveniebat, quia anima immediate uniebatur Verbo; unde decens erat ut gloria repleretur ab ipso Verbo: sed corpus uniebatur Verbo mediante anima."

merit for himself glorification of the body and other such secondary features of the attainment of the ultimate end of human existence.[193]

This, however, is only the beginning of Thomas's discussion of Christ's merit for himself; the continuation of this discussion reveals to us a great deal about the significance of merit for Thomas Aquinas and why he finds it valuable to speak of people meriting the reward from God to which they are ordained. This chapter has been most concerned to locate the treatment of merit in the broader perspective of God's plan in creating. Thomas's principal concern in the *Summa* in affirming merit is to portray how merit accords with God's will to manifest the divine goodness outside of God and indeed how meritorious actions result from God's plan for individual rational beings. But there is a secondary theme to which Thomas at times refers in his analysis of merit that emerges from this account of merit in terms of the divine plan. Merit also discloses the special dignity and perfection of the one who merits. There are various kinds of agents in the universe, each of whom displays God in the way appropriate to it. The relative worth of these agents follows on how closely each imitates the divine causality. Hence, the inanimate instrument of God is farther away from God than is the agent who possesses free choice, who more closely in his freedom in action approximates God as agent. The more an agent is able to do, the more noble it is. Thus, the human being is more perfect than the inanimate instrument because the human will is not only moved to act, it also contributes something to the act by the exercise of its own causality. By like reason, the more noble cause has a greater perfection because it is by its own action that it attains the end of its action, while the inanimate cause is simply moved to its end. Thus, the affirmation of human freedom and of the merit that comes from it by which the end of action, God, can be attained is meant to illustrate the dignity and worth of human being. Because people are free to act and are able to reach their end through their acts, they are of greater perfection than agents simply moved to their acts.

In his discussion of the merit of Christ for himself, Thomas explicitly refers to these ideas about the greater perfection and dignity of one who acts of himself and who is able to achieve through his acts his reward. Thomas begins III 19, 3c, by asserting that it is more noble to possess some good through oneself (*per se*) than to possess it through another, and he defines "possesses through oneself" as meaning that one is in some way (*aliquo modo*) the cause of his own possession of it. The addition of the *aliquo modo* is, of course, to be expected from Aquinas. Thomas has written too much in the *Summa* about God as the author of every formal perfection

---

193   For affirmations of Christ's merit of the beatitude of the body, see III 34, 4 ad 1, and III 46, 1c. In the latter text, Thomas says that one of the reasons Christ "had" to suffer was "ex parte ipsius Christi, qui per humilitatem passionis meruit gloriam exaltationis." In III 15, 10c, Thomas "enumerates" the features of bodily beatitude by citing I Corinthians 15:42, which was quoted in note 190 above.

and as the one who applies all secondary causes to their action to suggest here that free agents are autonomous actors who do not require divine aid to move to their act; the *aliquo modo* of the present article recalls to us that the causality of the human being is firmly situated in subordination to and dependence on the primary cause of all that is and occurs, God. But as Thomas adds in the present text, while the role of God must not be neglected, the causality of the human being is nevertheless real. As he here writes, "it still remains that a person can be, in subordinate fashion, the cause of his own possessing some good; inasmuch, that is, as he works with God in the achievement of this effect" ("potest tamen secundario aliquis esse causa sibi alicuius boni habendi, inquantum scilicet in hoc ipso Deo cooperatur"). Thomas then relates this discussion of possessing a good through oneself directly to merit, and points out that the person who merits a reward in some degree (*quodammodo*) can be said to possess it "through himself." Consequently, he concludes this part of the corpus, it is more noble to possess something by merit than to possess it without merit ("et sic ille qui habet aliquid per meritum proprium habet quodammodo illud per seipsum. Unde nobilius habetur id quod habetur per meritum quam id quod habetur sine merito"), that is, as simply moved to this end.

Meriting, then, is a perfection. It illustrates the greater dignity and worth of the human being. When viewed in this way, Thomas adds, it is necessary to speak of merit when one speaks of Christ. It is a general principle of Thomas's Christology that every perfection and dignity must be attributed to Christ.[194] Hence, we must assert that Jesus Christ merited

194   For a brief example of Thomas's argument for Christ's perfection and the necessity for it, see III 9, 1c, in which Thomas asserts Christ's possession of a full created knowledge in addition to his knowledge as God: "Filius Dei humanam naturam integram assumpsit; idest, non corpus solum, sed etiam animam; non solum sensitivam sed etiam rationalem. Et ideo oportuit quod haberet scientiam creatam, propter tria. Primo quidem, propter animae perfectionem. Anima enim, secundum se considerata, est in potentia ad intelligibilia cognoscenda. Est enim *sicut tabula in qua nihil est scriptum*; et tamen possibile est in ea scribi propter intellectum possibilem. . . . Quod autem est in potentia est imperfectum nisi reducatur ad actum. Non autem fuit conveniens ut Filius Dei humanam naturam imperfectam assumeret, sed perfectam; utpote qua mediante totum humanum genus erat ad perfectum reducendum. Et ideo oportuit quod anima Christi esset perfecta per aliquam scientiam, quae esset proprie perfectio eius. Et ideo oportuit in Christo esse aliquam scientiam praeter scientiam divinam. Alioquin anima Christi esset imperfectior omnibus animabus aliorum hominum. Secundo, quia cum *quaelibet res sit propter suam operationem* . . . frustra haberet Chrsitus animam intellectualem, si non intelligeret secundum illam. Quod pertinet ad scientiam creatam. Tertio, quia aliqua scientia creata pertinet ad animae humane naturam, scilicet illa per quam naturaliter cognoscimus prima principia: scientiam enim his large accipimus pro qualibet cognitione intellectus humani. Nihil autem naturalium Christo defuit; quia totam humanam naturam suscepit. . . . Et ideo in Sexta Synodo damnata est positio negantium in Christo duas esse scientias, vel duas sapientias."

for himself everything which other people merited for themselves. This is part of the human dignity that Christ shared. The only exception to this "Christological rule" is when the ascription of some perfection to Christ would entail the absence of an even greater perfection and so detract from Christ's dignity. In terms of the rewards which I have already noted that Christ does *not* merit—the beatific vision and the increase of grace[195]—it is clear that their possession from the beginning was a greater perfection for Christ than not having them and subsequently acquiring them through his acts. It pertains to the special dignity of Christ, for example, that throughout his lifetime Christ enjoyed the vision of God and that he did not have to wait until the next world to experience this vision.[196] But the same does not hold for the rewards which Thomas does assert Christ merits for himself. Since these rewards are merely secondary rewards attendant on the essential reward of the beatific vision, and since these rewards devolve upon the body as the "overflow" of the beatification of the soul, their absence from Christ during his lifetime did not detract from Christ's dignity. Indeed, as Thomas says here, because merit proceeds from charity, a perfection of the rational will (which is higher in the hierarchy of beings than the body, the subject of these secondary rewards), it works to the

195　In the text of III 19, 3c, Thomas also mentions Christ's knowledge and divinity. With regard to the latter, Thomas argues in a number of places that the actions of Jesus Christ did not merit union of the humanity of Christ to the Word and that this union is the result of God's predestination without regard to foreseen merits. See, e.g., III 2, 11c, in which Thomas says that Catholics do not hold that Christ was first a man and then afterwards by his merits had it granted to him to become the Son of God. In this text, Thomas dismisses this position as the error of Photinus. For other references to the error of Photinus, see III 16, 1c, and III 35, 4c. In III 2, 11c. Thomas adds that the merits of other people (i.e., the Patriarchs) could not merit condignly the incarnation of the Son of God, although they could merit it congruently by seeking it from God. In this text, it is clear that the incarnation is a spiritual good which transcends the workings of people, but which God grants mercifully to the entreaties of God's faithful and obedient people.

196　III 19, 3c: "Habere aliqoud donum per se est nobilius quam habere illud per aliud. . . . Hoc autem dicitur aliquis habere per seipsum cuius est sibi aliquo modo causa. Prima autem causa omnium bonorum nostrorum per auctoritatem est Deus: et per hunc modum nulla creatura habet aliquid boni per seipsam, secundum illud I *ad Cor., Quid habes quod non accepisti?* Potest tamen secundario aliquis esse causa sibi alicuius boni habendi, inquantum scilicet in hoc ipso Deo cooperatur. Et sic ille qui habet aliquid per meritum proprium habet quodammodo illud per seipsum. Unde nobilius habetur id quod habetur per meritum quam id quod habetur sine merito. Quia autem omnis perfectio et nobilitas Christo est attribuenda, consequens est quod ipse per meritum habuit illud quod alii per meritum habent, nisi sit tale quid cuius carentia magis dignitati Christi et perfectioni praejudicet, quam per meritum accrescat. Unde nec gratiam, nec scientiam, nec beatitudinem animae, nec divinitatem meruit: quia cum meritum non sit nisi eius quod nondum habetur, oportet quod Christus aliquando istis caruisset; quibus carere magis diminuit dignitatem Christ, quam augeat meritum."

greater dignity of Christ that Christ obtained these rewards through his meritorious acts. Thus, Thomas concludes the present article, although Christ did not merit those rewards which are the more important objects of merit, Christ "gloriam corporis, et ea quae pertinent ad exteriorem eius excellentiam, sicut est ascensio, veneratio et alia huiusmodi, habuit per meritum."[197]

Ultimately of greater significance than Christ's personal merit is the merit of Christ for other human beings. Indeed, it is through Christ's saving work, which is meritorious, that the salvation of others has become possible. The basic thrust of Thomas's analysis of Christ's merit for others has already been indicated in I-II 114, 6, where he discussed whether people in general can merit for others. In that article, as we saw, Thomas offered a two-part answer. If we ask about merit for another *by condignity*, then the Christian cannot merit condignly for another because the person moved by grace can merit only eternal life, and all which leads to eternal life, for himself. But if we ask about merit for another *by congruity*, then it is possible for the Christian to so merit for another, on the basis of the friendship which exists between God and the person established in grace. In I-II 114, 6, however, Thomas also observed that Christ presented a single exception to the rule about condign meriting for another. Although the condign merit of ordinary Christians is restricted to themselves, Christ's condign meriting is of universal application. In I-II 114, 6c, Thomas argued that the case of Christ is unique because of the special role which Jesus Christ has been destined to play in the divine dispensation: Christ's merit can extend to others because Christ has been ordained to be the head of all who are saved. Hence, because God has chosen Christ to be the means of universal salvation, Christ's merit can obtain for others the first grace and the rewards which fall under merit.[198]

In the Tertia Pars, Thomas repeats this basic analysis. First, Thomas affirms that Jesus Christ possessed the "fullness of grace," meaning by this

---

197 As these examples suggest, Thomas's discussion of Christ's merit for himself is designed to provide an exegesis of the Christ hymn in Philippians. For example, in III 19, 3 sed contra, Thomas cites Philippians 2:8–9: "He became obedient unto death. For which cause God also hath exalted him." For Aquinas, Philippians cannot be referring to Christ's obtaining through his actions a higher ontological dignity. Rather, through his obedience in life and dying, Christ merits that his true ontological status be revealed to the entire creation and receive the veneration owed to the Son of God. The entire text of Philippians as quoted in the context of merit, of course, also suggests the intimate relation between humility and the reward owed to merit. It is in losing oneself in obedience to the will of God that one finds for oneself the achievement of the true end of one's being, as set for one by God. For other places in which Thomas has cited the Philippians hymn in regard to merit, see, e.g., III 48, 1 sed contra, and III 49, 6 sed contra.

198 I-II 114, 6c: "Anima Christi mota est a Deo per gratiam, non solum ut ipse perveniret ad gloriam vitae aeternae, sed etiam ut alios in eam adduceret, inquantum est caput Ecclesiae et auctor salutis humanae."

both that the man Christ possessed habitual grace as completely as possible by a creature, and that the man Christ was able to achieve the full range of grace's effects.[199] That Jesus Christ had the plenitude of grace naturally follows from the fact that the Son of God has become incarnate as this man. The closeness of this human to the divine has created in this person the highest intensity of grace. But the Son of God need not have been joined to human nature in the person of Jesus. God could have chosen to become incarnate in some other historical figure. Hence, to explain Christ's grace, Thomas suggests that it is necessary to refer to the divine plan. Christ had the fullness of grace because in accordance with the divine wisdom Jesus had been ordained to be the head of all who are saved.[200] Just as the grace of ordinary Christians follows upon God's ordination for

199 For the discussion in the text, see III 7, 9c. After writing that something is "fully" possessed in two ways, according to the intensity of the thing possessed and the range of performance available to a possessor of the attribute, Thomas states that Christ had the "fullness of grace" in both ways: "Utroque autem modo Christus habuit gratiae plenitudinem. Primo quidem, quia habuit eam in summo, secundum perfectissimum modum quo potest haberi. Et hoc quidem apparet primo, ex propinquitate animae Christi ad causam gratiae. Dictum est enim quod, quanto aliquod receptivum propinquius est causae influenti, abundantius recipit. Et ideo anima Christi, quae propinquius conjungitur Deo inter omnes creaturas rationales, recipit maximam influentiam gratiae eius. Secundo, ex comparatione eius ad effectum. Sic enim recipiebat anima Christi gratiam ut ex ea quadammodo transfunderetur in alios. Et ideo oportuit quod haberet maximam gratiam. Sicut ignis, qui est causa caloris in omnibus calidis, est maxime calidus. Similiter etiam quantum ad virtutem gratiae, plene habuit gratiam; quia habuit eam ad omnes operationes vel effectus gratiae. Et hoc ideo, quia conferebatur ei gratia tamquam cuidam universali principio in genere habentium gratias. Virtus autem primi principii alicuius generis universaliter se extendit ad omnes effectus illius generis. . . . Et sic secunda plenitudo gratiae attenditur in Christo, inquantum se extendit eius gratia ad omnes gratiae effectus, qui sunt virtutes et dona et alia huiusmodi."

200 Thomas relates Christ's possession of habitual grace in its fullest extent to Christ's especial dignity and primary role in human salvation in a number of places; see, e.g., III 7, 1c, and especially III 7, 11c. In the latter text, in discussing why Christ had the fullness of grace, Thomas writes: "Et sic gratia ipsa potest dici infinita, eo quod non limitatur, quia scilicet habet quidquid potest pertinere ad rationem gratiae, et non datur ei secundum aliquam certam mensuram id quod ad rationem gratiae pertinet; eo quod, *secundum propositum gratiae Dei* [Romans 4:5], cuius est gratiam mensurare, gratia confertur animae Christi sicut cuidam universali principio gratificationis in humana natura, secundum illud *Ephes., Gratificavit nos in dilecto Filio suo.* [1:6]. Sicut si dicamus lucem solis esse infinitam, non quidem secundum suum esse, sed secundum rationem lucis, quia habet quidquid potest ad rationem lucis pertinere." Thomas's discussion of Christ's predestination also places the union of the human and divine natures in Jesus in the context of the divine plan for human salvation. See, e.g., III 24, 4c, in which Thomas asks whether Christ's predestination is the cause of the predestination of other people. To answer this question, Thomas distinguishes between the act

them, so too the greater grace of Christ follows upon the divine ordination for him.[201] Thus, given the divine determination to use Jesus Christ as the means through which God works the salvation of all, Christ was given sufficient grace so that what Christ did could be applied to all who join themselves to Christ in the mystical body of Christ.[202]

Thomas's discussion of the merit of Jesus Christ for others completes the picture of the ordination that serves as the basis of merit in the *Summa*. In I-II 114, 1c, Thomas argued that merit is possible because of the divine ordination of rational creatures to God. It is because God has decided to

of predestining and the term or effect of predestination. With regard to the former, Christ's predestination is not the cause of ours because it is by one and the same act that God has predestined Christ and others. But, Thomas adds, "Si autem consideretur praedestinatio secundum terminum praedestinationis, sic praedestinatio Christi est causa nostrae praedestinationis: sic enim Deus praeordinavit nostram salutem, ab aeterno praedestinando, ut per Jesum Christum compleretur. Sub praedestinatione enim aeterna non solum cadit id quod est fiendum in tempore, sed etiam modus et ordo secundum quod est complendum ex tempore."

201 See III 48, 1c: "Christo data est gratia non solum sicut singulari personae, sed inquantum est caput Ecclesiae, ut scilicet ab ipso redundaret ad membra; et ideo opera Christi hoc modo se habent tam ad se quam ad sua membra, sicut se habent opera alterius hominis in gratia constituti ad ipsum. Manifestum est autem quod quicumque in gratia constitutus propter iustitiam patitur, ex hoc ipso meretur sibi salutem. . . . Unde Christus per suam passionem non solum sibi, sed etiam omnibus membris suis meruit salutem." III 7, 10 ad 2, should also be consulted. In this article, Thomas is considering whether it pertained to Christ alone to have the fullness of grace. In the second objection, it was argued that others too have this fullness, on the basis of Ephesians 3:19: ". . . that you may be filled with all the fullness of God," a saying which is directed not to Christ but to Christians. In response, Thomas notes that the "fullness of grace" can mean different things, in accordance with the different destinies or degrees of the beatific vision to which God has ordained different people: The fullness of grace of each person differs, just as the term of their existence differs, in accordance with the divine plan. Hence, given Christ's greater destiny, Thomas implies in this response that his "fullness of grace" will be qualitatively more significant than the "fullness" enjoyed by the saints. Thomas here writes: "Apostolus ibi loquitur de illa plenitudine gratiae quae accipitur ex parte subjecti, in comparatione ad id ad quod homo est divinitus praeordinatus. Quod quidem est vel aliquid commune, ad quod praeordinantur omnes sancti; vel aliquid speciale, quod pertinet ad excellentiam aliquorum. Et secundum hoc, quaedam plenitudo gratiae est omnibus sanctis communis: ut scilicet habeant gratiam sufficientem ad merendum vitam aeternam, quae in plena Dei fruitione consistit. Et hanc plenitudinem optat Apostolus fidelibus quibus scribit."

202 III 19, 4c: "In Christo non solum fuit gratia sicut in quodam homine singulari, sed sicut in capite totius Ecclesiae, cui omnes uniuntur sicut capiti membra, ex quibus constituitur mystice una persona. Et exinde est quod meritum Christi se extendit ad alios inquantum sunt membra eius: sicut etiam in uno homine actio capitis aliqualiter pertinet ad omnia membra eius, quia non solum sibi sentit, sed omnibus membris."

bring rational creatures to share in God's own life through their merits that people are able to merit God by their acts. Following upon the ordination of chosen human beings to come to God, God gives to these people the grace needed to attain the measure of the reward of God in accordance with the divine preordination. Similarly, angels too are ordained to come to God through merit. The case of angels and of humans diverge, however, in at least two respects. First, while people are ordained to achieve God through a number of merits, the angel reaches God, through the divine dispensation, by a single meritorious act. Secondly, the predestination of angels to eternal life coincides more neatly with their original institution in different species. In their case, it is acceptable to state straightforwardly that creation and predestination mark but two parallel moments in God's ordination of an angelic creature to a determined reward. Finally, the merit of Christ reveals an additional dimension of the ordination that constitutes the ground of merit. Humans and angels are ordained to merit God by their acts, but their merit in the strict sense is restricted to themselves. Jesus Christ, however, has been ordained to be the savior of the human race. Thus, in accordance with this divine ordination, Christ was given grace to such a degree that Christ's acts were meritorious not only for himself, but even meritorious condignly for others. In other words, then, in each discussion of the divine ordination and merit Thomas is able to perceive both the common features of the divine ordination and the nuances appropriate to the particular case. In every case, the divine ordination is responsible for the rational creature's ability to merit God as its reward, and moreover for the degree of this reward to which the creature's merits extend. But the divine ordination is not precisely the same in each instance. The differences between the merits of different rational creatures is to be ascribed to the different roles that God wills them and their merits to play in the divine plan for the manifestation of the divine goodness outside of God.

Section IV. Hope (and Merit)
A. Summa Theologiae

Just as his teaching about merit in the *Summa* differs from that offered in the *Scriptum*, so too Thomas offers a more developed analysis of hope in the later work. As was suggested in Chapter 2, to a limited extent the changes in the portrayal of hope in the *Summa* can be ascribed to Thomas's greater freedom in organizing the treatise on hope according to his own wishes.[203] But at bottom the changes in the treatise on hope in the *Summa*

203   The principal ways in which Thomas has re-organized the treatise on hope are as follows: He treats the passion in the Prima Secundae (q. 40), and the virtue in II-II 17–22; it is the latter set of questions with which I am here concerned. Second, he has taken the discussion of the virtue of hope out of the context of the problem of whether Christ possessed the theological virtues. Thomas does consider in the treatise on hope why Christ, who is both

are primarily due to the greater depth of reflection about hope by Thomas in his later career and to his desire to describe more thoroughly the reality of Christian hope. For our purposes, there are two novel features of his later discussion of hope directly relevant here. First, Thomas offers in the *Summa* a more nuanced account of the object of the theological virtue of hope. In the *Scriptum* and in the *Summa*, Thomas offers more or less the same material definition of hope. In the latter, he defines hope as the virtue by which the rational creature expects to attain a future good that is difficult but yet possible to attain.[204] The two works agree, of course, about the *future* good to which hope is directed. Both assert that this is God Who promises God to those who orient their love and efforts in the present life to God.[205]

But there is a significant difference in Thomas's description of the reason that makes the attainment of this future good *possible*. As we saw in Chapter 2, Thomas was content in the *Scriptum* to assert the possibility of coming to the object of one's hope on merely general grounds. It is possible to attain God because God has made available the grace that permits the individual to rise to the supernatural level and come to God. In the discussion of *possibility* in the *Summa*'s analysis of hope, on the other hand, Thomas exploits the advances made in his understanding of grace and accordingly accounts for the possibility of hope in terms that are more dynamic and of direct, personal application to the one who hopes. Referring to the words of Aristotle,[206] Thomas observes that there are two ways in which some end may be attained: through one's own powers and through the help of friends. It is clear that the object of hope cannot be attained through one's own powers. The entire treatise on grace was designed to show that eternal life surpasses the powers of the rational creature and that left to oneself, it would be impossible to attain God. Yet the treatise on grace also disclosed that God has not left the rational creature to his own impotence. Rather, in grace God is effectively involved in the life of the creature, raising this creature to the supernatural level in accordance with God's predestinating will and granting this creature all that is necessary for coming to God. Hence, recalling this earlier teaching, Thomas asserts in the treatise on hope that the attainment of the future good,

---

comprehensor and *viator*, does not have hope; see II-II 18, 2 ad 1. But the question of Christ's hope has faded in significance in the *Summa* and does not color the discussion of the virtue of hope in the Secunda Secundae. Thomas also treats formally of Christ's lack of hope in the treatise on Christology, III 7, 4.

204 II-II 17, 1c: "Objectum spei est bonum futurum arduum possibile haberi."
205 In II-II 17, 2c, Thomas states that "proprium et principale objectum spei est beatitudo aeterna."
206 Thomas refers to *Ethics* III, 3 in II-II 17, 1c: "Possibile autem est aliquid nobis dupliciter: uno modo per nosmetipsos; alio modo per alios, ut patet in 3 *Ethic.*" Thomas also alludes to this saying of Aristotle in the beginning of his discussion of presumption, in II-II 21, 1c.

although difficult, is possible precisely because of the grace of God. While
this end cannot be reached through one's own powers, it can be reached
because of the aid (*auxilium*) that God provides the individual in grace.
Thus, one can hope because one trusts in the God who has expressed God's
love for the individual in predestination and provides the help necessary
to attain the end of hope, eternal life, in accordance with this love.[207]

In its consideration of the possibility of hope, the treatise on hope as a
whole in the *Summa* reveals a considerable shift in emphasis when
compared to the analysis of hope in the *Scriptum*. In the earlier work,
Thomas was most concerned to relate hope to the future good to which it
tends. His references to the possibility of hope are relatively brief, made in
passing, and couched in general terms. In the *Summa*, on the other hand,
while continuing to evince an interest in the future good to which hope
tends, Thomas also devotes much greater attention to the reason for the
possibility of hope. In fact, the latter has assumed an importance in the
Summa equal to that of the discussion of the future good of hope. Indeed,
in the *Summa*, Thomas's preoccupation with the *auxilium* of God that
makes hope possible has caused him to assert that there is in fact a *twofold*
object of hope.[208] Thomas describes the two objects of hope in terms of the
Aristotelian system of causes. In the first place, the future good to which
hope tends is the ultimate *final* cause of hope. But secondly, there is a
"present" object of hope, the *auxilium* of God, and this is the *efficient* cause
of hope. By one's hope, one looks to the *auxilium* of God and indeed to the
God who is continually active in *auxilium*,[209] and one is thereby sustained

---

207 Thomas establishes the possibility of hope by referring to God's aid in moving
the one who hopes to God as to his final end in a number of places in the
treatise on hope. See, e.g., II-II 17, 1c; 4c; and II-II 18, 2c.

208 Thomas states that there is a twofold object of hope in a number of places in
this treatise. In II-II 17, 4c, he writes: "Spes . . . duo respicit, scilicet bonum
quod obtinere intendit, et auxilium per quod illud bonum obtinetur."
Similarly, in II-II 19, 1c, he begins the discussion of fear by stating: "Sicut
spes habet duplex objectum, quorum unum est ipsum bonum futurum eius
adeptionem quis expectat, aliud autem est auxilium alicuius per quem
expectat se adipisci quod sperat . . ." See also II-II 19, 9 ad 2, in this regard.

209 For the description of the two objects of hope in terms of final and efficient
causality, see II-II 17, 4c: "Bonum autem quod aliquis sperat obtinendum,
habet rationem causae finalis, auxilium autem per quod aliquis sperat illud
bonum obtinere, habet rationem causae efficientis." Thomas repeats this
analysis in II-II 17, 5c, and 17, 6 ad 3. For the statement that God Himself is
the second object of hope, see II-II 17, 1 ad 3, in which he states that hope in
the present life attains God, on whose help the one who hopes relies (". . .
Deum, cuius auxilio innititur"); II-II 17, 2c, where he affirms that hope
"attingit Deum, innitens eius auxilio ad consequendum bonum speratum";
II-II 17, 6 ad 3, where he states that hope makes one tend to God as to the
final end to be attained and "sicut in quoddam adjutorium efficax ad
subveniendum"; and II-II 18, 4 ad 2, in which he "explains" Peter Lombard's
difficult saying about the relation of hope and merits (see below in the text)
which is cited in ob 2 by stating that "spes non innititur principaliter gratiae

in the movement back to God. This recognition that there are two objects of hope will be retained in the other works of this period in which Thomas discusses hope (the *Compendium Theologiae* and *De Spe*), although in these works, as we shall shortly see, he uses terminology other than "final" and "efficient" causality to describe the two objects of hope.[210]

The affirmation of a second object of hope in the *Summa* is of great significance for our understanding of merit and its role in the soteriology of Thomas's mature period. When Thomas asserts that the second object of hope is the *auxilium* of God that makes possible the return to God, he is in fact picking up the thread of the discussion found in I-II 114, 9, and elsewhere, where he discusses the grace *not* merited by our acts. Thomas's use of the term *auxilium* in the treatise on hope is deliberate and well thought out: He wants to direct our attention explicitly to the modality of God's action in the spiritual life of the individual which is unearned and not due to our merits but which is necessary for the successful movement to God through human merit. Earlier, it was noted that Thomas affirms the necessity of *auxilium* on both metaphysical and "ethical" grounds. As Pure Act God must apply every potency to its act. And in terms of human nature afflicted by sin and sin's abiding effects, God must apply the rational creature to the correct use of its powers.[211] We also saw that Thomas was able to describe this *auxilium* of God in traditional Augustinian terms. As *operative*, *auxilium* moves the will to its correct act, and the will is only moved. As *cooperative*, *auxilium* confirms and supports the will when it moves itself to act.[212] Finally, we also saw that Thomas has woven his understanding of *auxilium* into the analysis of merit. Hence, in I-II 114, 5, he denied the possibility of meriting for oneself the operative *auxilium* of conversion, while in I-II 114, 9, he similarly denied the possibilty of

iam habitae, sed divinae omnipotentiae et misericordiae, per quam etiam qui gratiam non habet, eam consequi potest, ut sic ad vitam aeternam perveniat."
210 Merkt, "'Sacra Doctrina' and Christian Eschatology," p. 153ff., discusses Thomas's description of the objects of hope in his various writings. Merkt has also noted that in the later works, Thomas adopts different terminologies to characterize the twofold object of hope; see, e.g., p. 162ff., for the different approach offered in *De Spe*. Merkt's dissertation discusses Thomas's theology of hope to see whether Thomas applies his basic theological principles (as articulated in such texts as *ST* I 1) consistently. Merkt's purpose is to answer the charges of Moltmann and others that Thomas's theology of hope is subordinate to, and an expression of, his (real and dominant) philosophical interests and is not faithful to the authentic biblical concerns. For our purpose, Merkt's dissertation is of value inasmuch as he provides a straightforward account of Thomas's understanding of hope in his various works, employing intelligently the pertinent secondary literature.
211 For the discussion of the Aristotelian and Augustinian elements in Thomas's treatment of *auxilium*, see the second sub-section of the first section of this chapter and notes 51 to 54 above.
212 Recall the description of the teaching of I-II 111, 2c, in the second sub-section of the first section of this chapter.

meriting the operative *auxilium* of perseverance. When in the treatise on hope he affirms that God's *auxilium* is the second object of hope and that this *auxilium* is needed to make the attainment of the first object of hope possible, Thomas means for us to recall all that he has said about *auxilium* earlier in the treatise on grace and merit; his reflections on the hope of God's *auxilium* should be viewed as the complement of what he has earlier said about merit. Once someone has received grace, he can merit the increase of this grace considered as habitual. But he cannot merit that he will stay in the state of grace and so attain God. Rather, God's *auxilium* that maintains one on the course to God always remains God's free and unmerited gift. With regard to *auxilium* all one can do is hope. One trusts in the God who has initiated the movement back to God and prays that God will complete this work through the continued gift of grace.[213] Hence, the discussion of hope completes the treatment of merit in the *Summa*. By one's acts, done under the influence of God's grace, one merits coming to God; by one's hope, one is confident that God will in fact support this movement to God by continuing to grant the grace that is at the basis of every good and meritorious act.

There is a second way in which Thomas's revision of the treatise on hope in the *Summa* complements his teaching about merit. In the *Scriptum*, Thomas had not devoted separate questions to the vices opposed to hope in the treatise on hope. He discussed despair and presumption only briefly, not in the treatise on hope but in connection with the sins opposed to the Holy Spirit, at the end of the second book of the *Scriptum*. In the treatise on hope in the *Summa*, however, Thomas discusses these vices in separate questions and his teaching about despair and presumption helps us to grasp more surely the relation between hope and merit. For Thomas, despair is opposed to hope because it signifies the absence of hope in the God who saves. While Thomas allows that despair can arise because of a complete lack of faith,[214] he is most interested in the despair of one who believes and is cognizant of the truths of the Christian faith. Such a person believes that God has taken decisive action in Jesus Christ to overcome sin and to save the world. But while this person affirms this as a general truth, he is unable to apply God's action to himself. Here, says Thomas, the individual looks not to the power and mercy of God to forgive sins, but to the sin estranging him from God. Focusing on this sin, the individual becomes convinced that his sin is so grave that while God forgives sinners, God is unable to forgive him.[215] Thus, in despair, hope has become misdi-

213 For the need for prayer in the life of the Christian to complement his meritorious efforts, see the discussion of I-II 114, 9c, and note 165 above.

214 In II-II 20, 1c, Thomas asserts that despair can arise from a completely erroneous understanding of God. In this incorrect evaluation, the one who despairs may believe that God denies pardon to the repentant sinner or does not convert sinners to God through justifying grace.

215 Thomas explains that infidelity is not required for despair in II-II 20, 2c: "Infidelitas pertinet ad intellectum, desperatio autem ad vim appetitivam.

rected. When hope looks to its correct object, the *auxilium* of God, the individual is sustained on the journey to God, confident of God's power in his life. But when the individual turns to himself, he loses sight of the power and mercy of God. Knowing his own sin, he concludes that he cannot be saved. Despair, then, amounts to a lack of confidence in the grace and aid of God and to the conviction that one cannot expect a personal share in the divine goodness.[216] Thomas is telling us in this discussion that one must not underestimate or ignore the *auxilium* of God to initiate and sustain the return to God through one's merits.

The other vice opposed to hope, presumption, goes to the opposite extreme. Thomas explains the different kinds of presumption in terms of Aristotle's analysis of the two ways in which the attainment of an end is possible, through one's own powers and through the help of a friend. With regard to the former, there would be presumption when one trusts in one's own powers in an illegitimate way, such as when one thinks oneself capable of doing what lies beyond one's strength. In the context of the discussion of the attainment of God, one would be guilty of presumption if he thought that he could come to God without grace, by doing what lies in his natural power. The other kind of presumption occurs when one presumes too much in the help of a friend, leaving the achievement of a task completely to the friend. It is this presumption in which Thomas is most interested in the treatise on hope in the *Summa*. The attainment of God is possible because of the help of God, in grace. Without grace, it is impossible to reach God. But the necessity of grace does not permit the recipient of grace to leave the working out of salvation completely to God. This would be presumptu-

Intellectus autem universalium est, sed vis appetitiva movetur circa particulares res; est enim motus appetitivus ab anima ad res, quae in seipsis particulares sunt. Contingit autem aliquem habentem rectam existimationem in universali circa motum appetitivum non recte se habere, corrupta eius aestimatione in particulari, quia necesse est quod ab aestimatione in universali ad appetitum rei particularis perveniatur mediante aestimatione particulari.... Et inde est quod aliquis habens rectam fidem in universali deficit in motu appetitivo circa particulare, corrupta particulari eius aestimatione per habitum vel per passionem; sicut ille qui fornicatur, eligendo fornicationem ut bonum sibi ut nunc, habet corruptam aestimationem in particulari; cum tamen retineat universalem aestimationem veram secundum fidem, scilicet quod fornicatio sit mortale peccatum et similiter aliquis retinendo in universali veram aestimationem fidei, quod scilicet est remissio peccatorum in Ecclesia, potest tamen pati motum desperationis, quod scilicet sibi in tali statu existenti non sit sperandum de venia, corrupta aestimatione eius circa particulare. Et per hunc modum potest esse desperatio sine infidelitate." See also II-II 20, 2 ad 2: "Si quis in universali existimaret misericordiam Dei non esse infinitam esset infidelis. Hoc autem non existimat desperans, sed quod sibi in statu illo propter aliquam particularem dispositionem non sit de divina misericordia sperandum."

216 In II-II 20, 3c, Thomas states that despair indicates the cessation in the person of an expectation of a personal share in the divine goodness.

ous of God's aid. Thomas mentions in this regard the one who thinks it possible to please God without repenting sins or, most pertinently, who thinks eternal life can be attained without any effort or merit on his part.[217] With this teaching about presumption, then, Thomas warns his reader that confidence in the divine *auxilium* through hope must not result in the person's passivity before God. God's grace does initiate salvation and sustains it, and God's grace is most certain in its results. Yet God achieves God's goals through secondary causes. Hence, the gift and promptings of grace are designed to issue in human action. Under the influence of the grace in which one places his trust, one is enabled to do the good, the merits, by which the end of God's action, eternal life, is obtained. The emphasis on grace, Thomas here insists, cannot be at the expense of the individual's responsibility to yield himself, as it were, as an instrument of God's righteousness. God saves by grace, and people are strengthened and emboldened by their confidence in this grace. But they must respond to grace and act as God wills, in order to come to God, and this they do by their merits.[218]

The affirmation of a second object of hope and the addition of extended treatments of despair and presumption mark the most significant and innovative ways in which Thomas has attempted in the *Summa* to define the relations of hope and merit. However, in the treatise on hope in the *Summa*, Thomas also makes some other comments about hope which clarify how this virtue is related to meritorious action. First, as in the *Scriptum*, Thomas again is forced to explain the difficult saying of Peter Lombard, that hope "arises from grace and merits."[219] Thomas's analysis

217 The entire corpus of II-II 21, 1, is relevant to our discussion: "Praesumptio videtur importare quamdam immoderantiam spei. Spei autem objectum est bonum arduum possibile. Possibile autem est aliquid homini dupliciter: uno modo per propriam virtutem, alio modo nonnisi per virtutem divinam. Circa utramque autem spem per immoderantiam potest esse praesumptio. Nam circa spem, per quam aliquis de propria virtute confidit, attenditur praesumptio ex hoc quod aliquis tendit in aliquod bonum ut sibi possibile, quod suam facultatem excedit. . . . Et talis praesumptio opponitur virtuti magnanimitas, quae medium tenet in huiusmodi spe. Circa spem autem, per quam aliquis inhaeret divinae potentiae, potest per immoderantiam esse praesumptio in hoc quod aliquis tendit in aliquod bonum ut possibile per virtutem et misericordiam divinam quod possibile non est; sicut cum aliquis sperat se veniam obtinere sine poenitentia, vel gloriam sine meritis. Haec autem praesumptio est proprie species peccati in Spiritum Sanctum, quia scilicet per huiusmodi praesumptionem tollitur vel contemnitur adjutorium Spiritus Sancti, per quod homo revocatur a peccato."

218 In II-II 21, 1 ad 1, Thomas says that in presumption, "quis inordinate innititur Deo," and one presumes of God something which is out of keeping with the divine nature: "Aliquis innitatur divinae virtuti ad consequendum id quod Deo non convenit" and "hoc est diminuere divinam virtutem."

219 Thomas refers to Peter Lombard's saying about merit and hope in a number of places in the treatise on hope. See, e.g., II-II 17, 1 ob 2 and ad 2; II-II 17, 8 ob 3 and ad 3; and II-II 18, 4 ob 2.

in the *Summa* follows the lines taken in the *Scriptum*. He tells us that the words of the Lombard are incorrect if they are taken to suggest that the virtue of hope arises both through grace and merits. After all, as a theological virtue, hope is infused freely by God, without respect for preceding acts done in preparation of this virtue. But, he adds, this is not what the Lombard means to say. Rather, when he says that hope arises from grace and merits, he means that the *object* of hope, eternal life, is attained through grace and our response to grace, our meritorious actions. Or the Lombard is referring here to the act of hope that, as informed by the charity directing it to God as to its ultimate end, is itself meritorious— meritorious not of the *auxilium* on which it depends, but meritorious of the good that *auxilium* makes it possible to obtain.[220] Thus, in the *Summa*, as in the *Scriptum*, Thomas refashions the teaching of the Lombard in this regard, by offering his own benevolent interpretations of the Lombard's difficult saying.

Second, Thomas's teaching about the gift of fear also tells us a great deal about the relation between hope and merit. In the treatise on hope in the *Summa*, Thomas devotes an entire question (II-II 19) to this gift. "Gifts" are designed to facilitate the exercise of the virtues and, like the theological virtues, are freely given by God through the agency of the Holy Spirit.[221] In his discussion of "fear," Thomas notes that there are different kinds of fear, only one of which is truly a "gift." For example, there is the fear called "servile fear," according to which someone refrains from evil not because of the love of God, but because one fears the punishment attendant on sin.[222] When theologians speak of the gift of fear, however, they are referring especially to the gift of *filial* fear.[223] This is the fear proper to the children of God, who have been given the grace and the theological virtues which make possible action pleasing to God and appropriate for God's children. "Filial" fear, like other fears, is directed to an evil. The evil to which this fear responds, however, is not punishment, but instead is the

220 See II-II 17, 1 ad 2: "Spes dicitur ex meritis provenire quantum ad ipsam rem expectatam, prout aliquis sperat beatitudinem se adepturum ex gratia et meritis; vel quantum ad actum spei formatae. Ipse autem habitus spei, per quam aliquis expectat beatitudinem, non causatur ex meritis, sed pure ex gratia."

221 Thomas looks at the gifts of the Holy Spirit in general in I-II 68. In I-II 68, 1c, Thomas asserts that by these gifts infused by God, the possessor of the virtues and the gifts becomes more amenable to the promptings of God and hence more likely to act in a way pleasing to God.

222 Thomas distinguishes four kinds of fear in II-II 19, 2c: filial, initial, servile, and worldly. In II-II 19, 4c, he discusses servile fear in some detail.

223 Thomas states that it is filial fear which properly is the gift of the Holy Spirit in II-II 19, 9c. In this article, he provides an explication of the function of gifts on which the description in the text above has been based. In II-II 19, 10c, Thomas adds that the more our charity increases, the more of the gift of filial fear one has, and so one is more likely to want to serve God and remain in community with God.

threat of estrangement from God. By filial fear, one fears the separation from God that comes through sin.[224] Hence, filial fear perfects the virtue of hope to which it is attached by making its possessor more prompt to trust in the God who makes it possible to come to God. Since one does not want to be separated from the heavenly Father, one gives oneself ever more in hope to the God who sustains the movement back to God.[225] Yet, as we just saw in the discussion of presumption, by the virtue of hope the Christian acknowledges the need to do the good required by God in order to come to eternal life. To leave salvation utterly to God would be to presume on God's mercy. Hence, inasmuch as the gift of fear makes its recipient more apt to turn in hope to God and to maintain the correct attitude of hope toward God, the gift of fear itself also contributes to the doing of the merits that lead to God. Through the filial devotion associated with this gift, one works more strenuously to obtain the end for which Christians hope.

B. Other Writings of the Mature Period

There are but fleeting references to merit in the other writings of the mature period, and these add nothing substantial to Thomas's portrayal of merit in the *Summa Theologiae*.[226] Of much greater interest, however,

---

224 In II-II 19, 1c, Thomas states that in the highest form of fear, one fears being separated from God through sin. In II-II 19, 5 ad 2, he specifies that it is filial fear which fears being separated from God through one's fault.

225 Thomas makes this point explicitly in II-II 19, 9 ad 1, where he writes: "Timor filialis non contrariatur virtuti spei. Non enim per timorem filialem timemus ne nobis deficiat quod speramus obtinere per auxilium divinum; sed timemus ab hoc auxilio nos subtrahere. Et ideo timor filialis et spes sibi invicem cohaerent et se invicem perficiunt."

226 It is impossible (and unnecessary) to provide an exhaustive summary here of all of the references to merit in the other works of Thomas's mature period. The following examples suffice to demonstrate, however, that Thomas has retained most of the claims about merit made in the *Summa* in his contemporary writings. For example, the *Compendium Theologiae* part I, chapters 198 and 214, insists that justification is gratuitous and not granted for any preceding merits. The disputed question *De Virtutibus in Communi* a. 11c makes the same point. The same text in *De Virtutibus* also observes that once habitual grace is possessed, it is possible to increase it as well as charity by meritorious actions, which dispose the person for God's infusion of more grace. *De Virtutibus* a. 1 ad 2 stresses that merit is governed by justice: The proper definition of *mereri* is "to do an action by which one *iuste* acquires for oneself a reward." As might be expected, the disputed question *De caritate* emphasizes the need for love in meriting. In 1c, charity is called the "root of merit" (*radix merendi*), for its permits the correct exercise of human freedom (which is also required for merit), while in a. 3 ad 1 and a. 3 ad 3, charity is called the "form of the virtues" and the "principle of meriting," for it orients the acts of the other virtues to God and so makes these acts acceptable to God. Finally, the *Compendium Theologiae* part I, chapter 231, refers in some detail to the merit of Christ and states that since Christ as *viator* as well as *comprehensor*, it was possible for him to merit. The *Compendium* adds that

is Thomas's relatively detailed discussion of hope in other writings of his later period, especially in the disputed question *De Spe*.[227] *De Spe* replicates the basic thrust of the analysis of hope offered by Thomas in the *Summa Theologiae*. In particular, Thomas repeats in *De Spe* the principal new insight of the *Summa*, that there are in fact two objects of hope. "Hope" means the rational will's expectation of a future good which is arduous but yet possible to attain.[228] As he had from the beginning of his career, Thomas identifies God, the beatifying end of human existence, as this "future good" to which hope is directed and says in *De Spe* that the difficulty in attaining this good is posed by the transcendence of God. As in the corresponding passage in the *Summa*, in *De Spe* Thomas refers to the words of Aristotle to explain why the transcendent object of hope nevertheless can be attained. Aristotle had observed that something is "possible" in one of two ways: through one's own powers or through the powers of a friend. The transcendence of the God of Christians naturally precludes the fulfillment of one's hope in the first way, for God lies beyond the scope of the natural powers of the creature. But God is also the "friend" of those who seek God and thus provides the aid which makes possible the attainment of God.

Christ's merit was applied not only to himself but to others too, in accordance with the special dignity of his person and his designation by God as head of all those who are to be saved, and affirms that Christ merited in the first moment of his conception. However, in the other writings of the mature period, Thomas has not repeated his analysis of merit in terms of the divine ordination. This does not mean that Thomas abandoned the *Summa*'s crucial insight about merit. It simply reflects the *ad hoc* nature of Thomas's comments in these other works about merit. Only in the *Summa* has Thomas provided an *ex professo* examination of merit and so treated adequately all the salient features of this difficult concept.

227　According to Weisheipl, *Friar Thomas d'Aquino*, p. 365, *De Spe* was composed between 1269 and 1272. It is divided into four articles: Is hope a virtue (a. 1); is the will its subject (a. 2); is hope prior to charity (a. 3); and is hope only possessed by those on the way (a. 4)? I have used the Marietti edition of this disputed question. In addition to *De Spe*, there is another fairly detailed account of hope in the later period, in the *Compendium Theologiae*, written between 1269 and 1273. Thomas intended to describe the whole of Christian faith under the headings of the three theological virtues—faith, hope, and charity. He completed the first part on faith, but had come only to the tenth chapter of part two, on hope, when he ceased writing. Although the *Compendium* possesses only a partial description of hope, Thomas had completed enough of the book to show that his analysis of hope in this book retains the insights of the *Summa*. To avoid repetition, in the text I have concentrated on the teaching of *De Spe*, drawing attention in the notes to the parallel comments in the *Compendium*.

228　*De Spe* a. 1c: "Ergo sic in obiecto spei quatuor considerantur. Primo quidem, quod sit bonum. . . . Secundo, quod sit boni futuri. . . . Tertio, quod sit boni ardui. . . . Quarto, quod sit boni possibilis." See also *De Spe* a. 4c: "Spei autem obiectum . . . est bonum arduum futurum possibile." *Compendium Theologiae* part II, ch. 7, mentions as the notes of the object of hope that this object is difficult and yet possible to attain.

Hence, concludes Thomas in this passage, there are two objects to which hope is directed. Hope looks to God as the future object to whom the human person desires to come. Hope also looks to God as to the one who presently aids the person in this effort to come to God.[229]

While the *Summa* and *De Spe* agree that there are two objects of hope, *De Spe* employs slightly different terminology to describe these objects of hope. In the *Summa*, Thomas had stated that God as the beatific end is the "final" end of hope, while God (and God's *auxilium*) as the ground of hope is the "efficient" cause of hope. In *De Spe*, Thomas draws a parallel with the theological virtue of faith in his description of the two objects of hope. God is the object of faith in two ways. First, God is the *material* object of faith in the sense that faith holds certain truths about God. Second, God is also the *formal* object of faith in the sense that faith holds these truths on the basis of God's authority—the believer affirms these truths because they are revealed by God. Similarly, God can be said to be both the *formal* and the *material* object of hope. God is the material object of hope because God is the end to whom the Christian hopes to come. But secondly, God is the formal object of hope because the Christian is confident of coming to God as the end of his efforts through the aid of the God who actively sustains the movement to God.[230] While noteworthy, this shift in terminology does not mark a departure by *De Spe* from the insights in the *Summa* about the twofold object of hope. Whether he speaks of the objects of hope in terms of efficient and final or formal and material causality, in his

---

229 *De Spe* a. 1c: "Est autem possibile aliquod haberi ab aliquo dupliciter: uno modo per propriam potestatem; alio modo per auxilium alterius: nam quae per amicos sunt possibilia, aliqualiter possibilia dicimus, ut patet per Philosophum in III Ethic. Sic igitur quandoque sperat homo aliquid adipisci per propriam potestatem, quandoque vero per auxilium alienum; et talis spes expectationem habet, in quantum homo respicit in auxilium alterius. Et tunc necesse est quod motus spei feratur in duo obiecta: scilicet in bonum adipiscendum, et in eum cuius auxilio innititur. Sumum autem bonum, quod est beatitudo aeterna, homo adipisci non potest nisi per auxilium divinum, secundum illud Rom. VI: *Gratia Dei, vita aeterna*. Et ideo spes adipiscendi vitam aeternam habet duo obiecta, scilicet ipsam vitam aeternam, quam quis sperat, et auxilium divinum, a quo sperat." Thomas repeats his comments about the different ways in which something may be possible in *Compendium Theologiae* part II, chapter 7, where he adds that the divine aid which makes the attainment of God possible can be obtained only by prayer, not by merit.
230 *De Spe* a. 1c: "Fides autem non habet rationem virtutis, nisi in quantum inhaeret testimonio veritatis primae, ut ei credat quod ab ea manifestatur . . . unde et spes habet rationem virtutis ex hoc ipso quod homo inhaeret auxilio divinae potestatis ad consequendum vitam aeternam. . . . Sic igitur, sicut formale obiectum fidei est veritas prima, per quam sicut per quoddam medium assentit his quae creduntur, quae sunt materiale obiectum fidei; ita etiam formale obiectum spei est auxilium divinae potestatis et pietatis, propter quod tendit motus spei in bona sperata, quae sunt materiale obiectum spei."

mature contemplation of hope Thomas is insisting that the one who hopes is thereby related to God in a twofold way.

In *De Spe*, Thomas has also solved the problem posed by Peter Lombard's difficult saying about hope and merit along the lines suggested by the *Summa*.[231] Peter had asserted that hope "arises from grace and from merits." Thomas states that the Lombard is correct if by "hope" he is referring to the object of hope. One attains God, the end of one's hope, through the aid of grace and after the performance of graced acts. But, Thomas adds here, as he had in the *Summa*, Peter's words must not be taken as suggesting that one comes to possess hope as a result of meritorious actions. As a theological virtue, hope is a gift, freely infused in the person by God. Hence, one merits only after hope and the other theological virtues have been received.[232]

But while *De Spe* retains the most important innovation in the *Summa*'s discussion of hope and disposes of the difficulty posed by the Lombard in terms familiar to us from the *Summa*, the parallel between the two writings is not complete. The treatise on hope in the *Summa* is the most satisfactory treatment of hope in the Thomistic corpus precisely because it is the most exhaustive. Not only does it analyze thoroughly the objects of hope. It also devotes considerable attention to the vices opposed to hope, demonstrating thereby the uniqueness and principal characteristics of hope. The value of the consideration of despair and presumption in the *Summa* is that it completes the picture of the relation between hope and merit. In particular, by his teaching on presumption, Thomas makes absolutely clear his conviction that while the successful return to God is dependent on the freely given aid of God, the second object of hope, this does not remove the need for meritorious action in the movement to God. *De Spe* forgoes any protracted consideration of despair and presumption, and refers to them only in passing.[233] Lacking the discussion of the *Summa*

---

231   Peter's claim that hope "arises from grace and from merits" is cited in *De Spe* at a. 1 ob 2 and a. 3 ob 10.

232   *De Spe* a. 1 ad 2: "Cum dicitur spes esse expectatio futurae beatitudinis, ex gratia et meritis proveniens, dupliciter potest intelligi. Uno modo ut expectatio intelligatur ex meritis provenire ex parte expectantis; ut scilicet, expectatio talis causetur in homine ex praecedentibus meritis. Et in hoc sensu procedit obiectio, qui falsus est. Alio modo potest intelligi expectatio esse ex meritis ex parte rei expectatae; et hic est sensus verus: expectamus enim quod per gratiam Dei et bona merita beatitudinem consequamur." See also a. 1 ad 3 and a. 3 ad 2. In the *Summa*, Thomas adds another possible interpretation of the Lombard's words which would also be acceptable: Peter may mean that the act of hope done in grace and charity is itself meritorious in the sense that any act done in charity deserves eternal reward. That *De Spe* omits this second interpretation should not suggest a departure from the *Summa*. Rather, its absence merely reveals that we cannot always expect the detail in disputed questions which is found in the corresponding passage of the systematic work.

233   For brief references to despair in *De Spe,* see a. 1c and a. 3 ad 11, where

on these vices, the analysis of this disputed question thus remains somewhat unbalanced. In *De Spe*, Thomas tells us that God makes possible the attainment of God and that hope in the divine *auxilium* assures the Christian of coming to God. He has failed to tell us as forcefully, however, that the divine *auxilium* issues in good human action and that the morally good acts of the Christian resulting from grace make an important, if secondary, contribution to the fulfillment of one's hope.

Thomas notes that hope differs from despair, as well as a. 4 ob 4. In a. 1 ad 1, Thomas notes that one who has presumption thinks that he can be saved while persevering in sin (*cum praesumit se salvandum etiam in peccatis perseverans*).

Chapter Four

Concluding Observations: Thomas and His Authorities

THOMAS AQUINAS shares with other medieval scholastic writers a profound preoccupation with authoritative texts. Thomas has worked out his theology in dialogue with the writings of others, and his own compositions skillfully engage a wide variety of texts. The importance of authorities, patent on every page, is stressed by Thomas in the opening question of the *Summa Theologiae*, in the article in which he describes the place of argument in sacred doctrine; in the second response of that article (I 1, 8 ad 2), he has specified the relative weight that should be accorded to each kind of authority employed in theological inquiry. The second objection, which would eliminate argument entirely from sacred doctrine, possesses an initial plausibility, building on some of the central insights of earlier articles. There are, the objection observes, two kinds of argument—that from authority and that from reason. Neither is appropriate for sacred doctrine. As has become clear from the earlier articles, sacred doctrine is the body of truths about God, and about all other things in relation to God, revealed by God and necessary for human salvation: God has revealed in this doctrine the transcendent end of human beings and the way to this end, through Jesus Christ.[1] As patterned on God's own knowledge of God, these truths, summarized in the articles of faith, transcend human reason.[2] Thus, the present objection quite understandably proscribes arguments from reason in sacred doctrine. Moreover, since the source of sacred doctrine is God, its dependence on God's revelation of God would also militate against arguments from authority. Sacred doctrine, we have earlier been informed (a. 5), is thus the highest of sciences available to people. But, as Boethius has said, the argument from authority is charac-

---

1 Thomas refers to the revelation of the transcendent end of human beings, God, in the *corpus* of the first article, in establishing the necessity of sacred doctrine: Human beings would have no knowledge of this end, and hence would not know how to attain this end, apart from God's revelation. For the discussion of the formal unity of the science of sacred doctrine, see *ST* I 1, 3 ad 1, and 7c.

2 The notion of "subalternation," the patterning of the truths of sacred doctrine on God's knowledge of God, is introduced in *ST* I 1, 2c. That the principal truths of the Christian faith transcend reason is noted at the beginning of the question, in 1c.

teristic of the lowest, the least dignified, science, and so it too should find no place in sacred doctrine.[3]

In the *corpus* of the eight article, Thomas however does grant a legitimate, if circumscribed, role to argument in sacred doctrine. Practitioners of sacred doctrine will not, of course, seek to demonstrate its first principles, the articles of faith: These are received only through revelation and are accepted by faith. Yet argument can be employed in defense of the articles. The strategies of argument will differ from case to case. When one of the articles of faith is attacked by someone who accepts other articles, argument will proceed on the basis of the shared authority. Thus, the Christian heretic will be answered by reference to the other articles of the creed and to the Christian canon. The idea here is that there is a basic coherence of the faith: One article of faith assumes and builds on others, and the denial of one is ultimately impossible apart from the denial of the others. When, however, the attack on faith comes from outside, from one who does not adhere to the same scriptures or creed, argument must proceed in a different way, on the basis of reason. Here, the idea is that while Christian faith is above reason, it is not contrary to reason. Hence, arguments that suggest that it is can themselves be shown to be contrary to reason. Finally, Thomas grants to argument the capacity to illuminate. While eschewing the goal of demonstrating the articles of faith, by argument the Christian can show their coherence and can plumb ever more fully the basic meaning of the main Christian claims. In other words, Thomas seconds Anselm and Augustine on "faith seeking understanding." Beginning and ending with faith, the theologian through argument will come to understand more fully Christian truth.[4]

---

3   *ST* I 1, 8 ob 2: "Si sit argumentativa aut argumentatur ex auctoritate aut ex ratione. Si ex auctoritate, hoc non videtur congruere eius dignitati, nam *locus ab auctoritate est infirmissimus*, secundum Boetium. Si autem ex ratione, hoc non congruit eius fini . . ." The reference to Boethius apparently trades on the notion that it is better to reason to truth than to depend on the say-so of another.

4   *ST* I 1, 8c: "Sicut aliae scientiae non argumentantur ad sua principia probanda, sed ex principiis argumentantur ad ostendendum alia in ipsis scientiis, ita haec doctrina non argumentatur ad sua principia probanda, quae sunt articuli fidei, sed ex eis procedit ad aliquid ostendendum, sicut Apostolus 1 *ad Cor.* ex resurrectione Christi argumentatur ad resurrectionem communem probandum. Sed tamen considerandum est in scientiis philosophicis quod inferiores scientiae nec probant sua principia nec contra negantem disputant; sed hoc relinquunt superiori scientiae. Suprema vero inter eas, scilicet metaphysica, disputat contra negantem sua principia si adversarius aliquid concedit; si autem nihil concedit non potest cum eo disputare, potest tamen solvere rationes ipsius. Unde sacra Scriptura, cum non habeat superiorem, disputat cum negante sua principia, argumentando quidem si adversarius aliquid concedat eorum quae per revelationem divinam habentur, sicut per auctoritates sacrae doctrinae disputamus contra haereticos, et per unum articulum contra negantem alium. Si vero

ST I 1, 8 ad 2, repeats and extends the analysis provided in the *corpus*. It grants to the objection that argument from reason cannot demonstrate the truths of the faith. But it adds that arguments from reason can be employed in the illumination of faith, in the search for understanding, here putting the point in terms that would become dear to later Thomists: Since "grace does not destroy nature but perfects it," the resources of reason can be placed in service to the faith.[5] The second response, however, is more severe in rebutting the comments in the objection on argument from authority. Boethius's words have been poorly applied. Boethius is speaking about the human sciences, not about the science that derives from God. Indeed, when one considers the source of sacred doctrine and the means by which God communicates saving truth, it is clear that the argument from authority is most appropriate in this highest of the sciences. Thomas punctuates his teaching by limning the "hierarchy of authorities" operative in sacred doctrine, adding brief characterizations of the extent of authority enjoyed by each member of the hierarchy. The greatest authority is, of course, God's: God's word is most certain. Next comes that of the human authors of scripture, to whom God's revelation has been made. Their authority, participating in that of God, is also most certain. The authority of the church doctors, and of the philosophers, is considerably less. God has not revealed God's truth directly to either. Hence, while the authority of the human author of scripture is necessary, that of the others is only probable. Yet, Thomas adds, the authority of the church fathers is greater than that of the philosophers. Principally concerned with God's truth as disclosed in sacred doctrine, the authority of the church doctors is both "internal" and probable. That of the philosophers, on the other hand, is merely "extrinsic." Their truths, derived through reasoning and addressing for the most part issues outside the purview of faith, fall short of those of sacred doctrine. But philosophy can be drawn on for the purposes of sacred doctrine, brought into sacred doctrine in order to illuminate the truths of faith.[6]

---

adversarius nihil credat eorum quae divinitus revelantur, non remanet amplius via ad probandum articulos fidei per rationem; sed ad solvendum rationes, si quas inducit, contra fidem. Cum enim fides infallibili veritati innitatur, impossibile autem sit de vero demonstrari contrarium, manifestum est probationes quae contra fidem inducuntur non esse demonstrationes, sed solubilia argumenta."

5   *ST* I 1, 8 ad 2, here picks up the thread of 5 ad 2.
6   *ST* I 1, 8 ad 2: "Argumentari ex auctoritate est maxime proprium huius doctrinae, eo quod principia huius doctrinae per revelationem habentur; et sic oportet quod credatur auctoritati eorum quibus revelatio facta est. Nec hoc derogat dignitati huius doctrinae, nam licet locus ab auctoritate quae fundatur super revelatione humana sit infirmissimus, locus tamen quae fundatur super revelatione divina est efficacissimus. Utitur tamen sacra doctrina etiam ratione humana, non quidem ad probandum fidem, quia per hoc tolleretur meritum fidei, sed ad manifestandum aliqua quae traduntur in hac doctrina. Cum igitur gratia non tollat naturam sed perficiat, oportet

That Thomas's discussion of merit meets the expectations created by these programmatic comments—about the centrality of scriptural teaching for theological teaching, the secondary value of ecclesial authors for grasping and exploring the truths conveyed in scripture, the thoroughly subordinate role of philosophy—would seem clear. Aristotle, of course, figures in this teaching about theological merit. Throughout his career, Thomas has exploited the *Nichomachaean Ethics* to further the investigation of merit. Thus, for example, he often cites *Ethics* I, 9, to show that Aristotle also recognized that beatitude is granted to people as the reward of their virtue, although Aristotle's beatitude is a this-worldly phenomenon and the virtues of which he speaks are not the theological virtues which are necessary for attaining eternal life.[7] Similarly, Thomas has clearly drawn on his knowledge of the *Ethics* to determine the kind of justice operative in merit—Book V describes the proportionate equality involved in distributive justice, as well as the strict equality entailed in commutative justice, and Thomas uses Aristotle's reflections to support his own conclusions about justice in merit in the various stages of his teaching.[8] Finally, in the *Ethics* Aristotle has some pertinent comments about friendship (in books VIII and IX) which, as we have seen, is so important for Thomas's teaching about merit: It is Aristotle who provides Thomas (e.g., *ST* II-II 23, 1c) with the formal definition of the love of friendship (*amor amicitiae*) as "willing the good of another" and who insists that in such love there must be a "common good" uniting the two lovers (Book IX, 9), and Thomas has utilized these reflections in formulating his own analysis about the charity which is required for meriting.

quod naturalis ratio subserviat fidei sicut et naturalis inclinatio voluntatis obsequitur charitati: unde et Apostolus dicit II *ad Cor. In captivitatem redigentes omnem intellectum in obsequium Christi.* Et inde est quod etiam auctoritatibus philosophorum sacra doctrina utitur, ubi per rationem naturalem veritatem cognoscere potuerunt, sicut Paulus inducit verbum Arati dicens, *Sicut et quidam poetarum vestrorum dixerunt, genus Dei sumus.* Sed tamen sacra doctrina huiusmodi auctoritatibus utitur quasi extraneis argumentis et probabilibus. Auctoritatibus autem canonicae Scripturae utitur proprie, ex necessitate argumentando. Auctoritatibus autem aliorum doctorum Ecclesiae, quasi argumendo ex propriis, sed probabiliter. Innititur enim fides nostra revelationi apostolis et prophetis factae qui canonicos libros scripserunt, non autem revelationi, si qua fuit, aliis doctoribus factae. Unde dicit Augustinus in epistola ad Hieronynum: *Solis eis Scripturarum libris qui canonici appellantur didici hunc honorem deferre, ut nullum auctorem in scribendo errasse aliquid firmissime credam. Alios autem ita lego ut, quantalibet sanctitate doctrinaque praepolleant, non ideo verum putem quod ipsi ita senserunt."*

7   See, e.g., *ST* I-II 5, 7c; and I 62, 4c, where he cites the *Ethics* in connection with the beatitude of angels.

8   See, e.g, *In II Scriptum* d. XXVII, q. I, a. 4c, and *ST* I-II 114, 1c. It should hardly need observing that Thomas has also benefited from the ruminations of others, including Pseudo-Dionysius, in discussing the place of justice in merit.

Nevertheless, despite this use of Aristotle it is clear that Aristotle is a different kind of "source" for Aquinas than is the Bible or Augustine. Thomas advances a teaching on merit because he feels compelled to do so by the testimony of scripture, mediated to him through the analysis of Augustine; he does not affirm merit because this notion of reward for good action is found in Aristotle. Rather, *once* he perceives the need to affirm merit on other grounds he then turns to Aristotle to help him express his beliefs. One of the dangers of describing Thomas as a "Christian Aristotelian" is that the designation distorts the nature of Thomas's relation to Aristotle. Thomas is an "Aristotelian" if this means that he is familiar with the Aristotelian corpus, thinks that Aristotle has made valuable observations on many subjects, and finds Aristotle useful in grasping truth more intimately. He is not an "Aristotelian" if this means that Aristotle has provided Thomas with his basic outlook on life and approach to the crucial questions of theology. Thomas, instead, is a Christian theologian whose starting point is provided to him by the teachings of scripture and the tradition interpreting scripture: His vision of the world and of the relations of God and people is shaped by his Christian beliefs; it is from the vantage point of Christian revelation that he works out his thought, including the teaching on merit. [9]

---

9   For a surefooted consideration of the relations between Thomas and Aristotle, see Mark D. Jordan, "The Alleged Aristotelianism of Thomas Aquinas" (The Etienne Gilson Series 15; Toronto, 1992). It is worth noting that in his commentary on the *Ethics*, which is roughly contemporary with the Prima Secundae, Thomas says little about Christian merit. Here, Thomas does not apply Aristotle's words about justice or friendship to the Christian teaching on merit and does not inform us about how he has used the Aristotelian analyses in his own theological writings to delineate his teaching on merit. If he had read into the *Commentary* his own theological program, he would have contravened his own intention in commenting on Aristotle. In producing a commentary on Aristotle, Thomas wishes to do justice to the teaching of Aristotle himself. In his lectures on each book, Thomas gives a line-by-line appraisal of the Aristotelian text, and his purpose is to explain what Aristotle means and to defend Aristotle from possible misinterpretations of his text. Thomas's work, then, is designed to provide an authentic commentary on Aristotle and to establish the basic positions of Aristotelian philosophy. He is not trying to take the next step, to show the value which Aristotle can have in a Christian theology. This latter move he reserves to his theological work.

Thomas's reluctance in the commentary on the *Ethics* to go beyond what the text requires or permits is evident in his discussion of those few texts in which Aristotle himself discusses the notion of "merit." For example, in Book V, ch. 3 (lecture IV), Aristotle treats the merit involved in distributive justice. In this passage, Aristotle is concerned to show that the ruler(s) of a political community distribute the goods of the community in accordance with the deserts of different recipients. Aristotle notes here that while distributive justice recognizes merit, 'merit' (*dignitas*) means different things in different communities, according to the regulative order of the community and the values which it most prizes. Hence, people in a democracy situate merit in a

Recognizing that Thomas's discussion of this topic conforms in a general way to *ST* I 1, 8 ad 2, is, however, but a beginning. As the rest of this chapter will suggest, closer consideration of Thomas's approach to his principal sources in formulating a teaching on merit, scripture and Saint Augustine, can yield additional lessons about the character and inspiration of the mature teaching. While in both instances I attempt to depict the extent of Thomas's indebtedness to his principal sources, the task in the two cases is somewhat different. Thomas claims that his teaching on merit is biblically rooted. In particular, he suggests that his analysis of merit constitutes his attempt to reformulate in scholastic terms the biblical teaching on God's reward for human action. Thus, in evaluating Thomas's use of scripture, the principal question is that of Thomas's faithfulness in his teaching on merit to the biblical testimony on reward. In other words, does his teaching on merit in fact conform to the professed norm of Christian belief? The question assumes added urgency in light of the suggestion of some recent scholars about the flawed character of medieval discussions of grace and salvation. Karlfried Froehlich and Alister McGrath have independently suggested that medieval theologians were misled in their speculation by the Latin rendering of the biblical Greek and Hebrew for 'righteousness.' *Iustificare* and related words bear the connotation of "making just," of a moral transformation of the sinner, a note missing, at least in this modern reading, from the biblical teaching about justification. Hence, instead of speaking simply of God's declaration of forgiveness, the medievals shifted the focus to the result of this "transformation," to the good actions of the person endowed with grace, in the process creating a generous space for "merit."[10] My suggestion in this chapter about the way

condition of freedom, people in an oligarchy place it in riches or nobility of birth, and people in an aristocracy in a state of virtue. These brief comments by Aristotle could have provided Thomas with the opportunity to locate theological merit in the community of people with God established by God: According to the analysis of condign merit in the *Scriptum*, Thomas could have observed that God is the ruler of this special community who distributes to each according to his merit, giving equally for merits of the same kind (thus preserving the mean of distributive justice); or according to the analysis of condign merit in the *Summa Theologiae* he could have noted that the special community with God established by God, in which God's grace elevates the individual to God's own level, permits us to note that in theological merit God, the ruler of this community, continues to distribute the goods of the community but does so according to commutative, not distributive, justice. Yet Thomas makes no such comments in this commentary on the application of Aristotle's teaching about political merit and retribution to theological merit and the spiritual community of the elect and God. He simply adds a few comments to what Aristotle writes, to explain the set-up and governance of earthly, political communities.

10   See Karlfried Froehlich, "Justification Language and Grace: The Charge of Pelagianism in the Middle Ages," in E. A. McKee and B. G. Armstrong, eds., *Probing the Reformed Tradition: Historical Studies in Honor of Edward A.*

in which Thomas may stand in continuity with the scriptural proclamation thus also raises some doubt, at least indirectly, about the force of this "linguistic" argument. In terms of his use of Augustine, on the other hand, the degree to which Thomas was faithful to Augustine—who even during the Middle Ages lacked the normative status of scripture[11]—is a less compelling issue than when and how Augustinian ideas affected Thomas's thinking on merit. Generally, Augustine and Aquinas are in basic agreement about the need for merit in human salvation. More interesting, I believe, is that a good case can be made that the developments in Thomas's teaching about merit should in large part be attributed to his use in the later part of his career of the writings of Augustine unknown to him when he composed the *Scriptum* on the *Sentences*. In particular, the final form of Thomas's teaching on merit is in great measure due to his adroit use of crucial elements of the later Augustine's theology of grace. Thus, in studying here the relation between Augustine and Aquinas, I shall focus on the growing importance of Augustine in Thomas's teaching on merit. It is to the examination of the "Augustinian" character of the later Thomistic teaching on merit to which I now turn.

Section I. Aquinas and Augustine

Thomas's *ex professo* treatments of merit in the *Scriptum* and in the *Summa Theologiae* share, of course, a number of features, the most prominent of which is the claim that once in the state of grace people can in fact merit in some sense the end of the spiritual life, the direct and immediate vision of God.[12] But even more striking than the common elements in these two analyses of merit in Aquinas are the differences which distinguish these accounts. There are two main ways in which the *Summa*'s discussion of merit differs from that found in the *Scriptum*. First,

Dowey, Jr. (Louisville, Ky., 1989), p. 36, n. 12; and Alister E. McGrath, *Iustitia Dei: A History of the Christian Doctrine of Justification*, vol. I (Cambridge, 1989), pp. 11ff. The connection that such a linguistic argument can have with more traditional ecclesiastical polemic seems clear from Froehlich's subsequent comment in the text (p. 24): "It seems that precisely the doctrine of grace was surrounded by the greatest ambiguity during the Middle Ages, an ambiguity that eventually led to a Reformation which made the theological meaning of the Pauline justification language the center of its own polemics—this time, however, on the basis of the original, the Greek Paul."

11   For some perceptive comments about the reasons for, and limits of, his importance, see James J. O'Donnell, "The Authority of Augustine," *Augustinian Studies* 22 (1991): 7–35. Leo Elders has surveyed the textual use of Augustine in Thomas's great *Summa* in "Les Citations de Saint Augustin dans la *Somme Theologique* de Saint Thomas d'Aquin," *Doctor Communis* 40 (1987): 115–67.

12   Material in this section has earlier appeared in my articles "'Perseverance' in 13th-Century Theology: The Augustinian Contribution," *Augustinian Studies* 22 (1991): 125–40, and "On the Purpose of 'Merit' in the Theology of Thomas Aquinas," *Medieval Philosophy and Theology* 2(1992): 97–116.

Thomas interprets merit in terms of the divine ordination. The term 'ordination' in the *Summa* bears a rich variety of meanings, each of which suggests something significant about merit in Aquinas. At one level, 'ordination' simply refers to God's ordering of all actions to appropriate effects. Consequently, merit is possible because the divine providence has ordained that acts of a kind will be recompensed by the appropriate reward. Those in grace who act in conformity with the demands of the Christian life will be rewarded because of the divine ordination, with eternal life in God's presence. At a deeper level, 'ordination' refers to the plan formulated by the divine wisdom for the manifestation of the divine goodness in the way appropriate to creatures. Ordination therefore denotes the sapiential dimension of merit. Human meriting contributes in the fashion determined by the divine wisdom to the manifestation of the divine goodness. Finally, ordination in the *Summa* is the equivalent of predestination, understood in the sense of God's decision to share God's own life with certain people. As the equivalent of predestination, ordination also suggests the execution of God's plan for the elect: Predestination issues in the gift of the grace bringing the elect to God. Thus, by 'ordination' Thomas has located merit securely in the context of God's predestining will. God has decided to save certain people and to do so through the meritorious acts to which they are moved by grace.[13] The *Scriptum* lacks the latter two ideas suggested by

---

13   Recognition that the ordination of *ST* I-II 114, 1, is basically Thomas's predestination, in turn, allows us to understand correctly a basic image which shapes the description of merit in the succeeding articles of this question. When speaking of merit in these articles, Thomas repeatedly refers to the life of the Christian as a "journey" or "movement." The basic idea here is that the Christian life can be viewed as a journey in which one who is in grace moves further away from sin and draws nearer to God through the good actions/merits which one performs. Eventually the Christian will attain in this way the ultimate destination of this journey, God Himself. And yet, as portrayed by Thomas in this question, it is at first glance a rather odd journey, for the journey itself is controlled principally not by the traveler, but by God. In light of the recognition of the equivalence of the ordination that grounds merit and predestination, however, Thomas's imagery becomes more intelligible. In God's plan, God has freely destined a human person to the goal which is God. But predestination is more than simply this plan or destining. It is also God's execution of this plan, by actually bringing the elect to the predestined goal. Hence, in the succeeding articles of I-II 114, Thomas is referring to God's execution of God's predestining plan by the gift of the grace which arises from God's predestining will and which applies the human person to the action which will bring the person to the good ordained by God for that person, God Himself. For a striking expression of the notion of human existence as a journey or movement to God, see *ST* I-II 114, 7c, the discussion of the possibility of a person in grace meriting a future restoration to grace after a subsequent fall. Here, Thomas denies that this is possible, for the movement of the individual under grace to the rewards for grace-inspired acts is interrupted by sin and so is "blocked" from obtaining any reward for these acts. There is frequent mention in *ST* I-II 114 of the "movement of grace" that

the ordination grounding merit in the *Summa*. In the early work, Thomas does not contemplate the sapiential dimensions of merit. More significant, he makes no attempt to relate merit to predestination or to explore the ramifications for a teaching on merit of the affirmation of a free decision by God to elect certain people. In this neglect of predestination, we have a particular instance of the early Thomas's basic reluctance to relate grace in general to God's efficacious predestining will.

In addition to predestination, there is a second significant way in which the *ex professo* treatment of merit in the *Summa* differs from that in the *Scriptum*. Thomas's discussion of merit in the *Scriptum* is a rather straightforward account, which concentrates on the actual objects or rewards of merit. Thus, he wishes to demonstrate that by their good acts people can merit not only the end of the spiritual life, God, but the increase of grace[14] and even the conversion of another person as well. In the *Scriptum*, Thomas is *not* interested in telling us which features of the spiritual life, if any, elude merit. The only possible exception in the *Scriptum* is Thomas's discussion of *conversion*, of the first entry into the state of grace: He seems reluctant to concede that the human person can merit the first grace. However, as I argued in Chapter 2, this is only an apparent exception to the claim that in the *Scriptum* Thomas deals only with the actual objects of merit. In this writing, Thomas affirms the *facere quod in se est*, according to which God grants grace to a sinner who by his freely initiated and performed actions tries to amend his life. Moreover, although he stresses that congruent merit is an imperfect merit which falls short of merit in the strict sense—that is, falls short of the condign merit which is governed by justice—in this writing Thomas *does* admit that congruent merit is a real merit and in fact discusses the *facere* in terms of such a congruent merit. Thus, in his discussion of the merit of the first grace in the present distinction, all Thomas probably wants to do is exclude the *condign* merit of first grace, while wishing us to understand that the sinner nevertheless does merit this grace *congruently*.

---

impels the individual on the path to God. See, e.g., I-II 114, 7c and 8c, referring to the motion of grace; I-II 114, 6c and 9c, referring to a divine motion which controls the journey to God; and I-II 114, 3c, speaking of the power of the Holy Spirit that moves the person to God.

14   As I observed in Chapter 2, Thomas understands the merit of the increase of grace differently in the *Scriptum* than in the *Summa Theologiae*. In *In II* d. XXVII, q. I, a. 5c, Thomas introduced a distinction between a reward which "accompanies" the doing of a meritorious act and a reward which comes from outside, from God, for that act, and he states that the increase of habitual grace falls under the first kind of reward. In the *Summa*, Thomas abandoned the distinction between internal and external rewards, and in I-II 114, 8c, he explains the growth in grace according to his basic image of movement. One not only merits the end of the journey by good action, one also "passes through" all the "places" on the way to the end and so merits them. Hence, since (habitual) grace is needed to attain the end who is God, one must be able to merit the increase of this "intermediate" grace.

The situation is rather different in the *Summa*. Thomas naturally enumerates in I-II 114 the rewards which do fall under merit and again tells us that people can merit the end of the spiritual life, as well as the increase of (habitual) grace and conversion for another. But in the *Summa* Thomas is not content just to tell us which rewards Christians can merit by their acts. He also devotes considerable space to telling us which aspects of the spiritual life *cannot* be merited through good action. Thus, for example, whatever hesitations he might have had on this question in the *Scriptum*, in I-II 114, 5, Thomas unequivocally rejects any merit of the first grace. In keeping with his affirmation of gratuitous election to salvation, in this article Thomas stresses that conversion itself is worked freely by God alone, apart from any kind of merit of the sinner. Similarly, in the ninth article, Thomas argues for an unmerited grace of perseverance. Thomas's attitude toward perseverance in the earlier *Scriptum* is difficult to document, precisely because he hardly discusses the question. However, it is most likely that his position in the earlier work is that the one who perseveres on the path to God is the one who acts freely in accordance with the inclination of the habitual grace received in justification; perseverance in grace is left, as it were, in the hands of the justified. In the *Summa*, on the other hand, perseverance is a free gift of God by which God applies a person to good action and keeps the person away from sin, all in accordance with God's predestining will for that person. The result of Thomas's inclusion of these unmerited graces of conversion and perseverance in his description of merit is a more nuanced account. Their inclusion helps us to perceive the limits of meritorious action by bringing to our attention those features of spiritual existence which fall outside of merit, and most significantly, this revision of his teaching on merit underscores yet again the ultimate gratuity of salvation: that one gets into grace and then stays there is due to God's free decision to save the person.

Having described the principal differences between Thomas's two *ex professo* discussions of merit, the question naturally arises: Why did he revise his teaching in these ways? Why does he relate merit to predestination and refer to the unmerited graces of conversion and of perseverance in his description of merit? The literature on merit itself provides little help in answering this question. Indeed, the Thomists who have written about Thomas's understanding of merit have generally been oblivious to the changes in his later teaching. It is in the course of reconsidering the implications of ideas articulated in Henri Bouillard's important book on Thomas's theology, not of merit but of grace,[15] that hints toward an answer emerge. Bouillard's study of "conversion and grace in Thomas Aquinas" only incidentally touches on Thomas's teaching on merit and does not try to answer our question. His principal concerns, rather, are to chart the

---

15   Bouillard, *Conversion et grâce.* I have discussed Bouillard's book at considerable length in Chapter 1. I offer here but a brief summary of his basic thesis.

changes in Thomas's descriptions of the sinner's conversion to God and to explain these changes. Bouillard notes that in the early *Scriptum* on the *Sentences*, Thomas in effect is willing to allow the initiation into the state of grace to be determined by human action: One will receive habitual justifying grace after preparing oneself through naturally good action for this grace. Moreover, Bouillard adds, at this stage of his teaching, Thomas nowhere asserts that it is God who works this preparation for grace: It is the sinner who freely decides to reform. By the 1260s, however, Thomas has modified his account of conversion. He still will speak of preparation for justifying grace. But Thomas now insists that it is God who takes the initiative in conversion and that it is God who in fact works the conversion of the sinner. Moreover, Thomas also now insists that conversion itself is due to predestination: God has freely decided to save the sinner and so converts the sinner to God.

How then, Bouillard asks, are we to explain this new approach to the question of conversion? Bouillard is aware that part of the answer lies in Thomas's maturation as a systematician and in his more complete understanding of such pertinent concepts as the nature of the human will. But Bouillard is convinced that these changes are especially to be attributed to Thomas's work as a historian. In particular, Bouillard argues that Thomas had benefited from his reading in the 1260s of certain writings of the late Augustine, *De Praedestinatione Sanctorum* and *De Dono Perseverantiae*. According to Bouillard, these works of Augustine had been lost in their integrity for much of the Middle Ages. To the extent that they were known, they were known only through isolated passages which had passed into anthologies.[16] But, Bouillard postulates, Thomas Aquinas had come across these treatises in the early 1260s while he was connected with the papal court and had changed his own teaching on grace in the light of his close

---

16   Bouillard requires some qualification in this regard. For evidence of the availability of the two treatises at Paris in the last quarter of the thirteenth century, see the transcription of a fragment from the Sorbonne library, dated by Richard Rouse to c. 1275, in "The Early Library of the Sorbonne," in Mary A. Rouse and Richard H. Rouse, *Authentic Witnesses: Approaches to Medieval Texts and Manuscripts* (Notre Dame, Ind., 1991), p. 401. Bouillard (p. 122, n. 126) had suggested that Matthew of Aquasparta, in his disputed questions on grace, had been able to cite these treatises not because of a direct reading but through the mediation of Aquinas; on the basis of my own study of these questions, with their frequent, often-lengthy quotations, the proposal seems strained. See in this regard my "'Perseverance' in 13th-Century Theology," *Augustinian Studies* 22 (1991), especially pp. 133–35. Given the Italian locale of Thomas's probable rediscovery, it is also worth noting that M. Oberleitner, *Die Handschriftliche Überlieferung der Werke des Heiligen Augustinus*, Band I/1 Italien (Vienna, 1969) lists (pp. 62, 145–46) some thirteenth-century manuscripts of these works. Yet Bouillard's larger point does seem secure: These treatises were not widely known by medieval theologians and as the example of Matthew discloses, even when they were read, their import was not fully grasped. Thomas's distinctiveness in this regard seems assured.

study of Augustine's arguments in these writings. In these two writings (which had originally constituted two parts of a single work), Augustine had waged a polemic against what is now called "semi-Pelagianism," that is, the view that people can initiate their own conversion by their acts, although God must complete this conversion through God's infusion of grace. For Augustine, human sin makes it impossible for people to initiate conversion. Because of original and actual sin, people are bound by sin and indeed are inclined by sin to further sin. If people are to be saved from sin and oriented to God, says Augustine, God must initiate the process, for only God can smash the "heart of stone" created by sin and replace it with the "heart of flesh" which is open and submissive to God's promptings. And Augustine insists in these writings, God's intervention in human life to convert the sinner is itself due to God's free decision from eternity to save the sinner: God has freely pre-destined the sinner to conversion and has decided to make of the sinner a vessel of God's mercy. Of himself, the sinner deserves condemnation—this is the just payment of the sinner's "merits"— but God mercifully frees the sinner from this fate in accordance with the divine will and brings this person to the highest possible end, life in heaven with God.

Although Bouillard was not concerned to relate Thomas's work as a historian to Thomas's teaching on merit and more or less restricted himself to showing how Thomas's reading of the later Augustine had led Thomas to reconsider his own description of the respective roles of God's grace and of human freedom in conversion, by following Bouillard's lead, it is possible to see in Augustine's later writings an important stimulus to Thomas's revision of his own teaching on *merit*. In reading Augustine, Thomas was able to see the inappropriateness of leaving open the possibility of a merit of the first grace. Rather, conversion is worked by God alone, and the later Thomas unequivocally excluded every human merit from conversion. Moreover, emulating Augustine, Thomas in the works from the early 1260s wished to stress that salvation be seen as the gift of God, and thus as had Augustine Thomas insisted that the conversion of the sinner is itself due to God's predestination of this person to the attainment of God.

But what about the final new feature of Thomas's later teaching on merit, the insistence that *perseverance* in grace until the end of life is the unmerited gift of God and that it, like conversion, is also the result of God's predestination of the human person to salvation? Did the reading of Augustine contribute to this innovation as well? Naturally, given the limits of his topic, Bouillard himself was not interested in examining Augustine's teaching about the operative grace of perseverance or, in turn, in examining its inclusion in Thomas's theology of grace. But in these later works Augustine is very much concerned to emphasize that the successful completion of the spiritual life is the consequence of God's predestination of the justified person to perseverance. Apart from God's will, the justified person will lapse yet again into sin. Thus, in reading Augustine, Thomas would have encountered an operative grace of perseverance that he then incorporated into his description of the *limits* of merit. Indeed, in a way that Bouillard did not perceive, it was really only in the writings from the last stage of Augustine's career that Thomas could have encountered a teaching about a grace of perseverance that eludes merit and that is due to God's free decision about the human person. As Patout Burns has observed, Augustine had affirmed in writings earlier than the two which most concern us here an operative grace of *conversion* tied to predestination. But it was only in the writings after 426—that is, these two works, plus *De Gratia et Libero Arbiitrio* and *De Correptione et Gratia*—that Augustine had attained to the additional insight about an operative grace that works perseverance. Just as God must work the conversion of the sinner, so too, Augustine says, God must freely keep the justified in the state of grace, moving the justified to reject the continued temptations of sin and to perform the good works which God desires.[17] In other words, what is truly

---

17   J. Patout Burns, *The Development of Augustine's Doctrine of Operative Grace* (Paris, 1980), is enormously helpful for the development in Augustine's theology of grace. Without claiming here to provide an exhaustive summary of Burns's richly textured argument, it should be noted that Burns perceives three stages in Augustine's theology of grace. In the first stage, from 396 on, Augustine's starting point is the human person's desire for the good, for completion in God. The Augustine of this period acknowledged that sin can, and does, misdirect this desire for the good so that the person now seeks the good in the wrong places, that is, not in God. But the effects of sin can be overcome, and are overcome, by God, through the manipulation of the circumstances of a person's life in such a way that the person now comes to desire God as his good. In this first stage of his teaching, represented by the *Confessions*, divine predestination is generally left out of account. In the next stage of his theology of grace, from 418 on, Augustine has become more impressed by the seriousness of sin. From 412 on, he had recognized original sin and the hardening of the human heart which is caused by this and other sins. His analysis of sin, in fact, has caused him now to find unsatisfactory the merely external grace of the first stage of his teaching. Earlier, Augustine had believed that the person would turn away from sin if God changed the circumstances of his life. Now, Augustine acknowledged that because of sin the heart will be so hardened that it will inevitably reject the "external" entreaties of God to repent. Hence, in this second stage of his teaching, Augustine posited an interior grace which is required to work the conversion of the sinner: This inward grace smashes the heart of stone and replaces it with the heart of flesh which is amenable to the promptings of God. Along with this operative grace of conversion, Augustine also now emphasized predestination: That a sinner is converted is due to God's free, merciful decision to convert the sinner and to give the grace needed to overcome sin. Finally, in the final stage of his theology of grace, from 426 on, Augustine concluded to a second operative grace, that of perseverance, which complements the first and which is also tied to predestination. Since the justified person remains tormented by the temptations of this world, unless God provides a further grace which works the acts which will keep the person in grace, that person will inevitably fall from grace. It is this second operative

distinctive about the theology of grace of the later Augustine is precisely this positing of an operative grace of perseverance: Without it, the justified person will lapse into sin. And in reading these particular writings, Thomas had come to recognize as well the need for such a grace and thus had restructured his theology of grace in general and his description of merit in particular. Aware of this grace, the Thomas of the *Summa* insists that the good that the justified do and that brings them deservedly to God does not work the perseverance in grace; that the justified stay in grace is not caused by human action but is due to the predestinating will of God.[18]

Yet, if we can speak in this way of "Augustinian sources" of Thomas's later teaching about merit, it is crucial to be clear about the exact nature and the limit of these sources. Thomas has learned much from Augustine about what does *not* fall under merit. In particular, he exploits Augustine's ideas about the absolute significance of predestination and about the operative graces of conversion and of perseverance to re-structure his own teaching about merit. The later Augustine's comments directly on *merit*

---

grace, that of perseverance, which Augustine affirms and emphasizes in the works which most interests us here.

18   It is perhaps not inappropriate to mention here a possible alternative source of inspiration for the new developments in Thomas's teaching on merit. Many features of Bouillard's book have been criticized, but few, if any, have challenged his suggestion that the changes in Thomas's theology of grace are due especially to his reading of these writings of Augustine. Indeed, even such an acute critic as Deman has acknowledged the value of this suggestion: It plausibly accounts for the new features of Thomas's later thought about grace, and moreover there are verbal clues in Thomas's later discussion of grace which suggest his first-hand reading of these writings of Augustine. However, it may be claimed that Bouillard has mis-identified the writings which Thomas "rediscovered" and which were in reality so crucial for his theology. The canons of the Second Synod of Orange (529) were similarly inaccessible for much of the Middle Ages. Thus, it may be these canons, rather than Augustine's *De Dono Perseverantiae* and *De Praedestinatione Sanctorum* which Thomas located while in Italy in the 1260s and which figured so prominently in Thomas's re-structuring of his theology and grace. Whatever the value of this hypothesis in other respects, however, for our purposes the substitution of the canons of Orange for these Augustinian writings is but of limited value. The Synod of Orange does express some very important Augustinian notions, and it can be characterized as a victory for Augustinianism against the "remnants" of the Pelagians—the Synod, for example, affirms with Augustine the universality of sin (and hence the impossibility of people saving themselves), and the gratuity of salvation. But what we do *not* find in these canons are precisely those ideas which interest us and which were so crucial for the later Aquinas. That is, salvation is free and through grace, for Orange. But the Synod does not tie salvation directly or explicitly to *predestination*; and there is at best only an oblique and passing reference at this Synod (chapter 10) to an operative grace of perseverance which guarantees the successful completion of the spiritual journey. Thus, it is Bouillard's thesis, that it is the reading of Augustine's final writings on grace which Thomas found and studied, which remains most appealing.

itself, however, have been much less valuable or instructive for Thomas in his working-out of his teaching about merit. Indeed, the later Augustine makes but fleeting mention of merit. On the one hand, he engages in a polemic against the notion that one can "merit" the grace of conversion—as he says, the just reward of sin, the characteristic activity of fallen humanity, is not grace but damnation[19]. On the other hand, in a more positive vein, even in these final writings Augustine remains willing to speak of the merits of the justified and to allow that these good works of the justified do make a contribution to the salvation of the individual: Through merits,

19   Augustine makes the point that the grace of conversion is not given according to one's merits, for this would destroy its character as "grace," in numerous passages in these two writings. See, e.g., *De Praedestinatione Sanctorum* I, 1; II, 6; XII, 23; XIV, 27. In *De Praedestinatione Sanctorum* II, 4, he adds that Pelagius himself had condemned the view that the first grace is given according to our (good) merits. In *De Dono Perseverantiae*, Augustine repeats the claim that to be "grace," the grace of conversion cannot be given as a reward for one's merits: see, e.g., XX, 51, where he says that the absolute gratuity of the first grace has been the constant teaching of all the faithful since the beginning of the church; XVII, 42, where he says that to assert the bestowal of grace for merits is a "most pernicious error"; XX, 53, where he terms the notion that grace is given for merits the "complete negation of grace"; and XXI, 56, where he states that those who say that grace is rendered for merits are "ungrateful" to God for this grace. In these works, of course, the grace of conversion is ascribed to God's mercy, to God's free predestination of the sinner to repentance: see, e.g., *De Dono Perseverantiae* XI, 25, and XII, 28. For Augustine, the grace of perseverance is also a free, unmerited gift (*donum*) of God. See, e.g., *De Dono Perseverantiae* II, 2, and XVII, 41; and *De Dono Perseverantiae* XIII, 32, and XXI, 56, where he says that both conversion to grace and persevering in it are gifts of God, not the reward of merits. In *De Dono Perseverantiae* II, 3, Augustine observes that perseverance can be obtained only by one's prayer and, following Cyprian, goes through the petitions of the Lord's Prayer to show that this prayer is almost exclusively concerned with obtaining perseverance from God; according to V, 8, only the request for the forgiveness of sins is not concerned with perseverance. Augustine adds in *De Dono Perseverantiae* XIV, 35, and XXIII, 64, that only those who have been inspired by God will in fact pray for perseverance; all others will hear the biblical injunctions to pray for this gift but will fail to act on this exhortation.
      Augustine also argues against the merit of the first grace in two other contexts in these writings. First, he notes that Jesus Christ was predestined freely by God to be the savior of the race, without regard to any preceding merits—after all, he was elected savior even before he existed. See *De Praedestinatione Sanctorum* XII, 23, and XV, 30, and *De Dono Perseverantiae* XXIV, 67. Second, Augustine refers to the salvation of children who die in infancy. Why are some allowed to receive baptism before their death, and so are saved, while others die before regeneration? Augustine rejects the idea that the baptized infants have been allowed to receive baptism because of God's foreknowledge of their merits if they had lived. That they were baptized is due to God's free predestination of these infants to conversion and grace; see *De Praedestinatione Sanctorum* XII, 24.

the justified person is brought to the end of eternal life, although Augustine understandably insists here immediately that because these meritorious acts are themselves caused by grace, God's crowning of these merits with the reward of heaven must be viewed as in fact God's crowning of God's own grace.[20] But beyond these brief comments about merit Augustine is unwilling or unable to go. He retains merit-language in a positive sense even at the end of his career, and speaks of people "deserving" their reward of heaven through their good acts. He does not, however, explore merit in its various dimensions, or look at the various objects in addition to the end of the spiritual life which can be merited by the justified, or explain how the meriting of the Christian is fully compatible with the accompanying claims about perseverance and about the decisiveness of God's predestination to glory. In the end, then, in working out the positive side of his teaching on merit Thomas Aquinas has been left to his own speculative

---

20   Augustine continues to refer to the good acts of the justified as "merits" in these writings, while insisting that the good acts of the saints are themselves wrought by God. See, e.g., *De Praedestinatione Sanctorum* II, 5; and *De Dono Perseverantiae* II, 4, where he states that the merits of the saints are *dona Dei*. In *De Praedestinatione Sanctorum* XI, 22, in the course of arguing that first grace is not given for merits, he adds that there is a sense in which grace is given for "merits": It is given for *bad* merits in the sense that God confounds our expectations by "rewarding" the evil of the sinner with God's grace. Augustine adds here that grace is given the sinner so that good acts will follow and the justified will observe the commandments. Finally, in *De Praedestinatione Sanctorum* XII, 24, Augustine states that the present life is the time for meriting and doing good. After death, people will no longer merit but will receive rewards (*praemia*) for their good merits or be punished for their sins.

    Augustine's most sustained attempt in his post-426 writings to retain merit-language while emphasizing the gratuity of conversion and perseverance comes in *De Gratia et Libero Arbitrio*, especially from VI, 14, on. For example, in VI, 15, he states that the merits of the saints are God's *dona* and says that when God rewards these merits, God is simply crowning God's own gifts. Yet, even though Augustine makes an effort here to accommodate merit and the operative grace of perseverance, he has failed to make fully understandable how the human person does contribute to the meritorious act in such a way that the God-inspired act is also his. Rather, Augustine stays at a purely rhetorical level, making the case which had to be made against the Pelagians and the semi-Pelagians (that salvation is God's gift) without clarifying how God uses secondary causes, including the human person, in such a way that the actions worked by God through these causes is also theirs. Similarly, as I state in the text below, Augustine does not bother to offer in this writing any concerted attempt to enumerate the different rewards of merit, e.g., not just the end of eternal life but intermediary ends. Thomas knows *De Gratia et Libero Arbitrio*—he quotes it in the all-important *ST* I-II 111, 2 sed contra and corpus, where he outlines in his greatest detail the human and divine contributions to meritorious action—and it is likely that he had "rediscovered" this work, along with *De Praedestinatione Sanctorum* and *De Dono Perseverantiae*, in the 1260s.

resources. He agrees with Augustine's claims that salvation and its various parts are due to the free decision and grace of God. But in the remaining articles of I-II 114, Thomas completes the picture of human salvation, by showing precisely how it is meaningful to speak of people contributing to the attainment of their salvation through their good works and so fulfills in his own teaching on merit the task left unfinished by the later Augustine.

Section II. Thomas and Scripture (especially Paul)

In their response to the attacks of Luther and the Reformers, sixteenth-century Catholic theologians offered a variety of arguments in support of merit. Although the Latin translations of the New Testament lack the word *meritum* in the technical sense of an "act worthy of reward from God,"[21] the Counter-Reformation arguments for merit were primarily biblical in nature. Against the Lutheran claim to be advancing the true teaching of scripture on justification, Catholic apologists wished to show that the Bible itself teaches the possibility and need for people to contribute to their salvation through their acts. At Trent, at least three different kinds of biblical texts were cited to make the case for merit. First, the fathers of Trent referred to exhortations to righteousness in scripture as proof of the place of merit in the Christian life. In the Bible, the will of God for people is disclosed. Since scripture urges Christians to act in a way befitting their calling, God must want, and expect, Christians to act in a morally correct way; and when they do perform the moral good, their actions will gain them heaven. Second, Trent argued that merit must be upheld because it testifies to the greatness of Christ's work. Through Christ, the power and grace of God have been made available to Christians, and this grace will issue in new acts of righteousness, acts that will in turn deserve eternal reward from God. Finally, Trent asserted merit because of the reward texts

---

21   See Jerome D. Quinn, "The Scriptures on Merit," in *Justification by Faith*, ed. H. G. Anderson et al. (Minneapolis, 1985), pp. 82–83. Quinn notes that the word *meritum* does not appear in the Vulgate New Testament. It does appear in the Latin of Sirach in three places in the sense of a deserving of a reward. In his article on merit in scripture, Quinn makes the observation that the roots of the later teaching on merit must thus be sought elsewhere than in texts which would have affirmed merit directly and plainly. In particular, he draws our attention to reward-texts especially in Paul (p. 87ff.), thus continuing the Catholic tradition, described in the text below, of finding in the reward-language of scripture implicit support for the affirmation of merit. Quinn also observes (p. 92) that in scripture there is no simple or obvious correspondence between the works which one does, and their value, and God's reward—the amount of reward for merit remains for God alone to "calculate." Quinn's observation is of value in countering the tendency in post-Tridentine Catholicism to construct a precise calculus of merit and reward. However, Thomas Aquinas himself makes no attempt to calculate the exact worth of merits or to suggest that we need 'x amount' of merits to deserve a particular reward from God. His interest is simply to show that the good actions of the Christian do make a difference, a position which Quinn also adopts.

found in scripture. While the word 'merit' is not found in scripture, the concept of "reward" is found throughout the Bible: At the Last Judgment, Christians are told, God will render to each according to his works. For Trent, then, the affirmation of reward for morally good action implies that this good action is deserving of God's reward.[22]

22 For Trent's affirmation of merit, see the decree on justification of the Sixth Session of Trent, chapter XVI (I quote here the English translation by H. J. Schroeder, *The Canons and Decrees of the Council of Trent* [Rockford, Ill., 1978], pp. 40–42): "To men justified in this manner . . . are to be pointed out the words of the Apostle: *Abound in every good work, knowing that your labor is not in vain in the Lord.* [See I Cor. 15–58] *For God is not unjust, that he should forget your work, and the love which you have shown in his name;* [Heb. 6:10] and *Do not lose your confidence, which hath a great reward* [Heb. 10:35]. Hence, to those who work well *unto the end* [Matt. 10:22] and trust in God, eternal life is to be offered, both as a grace mercifully promised to the sons of God through Christ Jesus, and as a reward promised by God himself, to be faithfully given to their good works and merits [Rom. 6:22]. For this is the crown of justice which after his fight and course the Apostle declared was laid up for him, to be rendered to him by the just judge, and not only to him, but also to all that love his coming [See II Tim. 4:8]. For since Christ Jesus Himself, as the head into the members and the vine into the branches [John 15:1f.], continually infuses strength into those justified, which strength always precedes, accompanies and follows their good works, and without which they could not in any manner be pleasing and meritorious before God, we must believe that nothing further is wanting to those justified to prevent them from being considered to have, by those very works which have been done in God, fully satisfied the divine law according to the state of this life and to have truly merited eternal life, to be obtained in its time, provided they depart in grace [Apoc. 14:13], since Christ our Savior says: *If anyone shall drink of the water that I will give him, he shall not thirst forever; but it shall become in him a fountain of water springing up unto life everlasting* [John 4:13f.]. Thus, neither is our own justice established as our own from ourselves [Rom. 10:3; II Cor. 3:5], nor is the justice of God ignored or repudiated, for that justice which is called ours, because we are justified by its inherence in us, that same is of God, because it is infused into us by God through the merit of Christ. Nor must this be omitted, that although in the sacred writings so much is attributed to good works, that even *he that shall give a drink of cold water to one of his least ones,* Christ promises, *shall not lose his reward* [Matt. 10:42; Mark 9:40]; and the Apostle testifes that, *That which is at present momentary and light of our tribulation, worketh for us above measure exceedingly an eternal weight of glory* [See II Cor. 4:17]; nevertheless, far be it that a Christian should either trust or glory in himself and not in the Lord [See I Cor. 1:31; II Cor. 10:17], whose bounty toward all men is so great that He wishes the things that are His gifts to be their merits . . . the whole life of man is to be examined and judged not by the judgment of man but of God, *who will bring to light the hidden things of darkness, and will make manifest the counsels of the hearts, and then shall every man have praise from God* [See I Cor. 4:5], who, as it is written, *will render to every man according to his works* [Matt. 16:27; Rom. 2:6; Apoc. 22:12]." In affirming these reasons for merit, Trent is simply recapitulating the arguments against Luther made by earlier sixteenth-century Catholic apologists for merit. In

With sixteenth-century Catholics, Thomas Aquinas is convinced that merit is rooted in the Bible. However, in his various discussions of merit Thomas refers to only one of the arguments advanced by later Catholics to demonstrate the biblical basis of merit. Thomas, of course, believes that scripture provides the guidelines for shaping ethical behavior, and he is convinced that the Christian will act differently than the unjustified sinner. Moreover, Aquinas is thoroughly "Augustinian" in the sense of perceiving grace in transformational terms. Through union in faith and love to Christ, the Christian is transformed by God's grace and is enabled to do, as God's instrument, acts worthy of God. But when he speaks about merit, Thomas never suggests that he has been moved to affirm merit because of scriptural exhortations to righteousness or because of biblical references to transforming grace. Rather, it is the third "scriptural" argument for merit to which Thomas consistently turns to explain why he believes that the good acts of the Christian do contribute to the attainment of salvation. Thomas affirms merit because of the scriptural references to God's just judgment of people for their acts and rendering of eternal reward in accordance with their behavior. Hence, in both the early *Scriptum* on the *Sentences* and the later *Summa Theologiae* Thomas cites reward- and just-judgment-texts from scripture as evidence of the biblical origin of his own teaching on merit.[23] The question thus arises whether Thomas's use of such texts as the basis of his teaching on merit is in fact warranted.

---

his *Enchiridion of Commonplaces* (translated by F. L. Battles [Grand Rapids, Mich., 1979]), for example, John Eck argues (p. 51f.) for merit on the basis of reward-texts in scripture, as well as in the light of scriptural exhortations to righteousness. Cajetan, *Faith and Works—Against the Lutherans* (in *Cajetan Responds*, trans. J. Wicks (Washington, D.C., 1978) similarly refers to scriptural texts on reward as proof of merit (e.g., p. 230), but especially focuses on the power and grace of Christ which guide the Christian to condignly meritorious acts; see p. 231ff.

At Trent, a fourth argument is alleged for the need for merit in the Christian life. In chapter XIII (pp. 38–39), Christians are urged to do good works in order to remain in the state of grace, thereby insuring their calling. Thomas Aquinas, of course, expects the Christian to do good once in the state of grace; recall his comments on the vice of presumption reported in Chapter 3. However, in his later theology Thomas makes clear that the principal basis of the Christian's certainty of salvation lies in God: By one's hope in God, not by one's works, is one sure of coming to God. As I observed in the first section of this chapter, however, in the *Scriptum*, Thomas is probably closer to the teaching of Trent: That one perseveres in grace will be due, not to an operative grace of perseverance provided by God, but to one's continued, freely performed observance of the good.

23   Thomas's preferred "proof-text" for his teaching on merit is II Timothy 4:8, in which the author states that there is laid up for him a crown of justice which God, the just judge, will render to him on the day of judgment. See, e.g., *In II Scriptum* d. XXVII, q. I, a. 3, sed contra 1, and *ST* I-II 114, 3 sed contra. When discussing reward texts in his commentaries on scripture, Thomas often introduces merit. See, e.g., his *Commentary on Romans*, which is

Luther had rebutted the sixteenth-century Catholic argument for merit based on these reward-texts by drawing a distinction between 'worth' and 'consequence.'[24] A reward may be owed to a person because of an act which he has done and which has a value equal to that of the reward. In this case, we may speak of the good deed being "worth" the reward, and so as "meritorious" of it. For Luther, however, when scripture speaks of "reward," it is not referring to the "worth" of acts; such a correspondence of merit and reward is restricted to the everyday world of transactions between people. Rather, when scripture employs reward-language, it is speaking in "sequential" terms. God is in control of the entire process of salvation: God initiates it by God's action in Christ and by sending preachers to proclaim the Word; God moreover instills the faith needed to receive the Word in accordance with God's predestining will. For Luther, God also continues and completes the process of salvation by maintaining the justified person in faith until that person comes to God. Hence, when scripture refers to God's *reward*, it is referring to God's completion of what God has begun. As a consequence of the faith which the person holds as a gift of God, that person receives the further gift of heaven. In this analysis, the potential conflict posed by scripture's affirmation of the gratuity of salvation and of God's reward of people at the last judgment is dissipated. Even the references to reward in scripture for Luther bespeak the gratuity of salvation. At any rate, Luther's approach to the reward-texts of scripture seriously challenges the use of such texts in support of merit.[25]

contemporary with the Prima Secundae; here, Thomas interprets Paul's statements in Romans 2:1ff. about God's eschatological judgment of people in terms of Christian merit and reward; see *In Rom.* caput II, lectio II, #189ff. As was stated in Chapter 2, Thomas especially argues for the merit of Christ on the basis of such texts as Phillipians 2:6ff., where Christ's exaltation is rendered for the "merit" of humiliation.

24   For Luther's distinction between 'worth' and 'consequence,' see his writing against Erasmus, *On the Bondage of the Will*, in *Luther and Erasmus: Free Will and Salvation*, ed. and trans. E. G. Rupp and P. S. Watson (Philadelphia, 1969), p. 208ff. Calvin also utilized the distinction to counter the Catholic arguments based on reward-texts in the *Institutes* Bk. III, ch. 18. For a reconsideration of Calvin's teaching on sanctification in the light of Aquinas on condign merit, see my "John Calvin and Condign Merit," *Archiv für Reformationsgeschichte* 83 (1992): 73–90.

25   Luther also rejected the other "arguments" from scripture offered by Catholic proponents of merit which were mentioned in the text. Against Erasmus, he disputed the notion that scriptural exhortations to righteousness proved the freedom of the will or, consequently, the possibility and need for merit. On the contrary, such passages in scripture should be read in terms of the condemnatory function of the Law: Just as God gives the Law in order to humble the person and to turn the person away from the effort to justify himself and back to God, so too exhortations to righteousness are designed to humble the sinner by showing him his inability to save himself. God exhorts, and in failing to live up to this demand, the sinner comes to recognize his spiritual impotence. See *Bondage*, p. 188ff. Similarly, Luther was

Recent biblical scholarship, however, suggests that the New Testament assertion of divine retribution for good human action (and hence, by implication, the place of "merit" in the Christian life) can be taken more as Catholic tradition understands it without thereby jeopardizing the central biblical affirmation of the gratuity of salvation and the primacy of God in the redemption of the human person. In particular, the work of the Protestant scholar Ernst Käsemann discloses how the apostle Paul could allow for the contribution of the human person in coming to God through acts of obedience while insisting both that God controls the entire process of salvation and that salvation is indeed the gift of God. In his influential article on the "righteousness of God" in Paul,[26] Käsemann's purpose is to determine the exact meaning of this crucial term in the Pauline epistles. He notes that the genitive in this term has been interpreted variously as either subjective or objective. If the former, then by the term 'righteousness of God' Paul is referring especially to an attribute of God, by which God is righteous or just. If the latter, on the other hand, by the 'righteousness of God' Paul is designating the righteousness which is acceptable before God, that is, the gift of God by which God reckons humans as just before God. Contrary to the dominant Protestant interpretation since Luther, Käsemann argues in this article that in Paul the genitive construction is to be taken first of all as subjective, although he insists that this attribute of God is also active in the world, rendering fallen humanity righteous in the eyes of God.[27]

On the basis of pre-Pauline and of contemporary Jewish usages of the term 'righteousness of God,' Käsemann insists that in Paul the 'righteousness of God' has an especially eschatological reference.[28] The righteousness

---

unimpressed by Catholic claims about the transforming power of grace and the consequent performance of good acts which would be meritorious. Rather, he prefers to characterize justification in terms of the imputation of Christ's righteousness to the believer, in which Christ's genuine righteousness is ascribed to the sinner and covers his sins. In general, Luther combats merit because he perceives in the affirmation of merit human attempts at self-righteousness and a corresponding disrespect of the work of Christ. Christ has done all which is necessary for salvation. We must abandon the effort to save ourselves apart from Christ and trust in faith that Christ's grace suffices for human salvation.

26   E. Käsemann, "'The Righteousness of God' in Paul," in *New Testament Questions of Today*, translated by W. J. Montague (London, 1969), pp. 168–82. Käsemann has been one of the most influential scholars of the New Testament in recent years. I find his approach to Paul most congenial, for he offers an interpretation of the justice of God that credibly allows us to give full value to the reward texts in Paul without sacrificing the Reformation insight into the gratuity of justification.

27   For these two ways of interpreting the 'righteousness of God' in Paul, see *ibid.*, p. 169. Käsemann explicitly states that the righteousness of God describes an attribute of God which is active in the world on p. 174.

28   Käsemann refers to extra-Pauline usages of the term to clarify Paul's

of God refers to the power of God by which God will restore the world to complete obedience and submission to God at the end of time. Through sin the world has been removed from its correct order to God and in place of the harmony and peace desired by God have come the conflict and disharmony attendant on sin. Thus, at the end of time God's power/righteousness will be fully active, establishing the eschatological kingdom of God in which God's will will fully prevail and the world will be precisely as God wants. But, adds Käsemann, in Paul the righteousness of God is not wholly or exclusively future: God's righteousness is active even now, overcoming sin and summoning people to God's kingdom. It is at this point that faith comes into play. When God summons people to the kingdom, they must respond in faith to the call. Moreover, this faith is not restricted to the beginning of the Christian life. It is constantly required throughout existence in this world, as the appropriate response to God's promptings. For Käsemann, faith thus means more than "trust" in God, although it also means this: Faith especially means "obedience" to God, for by faith the person ceases to pursue his own goals and offers himself obediently in faith as the servant of God.[29] Thus, through faith and the obedience which faith promotes, the righteousness of God becomes manifest in the world, as all those called by God respond faithfully to the summons to work for God's kingdom. For the individual addressed by God, the correct response in faith determines his place in God's eschatological kingdom: It is the obedient servant who has been ruled by God's righteousness in this life who will enter the kingdom at the end of time. Thus, in Käsemann's reading of the 'righteousness of God,' it is possible to interpret reward-texts in terms of the "worth" of acts (to use Luther's language). The reward of the kingdom will be granted to those who have been steadfast in faith and obedience. By their service to God, they shall have "deserved" to enter into the kingdom.[30]

meaning in a number of places. See, e.g., *ibid.*, pp. 172, 174, 177, and 178; as in Paul, according to Käsemann, Jewish usages also speak of the righteousness of God as both future and present.

29 Käsemann stresses the centrality of Christian obedience throughout the article; see, e.g., *ibid.*, pp. 171, 177, and 182. He also repeatedly makes the point that faith/obedience is a constant task. See, e.g., p. 175: "We no longer exist simply for ourselves and cannot therefore simply dig in behind what we have received. Only so long as we keep on the pilgrim way and allow ourselves to be recalled daily to the allegiance of Christ, can we abide in the gift which we have received and can it abide, living and powerful, in us"; p. 176, where he states that "the possibility of choosing between the kingdom of Christ and the kingdom of Satan . . . is for ever demanding that the Christian should make this choice [for Christ] anew"; and p. 181, where Käsemann describes the "faithful" as "the world as it has been recalled to the sovereignty of God, the company of those who live under the eschatological justice of God, in which company, according to II Cor. 5:21, God's righteousness becomes manifest on earth."

30 In addition to the statement in *ibid.*, p. 175 quoted in the previous note, in which Käsemann observes that the Christian's place in the eschatological

Yet, Käsemann continues, his stress on Christian obedience and the call to act responsibly in order to come to the kingdom does not issue in a new "works-righteousness" or in the denial of the scriptural affirmation of the ultimate gratuity of salvation.[31] This becomes clear when we consider his rather difficult statements about the righteousness of God in Paul as both "power" and "gift." It is a "gift" because the offer of the kingdom come unexpectedly and undeservedly: God through Christ calls *sinners* to the kingdom. The righteousness of God is also a "gift" because the power of God is given over to the recipient in such a way that the recipient is enabled to act in a new fashion, in conformity to the requirements of the kingdom.[32] But the righteousness of God is "power" as well precisely because it always remains the power *of God*; it does not become the power or possession of the human person. According to Käsemann, in Paul the giver of the power to respond to God in faith and obedience always remains present with the gift of this power, and indeed it is God who works the correct use of this power, for the achievement of God's goals for the world.[33] This recognition

---

kingdom is dependent on continued obedience to God's righteousness, see Käsemann's *Commentary on Romans*, trans. G. W. Bromiley (Grand Rapids, Mich., 1980), pp. 53–61, in which Käsemann exploits his ideas about the righteousness of God and the need for faith/obedience in response to God's righteousness in the exegesis of Romans 2:1ff. Here, he states that Paul's argument is that God's favorable judgment of the individual at the Last Judgment is dependent on the person's faithfulness to God in this life, although this faithfulness is itself "worked" by God in the sense explained below in the text.

31   For Käsemann's polemic against the idea of merit, see "'Righteousness,'" pp. 175 and 180. As he makes clear here, Käsemann understands by 'merit' the attempt to save oneself and to pursue one's goal of salvation: It designates one's own achievement and is antipathetical to the idea that only God can, and does, save the world. For Käsemann, fixation on merit in this sense leads one to attempt to retain one's independence before God, even to achieve parity with God, and to refuse to offer oneself as the servant of God; see p. 180. It is clear that Käsemann has a rather stereotypical view of merit; I do not believe that his comments here apply to Aquinas. Indeed, as I shall argue shortly in the text, Käsemann's views on the righteousness of God, faith, and reward are in many ways compatible with Thomas's ideas about salvation and merit.

32   For the idea that in Paul, the righteousness of God is a gift which makes possible, and indeed requires, new action by its recipients, see Käsemann, "'Righteousness,'" p. 175 and especially p. 170: "The divine righteousness possesses us before we grasp it, and we retain it only as long as it holds us fast. The gift itself has thus the character of power. The meaning of this in concrete terms is quite clear. Paul knows no gift of God which does not convey both the obligation and the capacity to serve. A gift which is not authenticated in practice and passed on to others loses its specific content."

33   See *ibid.*, p. 173 and especially p. 174: "The gift which is being bestowed here is never at any time separable from its Giver. It partakes of the character of power, in so far as God himself enters the arena and remains in the arena with it. Thus personal address, obligation, and service are indissolubly bound up with the gift. When God enters the arena, our experience is, that he

that righteousness remains the power of the God who seeks to achieve the divine will in the world thus qualifies the call to obedience and affirmation of reward for this obedience. Obedience will be rewarded, but this obedience is itself the gift of God. God employs the God-inspired activity of Christians for the achievement of God's goals for the world and rewards Christians for their contribution, made possible by the divine power, to the establishment of the kingdom.

It would be relatively simple to draw up a lengthy list of the differences between Thomas Aquinas on human salvation and the apostle Paul (as presented by Käsemann). Käsemann, for example, argues that Paul thinks of salvation in communal terms—God's righteousness aims after all at the institution of the eschatological *kingdom*, not at the salvation of an individual—and thus would probably include Aquinas among those who have depicted salvation in excessively individualistic terms.[34] Similarly, at a different level, Käsemann and Aquinas would disagree about the exact interpretation of the term which stands at the origin of Käsemann's reflections on Paul. Despite Luther's claims that his Catholic predecessors tended to interpret the righteousness of God principally as the attribute of justice by which God is just, through punishing the evil and rewarding the good, Aquinas normally interprets the biblical righteousness of God not so much as an attribute of God as God's making the sinner just.[35] Hence, Aquinas would join Luther in rejecting Käsemann's claim that the genitive of this term should be taken as subjective, although he would appreciate Käsemann's additional argument that the righteousness of God entails God's transformation of human existence.[36]

maintains his lordship even in his giving; indeed, it is his gifts which are the very means by which he subordinates us to his lordship and makes us responsible beings."

34   In this regard, see *ibid.* against Rudolph Bultmann. According to Käsemann, Bultmann has erred by depicting Pauline theology too much in terms of the individual and has consequently lost sight of Paul's concern to proclaim the eschatological kingdom of God. See, e.g., p. 176.

35   In *In Rom* caput I, lectio VI, #102, Thomas in fact has offered two possible interpretations of Paul's *iustitia Dei*. It may refer to the justice by which God is just, *if* we are thinking here of God's fulfillment of the divine promise to save the world through the sending of Jesus Christ. Or it may refer to God's justification of sinners, by which God renders and considers people just. In the discussion of justification in the *Summa Theologiae* I-II 113, it is the justice of God which makes justification possible: This "justice" refers to God's free forgiveness of the sinner and introduction of the justified into the state of grace. On the other hand, I know of no passage in Aquinas in which he interprets the Pauline justice of God as an attribute of God according to which God punishes sinners and rewards the good.

36   In effect, Käsemann wants to have it both ways, although he insists that the genitive is primarily subjective. Against Luther, he wishes to interpret the righteousness of God in terms of an attribute of God; it is not primarily a gift of God by which the sinner stands righteous before God. But Käsemann adds that the Christian God is not self-contained: God is active in the world and

But much more significant than these differences is the fundamental similarity between Thomas Aquinas's analysis of salvation and that offered by Paul. Both Paul and Aquinas perceive the need for good Christian action in conformity with God's will. Moreover, both grant the religious significance of this action, Thomas by speaking of the Christian's meriting of the reward of eternal life, Paul by insisting on Christian obedience as the condition of entry into the kingdom. Yet in neither Thomas nor Paul is the affirmation of the need and value of good human action for salvation allowed to threaten the basic Christian insight into the divine sovereignty and pre-eminence in salvation. On the contrary, when they speak of God rewarding Christians for their acts, Paul and Aquinas insist that salvation always remains the gift and accomplishment of God, for it is God who works the acts rewarded by God. Above all, both thinkers speak of reward for good action in such a way that their statements testify, not to the greatness of the human person or to human "religious possibilities," but to the greatness and glory of *God*: Each subordinates the discussion of human salvation in general and of the human contribution to the attainment of this salvation in particular, to the broader discussion of God's purpose in the world. Hence, Thomas's explanation in the *Summa Theologiae* of the very possibility of merit in terms of God's will and ordination for the world and for the human person is designed to restate in scholastic terms Paul's understanding of reward. With Paul Thomas has recognized that responsible discourse on God's reward for human acts requires situating God's response to human activity in the broader context of the realization of God's plan for the world. It is this basic agreement between Paul and Thomas on the character of God's rewarding of Christians which permits the characterization of Thomas's teaching on merit, based as he says on the reward-texts of scripture, as fundamentally "Pauline." Especially in his later teaching, in which he clarifies the sapiential dimensions of merit, Thomas Aquinas has successfully incorporated the subtle nuances of Paul's understanding of reward into his own presentation of the place of merit in human salvation.

---

is active precisely because of the divine righteousness. By the divine righteousness, God enters into contact with the world, drawing it away from sin and into the service of God–God grants righteousness to people. Thus, there is, as he puts it, a "double bearing of the genitive construction" ("'Righteousness,'" p. 174): God is righteous (the subjective genitive), and therefore acts righteously, by covering the sins of the world by the gift of the divine righteousness and transforming people into the servants of God (the objective genitive). Although with Luther Thomas does not make the Pauline justice of God into an attribute of God, with Käsemann Thomas does assert that God's righteousness accomplishes the transformation of the sinner. God's forgiveness of sinners infuses in them the new reality which is grace, which changes them fundamentally and which makes it possible for them to act in a new way.

Selected Bibliography

I. Writings of Thomas Aquinas

A. *Latin*

Opera Omnia. Iussu Leonis XIII P. M. Edita. Rome, 1884–.

Compendium Theologiae. Leonine ed. Vol. 42. Rome, 1979.

De Caritate. In *Quaestiones Disputatae*, edited by P. Bazzi, et al. 8th ed. rev. Vol. 2. Turin and Rome, 1949.

De Malo. Leonine ed. Vol. 23. Rome, 1982.

De Potentia. In *Quaestiones Disputatae*, edited by P. Bazzi, et al. 8th ed. rev. Vol. 2. Turin and Rome, 1949.

De Spe. In *Quaestiones Disputatae*, edited by P. Bazzi, et al. 8th ed. rev. Vol. 2. Turin and Rome, 1949.

De Veritate. Leonine ed. Vol. 22 in 3 parts. Rome, 1972–75.

De Virtutibus Cardinalibus. In *Quaestiones Disputatae*, edited by P. Bazzi, et al. 8th ed. rev. Vol. 2. Turin and Rome, 1949.

De Virtutibus in communi. In *Quaestiones Disputatae*, edited by P. Bazzi, et al. 8th ed. rev. Vol. 2. Turin and Rome, 1949.

Expositio et Lectura super Epistolas Pauli Apostoli. Edited by R. Cai. 2 vols. Turin and Rome, 1953.

Expositio super Job ad litteram. Leonine ed. Vol. 26. Rome, 1965.

Liber de Veritate Catholicae Fidei contra errores Infidelium seu Summa Contra Gentiles. Leonine text annotated by C. Pera, P. Marc, and P. Caramello. Vols. 2 and 3. Turin and Rome, 1961.

Quaestiones quodlibetales. Edited by P. Mandonnet. Paris, 1926.

Scriptum super Libros Sententiarum. Edited by P. Mandonnet and M. F. Moos. 4 vols. Paris, 1933-47.

Sententia Libri Ethicorum. Leonine ed. Vol. 47 in 2 parts. Rome, 1969.

Summa Theologiae. Blackfriars ed. 61 vols. New York, 1964–.

B. Translations

Catena Aurea. Translated by J. H. Newman et al. 4 vols. Oxford, 1841–45.

Commentary on the Nichomachean Ethics. Translated by C. I. Litzinger. 2 vols. Chicago, 1964.

Compendium of Theology. Translated by C. Vollert. St. Loius, 1952.

On Charity. Translated by L. H. Kendzierski. Milwaukee, Wis., 1960.

On the Gospel of St. John. Translated by R. F. Larcher. Vol. 1. Albany, N.Y., 1970.

On St. Paul's Epistle to the Ephesians. Translated by M. L. Lamb. Albany, N.Y., 1966.

On St. Paul's Epistle to the Galatians. Translated by R. F. Larcher. Albany, N.Y., 1966.

On St. Paul's Epistle to the Philippians and First Thessalonians. Translated by R. F. Larcher. Albany, N.Y., 1969.

On the Power of God. Translated by L. Shapcote. 3 vols. in one. Westminster, 1952.

On the Truth of the Catholic Faith. Translated by A. Pegis, et al. 5 vols. Notre Dame, Ind., 1975.

On the Virtues in General. Translated by J. P. Reid. Providence, R.I., 1951.

On Truth. Translated by R. W. Mulligan, et al. 3 vols. Chicago, 1952–54.

II. Other Primary Sources

Augustine. *De Correptione et Gratia.* In *Aux moines d'Adrumète et de Provence.* Oeuvres de Saint Augustin. Vol. 24. Paris, 1962.

_____. *De Dono Perseverantiae.* In *Aux moines d'Adrumète et de Provence.* Oeuvres de Saint Augustin. Vol. 24. Paris, 1962.

_____. *De Gratia et Libero Arbitrio.* In *Aux moines d'Adrumète et de Provence.* Oeuvres de Saint Augustin. Vol. 24. Paris, 1962.

_____. *De Praedestinatione Sanctorum.* In *Aux moines d'Adrumète et de Provence.* Oeuvres de Saint Augustin. Vol. 24. Paris, 1962.

Cajetan. *Faith and Works—Against the Lutherans.* In *Cajetan Responds,* edited and translated by J. Wicks. Washington, D.C., 1978.

Calvin, John. *Institutes of the Christian Religion.* Edited by John T. McNeill. Library of Christian Classics, Vol. 20. Philadelphia, 1977.

Council of Trent. *The Canons and Decrees of the Council of Trent.* Translated by H. J. Schroeder. Rockford, Ill., 1978.

De Clercq, C., ed. *Concilia Galliae (A. D. 511-695).* Corpus Christianorum, Series Latina, Vol. 148A. Turnhout, 1963.

Eck, John. *Enchiridion of Commonplaces.* Translated by F. L. Battles. Grand Rapids, Mich., 1979.

Luther, Martin. *On the Bondage of the Will.* In *Luther and Erasmus: Free Will and Salvation,* edited and translated by E. G. Rupp and P. S. Watson. Philadelphia, 1969.

Peter Lombard. *Magistri Petri Lombardi Parisiensis Episcopi Sententiae in IV libris distinctae.* Edited by I. Brady. 3d ed. Grottaferrata, 1971.

III. Secondary Sources

Alszeghy, Z. *Nova creatura: La nozione della grazia nei commentari medievali di S. Paolo.* Rome, 1956.

Arfeuil, J.-P. "Le dessein sauveur de Dieu: La doctrine de la prédestination selon Saint Thomas d'Aquin." *Revue Thomiste* 74 (1974): 591–641.

Arges, Michael. "Divine Self-Expression Through Human Merit According to Thomas Aquinas." Ph.D. diss., University of Toronto, 1991.

Auer, Johannes. *Die Entwicklung der Gnadenlehre in der Hochscholastik.* 2 vols. Freiburg, 1942–51.

Bakhuizen van den Brink, J. N. "Mereo(r) and meritum in some Latin Fathers." *Studia Patristica* 3 (1961): 333–40.

Beer, T. "Lohn und Verdienst bei Luther." *Münchener theologische Zeitschrift* 28 (1977): 258–84.

Bernard, C.-A. *Théologie de l'espérance selon Saint Thomas d'Aquin.* Paris, 1961.

Bougerol, Jacques Guy. *La théologie de l'espérance aux XIIe et XIIIe siècles.* 2 vols. Paris, 1985.

Bouillard, Henri. *Conversion et grâce chez S. Thomas d'Aquin.* Paris, 1944.

Bourassa, F. "La liberté sous la grâce." *Sciences écclesiastiques* 9 (1957): 49–66; 95–127.

Boyle, Leonard E. "The Setting of the *Summa theologiae* of Saint Thomas," The Etienne Gilson Series 5. Toronto, 1982.

Burns, J. Patout. *The Development of Augustine's Doctrine of Operative Grace.* Paris, 1980.

Burrell, David B. *Aquinas, God and Action.* Notre Dame, Ind., 1979.

————. "Creation, Will and Knowledge in Aquinas and Duns Scotus." In *Pragmatik*, edited by H. Stachowiak, 1: 246-57. Hamburg, 1985.

————. *Knowing the Unknowable God.* Notre Dame, Ind., 1986.

————. Review of *Being and Goodness: The Concept of the Good in Metaphysics and Philosophical Theology,* ed. by Scott MacDonald. In *Faith and Philosophy* 9 (1992): 538–43.

Busa, R., ed. *Index thomisticus: Sancti Thomae Aquinatis operum omnium indices et concordantiae.* Stuttgart, 1974–.

Catão, B. *Salut et rédemption chez S. Thomas d'Aquin: L'acte sauveur du Christ.* Paris, 1965.

Cathrein, V. "Gottesliebe und Verdienst nach der Lehre des hl. Thomas von Aquin." *Geist und Leben* 6 (1931): 15–32.

Cessario, Romanus. *Christian Satisfaction in Aquinas: Towards a Personalist Understanding.* Washington, D.C., 1982.

Combés, A. "Le problème de la liberté d'après s. Thomas." *Divinitas* 18 (1974): 106–14.

Condit, A. "The Increase of Charity." *The Thomist* 17 (1954): 367–86.

Congar, Yves. "'Praedeterminare' et 'Praedeterminatio' chez saint Thomas." *RSPT* 23 (1934): 363–71.

————. Review of *Die Verdienstlichkeit der menschlichen Handlung nach der Lehre des hl. Thomas von Aquin,* by J. Weijenberg. In *Bulletin Thomiste* 1933: p. 772, #947.

Conlon, G. M. "The Certitude of Hope." *The Thomist* 10 (1947): 76–119; 226–52.

Czerny, J. *Das übernaturliche Verdienst für Andere.* Freiburg, 1957.

De Cousenongle, V. "Le 'Dieu de l'espérance' de saint Thomas d'Aquin." *Studia Theologica Varsaviensis* 12 (1974): 103–20.

De Ghellinck, J. "Pierre Lombard." In *DTC* 12:2. Paris, 1935.

De Letter, Prudentius. *De ratione meriti secundum Sanctum Thomam.* Rome, 1939.

_____. "Hope and Charity in St. Thomas." *The Thomist* 13 (1950): 204–48; 325–52.

_____. "Merit and Prayer in the Life of Grace." *The Thomist* 19 (1956): 446–80.

_____. "Merit of Congruity." *Bijdragen Tidschrift voor Filosofie en Theologie* 18 (1957): 262–67.

Delhaye, P. "La 'loi nouvelle' dans l'enseignement de s. Thomas." *Esprit et Vie* 84 (1974): 33–41; 49–54.

Deman, T. *Der Neue Bund und die Gnade.* Heidelberg, 1955.

_____. Review of *Conversion et grâce chez S. Thomas d'Aquin,* by H. Bouillard. In *Bulletin Thomiste* 7 (1943–44): 46–58.

De Margerie, B. "La sécurité temporelle du juste." *Studi Tomistici* 2 (Rome, 1974): 283–306.

Dettloff, Werner. *Die Entwicklung der Akzeptations- und Verdienstlehre von Duns Scotus bis Luther.* Münster, 1963.

_____. *Die Lehre von der Acceptatio divina bei Johannes Duns Scotus mit besonderer Berücksichtigung der Rechtfertigungslehre.* Werl, 1954.

Dhont, R.-C. *La problème de la préparation à la grâce.* Paris, 1946.

Donagan, Alan. "Thomas Aquinas on human action." In *The Cambridge History of Later Medieval Philosophy,* edited by N. Kretzmann, et al. Cambridge, 1982.

Edwards, S. A. *Interior Acts.* New York, 1986.

Elders, L. "Les Citations de Saint Augustin dans la *Somme Theologique* de Saint Thomas d'Aquin." *Doctor Communis* 40 (1987): 115–67.

Falanga, A. J. *Charity: The Form of the Virtues According to Saint Thomas.* Washington, D.C., 1948.

Fitzgerald, L. P. "The Divisions of Merit in the Early Scholastics." Ph.D. diss., Pontifical University of St. Thomas, Rome, 1972.

Flick, M. "Dialogo sul merito." *Gregorianum* 45 (1964): 339–48.

Froehlich, K. "Justification Language and Grace: The Charge of Pelagianism in the Middle Ages." In *Probing the Reformed Tradition: Historical Studies in Honor of Edward A. Dowey, Jr.*, edited by Elsie Anne McKee and Brian G. Armstrong, 21–47. Louisville, 1989.

Garrigou-Lagrange, R. *Grace: Commentary on the "Summa Theologica" of St. Thomas, Ia IIae, q. 109-14.* Translated by F. Eckhoff. St. Louis, 1952.

Gilson, Etienne. *The Mystical Theology of Saint Bernard.* Translated by A. H. C. Downes. New York, 1940.

Glenn, M. M. "A Comparison of the Thomistic and Scotistic Concept of Hope." *The Thomist* 20 (1957): 27–74.

Glorieux, P. "Le mérite du Christ selon S. Thomas." *RSR* 10 (1930): 622–49.

Grabmann, Martin. *Die Geschichte der scholastischen Methode.* 2 vols. Graz, 1957.

Guindon, A. *La pedagogie de la crainte dans l'histoire du salut selon Thomas d'Aquin.* Tournai, 1975.

Hamm, Bernd. *Promissio, Pactum, Ordinatio.* Tübingen, 1977.

Hankey, W.J. *God in Himself: Aquinas' Doctrine of God as Expounded in the Summa theologiae.* Oxford, 1987.

Heinz, J. *Justification and Merit: Luther versus Catholicism.* Berrien Springs, Mich., 1981.

Jordan, Mark D. "The Alleged Aristotelianism of Thomas Aquinas," The Etienne Gilson Series 15. Toronto, 1992.

Käsemann, Ernst. *Commentary on Romans.* Translated by G. W. Bromiley. Grand Rapids, Mich., 1980.

_____. "'The Righteousness of God' in Paul." In his *New Testament Questions of Today*, translated by W. J. Montague. London, 1969.

Klubertanz, G. "The Root of Freedom in St. Thomas' Later Works." *Gregorianum* 42 (1961): 701–24.

Kretzmann, Norman. "A General Problem of Creation: Why Would God Create Anything at All?" In *Being and Goodness: The Concept of the Good in Metaphysics and Philosophical Theology*, edited by Scott MacDonald, 208–28. Ithaca, N.Y., 1991

_____. "A Particular Problem of Creation: Why Would God Create This World?" In *Being and Goodness*, 229–49.

Kühn, Ulrich. *Via caritatis.* Göttingen, 1965.

Ladrille, G. "Grâce et motion divine chez saint Thomas d'Aquin." *Salesianum* 12 (1950): 37–84.

Lais, H. *Die Gnadenlehre des hl. Thomas in der Summa contra Gentiles und der Kommentar des Franziskus Sylvestris von Ferrara*. Munich, 1951.

Landgraf, Artur. *Dogmengeschichte der Frühscholastik*. Vol. I. Ratisbon, 1952.

Laporte, J.-M. *Les structures dynamiques de la grâce: grâce médicinale et grâce élevante selon Thomas d'Aquin*. Montreal, 1973.

Lawler, M. G. "Grace and Free Will in Justification: A Textual Study in Aquinas." *The Thomist* 35 (1971): 601–30.

Lonergan, Bernard. *Grace and Freedom: Operative Grace in the Thought of St. Thomas Aquinas*. Edited by J. Patout Burns. London, 1971.

Lottin, O. *La théorie du libre arbitre depuis S. Anselme jusqu'à S. Thomas d'Aquin*. Louvain, 1929.

Lumbreras, P. "Naturale meritum ad Deum." *Angelicum* 19 (1942): 139–78.

Lynn, William D. *Christ's Redemptive Merit: The Nature of its Causality according to St. Thomas*. Rome, 1962.

Marino, B. "La reviviscenza dei meriti secondo la dottrina del dottore Angelico." *Gregorianum* 13 (1932): 75–108.

McGinn, Bernard. "The Development of the Thought of Thomas Aquinas on the Reconciliation of Divine Providence and Contingent Action." *The Thomist* 39 (1975): 741–52.

McGrath, Alister E. *Iustitia Dei: A History of the Christian Doctrine of Justification*. Vol. 1. Cambridge, 1986.

McSorley, H. J. *Luther: Right or Wrong?* New York, 1969.

Merkt, J. T. "'Sacra Doctrina' and Christian Eschatology." Ph.D. diss., Catholic University of America, 1982.

Miralles, A. "El Gobierno Divino en la Teologia del Merito de Santo Tomas de Aquino." *Teresianum* 35 (1984): 73–97.

_____. "La Perspectiva sapiencial de la Teologia del Merito en Santo Tomas de Aquino." *Studi Tomistici* 13 (Rome, 1980): 293–303.

Neveut, E. "Des actes méritoires." *Divus Thomas* 33 (1930): 386–408.

_____. "Des conditions de la plus grande valeur de nos actes méritoires." *Divus Thomas* 34 (1931): 353–75.

_____. "Du mérite de convenance." *Divus Thomas* 35 (1932): 3–29.

_____. "Du mérite de convenance chez le juste." *Divus Thomas* 36 (1933): 337–59.

O'Donnell, J.J. "The Authority of Augustine." *Augustinian Studies* 22 (1991): 7–35.

Oberleitner, M. *Die Handschriftliche Überlieferung der Werke des Heiligen Augustinus*, Band I/1 Italien. Vienna, 1969.

Pernoud, M. A. "The Theory of the Potentia Dei according to Aquinas, Scotus and Ockham." *Antonianum* 47 (1972): 69–95.

Pesch, Otto Hermann. "Die Lehre vom 'Verdienst' als Problem für Theologie und Verkundigung." In *Wahrheit und Verkündigung: Festgabe M. Schmaus*, edited by L. Scheffczyk, et al., 2: 1865–1907. Paderborn, 1967.

_____. *Die Theologie der Rechtfertigung bei Martin Luther und Thomas von Aquin*. Mainz, 1967.

Pesch, Otto Hermann and Albrecht Peters. *Einführung in die Lehre von Gnade und Rechtfertigung*. Darmstadt, 1981.

Pfürtner, S. *Luther and Aquinas on Salvation*. Translated by E. Quinn. New York, 1964.

Philips, G. *L'Union personnelle avec le Dieu vivant*. Louvain, 1974.

Pinckaers, S. "La nature verteuse de l'espérance." *Revue Thomiste* 58 (1958): 405–42; 623–44.

_____. "La structure de l'acte humain suivant saint Thomas." *Revue Thomiste* 55 (1955): 393–412.

_____. "Les origines de la définition de l'espérance dans les Sentences de Pierre Lombard." *RTAM* 22 (1955): 306–12.

Quinn, Jerome D. "The Scriptures on Merit." In *Justification by Faith*, edited by H. G. Anderson, et al., 82–93. Minneapolis, 1985.

Reicke, B. "The NT Conception of Reward." In *Aux sources de la tradition chrétienne: Mélanges M. Goguel*, 195–206. Neuchatel, 1950.

Rivière, J. "Le mérite du Christ d'après le magistère ordinaire de l'Eglise. 2. Epoque médiévale." *RSR* 22 (1948): 213–39.

_____. "S. Thomas et le mérite 'de congruo.'" *RSR* 7 (1927): 641–49.

Rouse, Mary A. and Richard. *Authentic Witnesses: Approaches to Medieval Texts and Manuscripts*. Notre Dame, 1991.

Stegmüller, F., ed. *Repertorium commentariorum in Sententias Petri Lombardi*. 2 vols. Würzburg, 1947.

Synan, Edward A. "Brother Thomas, the Master, and the Masters." In *St. Thomas Aquinas, 1274–1974: Commemorative Studies*, edited by A. Maurer, et al., 2: 219–42. Toronto, 1974.

Tonneau, J. "The Teaching of the Thomist Tract on Law." *The Thomist* 34 (1970): 13–83.

Vignaux, P. *Justification et prédestination au XIVe siècle*. Paris, 1934.

Wawrykow, Joseph P. "'Perseverance' in 13th-Century Theology: the Augustinian Contribution." *Augustinian Studies* 22 (1991): 125–40.

_____. "On the Purpose of 'Merit' in the Theology of Thomas Aquinas." *Medieval Philosophy and Theology* 2 (1992): 97–116.

_____. "John Calvin and Condign Merit." *Archiv für Reformationsgeschichte* 83 (1992): 73–90.

Weijenberg, J. *Die Verdienstlichkeit der menschlichen Handlung nach der Lehre des hl. Thomas von Aquin*. Freiburg im Breisgau, 1931.

Weisheipl, James A. *Friar Thomas d'Aquino: His Life, Thought and Work*. Garden City, N.Y., 1974; reprint with addenda and corrigenda, Washington, D.C., 1983.

Wheeler, M. C. "Actual Grace according to St. Thomas." *The Thomist* 16 (1953): 334–60.

Wright, John H. *The Order of the Universe in the Theology of St. Thomas Aquinas*. Rome, 1957.

Ysaac, W. "The Certitude of Providence in St. Thomas." *Modern Schoolman* 38 (1961): 305–21.

Zimmerman, A. "Der Begriff der Freiheit nach Thomas von Aquin." In *Thomas von Aquin, 1274–1974*, edited by L. Oeing-Hankoff, 125–59. Munich, 1974.

Zychlinski, A. "De caritatis influxu in actus meritorios iuxta S. Thomam." *ETL* 14 (1937): 651–56.